UNSPEAKABLE AWFULNESS

Ma:
Tel:

The la   h century was a golden age for European travel in the United
States.   ous Europeans, a journey to America was a fresh alternative to
the m   ar 'Grand Tour' of their own continent, promising encounters with
a vast,   ape, and with people whose culture was similar enough to their
own t   ible, yet different enough to be interesting. Their observations
of Am   inhabitants provide a striking lens on this era of American history, a   ing glimpse into how the people of the past perceived one
anothe

In   Awfulness, Kenneth D. Rose gathers together a broad selection
of the   ons made by European travelers to the United States. European
visitor   ed upon what they saw as a distinctly American approach to
everyt   class, politics, and race to language, food, and advertising. Their
assessr   e 'American character' continue to echo today, and create a full
portra   nineteenth-century America as seen through the eyes of its visitors.

Inc   vid travelers' tales and plentiful illustrations, *Unspeakable Awfulness*
is a ric   that will be useful to students and appeal to anyone interested in
travel   narratives.

Kenn   se teaches history at California State University, Chico. He is
the au   *Myth of the Greatest Generation: A Social History of Americans in
World War II, One Nation Underground: The Fallout Shelter in American Culture*, and
American Women and the Repeal of Prohibition.

D1340034

UNSPEAKABLE AWFULNESS

America Through the Eyes of European Travelers, 1865–1900

Kenneth D. Rose

Routledge
Taylor & Francis Group

NEW YORK AND LONDON

First published 2014
by Routledge
711 Third Avenue, New York, NY 10017

Simultaneously published in the UK
by Routledge
2 Park Square, Milton Park, Abingdon, Oxon OX14 4RN

Routledge is an imprint of the Taylor & Francis Group, an informa business

© 2014 Taylor & Francis

The right of Kenneth D. Rose to be identified as author of this work has
been asserted by him in accordance with sections 77 and 78 of the
Copyright, Designs and Patents Act 1988.

Library of Congress Cataloging in Publication Data
Rose, Kenneth D. (Kenneth David), 1946-
Unspeakable awfulness : America through the eyes of European travelers,
1865-1900 / Kenneth D. Rose.
  pages cm
"Simultaneously published in the UK"–Title page verso.
1. United States–Description and travel. 2. United States–Foreign public
opinion, European. 3. Travelers' writings, European. 4. United States–
Social life and customs–1865-1918. I. Title.
E168.R795 2013
973.7'38–dc23   2013000906

ISBN: 978-0-415-81764-6 (hbk)
ISBN: 978-0-415-81765-3 (pbk)
ISBN: 978-0-203-79714-3 (ebk)

Typeset in Bembo
by Cenveo Publisher Services

Printed and bound by CPI Group (UK) Ltd, Croydon, CR0 4YY

To my Scottish friends David Newall and Steven Watson, and other intrepid travelers

There is no such thing as a stupid American. Many Americans are horrid, vulgar, intrusive, and impertinent, just as many English people are also; but stupidity is not one of the national vices. Indeed, in America there is no opening for a fool. They expect brains even from a boot-black, and get them.

—Oscar Wilde

In America, society is nothing; the individual is everything.

—A. Maurice Low

If they have sold their birthright of civility, they have not sold it for a mess of pottage.

—William Hepworth Dixon

No one is embarrassed for long in America.

—Jacques Offenbach

You may have seen the East, the South, the West, the Pacific States, and yet have failed to find America.

—Charles Wentworth Dilke

CONTENTS

ILLUSTRATIONS

ACKNOWLEDGMENTS

I owe a great debt of gratitude to persons known and unknown who have looked at my manuscript, and have made suggestions for how to improve it. Every writer naturally assumes that anything he puts down on paper is pure gold. Our readers and editors know better, and the virtues of this book are largely due to them, and the failings entirely due to me. My indebtedness begins with Michael Allen, who was good enough to go over my manuscript at a very primitive stage of development. He both encouraged me and steered me toward some wonderful material. Thanks Mike, I couldn't have done it without you. Among my colleagues at Chico State, Mike Magliari read my material on the West, and Robert Tinkler was very helpful on the Civil War material. Laird Easton also made many excellent suggestions on the overall shape of the manuscript. Robert O'Brien plowed through the entire manuscript, and his keen eye for inconsistencies and his understanding of what makes good writing were invaluable. Also at Chico State, Jo Ann Bradley and Flora Nunn at Interlibrary Loans and Debby Besnard at Special Collections were of great assistance.

Kimberly Guinta, my editor at Routledge, believed in this project from the beginning. She has been extremely patient with me, and I could not have asked for a better editor. Thanks as well to Genevieve Aoki and Rebecca Novack and others at Routledge. My brother-in-law John Lawrence and Ani Adjemian, both of Dongell Lawrence Finney (L.A.'s law firm nonpareil), were diligent in researching the permissions for this book. I am a complete idiot when it comes to computers, and I was extremely lucky to have August and Jim Connolly helping me out. They didn't even laugh (too much) when I tried to use the mouse backward. I also owe a debt of gratitude to Gary Kraus, who gave me a computer when my ancient Pentium IV gave up the ghost. I also want to put in a good word for Google, for scanning so many books from the nineteenth century (including a great number of obscure travel memoirs) and making them available to the public on archive.org. They have made an invaluable contribution to research.

I have saved the best for last, which is my wife, Jeanne Lawrence. Living with a writer is not easy, and I'm afraid that I'm no exception. Jeanne not only put up with a lot in our day-to-day lives, but also served as a shrewd reader and copy-editor. Of all the debts I owe, the one I owe to her is the greatest.

TRAVELERS TO AMERICA, BY YEAR

1860s

Charles Dickens, 1842, 1867–68; John Campbell Argyll, 1866; Charles Wentworth Dilke, 1866; William Hepworth Dixon, 1866; Henry Latham, 1866–67; Henry M. Stanley, 1867; Parker Gillmore, 1867; David Macrae, 1867–68; William A. Bell, 1867–68; F. Barham Zincke, 1867–68; W. F. Rae, 1869

1870s

George Augustus Sala, 1862–64, 1879–80; William Francis Butler, 1870; Robert Somers, 1870–71; Therese Yelverton, 1870, 1872–73; Baron Hübner, 1871; Rose G. Kingsley, 1871–72; Emily Faithfull, 1872–84; Windham Thomas Wyndham-Quin, 1872, 1874, 1877–88; Beatrice Webb, 1873, 1898; Isabella L. Bird, 1873; J. W. Boddam-Whetham, 1873; John Mortimer Murphy, 1875; Jacques Offenbach, 1876; Henry Sienkiewicz, 1876–78; Émile Levasseur, 1876, 1893; H. Hussey Vivian, 1877; R. W. Dale, 1877; Ernst von Hesse-Wartegg, 1877–78; W. G. Marshall, 1878–79; William Saunders, 1878–79; Robert Louis Stevenson, 1879–80, 1887–88; A. Maurice Low, 1879–1900

1880s

William Howard Russell, 1861–62, 1881; William A. Baille-Grohman, 1879, 1880–81; Sarah Bernhardt, 1880–81, 1886–87, 1898, 1900–01, 1905, 1910–11, 1916–18; Lady Duffus Hardy, 1880–81; Edward A. Freemann, 1881–82; Iza Duffus Hardy, 1881–83; Oscar Wilde, 1882; W. E. Adams, 1882; Herbert Spencer, 1882; Knut Hamsun, 1882–84; 1886–88; Lillie Langtry, 1882–93, 1903, 1906, 1912;

Horace Annesley Vachell, 1882–99; James Bryce, 1870, 1881, 1883–84, 1887; W. Henry Barneby, 1883; Rose Pender, 1883; Henry Irving/Joseph Hatton, 1883–84; Bram Stoker, 1883–84; Matthew Arnold, 1883–84, 1886; Frederick Delius, 1884–85, 1897; Lepel Henry Griffin, 1884; E. Catherine Bates, 1885–86; Isabelle Randall, 1885–1886; J. J. Aubertin, 1886–87; Harold Brydges, 1887; Léon Paul Blouet, 1887–88; Mary Rhodes Carbutt, 1888; Alexandra Gripenberg, 1888; Rudyard Kipling, 1889, 1892–96, 1899

1890s

James Fullarton Muirhead, 1888, 1890–93, 1898; Paul de Rousiers, 1890; Alexander Craib, 1891; Peter Tchaikovsky, 1891; Harry Kessler, 1892, 1896, 1924; Antoní Dvořák, 1892–94; Paul Bourget, 1893–94; William T. Stead, 1893; Marie Therese Blanc, 1894; S. Reynolds Hole, 1894–95; S. C. de Soissons, 1896; William H. Davies, 1893–99; Theodora Guest, 1894; Bertrand Russell, 1896; Hugues Le Roux, 1898; Charles C. Osborne, 1898; William Archer, 1877, 1899.

INTRODUCTION

America the Awful and the European Traveler

"Unspeakable awfulness" is a phrase that European travelers could have used to describe any number of things in America. The roads in the United States were universally condemned as terrible, as was American cuisine (French actress Sarah Bernhardt actually used the term "unspeakably awful" to describe American food).[1] Likewise, the American habit of spitting tobacco juice nearly every place (and in heroic quantities) sent European travelers reeling in search of metaphors that would adequately express their revulsion. The ubiquity of guns, the American obsession with making money, the viciousness of U.S. political campaigns, the rudeness of American children—all of these things could have earned the "awful" label.

As it happens, the "awfulness" in the title is used in perhaps its best sense of inspiring an awe impossible to articulate. Indeed, in European descriptions of the Western landscape, the word "awful" keeps recurring. William Howard Russell was stunned by Yosemite's "awful granite portals," while W. G. Marshall similarly referred to that site's "awful barrier of domes and peaks," and "the awful majesty of that huge background of mountains."[2] (See cover.) Isabella Bird also found in the West both great beauty and something disturbing, and her vain attempts to describe the stark magnificence of the Sierra Nevada Mountains finally coalesced in the phrase "unspeakable awfulness."[3] For European travelers, America would prove to be awful in every sense of the word.

The thirty-five-year period between 1865 and 1900 was the golden age for European travel in the United States. In 1869, one observer commented that the old British "grand tour" of Europe had grown stale and predictable, and that "the grand tour of the present day is a trip through America to St. Francisco," and then through Asia.[4] A journey through America was the opposite of stale and predictable, with Europeans encountering a terrain that was vast, wild and forbidding, and a people whose culture sometimes resembled their own, but was radically different in other ways. The intensification of European tourism to the United States coincided with what is arguably the most dramatic period of change in American history. The beginning of this period marked the conclusion of the Civil War, and when this era closed the American frontier had officially ceased to exist and the United States had made its first tentative steps toward colonialism with the Spanish–American War. In between, a massive shift of the American population took place with some 2.5 million moving from East to West between 1870 and 1900.[5] More territory was settled during this period than at any time in U.S. history.[6]

Of course, Europeans had always visited the United States and had been eager to write about their experiences. But in the first fifty years of the new republic, as Jane Louise Mesick has observed, more often than not these travelers described the same parts of the country, mainly because of the nation's wretched transportation system.[7] Another deficiency of these early accounts was that it was the unusual that garnered the most attention, while many of the details of ordinary American life were neglected.[8] And while the reminiscences of Tocqueville, Trollope, Martineau, Thackeray, and Dickens are well known, the number of European travelers in America before the Civil War was relatively small.

Dominating many antebellum accounts of American life was the slavery issue, with Europeans quite naturally taking the same keen interest in slavery as Americans. And, like most Americans, the views of European travelers toward slavery covered a wide gamut, from abhorrence of the institution of slavery and sympathy for the slave to sympathy for the slave owner and contempt for the slave.[9] The Civil War totally remade the South, and as one British traveler observed, "the change which it effected was not so much a change as a revolution."[10] While the legacy of slavery would haunt the South, and the rest of the nation, well into the future, at least by 1865 slavery itself had been abolished, allowing foreign travelers to take up other aspects of American life that might have been neglected before.

Both external and internal transportation improvements after the war would ease the way for the traveler. Fast steamships made travel from Europe to America what one European called "easy, pleasant, and expeditious," and a feverish period of railroad building in the United States allowed travelers internal access to almost every corner of the nation.[11] In 1871, there were 60,000 miles of railroad track in America. By 1890 there were 166,000 miles of track, and by the beginning of the twentieth century the United States had almost half of the total railroad trackage in the world.[12] Even early in this period, British curate F. Barham Zincke emphasized that "on the fifteenth day after leaving Liverpool you may dine in the Rocky Mountains on trout you have yourself caught, venison you have yourself stalked, and fruit you have yourself gathered."[13] It should be emphasized, however, that while travel in America was more convenient after the Civil War, it was not cheap. One guidebook, published in 1873, estimated that comfortable round-trip travel from the East to the West Coast, including expenses and with various side trips thrown in, cost at least $1,200 (just under $22,800 in today's currency).[14] The additional cash outlay for a voyage across the Atlantic and back meant that only fairly prosperous Europeans could undertake such a venture.[15]

Travel to the United States after the war started slowly. Henry Latham visited America in late 1866 and recorded the number of English travelers as "comparatively small," while in the following year F. Barham Zincke noted that he did not encounter a single traveler from England.[16] Even as late as 1872, when English social reformer Emily Faithfull made her first trip to America, "English visitors were few and far between."[17] By the next decade, the trickle of European visitors had become a flood. Sarah Bernhardt began her American tour in 1880, and Oscar Wilde and Herbert Spencer followed in 1882. In 1883, actor Henry Irving toured America along with his manager Bram Stoker (future author of *Dracula*).[18] By the following year, Matthew Arnold, Lillie Langtry, England's Chief Justice and Faithfull herself were all in America as well as, according to one New York newspaper, "a large number of poor but illustrious lords, who are anxious to draw closer the ties that unite the two countries by marrying American heiresses, together with speculators and capitalists innumerable."[19]

Famous visitors to America during this era also included Charles Dickens, Rudyard Kipling, Robert Louis Stevenson, Jacques Offenbach, Peter Tchaikovsky, and Antonín Dvořák. But the less-than-famous also descended upon America in droves. Whether famous or not, these visitors not only wanted to see the United States, but also wanted to write about it. William Hepworth Dixon and Charles Wentworth Dilke toured America together in 1866, and they *both* wrote books about their experiences. Mary Duffus Hardy and her daughter Iza Duffus Hardy took separate trips to America in the 1880s, and each produced a memoir of her travels.

Travel accounts covered a wide gamut, from the whimsical to the encyclopedic. In the latter category, the most exhaustive study by far was rendered by James Bryce, a member of Parliament for twenty-one years and ambassador to the United States beginning in 1907. Bryce first came to America in 1870. By 1884 he had made three trips to the United States and in 1888 he published his great work, *The American Commonwealth* (a revised version was published in 1908).[20] Bryce stated as his goal nothing less than "portraying the whole political system of the country in its practice as well as its theory, of explaining not only the National Government but the State Governments, not only the Constitution but the party system, not only the party system but the ideas, temper, habits of the sovereign people."[21] In his massive two-volume work, he succeeds to a remarkable degree.[22]

Isabella Bird was no less determined than Bryce to penetrate to the meaning of America, but rather than being drawn toward aspects of U.S. politics she was enticed by the American wilderness and by the lives of ordinary people that she found there. Her solo journeys through the wilds of the Colorado Rockies in 1873 made Bird as much of a local legend as any mountain man. Others came merely to skim the surface of American culture with as little discomfort to themselves as possible. A good example is Lady Theodora Guest, who suffered few privations during her three-month tour of America in 1894 because she was pulled around the country in a private Pullman car. William Howard Russell, who visited America in 1881 in the company of the Duke of Sutherland, the Marquis of Stafford and various other notables, was also provided with luxury travel arrangements. Russell admitted that this group was not likely to gain "much knowledge of the ordinary conditions in which people live in the United States."[23]

One of the first things one must ask is why the views of foreigners—by definition persons neither citizens of the nation nor immersed in its affairs—should carry any weight when trying to assess American culture and society. There were indeed dangers. First, there was the enormous scale of the land. French traveler Léon Paul Blouet (who wrote under the pseudonym Max O'rell) insisted that "in six months you cannot know America, you cannot even see the country."[24] British military officer William Francis Butler agreed, noting that it was frequently the case for travelers to America that "the thirty-seven states are run over in thirty-seven days; then out comes the book, and the great question of America, socially and politically considered is sealed for evermore."[25] Barrister W. F. Rae, who visited America in 1869, believed that too many books produced by the English about their experiences in the United States were "either bundles of prejudices artistically arranged, or else deliberate caricatures skilfully drawn."[26] The temptation to incline toward the gaudy was often irresistible. As one traveler put it, "quiet family-life is hard to describe; bowie knives and revolvers will make the dullest pages bristle into some kind of vivacity."[27]

By the mid-1880s, E. Catherine Bates (who would become best known for her interest in spiritualism) acknowledged that producing a book about one's travels in America was a reliable way to become "an unutterable nuisance to our friends and the public in general."[28] (This did not deter Bates, however, from producing a two-volume description of her own American travels.) Travel writers as a breed, according to historian Christopher Mulvey, "suffered from a kind of generic insecurity. This made them turn on their craft, on themselves, or on their readers at the least provocation."[29] Almost standard was a preface attached to the travel memoir that sought to justify the memoir's existence. By the end of the nineteenth century, American travel memoirs had been produced "in prodigious quantities," with each "literary Columbus" returning to Europe with "a newer and more untrustworthy tale" about life in the United States.[30] It is perhaps belaboring the obvious to observe that these travel tales reveal as much about Europeans as they do about Americans.

When the European visitor came to America, he was confronted with a nation the size of Europe, a population likely to be more than twice that of his own country, and political and social institutions that were totally alien to him. Without a long period of residency to fully understand this strange new world, often the European fallback position was to approve or criticize, as A. Maurice

Low expressed it, "according to temperament or preconceived prejudice."[31] Historian William H. A. Williams despairs that anything meaningful can come out of travel narratives, and of his own examination of the travel literature produced by the British touring pre-famine Ireland, he says it "provides an interesting case study of the limitations of tourism and the travelogue as vehicles for promoting understanding between people."[32] According to Williams, travelers always carry with them images of "home," which "help to shape their perceptions of the host country."[33] Consequently, "the familiar becomes a fetish; its presence reassuring, its absence shocking." Williams insists that until the individual can "step outside the role of tourist and go beyond the endless game of using 'them' to define 'us,' of seeking 'our' superiority in 'their' shortcomings, genuine understanding between host and guest will be elusive."[34]

While the differences between Europeans ("us") and Americans ("them") were significant after the Civil War, they were surely not as great as the gap between the British and the rural Irish before the famine. Americans were mainly middle class rather than poor, Protestant rather than Catholic, increasingly industrial rather than agricultural, independent rather than colonized. In addition, because of close cultural ties between Britain and the United States, Britons identified more with Americans and were much less likely to invoke the us–versus–them dichotomy that they applied in Ireland. Williams is certainly correct in asserting that travelers use the familiar to make sense of the unfamiliar, but he perhaps underestimates the observational skills and the sense of judiciousness that the traveler can bring to a foreign country.

Every European arrived in America with an image (mostly negative) of life in the United States. E. Catherine Bates was perhaps typical when she referred to the "dreary prophecies" of her acquaintances that she would find America a land of over-rated scenery, bad food, and pretentious people. But travelers, like the rest of us, are capable of overcoming their prejudices when presented with the evidence of their experiences. After a twelve-month sojourn in America, Bates concluded that she had never spent "a more enjoyable year than the one that has just passed away."[35] H. Hussey Vivian notes that before he left England for the United States, he was warned that "the manners and customs of Americans were rough, and that it was doubtful how far a lady ought to travel in the public railway carriages, or to stay at hotels." Vivian concluded that "a more unfounded idea was never entertained," and that "in no country have I ever seen greater politeness shown to ladies, or better breeding generally."[36] Indeed, travelers often compared the Europe with which they were familiar to the America with which they were unfamiliar, and found the former wanting. When he spoke of the residents of the American West, for instance, J. W. Boddam-Whetham said, "There is an absence among them of that narrowness, that mental tight-lacing, which squeezes all charity out of human nature, and which is so characteristic of the Old World; and there is the presence of an open-hearted fellowship between man and man, of a rare and generous kind."[37] Even though many European travelers were rude and sometimes even imperious when traveling in the United States (especially the English), when the time came to record their appraisals of America and Americans, the great majority made an honest effort to be fair. This view is seconded by historian Richard L. Rapson. In *Britons View America*, Rapson confirms not only the fairness and sympathy of British travelers, but claims that throughout American history, British commentators have "attempted to arrive at balanced critical estimates of the American scene."[38]

James Bryce believed that the stranger (especially one who is "an Englishman, with some practical knowledge of English politics and English law") had two advantages: "He is struck by some things which a native does not think of explaining, because they are too obvious" and he "finds it easier to maintain a position of detachment."[39] A. Maurice Low also claimed that a foreigner "who approaches his task with sympathy, who comes not as a critic but as a judicious investigator, who is neither a partisan nor a eulogist" and who refrains from measuring everything "by the narrow vision of its own national perfection" was in the best position to write a history of a people.[40] The tone of postbellum travel memoirs such as Bryce's and Low's are distinctly different from those of earlier eras. They are less likely to be condescending, and more likely to be analytical.[41] Bryce himself, looking back from 1898 at the previous forty years of British travel in the United States, concluded that Britons had not only come to America in "far larger numbers" than previously, but had also returned "with more accurate ideas about the United States than they had before."[42]

Agendas and Preconceptions

Most travelers arrived in America with an agenda of what they wanted to see, which usually did not coincide with what Americans wanted to show them. Americans took great pride in their civilization, but in his advice to Americans attempting "to amuse or edify" the sight-seeing European, Englishman Phil Robinson emphasized that the tourist would show little interest in factories, mills or busy streets because he could see plenty of those things where he came from. Instead, "he would much rather see a prairie-dog city, than the Omaha smelting-works, an Indian lodge than Pittsburg; one wild bison than all the cattle of Chicago; a rattlesnake at home than all the legislature of New York … He prefers cañons to streets, mountain streams to canals; and when he crosses the river, it is the river more than the bridge that interests him."[43] As environmental historian Roderick Nash puts it, "Nature, not civilization, was the actively traded commodity between America and its foreign visitors."[44]

It was in the American West that European travelers encountered the greatest challenges to their experiences and preconceptions. As Ray Allen Billington has noted, it was here that two radically different portraits of America emerged: the "Land of Savagery" and the "Land of Promise."[45] Certainly, the perception of the unsettled regions of America as places of almost palpable hostility had been part of European thinking for centuries. When he arrived in America in 1620, William Bradford described the land around Plymouth Colony as "a hideous and desolate wilderness," inhabited by "wild beasts and wild men."[46] Likewise, when she was abducted by Indians in 1676, Mary Rowlandson called the place where she was taken a "vast and howling *Wilderness*" [Rowland's emphasis] and the Indians "Barbarous Creatures."[47]

It was the Romantic movement of the late eighteenth and early nineteenth centuries that began to alter the adversarial relationship that Europeans had established with the American wilderness. The wilderness itself had not changed, but now it was endowed with godliness and purity. Likewise, the dwellers of the wilderness had been transformed from "Barbarous Creatures" into "noble savages."[48] In *René*, François-René de Chateaubriand's eponymous character sighs that, "In our endless agitation we Europeans are obliged to erect lonely retreats for ourselves."[49] In the American West, Europeans would seek out those retreats.

James Bryce claimed that the West was "the most American part of America" because that was where the differences between America and Europe came out "in the strongest relief."[50] It was also in the West, according to Paul de Rousiers, that the "merits and weaknesses" of Americans became most obvious.[51] For many Europeans, the West seemed to promise an Edenic existence free of the hypocrisy of modern life, what sportsman Oliver North called "the delightful feeling of grand unrestraint."[52] "Out West," said Robert Louis Stevenson, "the war of life was still conducted in the open air, and on free barbaric terms; as if it had not yet been narrowed into parlours, nor begun to be conducted, like some unjust and dreary arbitration, by compromise, costume, forms of procedure, and sad, senseless self-denial."[53] Parker Gillmore, who took an extended hunting trip through North America in the late 1860s, experienced "an irresistible fascination in solitary communion with Nature; for the sake of which I would abandon the most brilliant scenes of life and civilised society."[54]

Travelers' descriptions of the sheer physical beauty of the region are rapturous, bordering on the religious. When sportsman Windham Wyndham-Quin first gazed upon the Yellowstone River, he absorbed the scene "with something of the silent enthusiasm of a pilgrim who sees in the far distance St. Peter's dome or the minarets of Mecca."[55] In the Sierras, Isabella Bird described a sunset as "a carnival of color … delirious, intoxicating, a hardly bearable joy, a tender anguish, an indescribable yearning, an unearthly music, rich in love and worship."[56] But in their engagement with the Western wilderness, Europeans also found something darker for which their aesthetic sense had ill prepared them. Rudyard Kipling, for instance, was unnerved by the "reckless profusion of Nature" that he found in Oregon. It was, he said, "oppressively magnificent."[57]

As for the residents of the West, disappointment often followed when Europeans found that Westerners were not savage (or romantic) enough. William A. Baille-Grohman, who traveled in the United States in the 1880s, noted that the European newly arrived at a place like Cheyenne or Denver often "hides a feeling of defrauded curiosity at not finding dead men lying about the streets and festooning the odd trees about the town."[58] When he was in Leadville in 1881, William Howard Russell, who had covered both the Crimean War and the American Civil War as a correspondent, noted the presence of some Hungarian travelers who, he said, were "filled with enthusiasm, and with a great deal of curiosity in regard to the shootings of which they had heard so much."[59] The following year, Phil Robinson also visited Leadville, seeking out what he called "exercises with bowie-knife and pistol." He pronounced himself "agreeably disappointed" by the well-behaved miners.[60] Confessing to being armed "like some bandit in an opera," Polish writer Henry Sienkiewicz, a future Nobel laureate, spent his first months in the United States carrying a revolver, brass knuckles, and a sword concealed in his cane. But after passing nights without incident in the isolated dwellings of farmers, shepherds, and fishermen, Sienkiewicz abandoned his arsenal and concluded that he was safer in the United States than anywhere on the planet.[61]

Especially disappointing to Europeans were American Indians. Europeans had been fed a steady diet of novels celebrating the nobility of the Indian, and of all the promoters of this idea, James Fenimore Cooper came earliest and arguably had the greatest impact. While Cooper has not aged well under the scrutiny of the modern sensibility (somewhat anachronistically, Patrick Brantlinger calls Cooper's writings "intrinsically both racist and sentimental"), the publication of Cooper's *The Pioneers* (1823), and the four Leatherstocking novels that followed, created a sensation in Europe.[62] Multiple editions were translated into almost every European language as well as into the languages of Turkey, the Middle East, and North Africa. Cooper's success spawned a legion of imitators in Europe, and the Western flourished as a popular genre for over a century to come.[63] One of the Western's themes was that certain Indians were possessed of a somber dignity, which can be clearly seen in Cooper's description of the Delaware Indian Chingachgook:

> Notwithstanding the intense cold without, his head was uncovered; but a profusion of long, black coarse hair, concealed his forehead, his crown, and even hung about his cheeks, so as to convey the idea, to one who knew his present and former conditions, that he encouraged its abundance, as a willing veil, to hide the shame of a noble soul, mourning for glory once known. His forehead, when it could be seen, appeared lofty, broad, and noble.[64]

The enduring appeal of Cooper can be found in numerous travel memoirs. Windham Wyndham-Quin acknowledged "the illusions and youthful fancies that a severe course of study of Fenimore Cooper's works, of 'Hiawatha,' and books of that description engendered in my mind."[65] The cult of Cooper had penetrated to Poland, and when Henry Sienkiewicz first encountered the Sioux in America, he admitted that their appearance "did not correspond entirely to the mental picture of Indians which I had acquired from my reading of the novels of Cooper."[66] Edward A. Freeman also expressed disappointment in real

Indians, which he condemned as "repulsive from the utter lack of intellectual expression."[67]

Despite the testimonies of foreign travelers as to actual conditions in the United States, the notion of America as a realm of untamed savagery continued to have a hold on the European imagination well into the twentieth century. Horace Annesley Vachell, who was a rancher in California for seventeen years before returning to England in 1899, found that at even this late date most Britons pictured America as a land of barbarism. One woman, according to Vachell, "believed that I roamed my ranch clad in skins of wild beasts, that the plains were black with Apaches, the towns at the mercy of desperadoes!" Others assumed that Vachell must be happy to be back in a "civilised country," even after Vachell explained that the California town where he lived had a population of 30,000 and was better lit and maintained than two-thirds of English cathedral towns.[68]

Oscar Wilde famously noted that the British were more interested in American barbarism than American civilization, and indeed, the dominant European image of an American, established long before the Civil War, was a man who carried a bowie knife, spoke in a detestable twang, elevated his feet above his head, and squirted tobacco juice everywhere.[69] As we will see, there was some truth to this image, but the creation of it owed more to caricature than to analysis because while the former is easy, the latter is not. As one British commentator put it, "we can stick a bowie-knife into the hand of the American, and provide the German with a glass of Bavarian beer, though we are profoundly ignorant of the occult causes which make beer congenial to Germans or bowie-knives to Americans."[70]

Influential in establishing stereotypes about the United States were the novels and plays produced by European writers that purported to portray accurately the manners and mores of Americans. Looking back at the novels with American characters created by German writers in the nineteenth century, Lida von Krockow acknowledged the huge influence of James Fennimore Cooper, and observed that "a generation of writers has had time to flourish and decline since his day; yet the obscure levels of German fiction still swarms with Indians and adventurers whenever America is concerned."[71] R. W. Dale only needed two months in the United States to come to the conclusion that popular representations of Americans in British literature were "gross and slanderous libels."[72] Especially fanciful, according to an Englishman who spent a decade and a half in the United States, were depictions of American speech. Invariably, American characters in British literature spoke "in a dialect happily combining all the peculiarities of speech of each section of the country from Maine to Texas; and such as, it may safely be affirmed, was never yet heard from the lips of any one human being."[73]

While the British often accused Americans of being provincial, the Scotsman William Archer found that the American's knowledge of England "puts to shame the Englishman's ignorance of America."[74] Historian Christopher Mulvey even claims that the English traveler "came from a society that prided itself, if anything, on its ignorance of its ex-colony."[75] This was especially true in the realm of geography, where according to one long-time British resident of the United States, the English were "curiously ignorant."[76] Edith Nicholl, an Englishwoman who lived on a ranch in New Mexico for twenty years, cites one example in which a new arrival from England wrote home to express his disappointment in not being able to see Pike's Peak from New York.[77]

What was America? Who were the Americans?[78] These questions mattered to Europeans, who were both excited and anxious about this colossus in the West and what it might mean for themselves and their own world. Summing up the motivations of foreigners traveling in America, Walt Whitman noted in 1888 that "some have come to make money—some for a 'good time'—some to help us along and give us advice—and some undoubtedly to investigate, *bona fide*, this great problem, democratic America, looming upon the world."[79] Anthony Trollope called a trip to the United States "the best means of prophesying, if I may say so, what the world will next be, and what we will next do."[80] German geography professor Friedrich Ratzel saw a direct link between a people's "political intelligence" and "the amount of knowledge and appreciation they may possess of what is occurring, and is likely to occur, in America."[81] When Lepel Henry Griffin came to America in 1884, he already detested the United States. He produced *The Great Republic* as a warning against the creeping Americanization of Britain.[82] A French delegation came to the United States to study American machinery, and left with the gloomy assessment that French industry would have to be radically altered if it wanted to compete with the Americans.[83] Some visitors, such as James Bryce, came to school themselves in the American political system, while others, especially sportsmen, sought out communion with nature in the American wilderness. For many jaded Europeans, a trip to the United States was motivated by nothing more than the expectation of a novel experience.

In travelers' accounts it is easy to see key national differences. Europeans struggling to establish a national identity or concerned with the creation of a modern nation state looked to America for inspiration. Andrew J. Torrielli noted that what was important about the United States to visitors from Italy "was not a question of ice water nor rocking chairs nor bad roads nor insufferable manners" (as it frequently was for the British) but in gaining "something to carry back with them to their own people."[84] After praising the "ebullient, internal strength" of Americans, Henry Sienkiewicz proclaimed, "how happy I should be to send here for its health a certain nation known to me," meaning, of course, Poland.[85] Other Europeans, lamenting the complacency of their countrymen, pointed to Americans as role models worth emulating. Finnish suffragist Alexandra Gripenberg, for example, contrasted "vigorous and determined" Americans with the "passive apathy" of the Finns.[86] Dutchman Charles Boissevain even produced a tongue-in-cheek comparison of Dutch pigs, creatures of "unashamed ease, of sensual comfort, of cosy, delightful sleepiness," to the "independent" American pigs, with snouts that "are constantly mobile; they insert their noses into everything searching for a grain of wheat in the mud, noticing everything."[87]

While travelers from France were just as fascinated by the United States as other Europeans, the French reaction to Americans—and vice versa—presents a special case. Beginning with Tocqueville, the French have been among the most insightful analysts of American society. Carrying on this tradition into the late nineteenth century was Paul Bourget, a multi-talented writer whose poems inspired composer Claude Debussy. By the late nineteenth century, Bourget had come to the conclusion that the forces of democracy, science, and race represented a threat to Europe, but when he visited the United States in 1893–94, he found that these same forces had succeeded in building "out of whole cloth, a new universe." Bourget's trip to the United States became an odyssey to reclaim "a little faith in the future of civilization."[88] Like most travelers, the French felt that they received a warm welcome from Americans (S. C. de Soissons went so far as to call Americans "the kindliest people I have met") but a real love for the French was often conspicuous by its absence.[89] Why this has historically been the case is a matter of some debate, but historian Theodore Zeldin claims that "the basic problem has been that the French fascination with the USA has not been reciprocated ... Everything in the interactions between the two nations is overshadowed by the French sense of being undervalued and, worse, ignored."[90]

Most French visitors complained that English was the only language spoken, and when she was in the United States in 1894, Marie Therese Blanc could not help but notice that "France does not hold the first place" in the esteem of Americans.[91] Indeed, Norwegian writer Knut Hamsun observed that one of the most heinous terms of abuse that an American could levy was to call someone "a Frenchman." Invariably, this led to a fight, unless one actually was French.[92] Among the reasons that the French so often rubbed Americans the wrong way was the Catholicism of France. The presence of a French Catholic Canada was perceived as a real menace to Protestant British colonists, with friction between France and Britain in North America eventually resulting in the French and Indian War. (In an 1885 article, American philosopher and historian John Fiske called the victory of British general James Wolfe at Quebec "the greatest turning-point" in modern history because it was crucial in subduing "the neighboring civilization of inferior type," i.e. French Canada.[93]) And while French assistance was invaluable to the success of the American Revolution, this was a geopoltical marriage of convenience more than an alliance of like-minded peoples. The Terror, and the political instability of France (by one count France has had at least thirteen regimes since 1789) also played into negative American views of the French.[94]

The American animus toward the French owes a great deal to British influence. One revealing document is Ralph Waldo Emerson's *English Traits* (1856), a paean to English society and culture. Throughout *English Traits* Emerson emphasizes the differences between the English and the French, at one point observing that "France is, by its natural contrast, a kind of blackboard on which English character draws its own traits in chalk."[95] Thus, said Emerson, the English

are honest and true to their word while the French "are more polite than true …
in the French language one cannot speak without lying."[96] Additionally, Emerson
judged the French to be "frivolous" and even cowardly.[97] "I suppose that all men
of English blood in America, Europe, or Asia," said Emerson, "have a secret feeling of joy that they are not French natives."[98]

The ongoing reticence toward the French is no less real today than it was in
the nineteenth century. As Rosecrans Baldwin puts it, "France and America have
a long history of mutual loathing and longing. Americans still dream of Paris;
Parisians still dream of the America they find in the movies of David Lynch."[99]
The differences between the two nations is probably culturally based. American
culture, with its emphasis on practicality, egalitarianism, and popular pursuits, is
the very definition of modernism. But Denis Lacorne and Jacques Rupnik see
French culture as "intrinsically archaic," including a "distrust of pragmatism, a
passion for philosophical abstractions, and a taste for refined fashions and high-
brow culture." With the French additionally endowed with "uninhibited delu-
sions of 'grandeur' and a desire to set themselves up as a model for the rest of the
world," there is little wonder that Americans sometimes gave the French a reception that was less than enthusiastic.[100] French "style" was also anathema to many
Americans. From his travels in the United States in the 1870s and 1890s,
Frenchman Émile Levasseur concluded that Americans viewed the French as
"frivolous, noisy and dissolute."[101] Henry Sienkiewicz theorized that the reason
Americans disliked the French was because of the elaborate way they greeted each
other—"they prance about each other like two monkeys in ardent courtship."[102]

The British Traveler

An altogether different dynamic was at play in the case of the British, the most
numerous foreign visitors to America. America's historical closeness with Britain
and the enduring British impact on American society and politics prompted
Charles Dickens to declare that "the notion of an American being regarded in
England as a foreigner" was "uncommonly incongruous and absurd to me."[103]
Indeed, many travelers endorsed Matthew Arnold's idea that Americans were
"English people on the other side of the Atlantic," although it should be noted
that Arnold came to this conclusion before he had set foot in the United States.[104]

This closeness should not be overstated, however, because even though the
two societies were rooted in similar traditions, they were different enough that
they often created sparks when they came in proximity to each other. On the
diplomatic level, the argument could be made that Anglo-American relations
were even more nettlesome than Franco-American relations. Even setting aside
the War of 1812, there were a number of issues that caused friction between
America and Britain during the nineteenth century. The British treatment of the
Irish bedeviled relations between the two countries throughout this century, and
E. Catherine Bates found that Britain's "decided show of sympathy with the

South [in the Civil War] was looked upon as an unjustifiable piece of interference," at least by Americans in the North.[105] Much of this had to do with the so-called "*Alabama* Claims," in which America accused Britain of violating its stated neutrality during the war by allowing British shipyards to build Confederate ships (among them the *Alabama*). An international tribunal awarded the United States $15.5 million dollars in 1872.[106]

There was another dispute between the two nations over the boundary between British Guiana and Venezuela. Britain sought to extend Guiana's borders into an area that contained gold, and in 1895 U.S. Secretary of State Richard Olney declared that this was a violation of the Monroe Doctrine. Reporting from the United States in 1896, Henry M. Stanley tried to impress upon British readers the seriousness of the situation. He described Americans as "extremely angry" and warned that there was "a storm brewing in the West which would burst over these islands with the force of a hurricane."[107] By 1899, the Venezuelan dispute had been settled, the American victory in the Spanish–American War was being proclaimed as a triumph of Anglo-Saxonism, and relations between Britain and the United States had become decidedly cordial. But reaching this point had taken much of the nineteenth century.

The complicated relationship between the two countries translated into a sometimes awkward kinship, with Americans making a distinction between Britons as individuals and Britain as a symbol. Most British felt at ease in the United States because they were "so kindly received, so hospitably entertained" and "so affectionately treated," but the American regard for Britain as a nation was considerably cooler.[108] William Francis Butler, who was in America in 1870, claimed that the American hostility toward Britain was "universal," and was possessed of "the dogged strength of unreasoning antipathy."[109] (Part of the hostility toward Butler was no doubt related to the fact that he was a British military officer in transit to Canada.) More than a decade later (in 1883), Bram Stoker related a telling incident that occurred on the ship that took him from England to America. A tug of war was organized between English and Americans (hardly a competition that was likely to foster better international relations), which the English won. But when the contest was restaged, "we English were pulled right over the line with a rapidity which we could not understand." Upon investigation, the English discovered that some seventeen American women had been added to the opposing side. "There they stood, with panting bosoms and flashing eyes"—a tribute, said Stoker, to the "national sentiment."[110]

It should also be noted that the British from England were more likely to receive a guarded reception than the British from Scotland, whom most Americans seemed to like. The Scots had made some of the same egalitarian commitments as the Americans, especially in the realm of education, and for many English people Scotland was as alien as the United States.[111] James Fullarton Muirhead, author of *Baedeker's Handbook* for the United States and Great Britain, even claimed that the Scots and Americans shared a sense of humor that was distinctly different from the English.[112] It was no great surprise, then, that Englishman Horace Annesley Vachell found that "abuse of England is greedily gobbled up" in the United States, while David Macrae claimed that as a Scotsman he received a kindly welcome everywhere in America.[113]

The most steadfast abuses of the British, according to Macrae, came "from the Irish, and from a few renegade Scotch and English."[114] (In a slightly different analysis, F. Barham Zincke blamed the Germans and the Democratic Party [because of that party's heavy Irish contingent] for the American hatred of the British.[115]) There is little doubt that the Irish question played an especially prominent role. William Howard Russell claimed that Americans believed that the British government had been unwise and unjust in its dealings with the American colonies, and that the same government was "treating with harshness and injustice the whole of the Irish race in Ireland." Russell claimed that "the head, perhaps the heart, and certainly the purse of this development of Irish discontent are in the United States."[116] Quite aside from Britain's relations with Ireland, there was the generalized American view that the British were undemocratic, and that Britain "lies prostrate under the heel of a tyrant."[117]

A number of English travelers in America also detected a hostility toward them on a personal level, but Lepel Henry Griffin admitted that one mitigating factor might be that the English were "often unendurable to each other."[118] James Fullarton Muirhead concluded that while Americans tended to view the stranger as "a good fellow until he proves himself the contrary; with the Englishman the presumption is rather the other way."[119] One motivation for the English to travel, as E. Catherine Bates suggested, was "to find fertile soil for that cherished English growth—a grievance."[120] Harold Brydges likewise observed that the English in America often did not leave a favorable impression because they were constantly grumbling, a propensity that they had brought with them from England.[121] One thing they grumbled about was what they saw as excessively heated American hotels, trains, and public facilities. When an American overheard a member of Henry Irving's troupe complaining about the heat on a ferry, he observed to his companion, "Our English friends would complain of heat at the North Pole."[122] As one long-term British resident of America put it, "An Englishman is never seen to worse advantage than when he is insisting upon what he is pleased to call his—rights."[123]

A notion revered by the English, according to E. Catherine Bates, was that foreigners were, after all, only a "'very poor imitation of the real thing.'"[124] Another commentator put it more bluntly: "Every true Englishman at the bottom of his soul hates a foreigner," and the American was "a bad imitation of a Briton."[125] It seemed a natural attitude for the Briton abroad to adopt. Even Scotsman Robert Louis Stevenson, who was more aware of the impression he was making than most, was appalled to discover that he himself had become the ugly British traveler that he detested—eager to find fault with the country that hosted him and discounting its virtues.[126] In an article representing a Scottish point of view that was probably penned by Stevenson (it appeared under the initials "R. L. S."), the writer confessed that "I do not know where to look when I find myself in company with an American and see my countrymen unbending to him as to a performing dog."[127]

This trait was nowhere more fully developed than in the case of Beatrice and Sidney Webb, who toured America in 1898 (ostensibly to gather information about municipal government). They were granted access to the highest offices and persons and were honored guests at American homes. But the Webbs learned nothing in America because they knew it all already. Instead, Beatrice, through her diary, contented herself with cutting personal remarks about the Americans who took the time to speak to her. She referred to Theodore Roosevelt's "vulgarity," called Vice-President Garret A. Hobart "a common looking man," described Speaker of the House Thomas Reed as "destitute of any culture" and "an ideal philistine," and characterized House Democratic Leader Joseph W. Bailey as "a cad of the worst description."[128] Nor did those who extended to the Webbs the hospitality of their homes fare any better. At Ithaca, the Webbs stayed at the home of Professor Jeremiah W. Jencks, who was on his way to becoming an eminent economist. Beatrice, however, speculated that Jencks might have done better as "a corn dealer or timber merchant," and described Jencks' wife and children as "ultra lower-middle class, talking with a detestable twang."[129] While such views might be expected from the unreconstructed British aristocracy, the Webbs were leading lights in the cause of Fabian socialism.

Bringing a unique perspective to the Briton abroad was Frenchman Léon Paul Blouet. As French master at St. Paul's School, London, Blouet was well acquainted with the English, and had married an English woman. He also had the opportunity of viewing English behavior both in France and in America during his own trip to the United States. According to Blouet, the Englishman looked at everything he saw "with a patronising air; with the arrogant calm that makes him, amiable as he is at home, so unbearable when he travels abroad."[130] Indeed, often what set Americans on edge was the commanding tone preferred by the English. The American James Russell Lowell referred to their "easy air of superiority" (which Blouet described as the Englishman's "haughty disdain").[131]

Americans could not help but see the English looking with contempt on "any one who is not of his caste," which was one reason why Americans were rude to them in return.[132] In one example, W. F. Rae observed a fellow Briton, who happened to be a well-known solicitor, adopting a manner that Rae described as "a little too abrupt" to customs officials. This display of impertinence met with a swift reaction. The solicitor was hustled off to an adjoining room, where he was subjected to a thorough personal search. Rae commented that "patience and courtesy" went a long way toward ensuring considerate treatment.[133]

Often Anglo-American conflicts came down to sensitivities about class. This could be seen in virtually every encounter between the British and what they saw as the American "servant class." It began when the Briton checked into a hotel.

"No one in the world teaches you your place so well as the American hotel-clerk," said Edward A. Freeman. It was not that the clerk was uncivil, but his was "a stately and lordly civility," such as might come from "a well-disposed Czar or Sultan" responding to one of his subjects.[134] Another traveler warned that a hotel guest should not expect "the obsequious attentions which greet a new arrival at an English hotel [or] the double doses of flunkeyism" that prevailed among hotel staff on the continent.[135] In one example, William Howard Russell's distinguished group ran afoul of the proprietor of a Kansas City hotel when one of the party complained about the absence of a mirror. According to Russell, the proprietor seemed remarkably unimpressed by the lofty stature of these guests, and told them, "'And if you don't like what you get here, there are other hotels in Kansas City, and you can go to them if you please.'"[136]

The British education in the American class system continued as the Briton encountered waiters, conductors, sales persons, domestics, and people on the streets, none of whom displayed the requisite servility.[137] Englishman "W. C. M.," who lived in New York for seventeen years, was constantly being regaled by his countrymen about the rudeness of the American working class. In one example, a British traveler walked up to an American mechanic and said, "'My good man, I want to go to Franklin Street.'" The reply was, "'Then why the devil don't you go there?'" What went wrong with this exchange, according to W. C. M., was "the unlucky phrase 'My good man,' and the patronizing tone in which it may be inferred that such words would be uttered." Had the Briton framed his inquiry in a less condescending way, any American laborer would have "shown a courteous readiness to afford him any information in their power." In W. C. M.'s experience, the working-class American was not only better mannered than his English counterpart, "but so superior is he in this respect, that no comparison can fairly be instituted between them."[138] Summing it up, David Macrae noted that "the man in America who grooms your horse must not be considered your inferior on that account."[139]

These issues were especially prominent in the American West, where material comforts were often lacking, and where the wealth of the British traveler (and his sense of entitlement) stood in stark contrast to the humble means of the locals.[140] When he was in the West, Rudyard Kipling met what he called "a young English idiot" who, with valet in tow, told Kipling that you couldn't be too careful whom you spoke to in those parts. This unsolicited advice enraged Kipling, who called the man "a barbarian."[141] According to William Baille-Grohman, who made four trips to the United States in the 1880s, "the true gentleman is heartily liked, but the swell is as heartily hated." Baille-Grohman found that Americans had no objection to good clothes, as long as they were worn "without ostentation," but when the Westerner sees you "in all the brand-new finery of your West-end outfitter, his mouth puckers up more than usually as he squirts from it a stream of tobacco juice."[142] The British sportsman who adapted to life in the West rather than insisting that the West adapt to him was held in high esteem by Westerners.

"Buffalo Bill" Cody, for instance, expressed admiration for Sir John Watts Garland who, despite his wealth, "roughed it like the rest of us, slept in the open on his blanket, [and] took his turn at camp duty." Garland's adoption of the Western saddle and his endorsement of the notion that "a cocktail before breakfast was considered entirely the thing on the prairie" also earned him considerable good will among frontiersmen.[143]

Unfortunately, the English in the West more often than not alienated those whom they encountered. In one case, a newly minted English college graduate arrived in New Mexico and refused to eat with what he called "the cow servants." This phrase delighted the locals, who were soon referring to themselves as "cow servants."[144] During her extended travels in the Rockies, Isabella Bird had the opportunity to observe a number of English travelers, who left behind a less than pleasing impression. One young Englishman had acquired the nickname "The Earl" because he rode on an English saddle and clung "to some other insular peculiarities."[145] In another case, two refined Englishmen who were camping in Estes Park contemptuously rejected the warnings of the locals about hostile Indians, crossed the mountains into North Park looking for gold, and were never seen again.[146] Bird was also staying at some rough lodgings in Colorado when a hunting guide brought in a young English hunter:

> This gentleman was lording it in true caricature fashion, with a Lord Dundreary drawl and a general execration of everything; while I sat in the chimney corner, speculating on the reason why many of the upper class of my countrymen—'High Toners,' as they are called out here—make themselves so ludicrously absurd. They neither know how to hold their tongues or to carry their personal pretensions.[147]

One person Bird became acquainted with during her time in the Rockies was a trapper named "Mountain Jim" Nugent, one of Colorado's legendary characters of the 1870s. When Bird introduced him to an English sportsman, the Englishman "put out a small hand cased in a perfectly-fitting lemon-colored kid glove. As the trapper stood there in his grotesque rags and odds and ends of apparel, his gentlemanliness of deportment brought into relief the innate vulgarity of a rich *parvenu*."[148]

Assessing Americans

This book will spend some considerable time looking at that elusive quality known as "the American character" that foreigners and, indeed, natives have been analyzing since colonial days. One popular strain has been an argument that U.S. society, especially in the nineteenth and twentieth centuries, was dominated by the "ugly American." This assertion, too frequently based on lazy preconceptions rather than fact, has persisted into the twenty-first century, and a grievous offender (and one who should know better) is Simon Schama. In a 2003 article for the *New Yorker* called "The Unloved American," Schama claims that "by the end of the nineteenth century, the stereotype of the ugly American—voracious, preachy, mercenary, and bombastically chauvinist—was firmly in place in Europe. Even the claim that the United States was built on a foundation stone of liberty was seen as a fraud."[149]

Schama based his assertions on what can only be called a highly selective reading of the travel memoirs of Knut Hamsun and Rudyard Kipling.[150] But the stereotype that Schama both identifies and endorses cannot be maintained if one actually spends some time with the vast literature produced by European travelers in the United States (rather than forcing the facts to fit a thesis). These writings are dominated not by complaints of ugly Americans, but by accounts of the great kindness and courtesy that Americans extended to Europeans. "Nowhere is there a greater desire to make the stranger at his ease than in America," said Britisher A. S. Northcote, "and no foreigner who has made even the shortest sojourn in this country but will affirm what I say."[151] W. Henry Barneby added, "I think there is no one in the world so hospitable and kind as the American gentleman."[152] James Fullarton Muirhead, who spent many years in America, found it "almost impossible to believe that the whole nation can be so good as the people who have been so good to me."[153]

The traveler did not, of course, praise every aspect of American life, and had plenty of criticisms to offer. Not only were American food, roads, and the chewing tobacco habit reviled, but most Europeans also condemned America's utter lack of an aesthetic sense. The single-minded drive for money in the United States came under heavy criticism. As Norwegian traveler Knut Hamsun put it, in America "it is the scale and cash value of things" that constitute their substance.[154] In addition, America's rampant egalitarianism—and the sturdy resistance of America's "servant class" to behave like servants—was totally alien to European experience. Some found it exhilarating, but more often than not Europeans saw it as threatening because it called into question their basic assumptions about the social order. For instance, when Austrian visitor Baron Hübner toured California, he complained of the "insolence of the miners and servants" and the "infamous treatment to which we are subjected."[155]

The idea of an American character is an important one as it runs counter to the notions of our own time. The trend among academics has been to flee from the suggestion of a distinctive American type and instead embrace concepts such as multiculturalism that emphasize class, racial, and ethnic divisions. But the scholar always has the obligation to follow where the evidence leads, rather than where the theory leads, and I emphasize that a distinctly American character did indeed exist not because of my own historical bent, but because the travelers that I have looked at overwhelmingly endorsed this idea. While many twenty-first century historians would no doubt feel more comfortable if these nineteenth-century travelers had thrown up their hands and proclaimed that the United

States was so economically, racially, and ethnically diverse that it was impossible to make any general statements about Americans, that is not what they did. The critic can make the dubious claim that these travelers insisted on the reality of an American character because they were slaves to their acculturation and incapable of rational thought (a hideous, totalitarian notion that removes any possibility of human agency), but the critic cannot finesse away the words themselves.

For a moment, then, let's deviate from the academic collective wisdom and instead of concentrating on what these travelers may or may not have been thinking or how their societies may or may not have molded them, look at who these travelers were and what they actually said. Somewhere over half of them wrote for a living, so they tended to be educated, skilled in observation and critical analysis, and fully able to articulate their thoughts. As noted earlier, travel in the United States was not cheap, so most of these travelers were at least middle class, with some from the upper class. They could be found across a wide political spectrum, from socialist to high Tory, and while most were Protestant, there was also a large number of French and Italian Catholic visitors. They came from all over Europe to visit America, and while they had differing opinions on many aspects of American culture, on the things that really mattered—that is, on the essentials of life in the United States—there was a near unanimity of opinion. Men and women, Catholics and Protestants, liberals and conservatives, from countries that included France, Poland, Germany, Finland, England, Italy, and elsewhere, not only agreed that an American character existed, but were also in wide agreement on its structural components.

Not only in the era that I am examining, but also throughout American history, travelers found that life in America was conducted on a radically different premise than it was in Europe.[156] They saw a uniquely American approach to things that included class, work, gender relations, child rearing, education, politics, religion, and even food and alcohol consumption. Speaking of the British travelers to America that he examined in *Observing America: The Commentary of British Visitors to the United States, 1890–1950*, Robert Frankel notes that they "examined American society in all its rich detail, but they also pulled back to look at the larger picture. In fact, they were more prone than Americans themselves to attempt to capture what used to be called the American 'character' but is now more commonly referred to as the national 'identity.'"[157] Richard L. Rapson prefers American "values" to American character, but he too emphasizes that the British travelers to America that he studied "presented a picture of a society which held to a certain group of values from as early as 1830 until around 1900."[158] Alexander Craib was one among many European travelers who could not help but notice that "the Americans are a go-ahead people; they do things differently from us."[159]

Because of their outsider status, European travelers were in a position to make keen observations on the virtues and failings of Americans and their society that the natives, because of their too close proximity, often missed. As A. Maurice Low put it, "it is axiomatic that we do not see ourselves as others see us, and what is true of the individual is even in a larger sense true of a people."[160] European travelers were frequently wrong about the United States especially, as Richard L. Rapson observes, in the areas of politics, economics, and history—all of which rely on extensive study rather than simple observation.[161] But where "a fresh vision and a willingness to say the obvious are in order," these visitors had a lot to tell us.[162] W. G. Marshall, who visited the United States in the late 1870s, included in his account a quote from a *San Francisco Chronicle* article. It is worth reprinting as it is a reasonable assessment of at least the Briton in America:

> His lungs are always sound, his views are positive, and his self-possession is impregnable. He has a faint idea that the American language is as foreign as Greek or Italian, and the accompanying impression that all foreigners are slightly deaf. He gives his order at the *table d'hôte* in a voice distinctly audible to everyone in the room. He looks at the women as if they were a portion of Mme. Tussaud's exhibition. He is more careful of the *convenances* than when at home. But he is withal an exceedingly intelligent observer, and if he remains with us any length of time, carries away with him a very fair general impression.[163]

One of America's shrewdest social observers, Walt Whitman, endorsed this point of view, noting that in regards to coming to a true understanding of the United States, "I have occasionally found the clearest appreciation of all, coming from far-off quarters."[164]

A scholarly focus on travel and tourism is relatively new, and like most new fields the results have thus far been uneven. Much of this literature is good, but the worst of it makes a martyr of the reader by employing mind-numbing jargon (we could all benefit from a lifetime ban on the word "liminoid") and pretentious name dropping (multiple references to Derrida, Lacan, Baudrillard, Saussure, etc.). It's also unfortunate that some concepts associated with tourist studies either falter because of underwhelming premises, or because they simply do not work for the America of the late nineteenth century. One prominent, but not very useful, analytical device is the "tourist's gaze," a conceit borrowed from Foucault by John Urry.[165] William H. A. Williams claims that, "Through that gaze the tourist isolates, classifies, and judges the characteristics and qualities, not only of the host country's scenery but of its natives as well, turning them into specimens to be scrutinized, identified, and described."[166] In addition, John Urry tells us that the photograph is an ominous extension of the tourist's gaze ("To photograph is in some ways to appropriate the object being photographed. It is a power/knowledge relationship").[167]

Even setting aside the dreary postmodernist formulations, a number of problems are apparent with this line of inquiry. First, every human being classifies and makes judgments about things and people as we move through life, which makes the tourist gaze less than revelatory. Second, unless the scholar is also a swami, it is impossible to know what exactly gazers are thinking about at a given moment unless they tell us. In addition, gazing at things is the principal occupation of the tourist and, as far as I know, no one has raised the question of what we would otherwise have the tourist do. Not look at things? Not take photographs? Give up traveling altogether?

A more fruitful approach has been to explore the concept of the "picturesque" and its influence on travelers. Defining what it is we mean when we use this term is difficult, with some seeing the picturesque as a historical period bridging classical and romantic art, while others see it as a flexible concept used by the tourist to interpret and "frame" (literally, in the case of photographs and postcards) his experiences. As the scholar Malcolm Andrews puts it, we say that something is "picturesque" if it "conveys the sense that what we are seeing is gratifyingly similar to the familiar images of an idealised rural beauty."[168] At the heart of original notions of the picturesque was a connoisseurship that was reserved for those with a certain aesthetic education and denied to the hoi polloi (the "man of taste" as opposed to "the clown").[169] Under the spell of the picturesque, the viewer looked backward to an idealized era before the ravages of modernity, and experienced a gratifying melancholy as he contemplated the impact of time and nature on the rural built environment (what Ann Bermingham calls the "love of the ruined and dilapidated").[170]

Was there anything in nineteenth-century America that qualified as picturesque? Certainly in the realm of art, the painters of the Hudson River School were greatly influenced by English landscape painters in their idealization of nature, and both European and American travelers were familiar with the language of the picturesque.[171] But the lack of an ancient was a chronic problem in America (Rose Pender, for instance, complained of San Antonio that it was neither "modernly clean and comfortable" nor "picturesquely old"), and travelers were united in observing that rather than letting things decay, Americans quickly replaced the old with the new.[172] Among the many deficiencies of American civilization that he identified, Henry James included "no castles, nor manors, nor old country-houses, nor parsonages, nor thatched cottages, nor ivied ruins."[173] And while the natives of a locale could also be judged "picturesque," here America disappointed again because American Indians—the closest analog to the gypsies, beggars and other rustics that were deemed picturesque in Europe—did not conform to the image created for them by James Fennimore Cooper.[174] Theodora Guest, for instance, who visited America in 1894, experienced a keen disappointment when she encountered the Utes, and judged them to be a degraded race "with no picturesqueness."[175]

There is also some debate among those involved in tourist studies over whether a distinction should be made between the traveler and the tourist. This issue was raised some fifty years ago by Daniel J. Boorstin. Somewhere past the mid-nineteenth century, according to Boorstin, the nature of travel changed. Driven by transportation improvements and the rise of the travel agency, "foreign travel ceased to be an activity—an experience, an undertaking—and became a commodity." It was, said Boorstin, "the decline of the traveler and the rise of the tourist."[176] Summing up the perceived differences between traveler and tourist, James Buzard observes that, "The traveller exhibits boldness and gritty endurance under all conditions (being true to the etymology of 'travel' in the word 'travail'); the tourist is the cautious, pampered unit of a leisure industry."[177] Activating the scorn of the traveler were the packaged tours offered by agencies such as the Cook Company and American Express, as well as the tourist's reliance on the Murray or Baedeker travel guides to tell him what to see and how to experience it.

Surely there is an element of class elitism here. As scholar Pam Palmowski notes, "the guidebook was a great leveler of knowledge and of culture … for those who had not received a good classical education, among them many women travelers, the guidebook was a great emancipatory tool."[178] Thomas Cook himself defended his tours on the grounds that they were "agencies for the advancement of Human Progress," and rejected the idea that "places of rare interest should be excluded from the gaze of the common people, and be kept only for the interest of the 'select' of society."[179] Modern critics tend to endorse Cook's point of view. Orvar Löfgren refers to "the tired stereotypes that set 'the real traveler' against the *turistus vulgaris*," and James Buzard finds an obvious element of snobbery in an argument in which the traveler regards his "own cultural experiences as authentic and unique, setting them against a backdrop of always assumed tourist vulgarity, repetition and ignorance."[180] Historian Cindy S. Aron observes that "tourism may appear to be a shallow and mind-numbing enterprise, but compared to what?" After all, tourists could claim that they had spent their time far less frivolously than mere vacationers, who devoted themselves to "idling away time at a resort, drinking juleps and flirting with strangers."[181] While the centuries-old tradition of the European Grand Tour (and the tourist infrastructure that was created to serve it) makes it at least feasible to distinguish between traveler and tourist in nineteenth-century Europe, this was less easy to do in America.

I will be endowing my subjects with the dignity of the word "traveler" simply because for much of the nineteenth century the American tourist industry was in a fledgling state. Tourist facilities were established by the 1820s to serve Europeans and Americans who traveled through the Hudson River Valley, and those who ventured further afield could visit Kentucky's Mammoth Cave and New Hampshire's White Mountains. But for the greater portion of this century, the only bona fide tourist trap in America was at Niagara Falls.[182] One European traveler complained in 1891 that "guides, touters, sellers of relics, infest Niagara," while others referred to Niagara as "a nest of harpies" and the place where one is "continually pestered."[183] William Francis Butler described the habitues of Niagara as, "Vendors of Indian bead-work; itinerant philosophers; camera-obscura men; imitation squaws; free and enlightened negroes; guides to go under the cataract, who should have been sent over it; spiritualists, phrenologists, and nigger minstrels."[184] Travelers who ventured elsewhere in the United States would have a much less tailored experience.

This brings up another issue that scholars of tourism have examined, namely, the transformation of a site by tourism itself.[185] While the falls at Niagara have not changed, it is obvious that tourism has changed everything around the falls. Most nineteenth-century travelers found the American side of the falls more vulgar than the Canadian side, and one of their biggest complaints was that Americans lit up their side of the falls at night with colored calcium lights.[186] Today, the opposite trend seems to be at work. In a recent *New York Times* article, Barbara Ireland notes that "casinos, high-rise hotels and hucksterish come-ons have so proliferated in Niagara Falls, Ontario, that it risks feeling like a tired amusement park. Meanwhile, in Niagara Falls, New York, the visitor who ventures inside the shabby, underfinanced state park is surprised to discover vestiges of something like a natural landscape."[187]

Niagara Falls was the exception rather than the rule in nineteenth-century America because the tourist industry was in its infancy. In the East, there were often ample accommodations for the traveler, and sometimes even the smallest American community could boast of a substantial hotel. But as we shall see, the majority of guests were locals and American business travelers rather than tourists. The first Western resort sites (at Colorado Springs and nearby Manitou Springs) did not begin construction until the early 1870s, nor did Thomas Cook and Son open up a U.S. branch until 1874.[188] Tourist facilities in the West were often quite rudimentary at the beginning. Rose G. Kingsley noted of the temporary hotel that was put up at Manitou in 1871 that there were large spaces between the boards.[189] When British traveler J. W. Boddam-Whetham was in Yosemite in 1873, he said of Yosemite's tourist cabins that "too strong a gale might blow them away," and that "the partitions of the bedrooms are of cotton cloth, and the doors are sheets."[190] Ten years later, things had not markedly improved when Rose Pender visited Yosemite. She described the hotels as "very bad at present … The walls are merely lath and paper."[191] Entrepreneurs moved aggressively to establish luxury Western resorts in the decades ahead, but progress was neither swift nor uniform. There was not a first-class hotel in western Colorado (at Glenwood Springs) until 1893. As historian Earl Pomeroy has noted, as late as 1887 travelers seeking out the waters at Glenwood encountered "bathhouses [that] were crude sheds, the tubs no more than holes excavated with a shovel and rented for fifteen cents a customer."[192] Inevitably, tourism would wrought the same transformations in the American West as it did in Europe, but it would come at a much later date.

The accounts of travelers have always been useful in uncovering the intricacies of a society. Fernand Braudel, in the introduction to his magisterial three-volume study *Civilization and Capitalism, 15th–18th Century*, noted that, "Through little details, travelers' notes, a society stands revealed. The ways people eat, dress, or lodge, at the different levels of that society, are never a matter of indifference."[193] This is no less true of America than it is of Europe.

The United States in this period was arguably the most dynamic nation on the planet. W. E. Adams said of America in the early 1880s that no other country "undergoes such rapid and marvellous changes," and what was true of one decade "may be very unlike the truth the next."[194] More succinctly, Charles Dickens observed that "nothing in this country lasts long."[195] But while change over time is inevitable, the "little details" supplied by European travelers during this era reveal a undeniable continuity, not only in the day-to-day activities of Americans, but in their general outlook on life. And surely, one of the most important constants of American life, going back to colonial days, was the idea that in America one had the opportunity to succeed, or fail, based not on his social class, but on his own abilities. As Lady Duffus Hardy put it,

> There has been no effete civilization here. Every man has depended on his own brains, his own hand for his well-doing. It may truly be said, in this land above all others, that every man is the architect of his own fortunes.[196]

Notes

1. Sarah Bernhardt, *Memories of my Life* [1907] (Grosse Pointe, MI: Scholarly Press, 1968), 393.
2. W. G. Marshall, *Through America: Nine Months in the United States* (London: Sampson, Low, Marston, Searle & Rivington, 1881), 353, 373.
3. Isabella L. Bird, *A Lady's Life in the Rocky Mountains* [1879] (Norman: University of Oklahoma Press, 1969), 83.
4. Anonymous, "Some Remarks on Travelling in America," *The Cornhill Magazine* 19 (March 1869), 323.
5. Thomas J. Schlereth, *Victorian America: Transformations in Everyday Life, 1876–1915* (New York: Harper Perennial, 1992), 13.
6. See Philip Weeks, *Farewell, My Nation: The American Indian and the United States, 1820–1890* (Arlington Heights, IL: Harlan Davidson, 1990), 110.
7. Jane Louise Mesick, *The English Traveler in America, 1785–1835* [1922] (Westport, CN: Greenwood Press, 1970), 336.
8. Ibid., 339, 337.
9. See Christopher Mulvey, *Transatlantic Manners: Social Patterns in Nineteenth-Century Anglo-American Travel Literature* (Cambridge: Cambridge University Press, 1990), 76–102.
10. Anonymous, "Some American Notes," *MacMillan's Magazine* 53 (November 1885), 48.
11. W. E. Adams, *Our American Cousins: Being Personal Impressions of the People and Institutions of the United States* (London: Walter Scott, 1883), 3.
12. U.S. Department of Commerce, Bureau of the Census, *Historical Statistics of the United States: Colonial Times to 1957* (Washington, D.C.: GPO, 1961), 427; James Fullarton Muirhead, The Land of Contrasts: A Briton's view of his American Kin (London: Lanson, Wolffe and Co., 1898) 12.
13. F. Barham Zincke, *Last Winter in the United States: Being Table Talk Collected During a Tour Through the Late Southern Confederation, the Far West, the Rocky Mountains, &c.* [1868] (Freeport, NY: Books for Libraries Press, 1970), 251. As for expense, Zincke noted that "it will not have cost you so much as it would have done to have hired a moor and forest in Scotland, and paid a parcel of gillies, and kept house besides for two or three months; and you will have killed twenty times as much game, and had much more varied and interesting sport, and have had the choice of a district larger than the whole of Scotland, and seen some of the greatest sights the world has to show." Ibid., 253.

14. It may have been cheaper for an American on the East Coast to travel to Europe than to travel to California. See Anne Farrar Hyde, *An American Vision: Far Western Landscape and National Culture, 1820–1920* (New York: New York University Press, 1990), 108. For historical currency conversions, see www.futureboy.us/fsp/dollar.

15. In 1874, J. W. Boddam-Whetham complained that "travelling is much cheaper in Europe than in the United States, and that the cost of living at American watering-places and at all favourite resorts is so enormous that a whole family can enjoy some months of European travel for the same sum that a short sojourn at any of these fashionable places would entail." J. W. Boddam-Whetham, *Western Wanderings: A Record of Travel in the Evening Land* (London: Richard Bentley and Son, 1874), 362.

16. Henry Latham, *Black and White: A Journal of a Three Months' Tour in the United States* [1867] (New York: Negro Universities Press, 1969), v; Zincke, 119.

17. Emily Faithfull, *Three Visits to America* (New York: Fowler & Wells, 1884), 1.

18. Joseph Hatton, *Henry Irving's Impressions of America, Narrated in a Series of Sketches, Chronicles, and Conversations*, v. 1 [1884] (New York: Benjamin Blom, 1971), 60.

19. Quoted in Faithfull, 2.

20. James Bryce, *The American Commonwealth* [1888], v. 1 (New York: The Commonwealth Publishing Co., 1908), 4.

21. Ibid., v. 1, 2.

22. In an 1889 review of James Bryce's *The American Commonwealth*, Edward Eggleston claimed that of the hundreds of books written by foreigners on life in the United States, only Bryce and Tocqueville had produced "real books." According to Eggleston, other treatments of this subject were "superficial observations of men who could not penetrate beyond the cuticle of the strange world in which they found themselves, and who were unable to divest themselves of the prejudices in which they had been cradled." Edward Eggleston, "A Full-Length Portrait of the United States," *The Century Magazine* 37, no. 5 (March 1889), 789.

23. William Howard Russell, *Hesperothen, Notes from the West: A Record of a Ramble in the United States and Canada in the Spring and Summmer of 1881*, v. 1 (London: S. Low, Marston, Searle & Rivington, 1882), 54.

24. Max O'rell and Jack Allyn, *Jonathan and His Continent: Rambles Through American Society*, trans. Madame Paul Blouet (Bristol: J. W. Arrowsmith, 1889), 6.

25. William Francis Butler, *The Great Lone Land: A Narrative of Travel and Adventure in the North-West of America* (Rutland, VT: 1968), 79.

26. W. F. Rae, *Westward by Rail: The New Route to the East* [1871] (New York: Promontory Press, 1874), 371.

27. Anonymous, "Some Remarks on Travelling in America," 324.

28. E. Catherine Bates, *A Year in the Great Republic*, v. 1 (London: Ward & Downey, 1887), x.

29. Christopher Mulvey, *Anglo-American Landscapes: A Study of Nineteenth-Century Anglo-American Travel Literature* (Cambridge: Cambridge University Press, 1983), 20.

30. A Maurice Low, *The American People: A Study in National Psychology*, v. 1 (Boston: Houghton Mifflin, 1909), 4.

31. Ibid., v. 1, 5, 6.

32. William H. A. Williams, *Tourism, Landscape, and the Irish Character: British Travel Writers in Pre-Famine Ireland* (Madison: University of Wisconsin Press, 2008), x.

33. Ibid., 113. Others have endorsed Williams' point of view. James Fullarton Muirhead said of the United States that, "More, perhaps, than in any other country that I know of will what the traveler find there depend on what he brings with him." Muirhead, 1. Historian Christopher Mulvey noted that, "The Englishman in America was on the look out for England. When he found a deferential servant, he recorded it as a sign of improvement; when he found a rude one, he recorded it as a sign of progressive decay." Mulvey, *Anglo-American Landscapes*, 10. Historian Ray Allen Billington claimed that visitors found ways to confirm "not what was there, but what their

experiences, beliefs, prejudices, and convictions convinced them should be there." Ray Allen Billington, *Land of Savagery, Land of Promise: The European Image of the American Frontier in the Nineteenth Century* (New York: W. W. Norton, 1981), 74.

34. Williams, 199, 200.

35. Bates, v. 1, xi–xii.

36. H. Hussey Vivian, *Notes of a Tour in America from August 7th to November 17th, 1877* (London: Edward Stanford, 1878), 211, 212.

37. Boddam-Whetham, 364.

38. Richard L. Rapson, *Britons View America: Travel Commentary, 1860–1935* (Seattle: University of Washington Press, 1971), 203–204, 205.

39. Bryce, v. 1, 8.

40. Low, v. 1, 14.

41. Allan Nevins, in his compilation of literature produced by British travelers from 1789 to 1946, argues that what makes the period from 1870 to 1922 different is that, Tocqueville notwithstanding, "for the first time analysis became the dominant note. It completely triumphed over mere narration and description." *America Through British Eyes*, ed. and compiled by Allan Nevins (Gloucester, MA: Peter Smith, 1968), 305.

42. James Bryce, "The Essential Unity of Britain and America," *Atlantic Monthly* 82, no. 489 (July 1898), 26.

43. Phil Robinson, *Sinners and Saints: A Tour Across the States, and Round Them; with Three Months Among the Mormons* (Boston: Roberts Brothers, 1883), 304–305. One British traveler, Edward A. Freeman, expressed relief that his American friends had spared him the "fearful grind" of being led through factories, prisons and hospitals. Edward A. Freeman, *Some Impressions of the United States* (London: Longmans, Green, and Co., 1883), 4.

44. Nash notes that "no European would journey to Arizona or Wyoming in 1900 to see cities, museums, and churches. But Indians, the Rocky Mountains, Yosemite and the Grand Canyon were compelling." Roderick Nash, *Wilderness and the American Mind* (New Haven: Yale University Press, 1982), 350.

45. Billington, 78.

46. William Bradford, *Of Plymouth Plantation, 1620–1647* (New York: Modern Library, 1981), 70.

47. Mary Rowlandson, *The Sovereignty and Goodness of God* [1682] (Boston: Bedford Books, 1997), 80, 70. In 1662, Michael Wigglesworth used similar words:

    Waste and howling wilderness,
    Where none inhabited
    But hellish fiends, and brutish men
    That devils worshiped.
    Quoted in Henry Nash Smith, *Virgin Land: The American West as Symbol and Myth* (Cambridge, MA: Harvard University Press, 1950), 4.

48. See Nash, 44–48. The religious element of the wilderness is made explicit in *The Prairie* when someone asks James Fenimore Cooper's character Natty Bumppo if he actually lived on the prairie. Bumppo replies, "'I have been long on earth, and never I hope nigher to Heaven than I am at this moment.'" James Fenimore Cooper, *The Prairie* [1827] (New York: Library of America, 1985), 910.

49. François-René de Chateaubriand, from *René*, in *Norton Anthology of World Masterpieces*, v. 2, sixth edition, ed. Maynard Mack et al. (New York: W. W. Norton, 1992), 583.

50. Bryce, v. 2, 82.

51. Paul de Rousiers, *American Life*, trans. A. J. Herbertson (New York: Firmin-Didot, 1892), 15.

52. Oliver North, "Quail Shooting in California," in Oliver North, *Rambles After Sport, or, Travels and Adventures in the Americas and At Home* (London: The Field Office, 1874), 43.

53. Robert Louis Stevenson, "The Amateur Emigrant," in *From Scotland to Silverado* [1892] (Cambridge, MA: Belknap Press, 1966), 90.

54. Parker Gillmore, *A Hunter's Adventures in the Great West* (London: Hurst and Blackett, 1871), 218.

55. Windham Thomas Wyndham-Quin, *The Great Divide: Travels in the Upper Yellowstone in the Summer of 1874* (London: Chatto and Windus, 1876), 60.

56. Bird, 21.

57. Rudyard Kipling, *American Notes* [1891] (Norman: University of Oklahoma Press, 1981), 55.

58. William A. Baille-Grohman, *Camps in the Rockies: Being a Narrative of Life on the Frontier, and Sport in the Rocky Mountains, with an Account of the Cattle Ranches of the West* (New York: Charles Scribner's Sons, 1884), 12.

59. Russell, v. 2, 99.

60. Robinson, 43.

61. Henry Sienkiewicz, *Portrait of America: Letters of Henry Sienkiewicz*, ed. and trans. Charles Morley (New York: Columbia University Press, 1959), 103. Other Europeans who came to America heavily armed included Paul de Rousiers, who brought with him a revolver "with the latest improvements" and enough cartridges "to make fifty of my fellow-beings bite the dust." But with no opportunity to use them, they lay abandoned in the bottom of his luggage until he rediscovered "these traces of vanished apprehensions." Rousiers, 160, 161.

62. Patrick Brantlinger, *Dark Vanishings: Discourse on the Extinction of Primitive Races, 1800–1930* (Ithaca: Cornell University Press, 2003), 60.

63. See Billington, 30–32. Billington notes that Karl May, the most popular German writer of Westerns, sold thirty million copies of his books, and was the favorite author of both Adolf Hitler and Albert Einstein. Ibid., 56.

64. James Fenimore Cooper, *The Pioneers* [1823] (New York: Library of America, 1985), 85.

65. Wyndham-Quin, 112–113. Even though Wyndham-Quin confessed that he was "not disposed to be over fond of Indians," he went on to say, "still I am fond of them; I respect their instinct, I admire their intense love of freedom; and, while admitting that Cooper's heroes are somewhat imaginary, I must confess that the 'noble Red man' is not altogether such a mythical being as one school of writers would have us believe." Ibid., 113. Henry M. Stanley, who accompanied General Hancock on his expedition to the Great Plains in 1867, had many opportunities to see Indians up close. He said, "We were formerly under the impression that there were no noble-looking Indians, save in the fervid fancies of Fenimore Cooper, but we must confess that they do exist, even at the present day, and that we have seen them." Henry M. Stanley, *My Early Travels and Adventures in America* [1895] (Lincoln: University of Nebraska Press, 1982), 35.

66. Sienkiewicz, 61.

67. Freeman, 151.

68. Horace Annesley Vachell, *Life and Sport on the Pacific Slope* (New York: Dodd, Mead and Co., 1901), 7. Reporting from San Francisco in 1871, R. H. Inglis Synnot observed that "many worthy English people still look on San Francisco as a den of murderers, ignorant that the citizens there are quieter, the police better (as it very easily may be), and life safer, than in dear old London." R. H. Inglis Synnot, "The Pacific Express," *The Contemporary Review* 17 (June 1871), 441.

69. Oscar Wilde, "Americans in London," in Oscar Wilde, *The Essays of Oscar Wilde* [1916], ed. Albert and Charles Boni (New York: Bonibooks, 1935), 197; David Macrae, *The Americans at Home* [1870] (New York: E. P. Dutton, 1952), 11.

70. A Cynic, "National Antipathies," *The Cornhill Magazine* 21 (February 1870), 158.

71. Lida von Krockow, "American Characters in German Novels," *Atlantic Monthly* 68, no. 410 (December 1891), 833.

72. R. W. Dale, "Impressions of America," pt. 1, *Eclectic Magazine* 27, no. 6 (New Series, June 1878), 666.

73. Literary works whose American characters were presented "in either an odious or a ridiculous aspect" included Edward Bulwer's *My Novel*, Charles James Lever's *One of Them*, Edward Hodgson Yates' *Black Sheep*, and Charles Dickens' *Martin Chuzzlewit* and *Mugby Junction*. W. C. M., "American Traits," *Eclectic Magazine* 16, no. 1 (New Series, July 1872), 58.

74. William Archer, *America To-Day: Observations and Reflections* [1899] (New York: Arno Press, 1974), 89. Archer noted that in American gentlemen's clubs "one or two English daily papers and all the more important weekly papers are taken as a matter of course." Ibid., 88.

75. Mulvey, *Anglo-American Landscapes*, 9.

76. W. C. M., 58.

77. Robert G. Athearn, *Westward the Briton* (Lincoln: University of Nebraska Press, 1953), 158.

78. As historian William H. A. Williams suggests, "The tourist's question about his hosts—'Who are they?'—inevitably prompts the query 'Who am I?'" Williams, 7.

79. Walt Whitman, "Our Eminent Vistors Past, Present and Future," in *November Boughs*, collected in Walt Whitman, *Prose Works 1892*, v. 2, ed. Floyd Stovall (New York: New York University Press, 1964), 541–542.

80. Anthony Trollope, *North America* [1862] (New York: Alfred A. Knopf, 1951), 537.

81. Quoted in "A German Appraisal of the United States," *Atlantic Monthly* 75, no. 447 (January 1895), 124.

82. Lepel Henry Griffin, *The Great Republic* [1884] (New York: Arno Press, 1974), 4, 35.

83. Paul Bourget, *Outre-Mer: Impressions of America* (London: T. Fisher Unwin, 1895), 113; French labor delegates quoted in Émile Levasseur, *The American Workman*, trans. Thomas S. Adams (Baltimore: Johns Hopkins University, 1900), 63.

84. Andrew J. Torrielli, *Italian Opinion on America, As Revealed by Italian Travelers, 1850–1900* (Cambridge, MA: Harvard University Press, 1941), 292.

85. Sienkiewicz, 166.

86. Alexandra Gripenberg, *A Half Year in the New World: Miscellaneous Sketches of Travel in the United States* [1889], trans. and ed. Ernest J. Moyne (Newark: University of Delaware Press, 1954), 207, 194.

87. Quoted in A. N. J. den Hollander, "Charles Boissevain, 1842–1927," in *Abroad in America: Visitors to the New Nation, 1776–1914* (Reading, MA: Addison-Wesley, 1976), 187.

88. Bourget, 4–7.

89. S. C. de Soissons, *A Parisian in America* (Boston: Estes and Lauriat, 1896), 41.

90. Theodore Zeldin "Foreword," in *The Rise and Fall of Anti-Americanism: A Century of French Perception*, ed. Denis Lacorne et al. (New York: St. Martin's Press, 1990), x–xi.

91. Marie Therese de Solms Blanc, *The Condition of Woman in the United States: A Traveller's Notes*, trans. Abby Landdon Alger [1895] (New York: Arno Press, 1972), 76.

92. Knut Hamsun, *The Cultural Life of Modern America* [1889] (Cambridge, MA: Harvard University Press, 1969), 10. Hamsun claimed that the only foreigners Americans respected were the British, and that Americans had devoted themselves to "the tag ends of the old English civilization." Ibid., 14.

93. John Fiske, "'Manifest Destiny,'" *Harper's* 70, no. 417 (February 1885), 583, 584.

94. Crane Brinton, *The Americans and the French* (Cambridge, MA: Harvard University Press, 1968), 50–51, 40.

95. Ralph Waldo Emerson, *English Traits* [1856] (Cambridge, MA: Belknap Press of Harvard University Press, 1966), 94.

96. Ibid., 76–77.

97. Here Emerson repeats the anecdote of the Frenchman and Englishman who quarrelled. Neither one of them wanted to fight, but their friends insisted and arranged that the

two would fight in the dark with pistols. "the Englishman, to make sure not to hit anybody, fired up the chimney—and brought down the Frenchman." Ibid., 79, 96–97.

98. Ibid., 94.
99. Rosecrans Baldwin, "The American in Paris," *New York Times*, May 7, 2012.
100. Denis Lacorne and Jacques Rupnik, "Introduction: France Bewitched by America," in *The Rise and Fall of Anti-Americanism: A Century of French Perception*, ed. Denis Lacorne et al. (New York: St. Martin's Press, 1990), 1–2.
101. Levasseur, 437.
102. Sienkiewicz, 226.
103. Charles Dickens, *The Speeches of Charles Dickens*, ed. K. J. Fielding (Hemel Hempstead, Hertfordshire: Harvester Wheatsheaf, 1988), 381.
104. Matthew Arnold, "A Word About America," in *Civilization in the United States: First and Last Impressions of America* [1888] (Freeport, NY: Books for Libraries Press, 1972), 72. Bram Stoker said in 1886 that Americans were "not merely like ourselves, but ourselves—the same in blood, religion, and social ideas, with an almost identical common law." Bram Stoker, "A Glimpse of America" [1886] in *Bram Stoker's A Glimpse of America and Other Lectures, Interviews and Essays*, ed. Richard Dalby (Westcliff-on-Sea, UK: Desert Island Books, 2002), 11. By the time he published *The American People: A Study in National Psychology* in 1909, A. Maurice Low proclaimed that "America is no longer England or even a reflex of England. America is American, and if the character of the American people is to be understood and their civilization is to be correctly interpreted they must be measured by their own standards and not weighed in the scales of foreign make." Low, v. 1. 27.
105. Bates, v. 1, xix.
106. See Amanda Foreman, *A World On Fire: Britain's Crucial Role in the American Civil War* (New York: Random House, 2010), 802–805.
107. Henry M. Stanley, "The Issue Between Great Britain and America," *The Nineteenth Century* 39, no. 227 (January 1896), 1.
108. Adams, 6.
109. Butler, 81.
110. Stoker, 27.
111. See Rapson, 14–15. In his novel *Humphrey Clinker*, the Scottish author Tobias Smollett observes of the English that "between want of curiosity, and traditional sarcasms, the effect of ancient animosity, the people at the other end of the island know as little of Scotland as of Japan." Tobias Smollett, *Humphrey Clinker* [1771] (London: Penguin, 2008), 238.
112. Muirhead related the following joke that he had read in an American comic journal:

> *Tomkyns* (of London). — I say, Vanarsdale, I told such a good joke, don't you know, to MacPherson, and he didn't laugh a bit! I suppose that's because he's a Scotsman? *Vanarsdale* (of New York). — I don't know; I think it's more like that it's because you are an Englishman!
> Muirhead, 129.

113. Vachell, 208; Macrae, 19.
114. Macrae, 19.
115. Zincke, 199, 101. Rudyard Kipling also concluded that the "Germans and Irish who are more Americans than the Americans are the chief offenders." Kipling, 86. William Archer claimed that by 1899 American attitudes toward the English could be narrowed to three classes: "The cultured and travelled" class who revered the English, the "hyphenated Americans whose hatred of England is partly a mere plank in a political platform," and "the great mass of the American people, who neither love nor hate England, any more than they love or hate (say) Italy or Japan." Archer, 176, 177.

116. Russell, v. 2, 146.

117. Robinson, 4.

118. Lepel Henry Griffin, *The Great Republic* [1884] (New York: Arno Press, 1974), 10, 14.

119. Muirhead, 92.

120. Bates, v. 1, xi.

121. Harold Brydges, *Uncle Sam at Home* (New York: Henry Holt and Co., 1888), 215. George Augustus Sala said of the English that "we are always snarling and grumbling and bringing actions against our brothers and sisters." George Augustus Sala, *America Revisited: From the Bay of New York to the Gulf of Mexico and from Lake Michigan to the Pacific* (London: Vizetelly & Co., n.d.), 76. F. Barham Zincke contended that because Americans were so careful about giving offense, "where an Englishman is the complainant, I should be disposed to think that, in most cases, he had provoked the treatment he complains of." Zincke, 175.

122. Quoted in Hatton, v. 2, 66. George Augustus Sala compared the experience of enduring an over-heated railway waiting room in Jersey City on a rainy day to being "so much barley that had been well sprinkled and had germinated, and were now being roasted, as malt, in a kiln." Sala, 91.

123. Vachell, 28. Vachell added that "the Englishman is so morbidly afraid of making a fool of himself that he is often blind to the fact that others have performed that office for him." Ibid., 201. G. K. Chesterton noted that "when I think something in America is really foolish, it may be I that am made a fool of." G. K. Chesterton, *What I Saw in America* [1922], in *The Collected Works of G. K. Chesterton*, v. 21 (San Francisco: Ignatius Press, 1990),

124. Bates, v. 2, 312.

125. A Cynic, 154.

126. Stevenson, 93.

127. R. L. S., "The Foreigner at Home," *The Cornhill Magazine* 45 (May 1882).

128. Beatrice Webb, *Beatrice Webb's American Diary* (Madison: University of Wisconsin Press, 1963), 14, 16, 23, 31.

129. Ibid., 69, 68.

130. O'rell, 7.

131. J. R. Lowell, "On a Certain Condescension in Foreigners," *Atlantic Monthly* 23 (January 1869), 89; O'rell, 8. In its obituary of Englishman William Hepworth Dixon, the *New York Times* contrasts Dixon with other British travelers to America: "He was a very accessible person, having much more ease and freedom of manner, more fluency of speech, and outward geniality than most of his compatriots." *New York Times*, December 28, 1879.

132. Low, v. 2, 151.

133. Rae, 16–17.

134. Freeman, 235.

135. Quoted in A. K. Sandoval-Strausz, *Hotel: An American History* (New Haven: Yale University Press, 2007), 185.

136. William Howard Russell observed that "a stranger accustomed to have his own way in his inn, and to have his orders attended to with dispatch, might perhaps have his temper ruffled by the divine calm of the coloured citizens who officiated as helps, or by the haughty composure of the landlord." Quoted in Russell, v. 1, 209.

137. James Fullarton Muirhead concluded that, "Almost the only field in which the Americans struck me as showing anything like servility was their treatment of such mighty potentates as railway conductors, hotel clerks, and policemen." Muirhead, 97.

138. W. C. M., 56.

139. Macrae, 511.

140. Commenting on the English sense of entitlement, G. K. Chesterton noted that "an Englishman will go poking about in little Swiss or Italian villages, in wild mountains

or in remote islands, demanding tea; and never reflects that he is like a Chinaman who should enter all the wayside public-houses in Kent or Sussex and demand opium." Chesterton, 79.

141. Kipling, *American Notes*, 107.

142. Baille-Grohman, 213, 29, 30.

143. William F. Cody, "Famous Hunting Parties of the Plains," *The Cosmopolitan* 17, no. 2 (June 1894), 134.

144. Quoted in Athearn, 110.

145. Bird, 112.

146. Ibid., 112, 113.

147. Ibid., 176.

148. Ibid., 248–249.

149. Simon Schama, "The Unloved American," *New Yorker*, March 10, 2003, 34.

150. As "evidence," Schama cites the American experiences of Rudyard Kipling and of the Norwegian Knut Hamsun, without mentioning that the latter called his book on America "appallingly badly and childishly written," and a "youthful sin." Hamsun refused to allow it to be republished. As for Kipling, he despised Americans so much that he married one, and said of Americans as a whole (in the same memoir from which Schama quotes) that "I love them, and I realized it when I met an Englishman who laughed at them." Or, he might have added, by a historian who misrepresents them. Hamsun quoted in Barbara Gordon Morgridge, "Editor's Introduction," in Knut Hamsun, *The Cultural Life of Modern America* [1889] (Cambridge, MA: Harvard University Press, 1969), xxx, xxiv. Kipling, *American Notes*, 124.

151. A. S. Northcote, "American Life Through English Spectacles," *The Nineteenth Century* 34, no. 199 (September 1893), 487.

152. W. Henry Barneby, *Life and Labor in the Far, Far West: Being Notes of a Tour in the Western States, British Columbia, Manitoba, and the North-West Territory* (London: Cassell & Co., 1884), 9. Alexander Craib took note of "the erroneous impression" in Britain that Americans were "impolite to strangers, and rude in speech and behavior … My impression of Americans is this—they are intelligent, free, and frank, of a kindly disposition, without restraint, and obliging to a degree." Alexander Craib, *America and the Americans: A Tour in the United States and Canada, With Chapters on American Home Life* (London: Alexander Gardner, 1892), 53–54.

153. Muirhead, 6.

154. Hamsun, 140.

155. Baron Hübner, *A Ramble Round the World, 1871*, trans. Lady Elizabeth Herbert (London: MacMillan and Co., 1878), 180.

156. See Jane Louise Mesick, *The English Traveler in America, 1785–1835* [1922] (Westport, CN: Greenwood Press, 1970); Max Berger, *The British Traveller in America, 1836–1860* (Gloucester, MA: Peter Smith, 1964); Richard L. Rapson, *Britons View America: Travel Commentary, 1860–1935* (Seattle: University of Washington Press, 1971).

157. Robert Frankel, *Observing America: The Commentary of British Visitors to the United States, 1890–1950* (Madison: University of Wisconsin Press, 2007), xiii.

158. Rapson, 53.

159. Craib, 49. In 1782 Hector St. John de Crèvecoeur declared that, "The American is a new man, who acts upon new principles; he must therefore entertain new ideas, and form new opinions." Hector St. John de Crèvecoeur, "What Is An American," in *Letters From An American Farmer* [1782] (London: J. M. Dent and Sons, 1926), 44.

160. Low, v. 1, 14.

161. Rapson, 211–212.

162. Ibid., 193.

163. Marshall, 256.

164. Whitman, 542.

165. Foucault famously noted that, "I am well aware that I have never written anything but fictions ... One 'fictions' history on the basis of a political reality that makes it true, one 'fictions' a politics not yet in existence on the basis of a historical truth." Michel Foucault, *Power/Knowledge: Selected Interviews and Other Writings, 1972–1977*, ed. Colin Gordon (New York: Pantheon, 1980), 193. Important to postmodernist thinking is the idea that humans create their own reality through social constructs. A key document in the development of this notion is Peter L. Berger and Thomas Luckman, *The Social Construction of Reality* (New York: Anchor Books, 1966). Postmodernism's lack of logic is a chronic problem, which Mark Goldblatt illuminates in his critique of Jacques Derrida's *Positions*: "For Derrida winds up his analysis with another logical throwaway; 'Neither/nor, that is, *simultaneously* either *or*.' In other words, whatever Derrida is affirming he is also simultaneously denying. From a humanist perspective, the only way to read Derrida on his own terms is mentally to insert the phrase 'or not' after every one of his statements." Mark Goldblatt, "Can Humanists Talk to Poststructuralists?" *Adademic Questions* 18, no. 2 (Spring 2005).

166. Williams, 52.

167. John Urry, *The Tourist's Gaze: Leisure and Travel in Contemprary Societies* (London: Sage Publications, 1990), 138. In a later article, Urry and co-author Carol Crawhaw repeat the idea that "the travel photographer and the tourist seem to engage in a mutually reinforcing social process of constructing and altering images of places and experiences." See Carol Crawhaw and John Urry, "Tourism and the Photographic Eye," in *Touring Cultures: Transformations of Travel and Theory*, ed. Chris Rojek and John Urry (London: Routledge, 1997), 194.

168. Malcolm Andrews, *The Search for the Picturesque: Landscape Aesthetics and Tourism in Britain, 1760–1800* (Stanford: Stanford University Press, 1989), 239.

169. Ibid., 4.

170. Ann Bermingham, *Landscape and Ideology: The English Rustic Tradition, 1740–1860* (Berkeley: University of California Press, 1986), 70.

171. Cindy S. Aron observes that, "Well-read Americans knew well the concepts of the beautiful, the picturesque, and the sublime that eighteenth-century English philosophers and writers had elaborated." Cindy S. Aron, *Working at Play: A History of Vacations in the United States* (New York: Oxford University Press, 1999), 130.

172. Rose Pender, *A Lady's Experience of the Wild West in 1883* (London: George Tucker, 1888), 10.

173. James quoted in Christopher Mulvey, *Transatlantic Manners*, 214.

174. The picturesque barely masked what Bermingham calls "a social disdain" and what Andrews calls a "moral detachment." Bermingham, 69; Andrews, 236.

175. Theodora Guest, *A Round Trip in North America* (London: Edward Stanford, 1895), 86, 85. Rose Pender entertained the idea that cowboys might qualify as picturesque ("Such picturesque wild-looking fellows these cowboys were, in their wide-brimmed sombreros and leather chaps, all fringed, and wearing big Mexican spurs"), but after meeting a few, Pender concluded, "I do not like the cowboys; they impressed me as brutal and cowardly, besides being utterly devoid of manners or good feeling." Pender, 30–31, 46.

176. Daniel J. Boorstin, *The Image: A Guide to Pseudo-Events in America* [1961] (New York: Atheneum, 1987), 84–87.

177. James Buzard, *The Beaten Track: European Tourism, Literature, and the Ways to Culture, 1800–1918* (Oxford: Clarendon Press, 1993), 2. Among those insisting on making such a distinction is Paul Fussell. Paul Fussell, *Abroad: British Literary Traveling Between the Wars* (New York: Oxford University Press, 1980).

178. Jan Palmowski, "Travels with Baedeker—The Guidebook and the Middle Classes in Victorian and Edwardian Britain," in *Histories of Leisure*, ed. Rudy Koshar (Oxford: Berg, 2002), 117.

179. Cook quoted in Boorstin, *The Image*, 88.

180. Orvar Löfgren, *On Holiday: A History of Vacationing* (Berkeley: University of California Press, 1999), 8; Buzard, 5.
181. Aron, 155.
182. On tourism in the Hudson River Valley, see Mulvey, *Anglo-American Landscapes*, 173–186; Löfgren 37–38. See also Aron, 130.
183. Craib, 45; Russell, v. 1, 156; Marshall, 76–77. Marshall, who held Indians in contempt, nevertheless complained that the Niagara shops that featured "'Indian' curiosities are no more Indian than the clothes you are wearing. They are made in New York and are palmed off on you as Indian." Ibid., 77.
184. William Francis Butler, *The Great Lone Land: A Narrative of Travel and Adventure in the North-West of America* [1872] (Rutland, VT: Charles E. Tuttle, 1968), 26.
185. See Buzard, 12; Löfgren, 277.
186. See Lady Duffus Hardy, *Through Cities and Prairie Lands: Sketches of an American Tour* (London: Chapman and Hall, 1881), 54; Iza Duffus Hardy, *Between Two Oceans: Or, Sketches of American Travel* (London: Hurst and Blackett, 1884), 39.
187. Barbara Ireland, "36 Hours: Niagara Falls," *New York Times*, May 29, 2011.
188. It was not until 1884 that the first Cook excursions to Yellowstone took place. See J. Valerie Fifer, *American Progress: The Growth of the Transport, Tourist, and Information Industries in the Nineteenth-Century West* (Chester, CN: Globe Pequot Press, 1988), 257, 302, 301–306.
189. See Rose G. Kingsley, *South by West, or Winter in the Rocky Mountains and Spring in Mexico* (London: W. Isbinster and Co., 1874), 55–56.
190. Boddam-Whetham, 123.
191. Pender, 19.
192. Earl S. Pomeroy, *In Search of the Golden West: The Tourist in Western America* (New York: Knopf, 1957), 22.
193. Fernand Braudel, "Introduction," in Fernand Braudel, *Civilization and Capitalism, 15th–18th Century, Volume One: The Structures of Everyday Life* (New York: Harper & Row, 1981), 29. In another example, Grady McWhiney found that little material had been generated by the "Crackers" (antebellum Southerners of Celtic origins) that were the focus of his excellent study, *Cracker Culture*. But he did find a wealth of travel accounts, and because travelers were outsiders, "they often found Crackers unusual and therefore noticed and remarked upon things that Crackers took for granted and would not have thought worth pointing out." Grady McWhiney, *Cracker Culture: Celtic Ways in the Old South* (Tuscaloosa: University of Alabama Press, 1988), xviii.
194. Adams, 1.
195. Charles Dickens to Miss Georgina Hogarth. 27 and 28 February 1868. Charles Dickens, *The Letters of Charles Dickens*, v. 3, ed. Graham Storey (Oxford: Clarendon Press, 2002), 61.
196. Lady Duffus Hardy, 158.

1

CHARACTER, CLASS, DRESS, MONEY, AND ADVERTISING

Character

Nearly every traveler in America, whether friendly or hostile to the United States, took note of the national energy. Horace Annesley Vachell described Americans as "a people not to be matched in energy, patience, pluck, and executive ability."[1] Harold Brydges called American energy "superabundant" (he described the national motto as "hurry up"), and J. W. Boddam-Whetham said of Americans that they were "bent on making amends, as they say here, for having come into the world half-an-hour too late."[2] The pace was especially frenetic in American cities. In the vicinity of New York's elevateds, for instance, Americans were constantly running—running up and down the stairs of the platform, running to catch a train, running after leaving the train.[3]

Even when an American died, according to Paul de Rousiers, the hearse carried his body to the cemetery "at a trot" because those attending the funeral did not have the time for a slower-paced ceremony.[4] As evidence of the eternal restless energy of Americans, Léon Paul Blouet cited the popularity of the rocking chair in the United States, where even in repose Americans were on the move.[5] One observer even claimed that the American propensity to rush through life had resulted in the shortening of words to save time (thus "bike" for bicycle, "ave" for avenue, and "gents" for gentlemen).[6] Francesco Carega believed that the rapid progress of American society could be distilled down to a single word: "industriousness."[7] In one example, when his train was delayed in the Rocky Mountains in 1883, W. Henry Barneby watched a goodly number of passengers jump down and begin looking for signs of minerals, illustrating the "restless activity" of Americans and their insistence on turning every minute to account.[8]

Tocqueville had noted of Americans that they were "constantly on the move," and that there was something "improvised about their lives."[9] This national restlessness carried forward into the postbellum period and included both sexes. Maria Theresa Blanc contrasted the French woman, who clung to the familiarity of her home, with the American woman, who had no hesitation in leaving her residence for extended periods.[10] E. Catherine Bates was also struck by the willingness of even elderly American women "to uproot themselves at a moment's notice" to go live in some distant city.[11] Another commentator called Americans the "most locomotive people in the world," and suggested that foreigners visit the United States during the winter, otherwise they ran the risk that no one would be home.[12] "The American," said Baron Hübner "is essentially nomad."[13]

But to many Europeans, this energy and constant movement amounted to a manic obsession with no clear objective. When he visited America in 1892, Harry Kessler condemned "the endlessly prosaic and monotonous busyness of life" in the United States.[14] Six years later, Italian traveler Ugo Ojetti found himself on the same American train with the Spaniard Captain Mereu, a recently released prisoner from the Spanish–American War. Referring to Americans, an exasperated Mereu said to Ojetti, "They are crazy, they are crazy! Once they have run so much, where do they think they will get to?"[15]

The national energy and the American business ethos were directly linked to the rapid adoption of new inventions and innovations. One good example is electric lighting, which was being installed in American hotels by the early 1880s.[16] Joseph Hatton was struck by what he called "the new and beautiful light" when he toured America in 1883.[17] As early as 1881, the Philadelphia hotel where William Howard Russell stayed featured electric lighting, which Russell sarcastically predicted would "come into use in similar establishments in London in a generation or so."[18] Resistance to the new in Britain was considerable. As late as 1890, an article in the British publication *The Nineteenth Century* took pains to emphasize not the considerable advantages of electrical generation but "deaths from artificially produced electricity" in America.[19] In contrast, business leaders in even the smallest American towns quickly installed electricity, water works, and street cars as a way of raising property values and enhancing speculative opportunities. Paul de Rousiers noted of tiny Guthrie, Oklahoma, in 1890 that it had electric light that illuminated little more than "plank barracks" and the prairie flowers that still grew in the streets.[20]

Other innovations included the elevator, which was so ubiquitous by 1886 that J. J. Aubertin called it the "only recognized American staircase."[21] Within a few months of its invention, the telephone was in operation in most of America's cities, while years later, noted a rueful William Saunders, almost no phones were in service in England.[22] Herbert Spencer likewise found the telephone in general use in American cities as small as 10,000 in the early 1880s, while in Britain's "unenterprising towns" telephone service in communities of 50,000 or more was unknown.[23] Americans had also perfected other innovations that European travelers found remarkable. When his train was run onto a steamer that carried the passengers across the St. Clair River without anyone having to move from their seats, Alexander Craib was astonished. "'How clever you Americans are!'" said Craib to a nearby Yankee. The unimpressed American replied, "'Yes, I guess we know how to go about things.'"[24]

It is not surprising that by the last decade of the nineteenth century, Europeans were increasingly concerned that a gap was opening up between American and European industry, and that the constant upgrading to the most modern machinery by American manufacturers was leaving European industries behind. The American factory system evolved partly out of necessity (such as the substitution of water power for coal power in New England where coal was expensive), and partly because the United States had no entrenched tradition of manufacturing as was the case in Europe. Also, it must be admitted, the U.S. approach to manufacturing owed a great deal to naivety—Americans simply didn't know any better. Hence, Americans brought every manufacturing process needed for a product under a single roof (rather than separating the processes geographically) and created machines to do specialized work (rather than depending on skilled craftsmen).[25]

Machinery in America was quickly deemed obsolete and was replaced as soon as possible. When Émile Levasseur toured a sawmill in Minnesota, the manager apologized for not being able to show him one of the newer facilities. The mill that was on display was two years old, and would soon have to be scrapped.[26] "The mechanical skill of the Americans," said one British observer, "is unequalled in the world, and never likely to be rivalled in the old countries of Europe where labour is cheap."[27] Paul Bourget found among American businessmen a totally unexpected "technical genius," and French labor delegates to the United States concluded that if France wanted to compete with the "perfection" of U.S. machinery, it would either have to adopt a protective tariff or "relegate our machines to the garret and get modern types."[28]

Many travelers came to the conclusion that where Americans had problems was not in their work, but in their leisure. "The true American cannot understand the delights of repose," said Hamilton Aïdé, "to him inactivity is irritating."[29] Tocqueville had earlier described Americans as "grave and almost sad even in their pleasures," and Madame de San Carlos claimed that the American was admirable as long as there was a task at hand, but when called upon to enjoy himself, he was "pitiable."[30] Here there was a split between the sexes. American men were totally consumed with their work, and it seemed to be the case that only women in America had any leisure.[31] James Fullarton Muirhead noted that "the leisured class of England consists of both sexes, that of America practically of only one," and that the American response to the Englishman trying to explain the concept "gentlemen of leisure" would most likely be, "'Ah, we call them *tramps* in America.'" This was not merely a joke, according to Muirhead, but reflected a deep "ethical principle."[32]

Where the Englishman of leisure would probably have felt most at home in the United States was the South. Looking back to the estates maintained by the aristocracy of the antebellum South, William Hepworth Dixon observed that "a tourist from the Old World—one of the idler classes—found himself much at home in these country mansions … no man was busy, no woman was in haste. Every one had time for wit, for compliment, for small talk."[33] After the war, Scottish visitor David Macrae claimed that a certain indolence still seemed to prevail among white Southerners and attributed it to the corrupting influence of the slave system.[34] But historian Grady McWhiney has forcefully argued that from the beginning, the cultures of North and South were radically different from each other. The South was rural, while increasingly the North was urban.[35] Puritanism had forged attitudes toward work and life in the North, while the South had established "a leisure-oriented society that fostered idleness and gaiety."[36] Ernst von Hesse-Wartegg visited a number of Louisiana plantations in the late 1870s, and found residents there living lives that were not greatly different from the lives they had led before the war. Still presiding were the "proud, placid, pale women vegetat[ing] in easy chairs" who suddenly came to life when a visitor arrived ("with what grace she greets them, such kindness!").[37]

But for most European travelers, the South after the Civil War was an unknown quantity simply because the South was visited less often. There were a number of factors that discouraged European travel in the region. First, the devastation of the South in the immediate aftermath of war was hardly an inviting prospect for the visitor. Also working against greater tourist penetration of the South was that it had a less developed transportation system, and fewer first-class hotels.[38]

It was a nearly universal opinion among European travelers that Americans had a kindly disposition. R. W. Dale said of Americans that "there are no limits to their kindness," and Léon Paul Blouet called good society in America "the wittiest, most genial, and most hospitable I have met with."[39] The helpfulness and courtesy of Americans was described by William Archer as a "national instinct," and others, including Oscar Wilde, S. C. de Soissons, and Theodora Guest were extravagant in their praise of the kindness of Americans.[40] This was especially true in the West, where even the poorest resident exhibited "an unselfish and genuinely hearty hospitality," which was only found where civilization has not yet cast "her gloomy and repellent shroud, of so called 'good manners.'"[41] Peter Tchaikovsky contrasted the American hospitality without subtext with what he had encountered in Paris, where every kindness camouflaged an attempt at exploitation.[42] Paul Bourget was forced to admit that in America there was "a warm spontaneity of welcome of which we have no notion in Latin countries."[43]

The kindness that James Bryce found in America he attributed to the pervasiveness of hope, and "a land of hope is a land of good humour."[44] Bryce was not the only traveler to identify this trait. According to Henry Latham there was hope in the very air that Americans breathed: "All the air above this great continent is full of magnificent castles, with cloud-capped towers and gorgeous palaces."[45]

A corollary to the kindness of Americans was politeness. During thousands of miles of travel through the United States, J. J. Aubertin claimed that he had "never met with anything but great civility and good feeling."[46] William Howard Russell took note of the custom of Americans to repeat the name of someone to whom they had just been introduced. While initially puzzling to the traveler, Russell called this practice "eminently utilitarian" because a mispronunciation of a name could be immediately corrected.[47] A number of visitors were struck by the American proclivity for shaking hands with everyone, and Harold Brydges, for one, was taken aback by the affection that the American lavished on the foreigner: "He takes your hand in a hearty grip, calls you by name, and inquires after your health with a tenderness approaching anxiety."[48] There were some limits to the affection of the American male. Peter Tchaikovsky observed that while America men would embrace him, "here men never kiss."[49]

The Englishman William H. Davies came to many of the same conclusions as his contemporaries, but Davies was operating from a radically different premise than most travelers in America.[50] A self-described "super-tramp," Davies was determined to do as little work as possible in the United States, and over the course of a five-year stay succeeded admirably. Certainly, his sojourn in America seemed to be poorly timed, as he arrived in the United States in the midst of the depression of the 1890s. Still, Davies and his comrades had little trouble obtaining what they needed, and in one glorious summertime stretch in New England, "the people catered for us as though we were the only tramps in the whole world, and as if they considered it providential that we should call at their houses for assistance."[51] During one of Davies' few flirtations with gainful employment, he worked as a wrangler on cattle ships sailing between America and England, and in places like Liverpool he witnessed the American instinct for generosity even among poorly paid wranglers. According to Davies, these Americans would be so moved by the poverty that they encountered in England that they would give away what little money they had until they too were destitute.[52]

From an early date Americans had gained the reputation of being talkative, loud, and even obnoxious, but this seemed to be a minority opinion among Europeans visiting the United States. "Of the pushing, meddling, questioning, American," said Edward A. Freeman, "I have seen nothing."[53] Thomas Hughes claimed that you could travel hundreds of miles with an American before he would strike up a conversation with you.[54] Americans were "the reverse of talkative," said one traveler, while another referred to "long, grave journeys" and "a thousand miles in silence."[55] "A car full of travelling Americans," said George Augustus Sala, "is about the quietest company in which you could possibly find yourself."[56] On Baron Hübner's railroad car the only ones who were speaking loudly were Germans, while "the American is silent in general and only speaks in a whisper."[57] Even in intimate proximity over long periods of time, foreigners were struck by the American proclivity for silence. In Montana, Roger Pocock noted that the cowboys he rode with "rarely speak on the trail," and Parker

Gillmore said of his hunting partner of many weeks that "a more taciturn companion than my present one I do not think I ever met with."[58]

Dining areas in hotels were "dotted with silent solitary feeders," each of whom had seemingly removed himself as far away as possible from other diners in order to avoid the possibility of being spoken to.[59] William Saunders was unnerved by the oppressive silence of Americans, who would sit through an entire meal without saying anything. Saunders claimed that he never encountered what he called a "buzz of conversation" during his time in the United States.[60] Another Briton noted that even when American theatre-goers found a play dull or objectionable, "they show their dissatisfaction only by silence."[61]

Class

Of all the factors that forged the American character, perhaps the most important was egalitarianism. Alexis de Tocqueville had called the "equality of conditions" in America "the focal point" toward which all his observations converged.[62] Indeed, the American resistance to any notion that they belonged to a "servant" class had been noted by European travelers from the earliest days of the republic. During her stay in Cincinnati in 1827, Frances Trollope complained that one of the greatest difficulties in establishing a household in Ohio was acquiring servants. According to Trollope, the word "servant" was simply not used in the United States because it was deemed an insult to a free citizen. Instead it was called "getting help."[63] When one of Trollope's servants was told that she would eat in the kitchen rather than dining with the family, the girl responded, "'I guess that's 'cause you don't think I'm good enough to eat with you. You'll find that won't do here.'"[64] Tocqueville described the dynamic between servant and master perfectly when he wrote, "The servant always sees himself as a temporary visitor in the home of his masters."[65]

Egalitarianism was no less central to American society after the Civil War, with Lepel Henry Griffin claiming that American notions of egalitarianism had forged most social institutions in the United States, and dominated American politics and even religion.[66] "The ruling note of good society," said James Fullarton Muirhead, "is of pleasant cameraderie, without condescension on the one hand or fawning on the other."[67] Democracy in America, according to Henry Sienkiewicz, "was not only political but also social ... Everyone here stands on the same social level, with no one towering above another."[68] This fact was vividly brought home to Sienkiewicz when he hired a coachman to drive him to the home of a millionaire rancher. Upon arrival at the ranch the coachman, instead of staying with the horses, entered the house, sat down on the sofa, and began to play with the host's daughter. At first, according to Sienkiewicz, "this incident refused to penetrate my European skull," but it seemed quite natural to both coachman and host. The lesson, said Sienkiewicz, was that while the millionaire American rancher might not have the refinement of the millionaire European, "the American coachman ranks ten times higher than his European counterpart."[69] It was "respect for labor," according to Sienkiewicz, that had given birth to egalitarianism, which in turn eroded class distinctions.[70]

As in the years before the Civil War, David Macrae observed that servants in America did not like the word, and instead preferred to be called "'ladies,' 'helps,' 'companions.'"[71] More than fifty years after Frances Trollope's time in the United States, another English woman living in America (in San Francisco), encountered the same servant dilemma as Trollope: when she told her American servant that she would not be dining with the family, the servant responded by dumping the family's meal in the sink and quitting.[72]

It was not just domestic servants who asserted their independence and considered themselves as good as their employers, but virtually every worker in the United States. Frenchman Paul de Rousiers noted that Americans were willing to endure every trial in life "in order to become their own masters."[73] Other visitors to America cited numerous instances where large companies of Americans tolerated considerable inconvenience rather than infringing on "the right of the individual to do as he will."[74] Central to the American character, said Hugues Le Roux, was the sovereignty of the individual and the love of independence.[75] The entire republic, argued Paul Bourget, was based on the proposition that "the individual is free and powerful" and the State is weak.[76]

Helping to establish the independence of Americans was the absence of what French visitor Émile Levasseur called "caste traditions," where an occupation was passed down from father to son. U.S. employers did not have to take this into consideration when they established their businesses, nor did American workers feel obligated to practice a certain profession in a certain locale.[77] The result was an independent American worker and a relationship between employer and employee that ended at the factory door.[78] Another important element, especially in the American West, was the abundance of land and the scarcity of labor. Property ownership in the United States did not confer any special distinction as it did in Europe, and because American workers were a valuable commodity they were not likely to pay elaborate deference to their employers.

Europeans residing in the West constantly fretted that their employees would desert them. Horace Annesley Vachell found that it was hard to keep servants on ranches even when they were well paid, and Emily Faithfull noted of Western servants that when their work was done they felt at liberty to go out without asking.[79] When the English couple Isabella and Jem Randall moved to a ranch in Montana in the mid-1880s, they brought along with them a servant couple that they had recruited from "the slums of London."[80] Isabella fumed when one of her neighbors invited the servants to tea. "How can anyone keep servants in their place," asked Randall, "when the people, whom we associate with, invite them to their houses as equals?"[81] Relations between the Randalls and their servants continued to deteriorate until the servants "got very independent." In the end, they quit their jobs, informing the Randalls on the way out that, "in this country, people won't be 'hired servants.'"[82]

European bewilderment at the behavior of the American "servant class" was considerable. One British observer called "a supply of good domestic servants" the "great social want of the United States." This commentator wistfully noted that "under the system of negro slavery, the Southern people had the best servants in the world," but now Americans had to endure Irish servants, who quickly became "impertinent and assumed airs of social equality."[83] H. Hussey Vivian asked his English readers to put themselves in the place of an American dealing with the terrible servant problem: "Imagine having to employ a raw Irish girl to 'clean' your house or 'cook' your dinner, to be thankful that you can get her at any wages she chooses to ask, and that you are not forced to do it yourself."[84] House servants often did not even answer the door (leaving that chore to the mistress of the house) and when they did perform this duty servants frequently disappeared shortly thereafter "without ever thinking of showing you into the room or announcing your arrival."[85]

E. Catherine Bates observed that American domestic servants were "exacting in their demands," and expected to be allowed to "sleep out" at least twice a week.[86] Disgruntled servants often vacated their posts without notice, and frequently became vengeful when fired. A Boston acquaintance of Bates told Bates that when she fired her cook, the cook responded by mixing cinder dust with several pounds of mincemeat that had been prepared for Christmas.[87] R. W. Dale found American servants to be "respectful and attentive," but added that "it is quite clear that they do not suppose that their master and their master's guests belong to a superior race."[88] Nobody in America, claimed Paul de Rousiers, "entertains the idea of living and dying a servant." As a consequence, "one must think twice before giving an order to an American servant."[89] Summing up the differences between American and English servants, historian Christopher Mulvey notes that "the American servant had the option of becoming a master and he appeared only to have himself to blame if he did not become a master. The English servant had the option of becoming a convict."[90]

At restaurants, Europeans used to obsequious service first had to deal with the steward, who, according to Baron Hübner, "fixes your place at table with an authority which no one dreams of disputing."[91] Next, diners encountered the waiter, who, according to one French visitor, was slow and acted as if he was rendering a favor.[92] In Rapid City, when one of Rose Pender's traveling companions asked the waitress to bring some beer, the waitress "exploded, told him to fetch it himself, and marched off, declining to wait on us any further."[93] According to another visitor, the American waiter never replied to a request to bring food, but instead "fetches it in silence, and then leans over your chair listening to your conversation."[94] The arrogance and presumption of American waiters, said Paul de Rousiers, could be explained because they "serve at table incidentally while waiting to become President of the United States."[95]

Emily Faithfull encountered the same impudence among American shopgirls, who chatted with each other while attending to their customers, and who nurtured the attitude that they were conferring a great service in providing the requested goods.[96] In her experience with shopgirls in the United States, French visitor Maria Therese Blanc found that "the more ordinary the shop, the more aggressive the sense of social equality" was among the employees.[97] The dynamic between American shopgirls and their customers, said Lady Duffus Hardy, was that "*you* wait their pleasure, not they *yours*," and that when they "do deign to attend you, it is with a sort of condescending indifference" [original emphasis][98]

There was probably no profession in the country where workers displayed what Europeans believed was a fitting servility. When German visitor Harry Kessler was in New York, he reported that the proprietor of a hat shop whistled while he waited on Kessler, and that when Kessler asked for his keys the hotel porter "cracked jokes with me."[99] Another traveler found that those hawking their wares on American city streets did so "with an air of almost aggressive independence" and never thanked those who bought from them.[100] A peeved William Francis Butler referred to "the very deep obligation which you owe to the man who thus deigns to receive your money," while William Hepworth Dixon complained that the traveler in America had to do everything himself, which would otherwise be done for him for a shilling in London or a franc in Paris.[101] Egalitarianism, as one disgruntled European put it, had become so ingrained in the American consciousness that serving another person with useful labor had become a "sort of sin, shame, and disgrace."[102]

The social system in America also dictated that honorific titles, previously conferred only on the genteel, be either dropped or extended to the masses because in the United States, the individual was given credit "for what he does, not for what he is."[103] One traveler confirmed that everyone in America should be presumed to be a lady or a gentleman, and even when addressing a waiter the proper form was, "'Are you the gentleman to whom I gave my order?'"[104] This view was slyly endorsed by Mark Twain. Contrasting the English spoken in America with that spoken in Britain, Twain observed that "your words 'gentleman' and 'lady' have a very restricted meaning; with us they include the barmaid, butcher, burglar, harlot, and horse-thief."[105]

One incident that reveals a singular class inversion occurred at an American hotel where James Fullarton Muirhead and his traveling companion were staying. According to Muirhead, he and his companion were referred to by a porter as, "You fellows," who then told them that "the other *gentleman* would attend to my baggage!" [original emphasis][106] Englishman "W. C. M." relates a similar anecdote in which a stagecoach driver entered a barroom containing a solitary person and asked, "'Are you the man that's going by this here stage?' adding as the reason for his making the inquiry, 'I'm the gentleman that drives it.'"[107]

Many Europeans used to the traditional class arrangements raged against this system, but it must be said that the English system was equally dismaying to Americans. In 1878, Bret Harte was staying at J. A. Froude's summer home in Devonshire, and in a letter home described the household. "Everybody here is carefully trained to their station—and seldom bursts out of it. The *respect* the whole family show toward me is something fine and *depressing*. I can easily feel how this deference is ingrained in all." [original emphasis][108] The lack of ingrained deference in America often produced elaborate sarcasm among wounded European travelers. During her time in the Rockies in the 1870s, Rose G. Kingsley was forced to submit to being kissed by the washerwoman's daughter (who was reeking of garlic). Kingsley had to endure this indignity because, as she sardonically observed, "this is a free country where the washerwoman is as good as I."[109] Taking note of a hotel chambermaid whose attitude toward him was consistently "one of inveterate hostility and unmitigated scorn," George Augustus Sala speculated that it must have occurred to this young woman at an early age that "she was at the very least a Duchess."[110] (Léon Paul Blouet also suggested that American domestic servants were best viewed as "reduced duchesses and noblemen."[111]) Phil Robinson asked why "an ill-bred, ill-mannered chambermaid is always spoken of as a 'lady'? If the name is only given in courtesy, why not call them 'princesses' at once and rescue the nobler word from its present miserable degradation?"[112]

The suspension of traditional class relations was especially marked in rough frontier areas, where American men often dropped their surnames altogether and went by first names or nicknames, thereby eliminating all social distinctions.[113] William Howard Russell noted that the man who was in charge of watering his party's horses at Yosemite referred to the Duke of Sutherland as "Sutherland," and even called upon the duke to help with the watering bucket. The duke pitched in, but often when Westerners treated visiting Europeans with a similar familiarity, an extreme case of ruffled feathers developed.[114] The Italian Felice Scheibler complained that "uncouth" American miners treated people in his party "like peers." This, he said, was "really not pleasant." Even more disturbing was that the guides on Scheibler's hunting trip refused to show the proper deference to his companion, Don Leone Caetani, Prince of Teano. The guides refused to address him as "Mister Prince," and the prince refused to address the guides as "sir." A compromise of sorts was reached when the guides agreed to call him "Mister Leo."[115] These Italian sportsmen might have had a more pleasant experience if they had had time to absorb the lesson that Horace Annesley Vachell had gleaned after seventeen years in America: "around the camp-fire all men are equal."[116]

Also disorienting to foreign travelers was that railroad cars were not divided by class. As W. Henry Barneby eloquently expressed it, "you may have either a New York senator or a nigger" as a fellow passenger.[117] W. G. Marshall counseled foreign travelers that if they wanted to get along with those with whom they were traveling, they would address every man as "sir" and every woman as "ma'am." Even the conductor who collected your ticket must be treated "with great civility." On no account, said Marshall, should a traveler attempt to tip a conductor.[118] David Macrae also took note of the classlessness of railroad cars in the West, but could not help but observe the segregated "nigger cars" that prevailed in the South.[119] Other trains made provisions for a "ladies' carriage," into which well-dressed gentlemen were admitted, and "a caboose for negroes, emigrants, and very dirty people."[120]

While Americans did not grant enhanced social status to those of great wealth, it would be misleading, according to James Bryce, to conclude that the bulk of Americans hated the rich.[121] Upper-class society in America was established on a radically different basis from it was in Europe. Members of "society" in America were all businessmen who, according to Paul Bourget, "were not born to social station, they have achieved it ... They made it themselves."[122] Matthew Arnold contended that rich men in the United States were regarded with "less envy and hatred than rich men are in Europe" because the government did not make "grandees of them," and because their condition was less set.[123] Baron Hübner also found great differences in attitudes toward the wealthy in the United States and Europe. There was little in the way of resentment of the rich in the United States because the American "seeks for equality in a higher sphere than that in which he was born and bred, and finds it." The European, however, despairing of attaining a higher position, "strives to drag down everyone else to his level."[124] In addition, as James Fullarton Muirhead pointed out, there was less "patronizing kindness" of the rich toward the poor in the United States because of fluid social conditions.[125] After all, it was quite conceivable that today's man of wealth came from humble means, and that "the rich gentleman we have learned to look up to was once the happy owner of no more than an acre of waste land on Main Street."[126] It worked the other way as well, when "men and women who have held their place in brilliant circles one year drop out of it the next, and sink down and are lost, no one knows how or where."[127] The United States had a shifting aristocracy in which Americans moved from occupation to occupation, and between the two poles of poverty and riches.[128] This served to eliminate condescension from the wealthy and servility from the working class.

Henry Latham insisted that America's "lack of caste distinctions and a freedom of manners and intercourse" made it possible to understand the people better in three months than an American traveler in England could in a year.[129] Of his time in the West, Henry Sienkiewicz observed that the daughters of ranch owners danced with ranch hands, that waiters chatted amiably with their customers, and that railroad conductors conversed freely with genteel lady passengers.[130] (James Fullarton Muirhead counseled "the stately English dame" not to be offended "if she is addressed as 'grandma' by some genial railway conductor."[131])

While there is little doubt that Americans admired the rich man, French visitor Léon Paul Blouet believed that this esteem was based as much on "the activity and talent he has displayed in the winning of his fortune as for the dollars themselves."[132] A person's wealth by itself, however, was not sufficient reason for others to defer to him. The highly placed understood this, said James Bryce, and did not adopt social pretensions because a person who displayed such vulgarity would be shunned by all segments of society.[133] As one traveler put it, the putting on of airs was the one "unpardonable offence" in America.[134]

W. E. Adams provided a specific example of how this rule played out socially in the person of Charles Crocker, railroad magnate, multi-millionaire and one of California's "Big Four."[135] Adams and Crocker were fellow passengers on the Atlantic steamer *Celtic* in 1882, and Adams observed that Crocker "mixed as freely with the company as the most affable among them, smoked and chatted with everybody who wanted a 'crack,' and joined as heartily as anybody in the amusements of the voyage." Crocker gave no indication of his enormous wealth, and indeed, "there was nothing even to indicate that he was more prosperous than the ordinary run of American citizens."[136]

The dominance of the middle class in America was striking. As historian Gordon S. Wood puts it, "middling sorts" in the United States absorbed "the gentility of the aristocracy and the work of the working class," and created a society in which, "Leisure became idleness, work became respectable, and nearly every adult white male became a gentleman."[137] Baron Hübner confirmed that "the prejudices which in the old world exclude the higher and middle classes from manual labour, entirely disappear" in America.[138]

A number of travelers contrasted the class alignment in the United States with the system that prevailed in Britain. Matthew Arnold described the British class system as "an upper class materialized, a middle class vulgarized, a lower class brutalized" (or "Barbarians, Philistines, and Populace") and argued that what the English called the middle class "is in America virtually the nation."[139] While it was hardly flattering to be called a nation of philistines, Arnold at least argued that the American middle class had produced "a livelier sort of Philistine than ours."[140] While the United States might not have the cultivation and refinement found in Britain, what America had that was lacking in Britain was, in Arnold's words, "an excellent thing—equality."[141] Equality in America, according to James Bryce, had raised the lower classes without lowering the upper, while inequality in England, said another European traveler, had created an atmosphere of "a dull, pompous, selfish, ungenial nature."[142]

One of the obvious examples of the impact of egalitarianism in America was the easy access that citizens had to political office. "The consciousness of having not simply the right to vote but the chance of being voted for," said A. Maurice Low, "must make every man feel within himself the power of sovereignty."[143] Egalitarianism also dictated easy access to politicians, which was no more the case in Europe than were opportunities to rise to political office. W. E. Adams called American public officials "courteous without being subservient," which reflected "the difference between a democratic and an aristocratic form of government."[144] Tocqueville perhaps put it best when he observed that "American democracy prospers not because of its elected officials but because its officials are elected."[145]

Dress

American notions of egalitarianism and the easy mixing of different social groups had an impact on daily life even in areas where it would seemingly have no bearing, including the realm of dress and fashion. When Paul de Rousiers attended a ball in the small town of Fremont, Nebraska, he was surprised that the dancers "danced in whatever costume they owned, instead of coming to yawn in a correct ball-room suit," and that even though there was an "absence of selectness" it did not result in any bad manners.[146] David Macrae remembered servants in the West dining with the family, and recalled off-duty hotel waiters "sitting down to supper with us in their shirt-sleeves."[147] "Shirt-sleeves" is an important detail, as servants typically rejected uniforms as menial.[148]

Even "public servants" were resistant to the idea of a uniform. In the 1850s, for instance, when police forces in America were being regularized, police officers in New York City objected to uniforms because they "conflicted with their notions of independence and self-respect." In Philadelphia, fifteen quit the force over the issue of uniforms, with one noting that he did not wish "to wear anything derogatory to my feelings as an American."[149] Edward A. Freeman reported that even in the upper echelons of American life, public officials were reluctant to wear "official dress," because of concerns with "republican simplicity."[150] American jury trials were notorious for their lack of decorum, with both jury members and attorneys lounging about without their coats.[151] Léon Paul Blouet described court proceedings in the United States as "no uniforms, no robes, no wigs, no trumpets, no liveried ushers."[152] Even at the Supreme Court, English traveler J. J. Aubertin complained that the justices were "only slightly discernible, as such, by the meagre robes they wear, and counsel are not discernible at all, except by their speeches."[153] Another British commentator observed that "it is a shock to the English traveller when he finds that American judges don't wear wigs; that their butchers don't dress in blue; and that their agricultural population have abandoned smock-frocks and gaiters."[154]

A number of Europeans in the first half of the nineteenth century had already taken note of the trend toward the democratization of luxury in American dress. Frances Trollope argued in the 1830s that "the luxuries they [Americans] have, and they are already many, are common to an infinitely greater proportion of the population than has ever been seen elsewhere."[155] The following decade, the British consul in Boston, Thomas College Grattan, lamented that American servant girls had been "strongly infected with the national bad taste for being over-dressed, they are, when walking the streets, scarcely to be distinguished from their employers."[156] This trend had fully matured by end of the century. When Bram Stoker was in the United States in 1883–84, he found that working-class men and women were better dressed than their counterparts in Britain, and that the traveler "could not possibly distinguish classes as at home."[157] Léon Paul Blouet claimed that not only did upper-class women wear diamonds in America, but also "the tradesman's wife, shop-girls, work-girls, and servants," and Paul de Rousiers, like Stoker, groused that "nobody's profession can be told from dress or look."[158]

On her ship to America in 1894, Marie Therese Blanc took note of a young American woman who was "dressed like a picture" and charmed everyone she came near. It was not until they landed that Madame Blanc discovered that she was "a mere shop–girl."[159] Blanc's impression that American women of even modest means spent a lot of money on their clothes was confirmed when Blanc was in Maine. Here, rural girls were adorned in the latest fashions, including expensive furs and jewelry.[160] In San Francisco, Rudyard Kipling witnessed the ritual that took place between 8:00 and 10:00 p.m. on Kearney Street where a parade of expensively dressed persons strolled about with the goal of seeing and being seen. According to Kipling, dress leveled distinctions in rank and that the only clues to class were the accents.[161] In a similar scene, the fashionable set of New York drove through Central Park, putting themselves on display every day between 3:00 and 6:00.[162] The park was chosen both because it was beautiful and because the generally wretched condition of New York's streets meant that there was no other place to go.[163]

The sartorial standards of Americans varied widely from city to rural areas and region to region. Among city-dwelling males, a number of groups developed reputations for sharp dressing. In New York, bartenders were renowned for spending a lot of money on their clothes, while other splendidly dressed young men assembled near New York's Windsor Hotel, where they sucked on tooth-picks and surveyed the crowds, especially the female portion. "These young men are dudes," explained Harold Brydges, "the American variety of the London masher" (Figure 1.1).[164] Fashionable young American men could also appreciate one of their own. When an ulster-wearing member of Henry Irving's acting troupe passed by a group of sharp-dressed men in Philadelphia, they noted approvingly, "Here's a dude!"[165] J. W. Boddam-Whetham took note of the pop-ularity among American males of jewelry, including enormous gold watchchains (especially beloved of railroad conductors), and diamond studs and stickpins.[166] The better-dressed American male also insisted on having his boots polished to a mirror-like sheen, which spawned boot black emporiums, with elaborately fitted rooms and comfortable chairs for the clients.[167] In the South, especially in the years immediately after the Civil War, gentlemen wore the long, black coat that prevailed throughout much of the United States, but rejected the Yankee stove-pipe hat in favor of a Panama or Palmetto.[168]

By the early 1880s, W. E. Adams noted of men in Eastern cities that they wore felt hats in the winter and straw hats in the summer.[169] He was also struck by the number of American men who got their hair cut extremely short during the warm months, and the trend toward shaving everything except the moustache. Unshaved men in America, said Adams, "are generally understood to be either strangers or immigrants."[170]

But with the exceptions noted, dress tended to be less important to American men than American women. Upper-class New York women ("carriage ladies") wrapped themselves in furs and wore their diamond earrings all day long—a ten-dency that one visitor called "a remnant of savagery."[171] When British actress Lillie Langtry first encountered the "chic, well-dressed women" of New York in 1882, she reported feeling "quite dowdy" and indeed, American women tended to scorn

THE FEUDS OF THE DUDES.
Let Them Hire "Sluggers" to Protect Them.

FIGURE 1.1 "Dudes." Chromolithograph by Frederick Burr Opper. *Puck*, 30 May 1883. Library of Congress. LC-DIG-ppmsca-28392.

English fashions in favor of the French.[172] Emily Faithfull found that even in Washington, D.C., the ordinary Congressman was "shabby in his invariable suit of black broadcloth," while his wife and daughters were "resplendent in Paris gowns."[173] There were some city-to-city differences. In one example of how Philadelphia differed from other East Coast cities, Emily Faithfull noted that the make-up that women applied freely in places like New York and Baltimore was frowned upon in Philadelphia. She cites the case of one Baltimore woman, recently transplanted to Philadelphia, who was forced to abandon the rouge she had formerly applied so liberally so that she did not "place herself in a mistaken position."[174]

Léon Paul Blouet described the standard dress of the American gentleman as "plain, even severe," consisting of a high hat, and black coat and trousers. Any deviation from this look was sure to excite attention. Indeed, there was no surer way to transform the tourist into the tourist attraction than by the adoption of what Americans considered an outlandish outfit. The reaction of the locals in a small Pennsylvania town to Blouet's decision to wear light-grey trousers included fits of giggling from waitresses, a trail of street urchins that followed Blouet around, and the general consensus that here was a species of "strange animal."[175] When John Fox appeared on the streets of Cheyenne in 1885 with English riding breeches and leggings and a brown Derby hat, he reported that he had never been so intensely scrutinized in his life. He immediately replaced this garb with a pair of overalls, a blue flannel shirt, a cavalry hat and a pair of cowboy boots.[176] There was a similar reaction to W. G. Marshall when he sallied forth into Sacramento sporting knickerbockers. A crowd gathered around him to "wonder at the remarkable costume of the 'Britisher.'"[177]

Europeans were appalled by the willingness of American men to resort to the most shocking informality in dress should the spirit move them. Knut Hamsun was surprised to see New York men during the summer strolling about without jackets or vests with "no more than suspenders over their shirts," while Jacques Offenbach was dismayed at the informal dress of American men at both the theatre and the concert ("frightful suits—such as we hardly dare to wear in the country or at the seaside").[178] Formal dress for men was a relative rarity. Even President Grant when he opened the Philadelphia exposition appeared "in a business suit without gloves."[179]

In the unsettled West, women did their best to maintain standards in dress, while men generally did not. On the Mississippi, Henry Sienkiewicz observed bearded raftsmen "dressed in flannel shirts and tattered hats" and armed with revolvers which gave them, according to Sienkiewicz, "a storybook, romantic, half-brigandish appearance."[180] On trains traveling through the West, James Bryce found that the poorly attired male was the rule, while his female relations were well turned-out.[181] Even in rough mining regions, women did their best to dress fashionably. In Helena, Montana, E. Catherine Bates was struck by "the really good innate taste" in the dress of women in that city.[182] At a boarding house in Utah, Baron Hübner contrasted the "smart *recherché* toilets" of miners' wives with their husbands, "who rush in straight from their mines, covered with sweat, mud, and dust."[183]

It can be argued, however, that Western men had a distinctive clothing style that had been forged out of necessity. Indeed, Oscar Wilde claimed that Western miners were "the only well-dressed men" that he saw in America:

> Their wide-brimmed hats, which shaded their faces from the sun and protected them from the rain, and the cloak, which is by far the most beautiful

piece of drapery ever invented, may well be dwelt on with admiration. Their high boots, too, were sensible and practical. They wore only what was comfortable and therefore beautiful.[184]

Phil Robinson also praised the Western miners' clothing as "refreshing and unconventional," with an emphasis on comfort and sturdiness of material.[185] Even in Western cities, male dress tended toward the unconventional. Lady Duffus Hardy claimed that the men of San Francisco were "supremely indifferent" on the subject of apparel—"each dresses to please himself, and consults only his own individual comfort and convenience."[186]

European descriptions of cowboy regalia were especially detailed, for here was a legendary American type (Figure 1.2).[187] Isabella Bird described a group of cowboys near Cheyenne as "four or five much-spurred horsemen, in peaked hats, blue-hooded coats, and high boots, heavily armed with revolvers and repeating rifles, and riding small wiry horses."[188] In Nebraska, Theodora Guest observed men on horseback with wide hats and enormous spurs, while the cowboys Emily Faithfull saw in New Mexico reminded her of Arab horsemen in stories she had thrilled to as a youth.[189] In Texas, Lillie Langtry met cowboys "garbed in their finest leathers and most flamboyant shirts."[190] Indians could also be quite exacting about their personal appearance. William A. Bell took note of the "brightly painted and fantastically dressed" Comanches, and Windham Wyndham-Quin said of young Crow men that they were "great dandies" who always stopped to spruce up their appearance before entering a strange village.[191]

The Western melting pot for male sartorial splendor was probably Denver. Isabella Bird was there in the early 1870s and described

> hunters and trappers in buckskin clothing; men of the Plains with belts and revolvers, in great blue cloaks, relics of the war; teamsters in leathern suits, horsemen in fur coats and caps and buffalo-hide boots with the hair outside, and camping blankets behind their huge Mexican saddles; Broadway dandies in light kid gloves; rich English sporting tourists, clean, comely, and supercilious looking; and hundreds of Indians on their small ponies, the men wearing buckskin suits sewn with beads.[192]

But Denver was rapidly being civilized, and by 1876 British novelist William Black expressed astonishment at the number of men wearing black coats and tall hats.[193] Looks could be deceiving, however. On her train to Montana in the mid-1880s, Isabelle Randall was struck by the appearance of "a couple of true desperadoes of the frontier" who were decked out in buckskin hats and leggings, huge Mexican spurs, embroidered velvet coats, and silver-mounted revolvers. The desperadoes, as it turns out, were former French noblemen who had taken up residence in the West.[194]

FIGURE 1.2 Buccaroos (ca. 1905). Lithograph by Charles M. Russell. Library of Congress. LC–USZC4–4081.

Money

European travelers were more or less united in their condemnation of the American obsession with making money, though none of these visitors mentioned their own comfortable levels of income that had made it possible for them to visit the United States in the first place. G. Sormani claimed that in America, "love of the dollar eclipses any other sentiment," and Isabella Bird concluded that "the 'almighty dollar' is the true divinity."[195] French travelers, beginning with Tocqueville, theorized that Americans had substituted the dollar for the social distinctions that egalitarianism had eliminated.[196] Human striving must have some goal, said S. C. de Soissons, and Americans had adopted the dollar to serve that end.[197] Composer Jacques Offenbach also believed that the dollar constituted the only aristocracy in the United States, and was of the opinion that what most excited the American was not Offenbach's musicianship but the salary he was being paid to conduct:

> "They gave him a thousand dollars!" That is the price, and in his American mind, it increases the stature of the master. And why shouldn't it be this way? As a child, "dollar" was the first word he heard; as a youth, it was his first love; as a man, it will be his only passion.[198]

This was more than a little disingenuous, as the reason Offenbach came to America was because he was offered a thousand dollars per performance ("such a flattering offer that I felt I did not have the right to hesitate").[199]

If any city epitomized the American hustle for money, it was probably Chicago. David Macrae said of that city that the "universal cry is the same—'Dollars and cents, dollars and cents!'"[200] At Chicago's Palmer House, Rudyard Kipling encountered a room crammed with people, with money being the only topic of conversation. They boasted about thousands of dollars worth of this and millions of dollars worth of that. It was, said Kipling, "like listening to a child babbling of its hoard of shells."[201] But Americans did understand the correlation between the getting of money and hard work, and this concentration on work from morning to night was, according to S. C. de Soissons, "the secret of their prosperity."[202] The American love of the immense, which will be examined later, could also be complemented by that other great American passion, the love of money. Lepel Henry Griffin, who was irritated by almost everything he found in America, was especially exercised by the American proclivity for "making money the standard of beauty and virtue."[203] As Léon Paul Blouet put it, the American admired talent because "it is a paying commodity," and "talent without money is a useless tool."[204]

While this argument has some merit, the dynamic between Americans and money was more complex because it was the pursuit of money, rather than the getting of it, that seemed to motivate most Americans. A byproduct of the hopefulness and confidence that Europeans found in America was the "reckless chances taken in the battle of life."[205] The American, said Baron Hübner, "must embark in something; and once embarked, he must go on and on for ever; for if he stops, those who follow him would crush him under their feet."[206] Paul de Rousiers said that American life resembled a ladder "up which everybody is climbing, hanging on, falling, and beginning the ascent again after each tumble … Nobody thinks of stopping; nobody rests contented on any step."[207] Horace Annesley Vachell even claimed that American men did not greatly care for what wealth could buy, and instead sought to live an intense life rather than a comfortable one.[208] Confirming this trait among his countrymen was Henry Adams, who said of the American male that "he never cared much for money or power after he earned them. The amusement of the pursuit was all the amusement he got from it; he had no use for wealth."[209] Tocqueville himself commented that the rich in America never became blasé about their wealth because they had waged a long battle to gain their fortune, and "the passions that had accompanied the struggle survived."[210]

The fortunes that Americans built up were often high-risk, unstable enterprises, and as Paul de Rousiers put it, "A man may go to sleep a millionaire and waken to find himself without a cent."[211] From Leadville, Phil Robinson reported that one could not throw a boot out a hotel window without striking a former millionaire, and that the residents there "prefer to be ruined rather than be merely rich."[212] Thus, even after achieving success, the American man was seldom idle. According to Henry Irving, this lack of an American "idle class" (which Irving defined as "a class of gentlemen who have little else to do but to be amused") constituted one of the important differences between America and Britain or, one could argue, between America and Europe.[213]

If the American of wealth had little interest in saving his money and little use for personal luxuries, what did he spend his money on? The answer, most observers agreed, was that he spent it on the luxuries that the American woman craved.[214] For him, as S. C. de Soissons put it, "his wife, rather than money, is his luxury."[215] One consequence of this emphasis on work, according to Herbert Spencer, was a race of American men with lined faces, prematurely grey hair and a predilection toward "nervous collapse."[216] Jose Martí believed that the concentration on money in the United States had created something worse: "It is each man for himself. Fortune, the only object of life. Woman, a luxury toy."[217] But there was also something uplifting in the pursuit of wealth that was rooted in an American's belief in himself, and in his country. Henry Latham marveled at the American conviction that "nothing appears impossible" and that "he would make a fortune before he dies" and contrasted it with the English agricultural worker, "whose highest dream of possible affluence is £1 a-week."[218]

In addition to employing the latest technology to facilitate their pursuit of wealth, Americans also created an efficient financial system. In the United States, for instance, the same currency was accepted over vast distances. The British system was much different. As William Saunders lamented, "Why is it that if you bring a bank note from Bristol to London no one will look at it, and if you take it from Minnesota to New York it finds currency as readily in one place as the other?"[219] Harold Brydges also noted that Americans could wire money by telegraph, "a convenience denied to Englishmen at home."[220]

Advertising

To help generate the wealth that they craved, American businessmen turned to advertising. The United States was triumphantly a nation of advertisements, and for many travelers, it appeared that American cities had been created for the sole purpose of providing platforms for promotions.[221] New York was the most extreme example. When John Campbell Argyll visited that city in 1866, he was struck by the "the vulgarity inseparable from large staring name-boards and advertisements."[222] Ten years later, Jacques Offenbach observed flags in New York hanging from windows with advertisements, arches over streets proclaiming coming sales, and walls covered with enormous posters.[223] Street railway cars featured "gigantic parasols" emblazoned with ads, and at night, gas, kerosene and electricity were used for advertising. This included men walking around the streets "enclosed in sheds made of paper, illuminated on the inside and bearing inscriptions on their four sides."[224] A decade after Offenbach was in New York, J. J. Aubertin found that almost every elevated railway station in that city featured the faces of three chubby children with the inscription, "Our mothers took Dr. Hood's Sarsaparilla."[225]

Additional promotions included the giant foot adorning the outside of the podiatrist's office, and a cigar-clutching wooden Indian in front of the tobacco shop, "his tomahawk poised for action in case you decline his invitation to 'Try them.'"[226] In the waters off Coney Island, sailing ships displayed "in enormous characters on their main-sails the names of quack medicines."[227] Advertising in New York probably reached its apotheosis when the Heinz Company erected a sign that was six stories tall and featured a forty-foot-long pickle illuminated by 1,200 electric lights.[228] Delivering one of the wittiest comments on New York's kaleidoscope of advertising lights was G. K. Chesterton, who observed, "What a glorious garden of wonders this would be, to any one who was lucky enough to be unable to read."[229] While the crass standard established by New York was not likely to be exceeded, other cities were not far behind. When she was in Chicago in 1894, Marie Therese Blanc took note of placards hung across broad streets and advertisements with "blazing bunches of every color," while in New Orleans Ernst von Hesse-Wartegg was assaulted by "signs in garish colors, messages over a building's front from top to bottom (gross advertisements screaming Buy! Buy!)."[230]

The blight was arguably worse outside the cities, where Europeans were appalled at the extent to which the American countryside had been "disfigured" by advertising.[231] What, exactly, was being advertised? In the 1860s, one of the most aggressively promoted commodities in America was bitters. Ads for bitters were to be found in every newspaper and on every shed, and painted on any fence, tree or rock that might attract the human eye. David Macrae claimed to have found bitters ads in the middle of Southern swamps and on lonely Western prairies, "where one would imagine the only customers could be polecats, 'bars,' or buffaloes."[232] Between New York and Philadelphia, William Howard Russell encountered a "plague of hideous advertisements" that were seemingly placed on every available surface, man-made and natural. There were promotions for tobacco, oils and the nostrums of "quack doctors," accompanied by illustrations "in flaming colours."[233] When he traveled this route, George Augustus Sala found that Schenck and "his pulmonic syrup, his gargles, and his many varieties of pills" dominated despite intense competition.[234] Along the banks near Niagara Falls advertisements for various refreshments proliferated, and between Chicago and Omaha, one traveler took note of the ubiquity of billboards that carried such messages as "Use Carboline for the Hair," "Smoke Vanity Fair," and "Chew Wood Tag Navy."[235]

Robert Louis Stevenson found that advertisements recommending tobaccos and cures for the ague dominated on the prairies, while Rudyard Kipling concluded that it was ads for land promotions that were dominant between San Francisco and Portland. Everywhere there were "rocks degraded by quack advertisements." Lepel Henry Griffin, for instance, complained that the cliffs near St. Paul (through which the Mississippi River flowed) might have been imposing were they not adorned with giant letters that proclaimed, "'*Smith' chewing tobacco is the best*'" [original emphasis].[236] In the West, even the most inspiring landscapes sometimes attracted the advertiser's art. In one example, J. W. Boddam-Whetham described how he and his companions made their way through the Rockies near "Pulpit Rock," surrounded by "vast circles of rocks" and "lofty precipices." Distracting these travelers from the beauty of this setting was a towering cliff where letters several feet high spelled out the message, "'A thing of beauty and a joy for ever'—'Try our rising sun stove-polish!'"[237] Phil Robinson claimed that even the grandest landscape lost its dignity if it included "'Bunkum's Patent' inscribed in the foreground in whitewash letters six feet high."[238] Total national expenditures for advertising, which stood at $50 million in 1867, had increased to $500 million by 1900.[239]

America did not have exclusive claim to vulgar promotions, and the culture of advertising that plagued America was also making rapid inroads in Britain. British writer Arnot Reid was surprised to discover that *The Times* of London contained about the same amount of advertising as *The New York Times, New York Herald*, and *Tribune* put together.[240] And as aggressive as was advertising in the United States, when William Archer visited America in 1899 he judged it no worse than "the illuminated advertisements of whisky and California wines that vulgarise the August spectacle of the Thames by night."[241] There were certain national differences. Missing from American advertisements but ubiquitous in Britain were nobility endorsements. An American traveling in England observed that "the trading Briton seems to have achieved glory enough if he can spread upon his signboard the fact that he is patronised by some prince or princess."[242]

★ ★ ★

Life in the United States was clearly befuddling to many Europeans, and some retreated to the posture of condemning everything that was American. The Norwegian Knut Hamsun described Americans as "a people without a national literature or art, a corrupt society, a materialistic mode of life, and flourishing inanity."[243] Joining Hamsun in his virulent hatred of everything American was Lepel Henry Griffin, who wrote in his travel memoir, *The Great Republic*, that America was "the apotheosis of Philistinism," and a country of "disillusion and disappointment" in its people, cities, art, literature, culture, politics and even "in its scenery."[244] But for a condemnation of an entire nation, it would be difficult to improve upon Therese Yelverton's *Teresina in America*. Yelverton (Vicountess Avonmore) called Americans "worshippers of money," found the American political system reprehensible because the office of the presidency could be occupied by "men taken from field labour and tailors' shops," claimed that "refinement and good-breeding" was rarely to be found in America, and insisted that drunkenness among the better classes in the United States was "more prevalent than in any other country." In fact, Yelverton "had seen nothing to like" in America.[245] Still, she seemed somewhat hurt and surprised that no one seemed to want to socialize with her.[246]

Rudyard Kipling saw some of the same flaws in Americans as others, and was consequently puzzled to find that he had developed a great affection for them:

> My heart has gone out to them beyond all other peoples; and for the life of me I cannot tell why. They are bleeding-raw at the edges, almost more conceited than the English, vulgar with a massive vulgarity which is as though the Pyramids were coated with Christmas-cake sugar-works. Cocksure they are, lawless and as casual as they are cocksure; but I love them, and I realized it when I met an Englishman who laughed at them.[247]

Notes

1. Horace Annesley Vachell, *Life and Sport on the Pacific Slope* (New York: Dodd, Mead and Co., 1901), 4.
2. Harold Brydges, *Uncle Sam at Home* (New York: Henry Holt and Co., 1888), 76, 103; J. W. Boddam-Whetham, *Western Wanderings: A Record of Travel in the Evening Land* (London: Richard Bentley and Son, 1874), 11.
3. Paul Bourget, *Outre-Mer: Impressions of America* (London: T. Fisher Unwin, 1895), 28.
4. Paul de Rousiers, *American Life*, trans. A. J. Herbertson (New York: Firmin-Didot, 1892), 308. When actress Lillie Langtry landed in New York in 1882, her strongest first impression was of crowds "hurrying and jostling each other." Lillie Langtry, *The Days I Knew* (New York: George H. Doran, 1925), 179.
5. Max O'rell and Jack Allyn, *Jonathan and His Continent: Rambles Through American Society*, trans. Madame Paul Blouet (Bristol: J. W. Arrowsmith, 1889), 221.
6. J. J. Aubertin, *A Fight with Distances: The States, the Hawaiian Islands, Canada, British Columbia, Cuba, the Bahamas* (London: Kegan Paul, Trench & Co., 1888), 262.
7. Francesco Carega quoted in Andrew J. Torrielli, *Italian Opinion on America, As Revealed by Italian Travalers, 1850–1900* (Cambridge, MA: Harvard University Press, 1941), 261. Trans. from Italian by Pietro Bonomi.
8. W. Henry Barneby, *Life and Labor in the Far, Far West: Being Notes of a Tour in the Western States, British Columbia, Manitoba, and the North-West Territory* (London: Cassell & Co., 1884), 26. W. E. Adams claimed that all classes in America worked harder and longer than in England. W. E. Adams, *Our American Cousins: Being Personal Impressions of the People and Institutions of the United States* (London: Walter Scott, 1883), 61.
9. Alexis de Tocqueville, *Democracy in America* [1835], trans. Arthur Goldhammer (New York: Library of America, 2004), 717.
10. Marie Therese de Solms Blanc, *The Condition of Woman in the United States: A Traveller's Notes* [1896], trans. Abby Langdon Alger (New York: Arno Press, 1972), 266. Paul de Rousiers defined the home of an American as "any spot where he may happen to find himself for the time being." Rousiers, 110.
11. E. Catherine Bates, *A Year in the Great Republic*, v. 2 (London: Ward & Downey, 1887), 198.
12. F. Barham Zincke, *Last Winter in the United States: Being Table Talk Collected During a Tour Through the Late Southern Confederation, the Far West, the Rocky Mountains, &c.* [1868] (Freeport, NY: Books for Libraries Press, 1970), 3. The transient nature of many Americans meant that they often did not maintain permanent addresses, and called for their mail at post offices. At the larger post offices, there were three separate windows of inquiry for English, French and German speakers. Ibid., 197
13. Baron Hübner, *A Ramble Round the World, 1871*, trans. Lady Elizabeth Herbert (London: MacMillan and Co., 1878), 128.
14. Harry Kessler, "The Kessler Diaries," manuscipt trans. and ed. Laird Easton, 3.

15. Quoted in Torrielli, 291–292. Trans. from Italian by Pietro Bonomi.
16. Luxury hotels installed electric lighting in the 1880s, but most other hotels did without electric light until the twentieth century. A. K. Sandoval-Strausz, *Hotel: An American History* (New Haven: Yale University Press, 2007), 164.
17. Joseph Hatton, *Henry Irving's Impressions of America, Narrated in a Series of Sketches, Chronicles, and Conversations* [1884], v. 2 (New York: Benjamin Blom, 1971), 16.
18. William Howard Russell, *Hesperothen, Notes from the West: A Record of a Ramble in the United States and Canada in the Spring and Summer of 1881*, v. 1, (London: S. Low, Marston, Searle & Rivington, 1882), 56.
19. Charles W. Vincent, "The Dangers of Electric Lighting," *The Nineteenth Century* 27, no. 155 (January 1890), 145.
20. Rousiers, 131, 132.
21. Aubertin, 56.
22. William Saunders, *Through the Light Continent, or, The United States in 1877–78* [1879] (New York: Arno Press, 1974), 379. Harold Brydges also noted the ubiquity of telephones, reporting that "I have heard ladies say they would as soon be without a cook as without the telephone." Brydges, 146.
23. Herbert Spencer, "Report of Mr. Spencer's Interview" in Edward Youmans, *Herbert Spencer on the Americans and the Americans on Herbert Spencer: Being a Full Report of his Interview, and of the Proceedings of the Farewell Banquet of Nov. 11, 1882* (New York: D. Appleton, 1883), 11.
24. Alexander Craib, *America and the Americans: A Tour in the United States and Canada, With Chapters on American Home Life* (London: Alexander Gardner, 1892), 49–50. Craib called this incident "significant of the Yankee character, and of the enterprise and of the speedy way things are done on the American continent." Ibid., 50.
25. See Daniel J. Boorstin, *The Americans: The National Experience* (New York: Random House, 1965), 21–33.
26. Émile Levasseur, *The American Workman*, trans. Thomas S. Adams (Baltimore: Johns Hopkins University, 1900), 62.
27. Anonymous, "The Education of the People in England and America," *Blackwood's Edinburgh Magazine* 653, no. 107 (March 1870), 116.
28. Bourget, 113; French labor delegates quoted in Levasseur, 63.
29. Hamilton Aïdé, "Social Aspects of American Life," *The Nineteenth Century* 29, no. 172 (June 1891), 889.
30. Tocqueville, 625; Madame de San Carlos, "Americans at Home," *Review of Reviews* 1, no. 6 (June 1890), 487. Henry Adams echoed this view in *The Education of Henry Adams*. Adams claimed that American men "knew not how to amuse themselves; they could not conceive how other people were amused." Henry Adams, *The Education of Henry Adams* [1907] (Boston: Houghton Mifflin, 1961), 298.
31. See Oscar Wilde, "The American Man," in *The Collected Oscar Wilde* (New York: Barnes and Noble Classics, 2007), 307. F. Barham Zincke believed that the chief reason that Americans had not embraced the English enthusiasm for athletics was to be found "in the almost total absence among them of a class possessed of leisure, which from the times of the barons to the present day has always been a large and constantly increasing class among us." Zincke, 73. Henry Trueman Wood also said of Americans that "people do not seem to have any holiday time. They have few or no outdoor amusements, little sport, no hunting, no yachting, no games. Public opinion seems to expect everybody to be busy making money, and disapproves of the pursuits of those who are otherwise occupied." Henry Trueman Wood, "Chicago and Its Exhibition," *The Nineteenth Century* 31, no. 180 (February 1892), 557.
32. James Fullarton Muirhead, *The Land of Contrasts: A Briton's View of his American Kin* (London: Lamson, Wolffe, and Co., 1898), 49, 100–101. Léon Paul Blouet also noted that, "In England, a man who does nothing goes by the name of *gentleman*; in Chicago he goes by the name of *loafer*" [original emphasis]. O'rell and Allyn, 222.

In Anthony Trollope's *The American Senator*, an American politician spends a season among Britain's country gentry. As participants gather for a fox hunt, "the Senator looked with curious eyes, thinking that he had never in his life seen brought together a set of more useless human beings." Anthony Trollope, *The American Senator* [1876–77] (Oxford: Oxford University Press, 1991), 58.

33. William Wentworth Dixon, *New America* (Philadelphia: J. B. Lippincott, 1869), 461–463.

34. David Macrae, *The Americans at Home* [1870] (New York: E. P. Dutton, 1952), 275.

35. Grady McWhiney notes that in 1860, only 10 percent of the residents of the South lived in urban places, compared with 36 percent of Northeasterners and 16 percent of Westerners. There were sixteen cities in the United States with populations over 50,000, with New Orleans being the only one located in the South. Grady McWhiney, *Cracker Culture: Celtic Ways in the Old South* (Tuscaloosa: University of Alabama Press, 1988), 251.

36. McWhiney argues that those who observed Southerners found them to be "more hospitable, generous, frank, courteous, spontaneous, lazy, lawless, militaristic, wasteful, impractical, and reckless than Northerners, who were in turn more reserved, shrewd, disciplined, gauche, enterprising, acquisitive, careful, frugal, ambitious, pacific, and practical than Southerners." Ibid., 268.

37. Ernst von Hesse-Wartegg, *Travels on the Lower Mississippi, 1879–1880*, trans. and ed. Frederic Trautmann (Columbia: University of Missouri Press, 1990), 196. In 1897, when describing the residents of tidewater Virginia and South Carolina, W. P. Trent, claimed that "there is a persistence in customs, a loyalty to beliefs and traditions, a *naïveté* of self-satisfaction that cannot be called conceit, a clannishness, an attachment to the soil, that are radically English and thoroughly picturesque, but are certainly not American." W. P. Trent, "Dominant Forces in Southern Life," *Atlantic Monthly* 78, no. 471 (January 1897), 44.

38. See Sandoval-Strausz, 103–104.

39. R. W. Dale, "Impressions of America," pt. 1, *Eclectic Magazine* 27, no. 6 (New Series, June 1878), 670; O'rell and Allyn, 291.

40. William Archer, *America To-Day: Observations and Reflections* [1899] (New York: Arno Press, 1974), 80; Wilde, "American Man," 310; S. C. de Soissons, *A Parisian in America* (Boston: Estes and Lauriat, 1896), 41; Theodora Guest, *A Round Trip in North America* (London: Edward Stanford, 1895), 257.

41. William A. Baille-Grohman, *Camps in the Rockies: Being a Narrative of Life on the Frontier, and Sport in the Rocky Mountains, with an Account of the Cattle Ranches of the West* (New York: Charles Scribner's Sons, 1884), 23. Rose G. Kingsley described Americans in the West as a "generous, affectionate, and high-minded people." Rose G. Kingsley, *South by West, or Winter in the Rocky Mountains and Spring in Mexico* (London: W. Isbinster and Co., 1874), ix.

42. Peter Tchaikovsky, *The Diaries of Tchaikovsky*, trans. Wladimir Lakond (New York: W. W. Norton, 1945), 301.

43. Bourget, 47.

44. James Bryce, *The American Commonwealth*, v. 2 (New York: The Commonwealth Publishing Co., 1908), 765.

45. Henry Latham, *Black and White: A Journal of a Three Months' Tour in the United States* [1867] (New York: Negro Universities Press, 1969), 191.

46. Aubertin, 50. Historian Christopher Mulvey observes that, "The distinguishing feature of the American manners of the nineteenth century—their good temper and restraint—was that they were good manners for doing business." Christopher Mulvey, *Transatlantic Manners: Social Patterns in Nineteenth-Century Anglo-American Travel Literature* (Cambridge: Cambridge University Press, 1990), 111.

47. Russell, v. 1, 78.

48. Zincke called hand shaking "a rational way of expressing goodwill without saying anything." Zincke, 132; Brydges, 25; See also Anonymous, "Some American Notes," *MacMillan's Magazine* 53 (November 1885), 44. W. F. Rae claimed that hand shaking in America had "no special significance" and that the American "cordially shakes hands with those whom he does not care to meet on terms of intimacy." W. F. Rae, *Westward by Rail: The New Route to the East* [1871] (New York: Promontory Press, 1974), 381. Baron Hübner observed that white persons did not shake the hands of black persons: "In this case, with a due consideration for the shade of his skin, there is no shaking of hands. In spite of the emancipation, we have not yet arrived at that!" Hübner, 34.

49. Tchaikovsky, 319. Robert Louis Stevenson judged Americans as individuals to be both "surprisingly rude and surprisingly kind," a characteristic Stevenson claimed cut across class and regional lines. Robert Louis Stevenson, "The Amateur Emigrant," in *From Scotland to Silverado* [1892] (Cambridge, MA: Belknap Press, 1966), 97.

50. William H. Davies, *The Autobiography of a Super-Tramp* (New York: Alfred A. Knopf, 1917), 25.

51. Ibid., 39–40.

52. Ibid., 98.

53. Edward A. Freeman, *Some Impressions of the United States* (London: Longmans, Green, and Co., 1883), 5. The Englishman W. E. Adams claimed that most Americans were "nearly as reticent and reserved as we are ourselves." W. E. Adams, 84. Americans may have garnered their reputation for loquaciousness from when they traveled in Europe. J. W. Boddam-Whetham observed that "Americans at home are much more reserved than when abroad … In their own country, they seem to have lost, in some measure, their colloquial propensities, not only amongst strangers but amongst themselves." Boddam-Whetham, 40.

54. Thomas Hughes, "A Week in the West," pt. 4, *MacMillan's Magazine* 25 (November 1871), 159.

55. Zincke, 62; Dixon, 433.

56. George Augustus Sala, *America Revisited: From the Bay of New York to the Gulf of Mexico and From Lake Michigan to the Pacific* (London: Vizetelly & Co., n.d.), 128.

57. Hübner, 32. While waiting for dinner at a boarding house in Utah, the men "smoke and spit, but no one talks. The women sometimes whisper to one another in a low voice, but conversation is evidently considered out of place." Ibid., 81. While he was traveling on a riverboat in 1879, Ernst von Hesse-Wartegg said of American travelers that "conversation as a rule is sparse." Hesse-Wartegg, 94.

58. Pocock quoted in Robert G. Athearn, *Westward the Briton* (Lincoln: University of Nebraska Press, 1953), 96; Parker Gillmore, *A Hunter's Adventures in the Great West* (London: Hurst and Blackett, 1871), 125.

59. Hughes, pt. 4, 159.

60. Saunders, 13. If Saunders found the silence of Americans unnerving, he praised the "straightforward honesty of the American people." During Saunders' travels in the United States, "no one ever tried to give short change," and among merchants "no one ever failed to do fully what he promised to do." Ibid., 359, 360. In contrast to his native Italy, Dario Papa detected an emotional reserve in the United States which he called "no whim of feelings." Quoted in Torrielli, 234. Trans. from Italian by Pietro Bonomi.

61. W. C. M., "American Traits," *Eclectic Magazine* 16, no. 1 (New Series, July 1872), 57. George Jacob Holyoake added that "an American audience, anywhere gathered together, make the most courteous listeners in the world. If a speaker has only the gift of making a fool of himself, nowhere has he so complete an opportunity of doing it." George Jacob Holyoake, "A Stranger in America," *The Nineteenth Century* 8, no. 41 (July 1880), 76.

62. Tocqueville, 3. Madame de Staël claimed in 1800 that only America could be described as "an enlightened nation, where liberty and political equality are established, and where customs are consistent with its institutions." Madame de Staël, "Literature Considered in Its Relation to Social Institutions," in *Madame de Staël on Politics, Literature, and National Character*, trans. and ed. Morroe Berger (Garden City, NY: Doubleday, 1964), 225.

63. Frances Trollope, *Domestic Manners of the Americans* [1832] (New York: Alfred A. Knopf, 1949), 52.

64. Ibid., 54.

65. Tocqueville, 675.

66. Lepel Henry Griffin, *The Great Republic* [1884] (New York: Arno Press, 1974), 73.

67. Muirhead, 29.

68. Henry Sienkiewicz, *Portrait of America: Letters of Henry Sienkiewicz*, trans. and ed. Charles Morley (New York: Columbia University Press, 1959), 92.

69. Ibid., 96–97. Léon Paul Blouet put a negative spin on this phenomenon, noting that, "Just so agreeable, obliging, and considerate as is the cultivated American; just so rude, rough, and inconsiderate is the lower-class one." O'rell and Allyn, 255.

70. Sienkiewicz, 98.

71. Macrae, 56.

72. See Lady Duffus Hardy, *Through Cities and Prairie Lands: Sketches of an American Tour* (London: Chapman and Hall, 1881), 252. While the "servant problem" took on its most extreme contours in America, it was sometimes also a part of British social relations. Virginia Woolf, for instance, described "sordid" and "degrading" screaming matches with servants, and condemned her cook, Nellie Boxall, as a "mongrel" possessed of a "timid spiteful servant mind." Quoted in "The Servant Problem," *Economist* 401, no. 8764 (17 December 2011), 48.

73. Rousiers, 110.

74. See Muirhead, 10. Muirhead admitted that the American spirit of independence often degenerated into the "needlessly boorish," but at least it was "sturdy and manly." Ibid., 99.

75. Hugues Le Roux, *Business and Love* (New York: Dodd, Mead and Co., 1903), 136.

76. Bourget, 419.

77. Levasseur, 64.

78. Ibid., 444.

79. Vachell, 126; Emily Faithfull, *Three Visits to America* (New York: Fowler & Wells, 1884), 295.

80. Isabelle Randall, *A Lady's Ranche Life in Montana* (London: W. H. Allen & Co., 1887), 31.

81. Ibid., 48.

82. Ibid., 63. Randall became considerably exercised on the subject of servants: "I don't want to be bothered with any more servants if I can possibly manage to do without them; it is no use trying to have them out here; even *good* English ones would be spoilt in a month. The natives are very queer and independent, and rough; it is no use trying to make them into *servants*, and very disagreeable to have half-educated, ill-mannered sort of people to eat and sit with you; and if you had English, the natives would soon make them discontented" [original emphasis]. Ibid., 70–71.

83. Anonymous, "The Antagonism of Race and Colour; or, White, Red, Black, and Yellow in America," *Blackwood's Edinburgh Magazine* 653, no. 107 (March 1870), 327, 328.

84. H. Hussey Vivian, *Notes of a Tour in America from August 7th to November 17th, 1877* (London: Edward Stanford, 1878), 135.

85. Craib noted that American domestic servants were likely to become "indignant if spoken to in the way of 'counselling on matters,' and will very soon leave the family, and make a change to another." Craib, 133. Paul de Rousiers commented that often he went to a house, gave his letter of introduction to the person who opened the door,

and asked to see the mistress of the house. When the person who opened the door began reading the letter, "I suddenly realized she was mistress of the house." Rousiers, 301.

86. Bates, v. 1, 273.

87. Bates observed that "as these and similar casualties are of constant occurrence, we can hardly wonder that so many American ladies shirk the responsibilities and annoyances of housekeeping, and take refuge in hotels." Ibid., 112.

88. Dale, pt. 1, 667. Dale contrasted "the friendly ease of the American `help'" with "the absolute self-suppression and mechanical deference which are seen in the servants of many English houses." Ibid., pt. 1, 668.

89. Rousiers, 299, 300.

90. Mulvey, 166.

91. Hübner, 26.

92. Soissons, 35.

93. Rose Pender, *A Lady's Experiences of the Wild West in 1883* (London: George Tucker, 1888), 56.

94. Aïdé, 896.

95. Rousiers, 124.

96. Faithfull, 322.

97. Blanc, 242–243.

98. Lady Duffus Hardy, 61.

99. Harry Kessler, *Journey to the Abyss: The Diaries of Count Harry Kessler, 1880–1918*, trans. and ed. Laird Easton (New York: Knopf, 2011), 51.

100. Hatton, v. 2, 45.

101. Dixon, 442.

102. Robert Somers, *The Southern States Since the War, 1870–71* [1871] (Tuscaloosa: University of Alabama Press, 1965), 130.

103. Vachell, 24.

104. Anonymous, "Some American Notes," 44.

105. Mark Twain, "Concerning the American Language," [1882] in *Collected Tales, Sketches, Speeches and Essays*, v. 1 (New York: Library of America, 1992), 832.

106. Muirhead, 20.

107. W. C. M., 56.

108. Quoted in Mulvey, 160.

109. Kingsley, 66–67.

110. Sala, 103.

111. O'rell and Allyn, 262.

112. Phil Robinson, *Sinners and Saints: A Tour Across the States, and Round Them; with Three Months Among the Mormons* (Boston: Roberts Brothers, 1883), 47.

113. See David T. Courtwright, *Violent Land: Single Men and Social Disorder from the Frontier to the Inner City* (Cambridge, MA: Harvard University Press, 1996), 80.

114. Russell, v. 2, 37–38.

115. Torrielli, 98, n. 32. Trans. from Italian by Pietro Bonomi.

116. Vachell, 392.

117. Barneby, 5. W. E. Adams claimed that "the common schools on the one hand, and the arrangements for railway travelling on the other, level all mere artificial distinctions in the United States." W. E. Adams, 291.

118. W. G. Marshall, *Through America: Nine Months in the United States* (London: Sampson, Low, Marston, Searle & Rivington, 1881), 62. There is evidence that the American hostility toward tipping decreased as the century wore on. When Emily Faithfull was first in America in 1872, she was told that tipping would be regarded as an "insult." By 1884, she claimed that "increasing civilization has disappeared all antipathy to gratuities." Faithfull, 217. Also in the mid-1880s, E. Catherine Bates claimed that the tipping that was expected in American hotels "was on a far more ruinous scale" than

in England. Bates, v. 2, 135. When he visited America in 1899, William Archer also had the impression that tipping would not be accepted. But when he failed to tip a barber, he received a chilly reception upon his next visit and was forced to patronize a new barber, whom he "tipped from the outset." According to Archer, one class that continued to eschew tips was railroad conductors. Archer, 86, 87. Phil Robinson added, "What is the 'conductor' of a Pullman car? Is he a private gentleman travelling for his pleasure, a duke in disguise, or is he a servant of the company placed on the cars to see to the comfort, &c., of the company's customers?" Robinson, 52.

119. Macrae, 458. It was not only in the South where this system prevailed. Traveling on a train through Ohio, William Hepworth Dixon was struck by the absence of blacks in the cars. He went forward to the front of the train and "there, between the tender and the luggage van, found a separate pen, filthy beyond words to suggest, in which were a dozen free negroes, going the same road and paying the same fare as myself. 'Why do these negroes ride apart—why not travel in the common cars?' I asked the guard. 'Well,' said he, with a sudden lightning in his eyes, 'they have the right; but, damn them, I should like to see them do it. Ugh!'" Dixon, 469–470.

120. Zincke, 259.

121. Bryce, 706.

122. Bourget, 54–55.

123. Matthew Arnold, "A Word More About America," in *Civilization in the United States: First and Last Impressions of America* [1888] (Freeport, NY: Books for Libraries Press, 1972), 123.

124. Hübner, 14, 15.

125. Muirhead, 13.

126. William A. Bell, *New Tracks in North America: A Journal of Travel and Adventure Whilst Engaged in the Survey for a Southern Railroad to the Pacific Ocean During 1867–8* [1870] (Albuquerque: Horn and Wallace, 1965), 13.

127. Lady Duffus Hardy, 157–158.

128. Arnold, "A Word More About America," 121–122.

129. Latham, vi.

130. Sienkiewicz, 97.

131. Muirhead, 2.

132. O'rell and Allyn, 26.

133. Bryce, v. 2, 697, 699, 700. Bryce believed that in England, "great wealth, skilfully employed, will more readily force these doors to open." Ibid., v. 2, 697. In *The Way We Live Now*, Anthony Trollope creates one of his most memorable characters in Augustus Melmotte, a crooked financier whose enormous wealth gains him entree into the highest levels of British society. Anthony Trollope, *The Way We Live Now* [1875] (New York: Barnes and Noble Classics, 2005). Horace Annesley Vachell claimed that in America, "The master seldom forgets that once he was the man, and the man never forgets that he in his turn may be the master. I cannot recall, during seventeen years, one single instance of a cruel and cutting rebuke from one in authority to a clerk or servant." Vachell, 32–33. Tocqueville also observed that, "In the United States, the most opulent citizens take great care not to isolate themselves from the people. On the contrary, they reach out to the people constantly, listen to them voluntarily, and speak with them daily." Tocqueville, 592.

134. Zincke, 230. Zincke concluded that Americans "measure others much more fairly than we do." "Ours is a system which isolates," said Zincke, "theirs is a system which brings everybody in contact with everybody." Ibid., 263.

135. The Big Four built the Central and Southern Pacific railroads. The other three were Leland Stanford, Collis P. Huntington, and Mark Hopkins. See Richard B. Rice et al., *The Elusive Eden: A New History of California* (New York: McGraw-Hill, 1988), 253–257.

136. W. E. Adams, 98, 99.
137. Gordon S. Wood, *The Radicalism of the American Revolution* (New York: Alfred A. Knopf, 1992), 347.
138. Hübner, 46.
139. Matthew Arnold, "A Word About America," in *Civilization in the United States: First and Last Impressions of America* [1888], 74, 79, 85.
140. Arnold, "A Word About America," 80. In another essay, Arnold clarified his use of the word "Philistine," arguing that "in my mouth the name is hardly a reproach, so clearly do I see the Philistine's necessity, so willingly I own his merits, so much I find of him in myself." Arnold, "A Word More About America," 128. A dreadful public speaker, Arnold sent Americans fleeing his lectures in droves including, on one occasion, General and Mrs. Grant. At the end of his tour of the United States, Arnold returned to England with $6,000 of the Philistines' money. See Richard L. Rapson, *Britons View America: Travel Commentary, 1860–1935* (Seattle: University of Washington Press, 1971), 12–13. An anonymous article in the British periodical *The Cornhill Magazine* declared that "the American Philistine differs fundamentally from our own variety in possessing, for all that, a spirit of fun, a certain notable quickness of intelligence, and a considerable fund of native geniality." Anonymous, "The Great American Language," *The Cornhill Magazine* 11 (New Series, October 1888), 376.
141. Arnold, "A Word About America," 102, 103.
142. Bryce, v. 2, 763; J. W. C., 125. Still, Emily Faithfull claimed that despite American proclamations that their country was free of class privileges, "all candid persons will acknowledge to a growing love of caste distinctions in that country." Faithfull, 36.
143. A. Maurice Low, *The American People: A Study in National Psychology*, v. 1 (Boston: Houghton Mifflin, 1909), 79.
144. W. E. Adams, 302, 127.
145. Tocqueville, 593.
146. Rousiers, 329. Hamilton Aïdé contrasted "the air of frank and hearty enjoyment" that prevailed at American balls with the "miasma of self-consciousness which infects half the young people" at similar gatherings in England. Aïdé, 898.
147. Macrae, 56.
148. Ibid., 398.
149. Quoted in Eric H. Monkkonen, *Police in Urban America, 1860–1920* (Cambridge: Cambridge University Press, 1981), 45.
150. Freeman, 202.
151. Sienkiewicz, 21.
152. O'rell and Allyn, 179.
153. Aubertin, 280.
154. Anonymous, "Some Remarks on Travelling in America," *The Cornhill Magazine* 19 (March 1869), 327.
155. Frances Trollope, "Selections from Mrs. Trollope's Notebooks and Rough Draft," in Frances Trollope, *Domestic Manners of the Americans*, ed. Donald Smalley (New York: Alfred A. Knopf, 1949), 431.
156. Quoted in Daniel J. Boorstin, *The Americans: The Democratic Experience* (New York: Random House, 1973), 91.
157. Bram Stoker, "A Glimpse of America" [1886] in *Bram Stoker's A Glimpse of America and Other Lectures, Interviews and Essays*, ed. Richard Dalby (Westcliff-on-Sea, UK: Desert Island Books, 2002), 14, 15.
158. Blouet added that "when you see diamonds in the ears of shop-girls and factory-girls, they are sham gems bought with well-earned money, or real ones bought with badly-earned money." O'rell and Allyn, 24; Rousiers, 322.

159. Blanc, 25.

160. Ibid., 269. In fact, most American women who lived outside the great metropolitan centers made their own clothes. Seamstresses made weekly visits to private homes, and by the 1880s, sewing machines were increasingly common. By the 1890s, women could order clothing from mail order catalogs (such as Sears and Roebuck), but such catalogs still devoted twice as much space to fabric over ready-made items. See Rachel H. Kemper, *Costume* (New York: Newsweek Books, 1977), 136, 137.

161. Rudyard Kipling, *American Notes* [1891] (Norman: University of Oklahoma Press, 1981), 21.

162. Lady Duffus Hardy, 61.

163. See Iza Duffus Hardy, *Between Two Oceans: Or, Sketches of American Travel* (London: Hurst and Blackett, 1884), 107–108.

164. Stephen Buckland, "Eating and Drinking In America—A Stroll Among the Saloons of New York," *MacMillan's Magazine* 16 (October 1867), 460; Brydges, 61; Knut Hamsun said of the dude that "to go around eyeing the latest cut in jackets, getting into loud discussions about the most recent nose-battering antics of two boxers, making wisecracks in the current lingo, flinging cynical gibes at the poor sinners from the back rooms—these are his life's interests." Knut Hamsun, *The Cultural Life of Modern America* [1889] (Cambridge, MA: Harvard University Press, 1969), 134.

165. Quoted in Hatton, v. 2, 179.

166. Boddam-Whetham, 355.

167. Marshall, 268.

168. Charles Wentworth Dilke, *Greater Britain: A Record of Travel in English-Speaking Countries* (London: Macmillan and Co., 1890), 4.

169. W. E. Adams, 86.

170. W. E. Adams, 87. Lady Duffus Hardy claimed that "no American, East or West, will shave an inch of his own chin." That was a chore they entrusted to a barber. Lady Duffus Hardy, 135.

171. See Hatton, v. 2, 46; O'rell and Allyn, 24. Blouet condemned the practice of American women to wear low-necked dresses even in the afternoon hours. Ibid., 100.

172. Langtry, 180; O'rell and Allyn, 98. In 1891, Alexander Craib described the dress of New York women as "showy, but neat and in good taste." Craib, 164.

173. Faithfull, 35. American women also wore what J. J. Aubertin called "tall, exaggerated head-dresses" even in theatres. Appeals to cease this practice had produced no practical result. Aubertin groused that "so long as passengers can be pushed off their seats in the cars, and men are to put on church faces in hotel elevators, tall head-dresses will be persisted in." Aubertin, 256. Léon Paul Blouet claimed that the elaborate, feathered hats of American women imparted the look of "an irate cockatoo." O'rell and Allyn, 98.

174. Faithfull, 88.

175. The local paper announced that "a Frenchman had landed in the town the day before in white trousers, and that his popularity had been as prompt as decisive." O'rell and Allyn, 97.

176. Athearn, 72.

177. Marshall, 255.

178. Hamsun, 5; Jacques Offenbach, *Orpheus in America: Offenbach's Diary of His Journey to the New World*, trans. Lander MacClintock (New York: Greenwood Press, 1969), 110.

179. Sienkiewicz, 119.

180. Ibid., 52.

181. Bryce, v. 2, 687–688. At a dance in Santa Fe in 1867, William A. Bell described women wearing "roboses, often gracefully thrown over their heads, gay coloured dresses, big brooches and pendant earrings, [they] smoked sigarettes [*sic.*] incessantly, and sat quietly on forms placed around the room, waiting for any one who should choose to ask them to dance." Bell, 149.

182. Bates, v. 2, 201.

183. Hübner, 81.

184. Oscar Wilde, *Decorative Art in America: A Lecture by Oscar Wilde Together with Letters, Reviews and Interviews*, ed. Richard Butler Glaenzer (New York: Brentano's, 1906), 8. Wilde himself had the temerity to show up at a polo match in Newport wearing a white slouch hat. Ibid., 183 n. 8. Henry M. Stanley provided a considerably less flattering description of the miners of Central City: "a mixed crowd of stalwart men, with huge bushy whiskers, sharp grey eyes, soiled features, lead-coloured hats, smutty blouses, and muddy boots." Henry M. Stanley, *My Early Travels and Adventures in America* [1895] (Lincoln: University of Nebraska Press, 1982), 183.

185. Robinson, 44.

186. Lady Duffus Hardy, 156.

187. David T. Courtwright observes that "for the cowboy to become a symbol of the American experience required an act of moral surgery. The cowboy as mounted protector and risk-taker was remembered. The cowboy as dismounted drunk sleeping it off on the manure pile behind the saloon was forgotten or transmogrified into a rough-edged, heart-of-gold fellow who liked an occasional bit of fun." Courtwright, 89.

188. Isabella L. Bird, *A Lady's Life in the Rocky Mountains* (Norman: University of Oklahoma Press, 1969), 27.

189. Guest, 56; Faithfull, 271.

190. Langtry, 196.

191. Bell, 146; Windham Thomas Wyndham-Quin, *The Great Divide: Travels in the Upper Yellowstone in the Summer of 1874* (London: Chatto and Windus, 1876), 63. The Crows, said Wyndham-Quin, carefully protected their head-dresses in band-boxes, and were "very proud of their ornaments, earrings, bracelets, and garniture." Wyndham-Quin called the Crow male the "greatest coxcomb on the face of the earth, not to be surpassed even in London for inordinate vanity, stupendous egotism, and love of self." Ibid., 64.

192. Bird, 140.

193. Athearn, 38.

194. Randall, 6–7

195. Quoted in Torrielli, n. 29, 268, Trans. from Italian by Pietro Bonomi; Bird, 182. Grady McWhiney claims that, "The importance that both premodern British Celts and antebellum Southerners placed upon leisure rather than work was perhaps the single most important cultural trait that separated them from Englishmen and antebellum Northerners." McWhiney, 49.

196. Tocqueville said of Americans that "money is virtually the only thing that still creates very visible differences among them and sets some apart from their peers. The distinction that is born of wealth is enhanced by the disappearance and diminution of all the others." Tocqueville, 722–723.

197. Soissons, 30.

198. Offenbach, 159–160.

199. See "Introducing Offenbach," in *Orpheus in America*, 18; Offenbach, 36.

200. Macrae, 439.

201. Kipling, 139, 141. It was no different in the Far West. From Portland, Kipling reported that "men were babbling of money, town lots, and again money." Ibid., 68.

202. Soissons, 25. Knut Hamsun agreed, declaring that "the combined manpower of sixty million people is concentrated on the promotion and sale of goods." Hamsun, 21.

203. Griffin, 18.

204. O'rell and Allyn, 19, 21.

205. A. S. Northcote, "American Life Through English Spectacles," *The Nineteenth Century* 34, no. 199 (September 1893), 485. Rose G. Kingsley also referred to the "seemingly reckless way people go on here." Kingsley, 107.

206. Hübner, 55.
207. Rousiers, 13.
208. Vachell, 23, 242.
209. Henry Adams, 297.
210. Tocqueville, 619.
211. Rousiers, 264.
212. Robinson, 41.
213. Hatton, v. 1, 129.
214. Soissons, 27; Zincke, 188.
215. Soissons, 28.
216. Herbert Spencer, "Mr. Spencer's Address" ("Proceedings of the Spencer Banquet") in Edward Youmans, *Herbert Spencer on the Americans and the Americans on Herbert Spencer: Being a Full Report of his Interview, and of the Proceedings of the Farewell Banquet of Nov. 11, 1882* (New York: D. Appleton, 1883), 30. Spencer said, "In brief, I may say that we have had somewhat too much of 'the gospel of work.' It is time to preach the gospel of relaxation." Ibid. 35. Edward Livingston Youmans acknowledged that "some have thought it incongruous that a chronic invalid—himself a victim of overwork—should venture to talk to a robust and irrepressible people about the effects of overwork." Youmans, "Preface" to *Herbert Spencer on the Americans*, 7.
217. Jose Martí, *Martí on the U.S.A.*, trans. Luis A. Barlat (Carbondale: Southern Illinois University Press, 1966), 197. One of the few European commentators who saw the showering of American women with luxury items as a form of oppression (or conspicuous consumption) was A. Maurice Low. Like Thorstein Veblen in *The Theory of the Leisure Class* (1899), Low claimed that such largess "ministered to the vanity of these men, and was more valuable even than a high rating at a commercial agency, to install their wives in great houses, to load them down with enormous diamonds, to see them expensively and garishly dressed." Low, v. 2, 94. Alexandra Gripenberg also noted that the American man "considers it a matter of honor that he has the most beautiful house, the best-dressed wife, and the best-paid servants in the whole neighborhood. He does not like to see his wife and daughters do any work, for it might appear that he is not man enough to support them." Alexandra Gripenberg, *A Half Year in the New World: Miscellaneous Sketches of Travel in the United States* [1889], trans. and ed. Ernest J. Moyne (Newark: University of Delaware Press, 1954), 209.
218. Latham, viii.
219. Saunders, 239; J. J. Aubertin was also impressed that American currency was legal tender "not only in the State to which the bank in question belongs, but throughout all thirty-eight States and Eleven Territories." Aubertin, 296. One exception was California, where in 1869 W. F. Rae discovered that, "The State stretched its legal rights to the extreme point of refusing to accept as currency what Congress had proclaimed legal tenders. Nothing passes current here save gold and silver coin." Rae, 267.
220. Brydges, 147.
221. Harry Kessler observed of New York in 1892 that on "every possible spot there are advertisements." Kessler, *Journey to the Abyss*, 50.
222. John Campbell Argyll, *A Trip to the Tropics and Home Through America* (London: Hurst and Blackett, 1867), 172.
223. Offenbach, 104–105.
224. Ibid., 58, 105.
225. Quoted in Aubertin, 261.
226. Archer, 30; Hatton, v. 2, 40–41.
227. Russell, v. 2, 129.
228. Thomas J. Schlereth, *Victorian America: Transformations in Everyday Life, 1876–1915* (New York: Harper Perennial, 1992), 161.

229. G. K. Chesterton, *What I Saw in America* [1922], in G. K. Chesterton, *Collected Works*, v. 21 (San Francisco: Ignatius Press, 1990), 62.

230. Blanc, 63; Hesse-Wartegg, 157.

231. "No one who has not travelled in the United States has the least idea how sadly the country is disfigured by the daubing I have referred to." Marshall, 113. Joseph Hatton also referred to extensive advertising as "a disfigurement of the land which every English visitor notices with regret." Hatton, v. 1, 251.

232. Macrae, 532. F. Barham Zincke also commented on the proliferation of bitters promotions: "There are 'Red jacket bitters,' and 'Planters' bitters,' 'French,' 'German,' 'Mexican' and 'American bitters,' but no English, which I am disposed to take as a compliment implying that Englishmen need no such restoratives, for it can hardly mean that the name would be no recommendation." Zincke, 77–78. William Howard Russell took note of the relationship between bitters and low-quality alcohol "in which the badness of the spirit is artfully disguised by a stimulant of a more active character and more pronounced flavour, known as 'bitters,' and kept in subjugation by the liberal use of ice." Russell, v. 2, 168.

233. Ibid., v. 1, 53.

234. Sala, 97.

235. Iza Duffus Hardy, *Between Two Oceans: Or, Sketches of American Travel* (London: Hurst and Blackett, 1884), 48; Marshall, 112. Marshall had the cryptic observation that the painted advertising notices that he saw on the way to Yosemite were "not fit to meet the eye of the man or woman who has the least regard for any decency or propriety." Ibid., 336.

236. Brydges, 151; Griffin, 28.

237. Boddam-Whetham, 70. James Burnley claimed that "Rising Sun Stove Polish haunts you by every railway side on the continent." Quoted in August Mencken, *The Railroad Passenger Car* (Baltimore: Johns Hopkins Press, 1957), 172.

238. Robinson, 8.

239. Boorstin, *The Americans: The Democratic Experience*, 146.

240. Arnot Reid, "The English and the American Press," *The Nineteenth Century* 22, no. 124 (July 1867), 227.

241. Archer, 28–29. Certainly, obnoxious advertising was a feature of the Old World as well as the New. At the River Reuss in Europe, "a giant boulder had been painted brown, with a chocolate firm's name on it. High on the Rigi were enormous gilt letters advertising a hotel. Even the remote hills of the Sudan carried slogans for soap." Rudyard Kipling was one of those who believed that the British landscape had been even more vulgarized by advertisements than the American. E. S. Turner, *The Shocking History of Advertising!* (New York: E. P. Dutton, 1953), 157.

242. Horace White, "An American's Impression of England," *Eclectic Magazine* 22, no. 5 (New Series, November 1875), 554.

243. Hamsun, 139.

244. Griffin, 4, 35.

245. Therese Yelverton, *Teresina in America*, v. 1 (London: Richard Bentley and Son, 1875), 3, 18, 30, 25.

246. Yelverton lamented the "dearth of hospitality" she encountered in America. Yelverton, 26.

247. Kipling, 124.

2

THE BUILT ENVIRONMENT

Cities, Boosterism, Accommodations, and Transportation

Cities

For the majority of European travelers, New York was the great port of entry to America and the place where most formed their first impressions of the United States. Those impressions were often complex because, as David Macrae put it, New York contained all that was best and worst in America.[1] It was a city unlike any other where, according to Charles Dickens, the natural order of things had been reversed, and "everything grew newer every day, instead of older."[2] Visitors were struck by the noise and the pace of life in New York and what Baron Hübner called "that agitation and preoccupation and that provisional state of things."[3] Lady Duffus Hardy said of New York that it was like "a human cauldron, with a restless multitude seething and bubbling from morning till night."[4] Oscar Wilde was overwhelmed by the intense noise and the spectacle of an entire city that seemed to be rushing to catch a train.[5]

New York contained a huge immigrant population, with only short distances separating the mansions of the rich from "the miserable shanty of the Irish squatter."[6] Ernst von Hesse-Wartegg said of New York that "Europe lies at one end of Broadway, America at the other. In a few miles Broadway unrolls a continent for us to see."[7] The slums of this city were, according to Léon Paul Blouet, "the dirtiest, roughest, one can imagine. Hard by this frightful squalor, Fifth Avenue, with its palaces full of the riches of the earth" (Figures 2.1 and 2.2).[8] When J. J. Aubertin was in New York in 1886 he reported that "the mixture of nationalities is enormous; it is not, in point of fact, an American city."[9] But of course it was precisely that mixture that made it an American city.[10]

Coexisting with New York's "splendour, luxury and pleasure" were garbage cans overflowing with "dust, ashes, cabbage stumps, fish bones, broken china" and filthy, pot-holed streets.[11] Public health was additionally threatened by the

FIGURE 2.1 Fifth Avenue New York (ca. 1903). Library of Congress. LC-D401–16267.

large number of horses kept in New York. According to one estimate, New York's horses deposited 2.5 million pounds of manure and 60,000 gallons of urine per day.[12] David Macrae claimed that New York streets made even the streets of Glasgow or London look good.[13] One advantage that New York did have over London was that it used clean-burning anthracite coal, while London relied heavily on smoke-producing bituminous coal. The result was that New York's air was "as pure, and the skies as bright a blue, as in Italy."[14] Another difference between New York and London, according to George Augustus Sala, was in the degree of social friction that prevailed in the two cities: "The truth is, that in New York there is room enough for Everybody; whereas in London, huge as it is, there is not sufficient room for Anybody."[15]

Other eastern cities did not excite the same passions as New York. Philadelphia was generally dismissed as backward or, as one traveler put it, "rustic."[16] Oscar Wilde called Philadelphia "dreadfully provincial," where everyone seemed to go to bed at ten o'clock.[17] Lady Duffus Hardy called it "a sedate matronly city," and Léon Paul Blouet described it as "monotonous."[18] More diplomatically, David Macrae observed of Philadelphia that there was "a grateful absence of the feverish high-pressure life of other great cities."[19]

Opinions were split on Boston. Wilde referred to it as a "paradise of prigs," but Marie Therese Blanc called Boston "the most polished city in America," and said

9898—"How the other half lives" in a crowded Hebrew district, lower East Side, N. Y. City.   Copyright 1907 by Underwood & Underwood. U-86189

FIGURE 2.2 Lower East Side New York (ca. 1907). Library of Congress. LC–USZ62–63967.

that the city "dazzled me as a dream of beauty."[20] Harold Brydges took pains to praise the accomplishments of Boston women, who were "equally expert at composing a bonnet or a sonnet."[21] In a similar vein, another visitor deemed Boston the "'clever woman'" of America: "inwardly respected but outwardly condemned."[22]

The nation's capital was more often than not singled out for rough treatment. Baron Hübner's summation of Washington was that "the air is heavy, the heat stifling, the dust and the mosquitoes pursue you without mercy."[23] Washington was variously described as a "straggling city" or a "skeleton city" because public buildings were placed so far apart.[24] According to Henry Latham, Washington lacked the "growth and vitality" of other American cities, and Sarah Bernhardt said that Washington had "a sadness about it that affected one's nerves."[25]

William Archer claimed that Washington presented to the viewer the air of "a magnified and glorified frontier township," and French geographer Élisée Reclus bluntly stated that, "The United States have, properly speaking, no capital."[26]

Baltimore generally elicited positive reactions. Tchaikovsky called it a "very pretty, neat city," and super-tramp William H. Davies rated Baltimore extremely high as a mecca for panhandling.[27] To E. Catherine Bates, it was one of the "brightest and freshest" of American towns.[28] Many visitors, such as Lady Guest, detected a decided Southern atmosphere in Baltimore with "as many darkies as whites in the streets." Baltimore's Southern connection could be found in the many balls and bazaars that were got up in that city to raise money for impoverished Southern families.[29] As for the social differences among the major Eastern cities, Léon Paul Blouet neatly summed it up by observing that "in New York it is your money that will open all doors to you; in Boston, it is your learning; in Philadelphia and Virginia, it is your genealogy."[30]

Two characteristics that separated Eastern cities from their European counterparts were a greater openness in the layout of private residences, and the planting of trees as a municipal obligation. George Jacob Holyoake was enchanted by the "acres of plantations [that] lie unenclosed between the beautiful houses," and nowhere in America did Lady Duffus Hardy encounter the walling in of private grounds "for the solitary gratification of the owner."[31] Like Hardy, W. E. Adams emphasized the tendency in Britain to surround homes with walls "sufficiently high to stand a siege," but after traveling 4,000 miles through America, he claimed never to have seen a single wall put up for exclusion or protection.[32] He was also struck by the number of trees that had been planted even in "ill-governed" cities such as New York.[33] In Cleveland, the unenclosed foliage produced an overall effect like "that of a large and beautiful park dotted with houses," while New Haven had the aspect of a "a town planted in a forest."[34]

Western Cities

The cities of the East had their own peculiarities, but in their essentials they were not markedly different from many cities in Europe.[35] When the Scotsman William Archer walked the streets of New York in 1899, he occupied himself by trying to identify differences in dress and manners between New Yorkers and Londoners. In dress, the differences were "trifling," in manners, "microscopic."[36] It was in the cities of the West where the greatest contrasts were to be found, and also where the greatest urban growth was taking place. In 1840, there was no city west of the ninety-fifth meridian that had a population of more than 5,000. By 1890, twenty cities in the West had populations of 20,000 or more.[37]

The West's gateway city was St. Louis, which had long thrived as a hub for river traffic. Because of the French influence, the atmosphere of St. Louis was different from that of other American cities. Here, according to one traveler, "trade is less wild and enthusiastic, pleasure is more sought after and enjoyed."[38]

Ernst von Hesse-Wartegg also claimed that St. Louis was a magnet for Western "riff-raff," who "enjoy a district all their own, of infamous hotels and notorious casinos, saloons and dance halls, and houses of the lowest sort."[39] Throughout its history, St. Louis was subject to periodic cholera outbreaks. (St. Louis lost one-tenth of its population during the 1849 epidemic.[40]) When Charles Wentworth Dilke and William Hepworth Dixon arrived in that city in 1866, St. Louis was suffering through another epidemic. According to Dixon, "fires were burning in every street; lime was being forced into every gutter," and Dilke claimed that cholera deaths were running at 200 a day.[41] Even in non-epidemic years St. Louis seldom received glowing reviews. When Sarah Bernhardt performed there in 1881, she called it "repulsively dirty," and said that St. Louis was "less to my liking than the other American cities."[42] Four years later, E. Catherine Bates described St. Louis as a "big black manufacturing smoky city," exceeding even Cincinnati in its urban horrors.[43]

The importance of St. Louis was rapidly giving way to Chicago because of Chicago's dominance as a rail center. Of American cities, it was Chicago that excited the most loathing—and the most admiration—among European travelers. (Sometimes it did both, such as the case of Giuseppe Giacosa, whose view of Chicago evolved from "abominable" to "admirable beyond words."[44]) If America was a land of high energy, Chicago was in overdrive, a "raw, crowded, noisy, daring, busy, bustling" city with people rushing madly about.[45] Even houses were on the move in Chicago, due to the cost of building. As his train entered Chicago, Thomas Hughes saw a house on rollers sitting at a crossing, patiently waiting for the train to pass to continue its journey.[46] Several travelers witnessed houses being moved in Chicago that were still occupied by the family, who were "carrying on all the domestic work they were accustomed to perform when the place was stationary."[47] In one case, the chimney was still smoking while within an aria from *La Traviata* mingled with the sounds of a piano.[48] House moving was a relatively minor feat compared to what was done in downtown Chicago. Because of occasional flooding there, entire blocks of buildings had been raised "by hydraulic machinery" with minimum interruption to business.[49] Famously, the flow of the Chicago River was reversed in its course from east to west as a sanitation measure.[50]

Some European visitors saw Chicago as *the* American city. In the estimation of Élisée Reclus, Chicago had "the fairest prospects of becoming the future metropolis of the Union."[51] Thomas Hughes called it "the busiest and one of the handsomest cities I was ever in," and another British traveler said it was the most impressive city in America.[52] The business fever of Chicago, according to Paul Bourget, was a "devouring flame," rushing through the streets and making itself visible "with an intensity which lends something tragical to this city, and makes it seem like a poem to me."[53] For Giuseppe Giacosa, Chicago was the "ultimate expression" of the nineteenth century.[54]

The negative reactions to this city were equally impassioned. S. C. de Soissons called Chicago "monstrous," while Rudyard Kipling declared that having seen it once, he had no wish to see it again because it was "inhabited by savages."[55]

Sidney Webb called attention to "the garbage and litter of some of the most crowded slums in the world," while another commentator claimed that the smoke produced from the soft coal that was burned in Chicago "would do credit to Manchester or Leeds."[56] Much of what revolted European travelers about Chicago was related to that town's great pride and joy, its stockyards and slaughterhouses. In the miles of stockyard pens, the shouts of the drovers mingled with the sounds of thousands of animals.[57] At nearby slaughterhouses, animals were being slain and dressed on a scale never before seen with what Léon Paul Blouet called "the rapidity of conjuring."[58] Phil Robinson visited a Chicago slaughterhouse in 1882, and was astonished to see a live pig turned into meat in thirty-five seconds, the speed of which "robbed it of all its horrors."[59] "Hog-killing," said J. W. Boddam-Whetham, "is now recognised in America as one of the fine arts."[60] Kipling was less mollified, remembering that slaughterhouse butchers were bathed in blood, and that blood ran in the gutters and thickly coated every surface.[61] When Lepel Henry Griffin declined the opportunity to view a slaughterhouse in action, he reported that his Chicago friends "were distinctly ruffled."[62]

The views of these observers would have been even more negative had they seen the city from the perspective of Chicago's army of unskilled workers. Here once again, super-tramp William H. Davies provided a novel point of view as part of "the riff-raff of America and the scum of Europe" doing canal work in Chicago in the 1890s.[63] The back-breaking labor was bad enough, but lounging in the vicinity were thugs waiting to rob the workers of their pay. Davies claimed that seldom a day passed without a murder victim being dragged out of the water.[64]

Among the most notable of the foreign chroniclers of Chicago was the English reformer William T. Stead. Stead developed an interest in the seamy underbelly of Chicago when he visited the city in 1893 for the World's Columbian Exposition. In 1894 he published his observations of that city under the title, *If Christ Came to Chicago!* In this work, Stead frequently employs the jeremiad and the language of moral uplift (e.g. "deadly is the system by which the daughters reared in American homes are lured to their doom," and "the gaming hell open and unashamed is one of the indigenous institutions of Chicago") making large portions of *Christ* virtually unreadable.[65] Stead's great contribution, and what makes him unique among most European travelers, is that he sought out people and places that others avoided. Stead recorded his conversations with saloon owners, machine politicians, alcoholics, policemen, and prostitutes, and by doing so left behind a rich source of information for the social historian.[66]

The other must-see Western American city was San Francisco. Responding to the European who claimed that all American cities were the same, Ernst von Hesse-Wartegg said, "Obviously he never saw San Francisco or New Orleans."[67] Visitors praised San Francisco's "handsomely built" streets and the cable cars which leveled the city's steep hills, and were amazed by local markets, where one could get strawberries in February and fruits and vegetables of a "startling size."[68] San Francisco even gained the imprimatur of the world's foremost aesthetician.

Oscar Wilde called it "a really beautiful city" and Chinatown "the most artistic town I have ever come across."[69]

The loose morals of San Francisco residents also attracted plenty of attention. Youth gangs were ubiquitous (W. G. Marshall referred to "young embryo criminals"), and a new word—"hoodlum"—was coined to describe these youthful troublemakers.[70] Moral laxness was not limited to the youth of San Francisco, with Emily Faithfull complaining that the city's privileged devoted themselves to extremes in the use of cosmetics and dress, and to the pursuit of empty pleasures.[71] Mrs. Frank Leslie (the Baroness De Bazus) noted that "in other cities the *demi-monde* imitates the fashions of the *beau-monde*, but that in San Francisco the case is reversed."[72] In addition, a number of visitors claimed that San Franciscans of every class seemed to be heavily involved in speculation. Pedestrians crowded around the windows of brokers to follow the progress (or lack thereof) of their stocks, with fortunes won or lost in a single day.[73] J. W. Boddam-Whetham witnessed a suicide on a public street when a San Francisco man put a pistol to his head after losing money in a speculative venture.[74] Still, most travelers would probably agree with Phil Robinson that there was "no place in the world more full of interesting incidents and stirring types than this noisy, money-spending San Francisco."[75]

In stark contrast to San Francisco, especially in its moral precepts, was Salt Lake City. The great center of Mormon life in America, Salt Lake City had been planted in the middle of a remote desert, and through the use of irrigation the desert had been made to bloom. There were irrigation streams on every street, producing "a luxuriant plantation in a once-waste wilderness."[76] One traveler claimed that the city possessed "a pastoral character" that was lacking from every other Western community. Dominating Salt Lake City was the Mormon Tabernacle, a singular structure that was variously described as looking like an upside-down pie dish, the back of a large turtle, a dish cover with a handle, and an egg.[77] While visitors came to this town not for its architecture, but to ogle at the results of the Mormon advocacy of polygamy, plural marriage did have an impact on the physical layout of the town. Many private residences were built in groups of three or four, with one house occupied by the husband while each of the other dwellings contained one wife (unless the husband was economizing).[78] In contrast to other Western towns, venues for drinking and gambling were noticeably absent from the main streets of Salt Lake City.[79]

The only other settlement in the West that could remotely be called a city was Denver. Like other Western communities, visitors were struck by the activity and bustle of people on the streets.[80] The "Queen City of the Plains" was judged by Phil Robinson as "one of the very cleanest and airiest" of towns.[81] But William Hepworth Dixon called it "a city of rakes and gamblers," and another traveler condemned "the great braggart city" for its saloons and its legion of loafers who seemed to find it impossible to submit to the constraints of civilization.[82] Emily Faithfull was less judgmental, admiring Denver's fine houses and fast horses and expressing fascination at the number of carriages emblazoned with heraldic crests, which she found a curious phenomenon in the land of egalitarianism.[83] Denver was rapidly being civilized. As early as 1881, William Howard Russell took note of Denver's many fine shops and the vogue for "Paris fashions and millinery."[84] By 1900 Denver had literary societies, charitable organizations, fraternal lodges, churches, and a host of clubs. Women actually outnumbered men. As historian Carl Abbott notes, visitors arrived in Denver "looking for the Wild West and found a city not terribly different from Indianapolis."[85]

Most other towns in the West received withering reviews.[86] Especially distressing to European travelers was the "uniformity" of Western towns. "Their monotony haunts one like a nightmare," said James Bryce.[87] Invariably, numbered streets were laid out running parallel with each other, which were intersected by other parallel streets named after trees.[88] One striking aspect of the architecture in Western towns was that almost every structure had a false front, often made of brick or stone, that was much grander than the rest of the building. Horace Annesley Vachell asked, "Is there not something pathetic in this?"[89]

But Western "town making" often had to be accomplished in just a few months rather than in a few hundred years. It was the railroads that platted towns at regular intervals as the lines pushed West. (The Burlington and Missouri River Railroad, for instance, "laid out Crete, Dorchester, Exeter, Fairmount, Grafton, and so on alphabetically across Nebraska."[90]) A town would be established at the end of the line for a period of two or three months, and if it had natural resources or other advantages, it would survive. If not, the town itself would be moved to the new terminus of the line, leaving only a train depot behind (Figure 2.3). This process was illustrated in a dramatic way in a story that an acquaintance of William A. Bell told. This person had been standing on a railroad platform in Denver when a large freight train arrived that was carrying frame houses, lumber, furniture and other items. The guard jumped off the train and "called out with a flourish, 'Gentlemen, here's Julesburg.'"[91] Bell received confirmation of this process himself when he and his party reached Ellsworth, Kansas, in 1867. Ellsworth had eight shops, two hotels, fifty private residences and a population of 1,000, and was exactly one month old.[92]

While the layout of these towns may have been monotonous, the life that was found there was anything but. Typically, the sacred coexisted with the profane in Western communities. Leavenworth, for instance, had a population of 20,000, with three daily papers, an opera house and 200 saloons in 1866.[93] Thomas Hughes observed of Sioux City in the early 1870s that this town of under 4,000 could boast of two daily and four weekly papers, a large number of churches, a new school that had been constructed at a cost of $40,000—and seventy-three saloons and four gambling houses.[94] The mining community of Garland City, which had grown from a population of zero to 800 in four years, was large enough to keep two lawyers and a justice of the peace employed. (On the negative side of Garland City's ledger was a dance hall whose walls were covered with what an indignant William Saunders called "outrageously indecent pictures."[95])

FIGURE 2.3 Railroad building—and town building—on the Great Plains (1875). Wood engraving by Alfred R. Waud. Library of Congress. LC-USZ62-132926.

Saunders did not have a more edifying experience in Kansas City, where his evening walk through the city was impeded by a large number of rats.[96]

Omaha received similarly unflattering notices, with one visitor describing it as "a dreary, depressing waste, comprising a few wooden houses stuck into one of the mud-banks above the Missouri."[97] Lady Duffus Hardy called it a "dreary, desolate-looking city, with wide, straggling, dusty streets," and Rudyard Kipling noted that Omaha revealed "horrors that I would not willingly have missed."[98] Especially impressed by the horrors of Omaha was Phil Robinson, who before breakfast witnessed "a murder and suicide, and between breakfast and luncheon a fire and several dog fights." His efforts to become better acquainted with that town were precluded by "a terrible dust-storm [that] raged in the streets all day."[99]

On the West Coast, Rudyard Kipling put in extensive time visiting cities from San Francisco to Vancouver, B.C. In Tacoma, which was in the middle of a boom in 1889, Kipling found a town of contrasts, with the foundations of a giant opera house sharing the cityscape with blackened tree stumps. The human population, according to Kipling, consisted of people hunting for two things: corner lots and drinks, with the drinks receiving the highest priority.[100] In every West Coast town, there was evidence of the intense energy of the residents. Moving north from Portland, Kipling arrived in Seattle in the aftermath of a fire that had destroyed much of the city. Despite "a horrible black smudge" a mile long that went through the heart of the business district, the enterprising spirit of Seattle merchants was undaunted, as they set up tents among the blackened landscape and sold the stock they had salvaged.[101]

It should be emphasized, however, that the energy commented on by so many travelers was primarily an *American* phenomenon, and did not extend to Canada. When Kipling visited Vancouver, B.C., he noted with approval that the spittoons were empty and that "men don't fly up and down the streets telling lies." But something was missing, and compared to an American town "a great sleepiness" enshrouded that Canadian city.[102] J. W. Boddam-Whetham found a similar state of affairs in Victoria, where everyone seemed to be "waiting for something to turn up."[103] In his comparison of Detroit and Windsor, William Howard Russell was impressed by the vitality of the former which, he said, was "in strong opposition to the air of rather amateur repose on the British side."[104]

There was a similar state of affairs in Eastern Canada, where Harry Kessler claimed that "the French Canadian is lazy, without entrepreneurial spirit."[105] Quebec made a "boring, respectable" impression on Kessler, and H. Hussey Vivian also took note of the "dullness" of that city, observing that Quebec's "want of active commerce was conspicuous even to us casual travelers."[106] "Everything moves slowly in Canada," said Lady Duffus Hardy. "They want waking up." Hardy believed that if Canadians were possessed of the same energy and ambition as Americans, they would soon be even with them, but "at present they are a century behind."[107] Also detecting a "want of energy" among Canadians was Charles Wentworth Dilke, who found that crossing the border between the United States and Canada was like passing "from a land of life to one of death."[108] Why there was this difference between the two sides of the border is difficult to pinpoint, but one visitor suggested that one could not travel thirty miles into Canada "without feeling that the shadow of the Crown is there."[109]

American Western towns may have had energy, but no amount of energy could readily transform the sow's ear of these new, rude communities into a silk purse. Among the most trenchant critics of Western towns in the early 1870s was Isabella Bird. A small sampling would include the following:

Truckee:	"fires blazing out of doors, bar-rooms and saloons crammed, lights glaring, gaming tables thronged, fiddle and banjo in frightful discord, and the air ringing with ribaldry and profanity."[110]
Boulder:	"a hideous collection of frame houses on the burning plain."[111]
Fort Collins:	"altogether revolting, entirely utilitarian, given up to talk of dollars as well as to making them, with coarse speech, coarse food, coarse everything."[112]
Sacramento:	"very repulsive."[113]

Leadville, and specifically Oscar Wilde's visit to that town, deserves a special mention because here we can see how at least one traveler projected on a town his own image of what that town should be. Leadville had initially attracted gold prospecters in the 1860s, and by 1877–78, a second boom began when deposits of lead-silver ore were discovered.[114] According to W. G. Marshall, who visited Leadville in 1879 (just three years before Wilde), Leadville had 100 paying mines (mostly silver and lead), 110 saloons, five churches, three schools, and a branch of the Young Men's Christian Association.[115] Like many towns in the West, Leadville had a look that was physically unsettled, including "masses of tree-stumps cropping up in the centre of the main thoroughfares, pitched over an undulating, rugged dusty ledge."[116]

In Wilde's descriptions of Leadville there is a heady mixture of fact and fantasy. When Wilde returned to England, he told audiences there that he had read to Leadville miners

> passages from the autobiography of Benvenuto Cellini and they seemed much delighted. I was reproved by my hearers for not having brought him with me. I explained that he had been dead for some little time which elicited the enquiry, 'Who shot him?'[117]

A reporter from the *Leadville Herald*, who covered Wilde's lecture at the Tabor Grand Opera House, heard Wilde say nothing at all on that subject.[118] Wilde also claimed that two men had recently been "tried and executed before a crowded audience" at the opera house.[119] In fact, two people had been hanged across the street, but certainly none in the opera house.[120] Whether Wilde was letting his fantasies run away with him or was serving up to his English audiences what they wanted to hear cannot be known.

On a more factual footing was Wilde's description of a tour he took of a Leadville mine. Wilde noted that after descending to the bottom of the mine shaft, "I had supper, the first course being whisky, the second whisky and the third whisky."[121] Wilde's legendary capacity for alcohol was confirmed by a *Denver Tribune* reporter who accompanied him. He observed that Wilde had been greeted

> by a dozen miners, each with a bottle. By invariable Western custom every bottle must make the rounds. Within a few minutes all have had twelve snorters. The miners without exception are rather dizzy, but Wilde remains cool, steady, and collected. He is cheered loudly and is voted a perfect gentleman.[122]

Wilde judged the miners to be "very charming and not at all rough."[123]

Boosterism

Closely allied with town making was boosterism—an inescapable element of American culture after the Civil War. While the boosterist impulse was found in every region of the country (Southern promoter Richard H. Edmonds, for instance, proclaimed that "the Eldorado of the next half century is the South"), the most outlandish claims were made for the West.[124] The Trans-Mississippi, said Linus P. Brockett in 1882, was "destined to be the garden of the world," but even this assertion was modest compared to the boosterist prose of Brockett's compatriots.[125] The largest corporate boosters by far were the railroad companies, who had millions of acres of land to dispose of, and whose efforts to do so were characterized by what historian David M. Wrobel has called a "creative presentation of statistics and a shameless willingness to print some of the more melodramatic prose of the century."[126]

Indeed, it would be difficult to top the description of Colorado contained in a publication put out by the Chicago, Burlington and Quincy railroad in 1882. This was a state where, according to the CB&Q, "rainbows cast their glittering coronets around the mountains, and radiant irises dance in many a romantic gorge." Colorado was "Fairyland, a region where elves and gnomes might sport and make their homes," with air as "pure and dry as that which fanned the cheek of sinlessness in primal Eden."[127] The Edenic was a prominent theme in boosterist prose, employed not only by large corporations, but also by local promoters as well. The boosters of Dakota County, Minnesota, speculated that, "Perhaps the eye of man never rested on a spot of land better fitted to supply his material wants and meet the necessities of his nature since shut out from the original Eden." Not to be outdone in the Eden metaphors, Arizonans claimed that their state contained "some of the richest and most friable land in the world" and was perhaps even "the Paradise of America."[128]

The eagerness with which locals proclaimed even the most woebegone backwater town as the site of a future Valhalla was dismaying to European travelers. When Ernst von Hesse-Wartegg visited Cairo, Illinois, in 1879, it presented "one of the gloomiest and most deplorable aspects of any city on earth." With overwhelming poverty, muck a foot deep in the streets, and with cholera a regular visitor, Cairo seemingly had little going for it. When Hesse-Wartegg commented to a local that Cairo must be quite unhealthy during the summer, the resident indignantly replied, "'Not at all, sir,'" "'No fever or cholera here, ever. One of the healthiest places on the whole river, sir. Bound to be a big city, sir'" [original emphasis].[129]

Rudyard Kipling was especially appalled by this tendency, observing that it was a poor town indeed that could not declare that it had no equal.[130] In Livingston, Montana ("a grubby little hamlet full of men without clean collars and perfectly unable to get through one sentence unadorned by three oaths"), the local paper impressed upon residents that they were living in the most progressive community in the nation.[131] In Tacoma, the hotel stationery proclaimed that this town was basking in the greatest blessings of civilization, while Pasco, a burg consisting of fifteen frame houses, was described by a local as "the Queen City of the Prairie."[132] In Minnestoa, the superlatives were especially purple. The Twin

Cities of Minneapolis/St. Paul were dubbed "the twin columns of the eastern gateway to the magnificent west," while Duluth proclaimed itself the "Zenith City of the Unsalted Seas."[133] Lamented Kipling, "I wish Americans didn't tell such useless lies."[134]

When James Bryce visited Bismarck, North Dakota, in 1883, that community had been in existence for a total of five years. The locals were ebullient about Bismarck's future, however, and Bryce heard a speech that asserted that because Bismarck was the center of Dakota, Dakota the center of the United States, and the United States the center of the world, Bismarck was destined to "be the metropolitan hearth of the world's civilization."[135] By the time J. J. Aubertin arrived in Bismarck in 1886, these expectations clearly had not come to fruition. Aubertin noted that Bismarck's chief architectural feature was "a large gaol," while its natural enticements included an alkaline lake and "baked prairie air and prairie dust."[136] Bismarck did not attain a population of 10,000 until the 1920s.[137]

W. F. Rae passed through Promontory, Utah, in 1869, and found a shanty that bore the sign "Pacific Hotel" and a tent that was labeled "Club House."[138] During Thomas Hughes' visit to Dubuque, Iowa, in the 1870s, Hughes encountered a community of wooden hovels, vacant lots with water-filled holes, and a main street that was often axle-deep in mud. Despite these disadvantages, the leading citizens of this town described to Hughes the wonders of the West, "and of the certainty of Dubuque becoming before long the chief of these wonders."[139] Towns in America were quickly promoted to city status (H. Hussey Vivian noted that "all places over 5,000 or so are 'cities' here").[140] Another way for boosters to anticipate the future greatness of their communities was by working the word "Empire" into the name. Thus was created Empire, Colorado, Empire City, Nevada, Empire City, Kansas, and Empire City, Oklahoma, none of which were able to achieve imperial status.[141] The droll George Augustus Sala claimed that "an infant American city" brought to mind "some Kindergarten for juvenile Colossi."[142]

Boosterism was to be found not only in America's small towns, but also in its great metropolises. Perhaps this phenomenon had its roots in America's decentralized nature which, according to A. Maurice Low, had produced a greater local pride than could be found anywhere else.[143] German traveler Harry Kessler referred to "the rivalry which exists everywhere in America between cities and regions ... The New Yorker, for example, nourishes a pricelessly comic hate against the Brooklynite whom he sees as a kind of lesser creature."[144] Léon Paul Blouet found that "nothing is more diverting than to hear the dwellers in each great American town criticise the dwellers in the others." Thus residents of Boston referred to the "pig-stickers" of Chicago, while the denizens of Chicago condemned the "prigs" of Boston.[145] By the 1870s, Chicago had replaced St. Louis as the chief city of the West, but the city fathers of St. Louis did not give up easily, and predicted with commendable modesty that once St. Louis' railroad network was completed, that city was destined "to equal London in its population, Athens in its philosophy, art and culture, Rome in its hotels, cathedrals, churches and grandeur, and to be the central commercial metropolis of a continent."[146]

Historian Daniel Boorstin claimed that the boosterist language that Europeans condemned as outright lies was intended by Americans to be "vaguely clairvoyant." Americans were speaking in "the future tense," when great transformations might indeed take place.[147] Among the few European travelers with a charitable analysis of American boosterism was David Macrae. Like others, Macrae had encountered preposterous claims for dismal settlements, including river towns with only one or two houses that announced themselves to be "Bowden City" or "New Babylon." But Macrae was oddly moved by "the spectacle of a man squatting in one of these vast solitudes, and calling his log cabin a city! It shows his belief in the future of his country."[148]

Accommodations

From an early date, travelers in America were impressed with the size, services and lavishness of American hotels. In 1848, future Argentina president Domingo Sarmiento commented on the sumptuousness of the Saint Charles in New Orleans, and what he called the "palaces" of American hotels.[149] When he toured America in 1861–62, Anthony Trollope was surprised to discover that the inns of America were "an institution apart" and totally different from accommodations anywhere else. They were not only larger than those in other countries, but were also to be found virtually everywhere. It seemed that no community was too small to support a hotel, and Trollope observed that in the United States, "the first sign of an incipient settlement is an hotel five stories high, with an office, a bar, a cloak-room, three gentlemen's parlours, two ladies' parlours, a ladies' entrance, and two hundred bedrooms."[150] While America did not have the royal palaces of Europe, it had its hotels, which historian Daniel J. Boorstin called "Palaces of the People."[151]

The number of American hotels greatly increased after the Civil War, as did the quality gap between luxury American hotels and their counterparts elsewhere.[152] Robert Somers stayed in Atlanta's Kimball House hotel in 1870, and described a breath taking lobby that was open in the center almost to the roof with tiers of galleries rising around it. It was "brilliantly lighted with gas," and featured a steam-powered elevator that whisked guests to their rooms.[153] Peter Tchaikovsky found the comfort of American hotels superior to anything he had encountered in Europe, and was entranced, like other European travelers, by the advanced technology that was employed in these places.[154] Harold Brydges, for instance, praised U.S. hotels because hot and cold water were found in every room "and often the electric light."[155] Indeed, the early appearance of electricity in American hotels was enthralling to Europeans. Of the things that amazed William Howard Russell about the Palace Hotel in San Francisco in 1881, chief among them were "electric lights flooding the court with brightness beyond description."[156] The opulence of these hotels was likewise stunning. Henry Sienkiewicz said of Chicago's Palmer House that "everything within it simply drips with gold, silk, and velvet."[157] The Ponce de Leon Hotel in St. Augustine, said Léon Paul Blouet, resembled "a scene from the *Arabian Nights*" with its elaborate onyx walls, cloisters, fountains, and towers (Figure 2.4).[158]

These facilities were huge. Sienkiewicz called New York's Central Hotel "a small city," while Lady Duffus Hardy described the Windsor Hotel in that city as a "monster"—a "mountain of cherry-red bricks and mortar" that occupied an entire city block.[159] The United States Hotel at Saratoga where H. Hussey Vivian stayed in 1877 had accommodations for 1,200, prompting Vivian to declare that American hotels were "on the largest scale I have ever seen."[160] When W. E. Adams stayed at the immense National Hotel in Washington, he confessed that more than once he became "as completely lost on the passage as any belated traveller in a forest."[161] Under what was generally described as the "American plan," these hotels also provided guests with five meals a day.[162] There were royal palaces in Europe, said W. F. Rae, where the residents were surrounded by fewer luxuries than those staying at first-class American hotels.[163] Luxury resorts were also being developed in the American West, beginning in Colorado Springs in the early 1870s. More Western resorts would follow, including the Hotel Del

FIGURE 2.4 Ponce de Leon Hotel, St. Augustine, Florida (ca. 1895–1919). Library of Congress. LC-D4-32448.

Monte in Monterey, the Hotel Del Coronado in San Diego, and numerous others. Tourist accommodations were also built in national parks, such as Yellowstone.[164]

The ground floors of American hotels served as community centers where local residents gathered "to do everything, to read, to write, to talk" rather than doing those things at home.[165] There was typically a large lobby, a bar, a dining room, a news stand, a tobacconist, a barber shop, shoeshine stand, a counter for railway information, and a billiard room with some ten to fifteen tables.[166] Elevators were in constant operation (sometimes in pairs), and one visitor noted that even for the lower floors "the staircase is scarcely ever made use of."[167] There were aspects of American hotels that European travelers found unsatisfactory. Hare Booth took the Knutsford Hotel in Salt Lake City to task because it had no egg cups, and there were numerous complaints about insolent hotel staff.[168] Perhaps the most frequent lamentation was that these hotels were overheated. Joseph Hatton claimed that the only equivalent to the heat of an American hotel was "an English hothouse, where they grow pine-apples."[169] Henry Latham developed what he called a "face-ache" because the inside of his hotel was heated to the level of "the tropics," while outside the temperature approached that of "the polar regions."[170]

Hatton called America "the most hotel-keeping nation in the world," but who were the guests?[171] Among travelers, the most numerous were the "drummers," or commercial businessmen. They were distinguished from ordinary travelers by the fact that they received a discount for their lodgings.[172] American hotels were not designed merely for the comfort of temporary guests, however, but were rather "gigantic boarding-houses" where locals—especially newly married couples—often took up residence. Some couples remained in hotels for years and even brought up their children there.[173]

European visitors posited a number of theories to explain the attractiveness of these accommodations to American newlyweds. Prominent among them was that residency in a hotel enabled Americans to avoid the terrible "servant question," which the less-than-diplomatic Charles Wentworth Dilke described as paying "rough unkempt Irish girls from £6 to £8 a month."[174] Even those who maintained their own homes sometimes spent their vacations at rented cottages that were maintained by hotels. Hotel staff brought meals to these cottages and did the cleaning, enabling the American housewife to momentarily escape "from the tyranny of the servant-girl."[175] Oscar Wilde claimed that hotel living also had the advantage of eliminating the "tedious tête-à-têtes that are the dream of engaged couples, and the despair of married men."[176] Even in the most out-of-the-way places in America, the tourist could find large substantial hotels populated for the most part by people from the community. At one hotel where David Macrae stayed, 400 people sat down for dinner but only a hundred were travelers.[177]

One service that was typically *not* available at American hotels was the cleaning of boots. The traveler from Europe who left his boots outside the door of his room in the expectation that he would find them cleaned and polished the next morning was invariably disappointed. One of these was Stephen Buckland, who began his first morning in his New York hotel room by ringing for his boots. According to Buckland, they were brought by an Irish-American employee, who contemptuously dumped them on the floor. When Buckland observed that the boots had neither been cleaned nor polished, the saucy hotel employee replied, "Now, you see if I clane [sic.] them again while you stop here." This incident ended with Buckland launching a boot at the man's head, and the servant beating a hasty retreat.[178] When W. G. Marshall found his own boots in a similar condition, he hailed a domestic who was sweeping the stairs and asked her how he might get his boots cleaned: "She replied curtly, resting her arm on her broom and looking up at me; whereupon I thanked her, and withdrew."[179] In Charleston, F. Barham Zincke had a confrontation with what he called "a Paddy" over the issue of uncleaned boots. Zincke was livid at the Irishman's "insubordination," and noted with disgust that this person's tenure in the United States had taught him to act with the same freedom as "the President himself."[180] Why it was that this particular chore seemed to be the one that Americans found most offensive to their dignity, and to their own sense of place in the social system, is somewhat of a mystery. But David Macrae theorized that servants refused to clean boots not because they objected to the task "but because doing it for you as your servant is considered menial work."[181]

There were portions of the country, especially in the West, where accommodations were much rougher than those offered by eastern cities. Charles Messiter reported that the Cheyenne Hotel where he stayed in 1868 consisted of one room with twenty-seven beds, each of which was meant for two.[182] At her hotel in Truckee, Isabella Bird found that the beds were continuously occupied by different persons throughout the day. In Bird's room, men's coats were hanging everywhere, boots littered the floor, and a rifle rested in the corner. Even though the streets outside were noisy, Bird managed to get some sleep until she was woken up by the sound of pistol shots.[183]

In other parts of the West the population was simply too thin to support any kind of hotel. Here, every private residence was potentially a place of shelter or a temporary hotel. In Colorado, for instance, it was the custom for local residents to take in travelers, and to charge them the normal hotel rate for accommodations.[184] In the rude frontier town of Ellsworth, Kansas, (population forty in 1867), Henry M. Stanley praised the "rough hospitality, geniality, and kindness" of the residents, who were always willing to extend to the stranger a "corner, with a buffalo robe."[185] In another instance, F. Barham Zincke was the guest of a rancher on the Plains who combined cattle-raising with inn keeping. Here, cowboys took their meals with the guests, but Zincke was careful to point out that ranch hands washed their faces and hands before sitting down, and that "there was nothing disagreeable in their conversation or manners."[186]

Transportation

There was general agreement that the most sumptuous form of travel in America was by steamboat, and that in the words of Ernst von Hesse-Wartegg, "Cleopatra's barge could not have been more cheerful, more luxurious, or more elegant."[187] One traveler described the steamboats that were plying the water near New York as "floating palaces," while another noted that the rich woodwork on steamboats had lifted carpentry to "the dignity of a fine art."[188] The Mississippi steamboat *Brandish Johnson* was praised for its "gilded luxury of saloon, boudoir, and sleeping chambers," and the *Robert E. Lee* was singled out for "her gorgeous saloon," as well as her rich carpets, tables and expensively appointed lounges.[189] It was, said David Macrae, "the most delicious and luxurious kind of travelling" that he had ever experienced.[190] The one possible drawback to this mode of transportation was the tendency of steamboats "to take fire or to burst their boilers."[191]

While Macrae was enthusiastic about river travel in the United States, he found American roads to be especially bad—"probably the worst roads on the face of the civilized earth."[192] This was the consensus of most other travelers as well, who condemned "the utter absence of decent roads," and the "evil of bad roads in America."[193] Paving, said one visitor, was "an unknown art."[194] American horrors included "corduroy roads" (consisting of logs laid together) through swampy regions, and prairie roads that turned into "a continent of mud" after a rain.[195] On the Great Plains, roads were frequently submerged under creeks, stalling stagecoaches that were chronically overloaded. Coach operators often addressed this problem by dumping the mail into the creek.[196]

Travelers found that getting from Point A to Point B could be more of an adventure than they had bargained for. While in a coach that was traveling along one of Richmond's main roads in 1866, Charles Wentworth Dilke and a fellow passenger were forced to get out, lay planks along a bridge, then sit on the planks to hold them down until the coach passed over.[197] On a journey from Virginia City to Salt Lake City, William A. Bell reported that the stagecoach routinely became mired in mud, obliging passengers to get out and help dig.[198] Theodora Guest used the word "astonishing" to describe the ruts in the roads near St. Louis, and also took note of what were called "thank you, ma'ams." These were roads that had scoops across them for drainage, forcing passengers in carriages that ran over them to involuntarily bow their heads.[199] H. Hussey Vivian observed that the roads of New Jersey "would have shaken any of my carriages to pieces."[200]

City streets were likewise wretched, and the nation's largest city was a prime example. Harold Brydges called New York's streets "execrable," and claimed that they were worse than those in a German village.[201] Another traveler concluded that even a rural corduroy road was less hard on the nerves than "the pitfalls of a down-town street in the Empire city."[202] When Henry Latham was in New York in 1866, he observed five horses down and two dead because of the combination of bad streets and icy conditions.[203] Lady Duffus Hardy described traveling a New York street in 1880 as "a jolting process" in which the individual ran the risk of "dislocating your neck."[204]

When the actress Lillie Langtry arrived in New York in 1882, a reporter asked her what she thought of the street paving. Langtry's private opinion was that it was "very bad," but she hesitated because she wanted to be diplomatic. Another reporter called out, "'Abuse it, Mrs. Langtry, it will be popular.'"[205] Because of New York's wretched pavement, according to Léon Paul Blouet, "the carriages appeared to rise and fall as if on a troubled sea."[206] Sanitation was also a problem, and as late as 1876, Henry Sienkiewicz claimed to have seen something in New York that Charles Dickens had commented on thirty-five years earlier: pigs roaming the streets.[207]

City thoroughfares were no better elsewhere. In Augusta, F. Barham Zincke saw "axles disappear in the main streets," while in Memphis Ernst von Hesse-Wartegg witnessed horses and mules sinking "knee-deep in mire and ruts."[208] With Memphis additionally endowed with stagnant pools of water on building sites and "the accumulation of months of garbage in the streets," Hesse-Wartegg dubbed Memphis "the Bulgaria of America."[209] Harry Kessler deemed the streets of San Francisco "somewhat worse even than those of New York," and William Howard Russell complained that San Francisco streets were "atrociously paved; the torture of driving over boulders is aggravated by the sharp ribs of the tram-ways."[210] Phil Robinson said of Chicago streets that they were "more like rolling prairie than streets," and William Saunders encountered signs in that city that proclaimed "'there is no bottom here.'"[211]

Street railways (both ground level and elevated) added an additional element of chaos and discomfort to city life. Those who lived in dwellings adjacent to elevateds had to put up with nineteen hours of daily rumbling, the blocking out of light into their rooms, splatterings of oil from the engines, and exposure of their personal lives to the full view of passengers. Glancing out from the window of an elevated, William Howard Russell confessed to feeling that he was "taking a great liberty with private life" as he "beheld the domestic arrangements of family after family carried out under my eyes."[212] Pedestrians walking underneath elevated trains were subject to oil drippings on their clothes.[213] Those inside street railway cars endured extreme overcrowding because there was no limit placed on the number of passengers. Jacques Offenbach noted that passengers "crowd onto the platform; if need be they climb onto the back of the conductor. As long as there is a platform or a step free, or a knee unoccupied, the conductor does not announce that the car is full."[214]

Street railways could also be dangerous. In Philadelphia, Theodora Guest found that they had claimed the center of almost every street, leaving only narrow margins on the side for private carriages.[215] New Yorkers addressed this problem by fashioning the wheels of their private carriages to run on the street railway tracks. The resulting smoother ride was offset by the frequency of accidents.[216]

There was something Darwinian in the carnage produced by both street railways and passenger and freight trains operating in American cities. "You sometimes hear a bell, a sudden rush," said Harold Brydges, "and before you know what is the matter, a train dashes through the street you are about to cross."[217] Emily Faithfull was dismayed by the apparent disregard for life in the vicinity of railroad tracks, with trains running through busy streets and "killing foot-passengers and scaring horses with equal impartiality."[218] William Howard Russell observed that "'killed by the cars' is a very ordinary head-line in American newspapers."[219] Americans, however, seemed remarkably unconcerned. When Alexandra Gripenberg inquired about the accident rate from trains in the city of New York, she was told, "'Only one human life per week.'"[220] Theodora Guest likewise raised the possibility that trains operating in cities might be dangerous, but her American guide replied, "'Not at all, though they do kill a good many children'"[221] (Figure 2.5).

On cross-country routes, railroad companies took great pains to assure travelers that they would be completely safe. One railroad stressed that it would "'surely afford as safe a travel as the midland counties of England and the

A TRAIN PASSING THROUGH AN AMERICAN CITY.

FIGURE 2.5 "A train passing through an American city." *Harper's* 71 (August 1885), 387.

Scottish highlands.'"[222] A conspicuous difference between rail travel in Britain and in America was that American cars were not divided by class. (Iza Duffus Hardy described the American railroad experience as "all classes and nations promiscuously pushed together in a limited space."[223]) W. G. Marshall advised prospective foreign travelers on railways to "be very polite and say 'sir' to every man and 'ma'am' to every woman, and then you will get on."[224]

The classlessness of train cars had its limits, however. There was little doubt that trains were race segregated by means both crude and subtle. A number of travelers took note of what David Macrae called "'nigger cars'" in the South, and by 1891 eight Southern states provided for separate railroad cars for blacks and whites.[225] George Augustus Sala commented on a less blatant arrangement in Baltimore. As Sala was preparing to board a train, the railroad clerk told him to take the "third car on the left." Despite the large number of black passengers, none chose this particular car.[226] On cross-country routes, Pullman cars were effectively first-class cars, with those unable to pay a premium price condemned to a remarkably low standard of travel. J. W. Boddam-Whetham entered one of these cars when he wanted to smoke, and discovered it "crowded indiscriminately with whites, blacks, and Chinese." Boddam-Whetham was appalled that those of "cultivated minds" were forced to travel with "the vulgar and low-mannered."[227]

There were also the "emigrant cars," with special low rates for those on a budget and those who were capable of enduring considerable misery. On the emigrant train that Robert Louis Stevenson took from New York to Ogden, Utah, one car was reserved for unmarried men, one for women and children, and one for the Chinese. After passengers had been cooped up for ninety hours, the cars began "to stink abominably."[228] Stevenson judged that the Chinese car smelled the least offensive, while the car for women and children was "by a good way the worst."[229] (Part of the problem may have been related to a characteristic of American train travel identified by Peter Tchaikovsky. Because American women were "afraid of drafts" there was no fresh air because the windows were always closed.)[230] Rudyard Kipling called the sleeping arrangements on emigrant trains "hard as a plank bed," and he was not speaking metaphorically.[231] The emigrant train bed consisted of a board wide enough for two, on top of which were placed three cushions stuffed with straw. After finding a "chum" to share the bed, the passenger paid two-dollars-and-a-half, and did his best to get a night's sleep.[232]

In contrast to the plank bed was the sleeping car. While railroad sleeping cars and the Pullman name are virtually synonymous, George Pullman was a somewhat late entrant in this business. By the end of the century, however, Pullman was the only manufacturer remaining.[233] Pullman sleeping cars had been added on almost every main line by the 1870s, and those who availed themselves of this travel option almost universally praised it. Thomas Hughes called his sleeper "as comfortable a little chamber as man could wish for, or woman either."[234]

One woman, Emily Faithfull, initially found the idea of sharing a Pullman berth with a stranger "distasteful," but soon learned to slumber so peacefully that she almost preferred to travel at night.[235] Isabella Bird called her sleeper berth a "Temple of Morpheus," and W. F. Rae claimed that "no royal personage can be more comfortably housed than the occupant of a Pullman car."[236] When Isabelle Randall was traveling to Montana in the mid-1880s, she began to doubt that the West was as wild as she had been told because her Pullman car had made the journey "so easily accomplished, and travelling brought to such a pitch of perfection."[237] Accommodations on a Pullman train often included a dining car, a drawing-room car, a smoking room, library, and even a barber's shop.[238]

The gender arrangements on sleeping cars seemed to vary widely. Henry Deedes could not help but notice that when his sleeping car crossed over the Ohio River and into the South, a curtain was put in place separating the men's portion of the car from an area reserved for women and couples. In the North, however, "this luxury is dispensed with and ladies have to take their turn with the lords of creation."[239] On one sleeping car, William Saunders claimed an upper berth, and complained that the lower one "was occupied by two women and a child."[240] James Fullarton Muirhead noted that women on Pullman cars were expected to tolerate "the legs of a strange, disrobing man dangling within a foot of their noses."[241] Jacques Offenbach commented on the "strangeness and picturesqueness of this American dormitory," and when the residents of his car were preparing for sleep, he was titillated by the "agreeable rustlings which mean skirts are being raised."[242] (William Francis Butler also referred to turning in "in rather a promiscuous manner with ladies."[243])

Sleeping cars had their own peculiar challenges. They were of heavier construction than ordinary railway cars, weighing in at between 20 and 30 tons. While H. Hussey Vivian praised the comfort of Pullmans, he noted that at about one ton per passenger, these cars represented "a frightful waste of locomotive power."[244] Pullman cars frequently broke down, as one did on Thomas Hughes' trip to Chicago. As E. Catherine Bates' Pullman car was pulling out of Albuquerque, the wheels caught on fire.[245] Inside, the lower berths were preferable to the upper ones because the upper ones were likely to get covered with dust and coal soot that came through the top ventilators.[246] There were pegs on which to hang clothes above the upper sleeping berth, and W. G. Marshall discovered another disadvantage of an upper berth when he awoke to find someone on top of him who was trying to retrieve his trousers from one of the pegs.[247]

The problem of dressing and undressing in a Pullman car was considerable. David Macrae compared it to "trying to dress under a sofa," and Kipling noted that "it is easier to get out of a full theater than to leave a Pullman in haste."[248] Dressing in a Pullman was especially challenging for women because, as E. Catherine Bates put it, men's clothes "are much more easily taken off or put on."[249] Women's washrooms were cramped and in constant demand, producing long lines of bedraggled females waiting their turn.[250] Another Pullman traveler complained that getting a good night's sleep was not always easy because of the constant door banging which everyone felt obliged to do on an American train.[251]

The progress of American trains was not always swift. W. G. Marshall claimed that there were 230 stations between Omaha and San Francisco, and that the train stopped at every one.[252] At such stations passengers could avail themselves of meals, which Emily Faithfull described as "difficult to eat and impossible to digest."[253] The standard charge for such fare was a dollar, and it seemed to be the case that American diners were less squeamish than Europeans. When W. G. Marshall's train stopped in Sidney, Nebraska, for a meal, he described the scene that unfolded as "a typical American feast, all ate as if for their very lives."[254]

Unlike railroad operations in Europe, trains in America departed promptly. Phil Robinson noted that on British trains, passengers waiting to board were used to a first, second and third bell, and even then they would not move "until the guard has begged them as a personal favour to take their seats." In contrast, the American conductor's cry of "All aboard" meant get on immediately or be left behind.[255] Some stations did provide some warning that the train was about to leave, if one knew the system. At the Utica and Albany stations, Jacques Offenbach encountered large black men playing tom-toms next to the restaurant. Enquiring as to the meaning of this mystery, Offenbach was told that as long as the drums were loud, boarding was not imminent. But as the sound diminished, travelers needed to hurry and, "when it almost fades away, the travelers know that they've got to rush to the train."[256]

Once on board, passengers discovered that train conductors were lords of their domains, and that travelers were well advised to acknowledge them as such. A conductor, according to Henry Sienkiewicz, was "a veritable captain of a ship."[257] W. G. Marshall emphasized the great civility with which conductors should be treated because they were gentlemen and expected to be regarded as such.[258] Emily Faithfull claimed that conductors and porters were "some of the most polite men to be found in the whole of America," but Isabella Bird said that when it was time to vacate, passengers were "unceremoniously" turned out of their berths.[259]

Conductors could be even more forthcoming with delinquent passengers. In one incident, a drunken passenger on Robert Louis Stevenson's train had a confrontation with the conductor, who forthwith grabbed the man by the shoulders, removed him from his seat, marched him through the car, and "sent him flying on to the track."[260] On the way to Yellowstone, a passenger on Rudyard Kipling's train who refused to pay wrestled with the conductor, "who neatly cross-buttocked him through a double plate-glass window." The passenger's head was deeply cut open. The conductor calmly observed that this person would probably die, and added that "there was no profit in monkeying with the North Pacific Railway."[261]

Railroads made their way through some of the wildest terrain in the West. In the Siskiyou Mountains, Kipling's train crawled over trestles a hundred feet high that looked like "a collection of match-sticks."[262] James Bryce also referred to trestle bridges that seemed as if they would collapse under a high wind, much less a heavy train.[263] In the Sierra, Isabella Bird argued that when the track curved around a precipice with a 2,500 foot drop, "it is correct to be frightened." She also took note of the railroad snow sheds in the mountains, one of which was 27 miles long.[264]

Wherever railroads went they seemed to act as agents of civilization, turning formerly wild towns into respectable communities.[265] A good example is Cheyenne, Wyoming. In 1873, it was described by Isabella Bird as a town that "abounds in slouching bar-room-looking characters" and "atrocious profanity."[266] Five years later, Cheyenne had been transformed, and according to W. G. Marshall the railroad had done the transforming. It had brought "civilization and enlightenment" to a once savage community, with churches and schools now taking the place of saloons and gambling halls.[267] Iza Duffus Hardy even postulated that the railroad would "vanquish polygamy" in Salt Lake City by bringing in the "Gentile element."[268]

Lost luggage was seldom a problem on American railways. Harold Brydges pronounced the American system of baggage handling "excellent," and David Macrae noted that he had had fewer difficulties in America with his baggage traveling thousands of miles on different railway lines than he had traveling from Edinburgh to Glasgow.[269] Emily Faithfull liked the fact that rail travelers could get off the train whenever they wanted, and resume their trips whenever they wanted, and concluded that "this, together with the system of checking baggage, are great improvements upon British regulations."[270] William Saunders also preferred this system, and noted of baggage on American trains that "any experienced traveller in this country would think you an idiot if you felt any anxiety about it."[271]

One "conspicuous feature" in American railway travel was the boy circulating through the cars selling a wide variety of products.[272] On the better trains these products included "newspapers, novels, cacti, lollypops, pop corn, pea nuts, and ivory ornaments," while the boys who worked the lower-class emigrant trains sold soap, towels, wash basins and canned goods.[273] On W. G. Marshall's train, the boys gave Marshall and his fellow passengers a slip which announced, "GREAT NATURAL CURIOSITY, IVORY THAT GROWS ON TREES. FOR SALE BY THE NEWSAGENTS ON THIS TRAIN, WHO WILL CALL ON YOU FOR THIS CIRCULAR, AND GIVE YOU AN OPPORTUNITY TO EXAMINE THE ARTICLE." Whether they wanted it or not, each passenger was given a specimen, but no one bought.[274] Most agreed that the boys made pests of themselves and, according to Phil Robinson, even had the effrontery to become "insolent" when passengers expressed annoyance.[275] In addition to the newsboys, other enterprising types plied their trades on American trains. On the train between Buffalo and New York City, Iza Duffus Hardy and the other passengers were harassed by a crippled man circulating through the cars who sought to sell a poem lamenting his condition.[276] On his train, Henry Latham was accosted by insurance agents trying to sell him a policy.[277]

★ ★ ★

In many ways, the American built environment exemplified the contradictions found throughout American life. In the great Eastern cities, dazzling skyscrapers and palatial private residences coexisted with primitive slums and wretchedly maintained streets. Efficient mass transit systems moved passengers by the thousands around these cities, but trains operating in cities killed horses and humans by the score because of the American unconcern for safety. In the West, entire towns could be assembled in a matter of weeks and immediately attract hundreds of residents, then be disassembled and deserted a few months later. Boosters conjured up magnificent castles in the air, telling anyone who would listen that their town was destined to become the Athens of the New World, while residents struggled to scratch a meager living from the land. A traveler could spend the night in a lavish hotel with gas, electric lights, and hot and cold running water, or find himself in the corner of someone's hovel wrapped in a buffalo robe. They could travel in luxury in a Pullman sleeping car, or take the overland route on bone-breaking corduroy roads. America offered many realities, and the ones to which the traveler was exposed naturally colored his overall impressions of the United States.

Notes

1. David Macrae, *The Americans at Home* [1870] (New York: E. P. Dutton, 1952), 75.
2. See *Abroad in America: Visitors to the New Nation, 1776–1914*, ed. Marc Pachter and Frances Wein (Reading, MA: Addison-Wesley, 1976), 91
3. Baron Hübner, *A Ramble Round the World, 1871*, trans. Lady Elizabeth Herbert (London: MacMillan and Co., 1878), 180, 17.
4. Lady Duffus Hardy, *Through Cities and Prairie Lands: Sketches of an American Tour* (London: Chapman and Hall, 1881), 63.
5. Oscar Wilde, "Impressions of America," in Oscar Wilde, *The Works of Oscar Wilde* (New York: AMS Press, 1972), 252.
6. W. F. Rae, *Westward by Rail: The New Route to the East* [1871] (New York: Promontory Press, 1974), 22.
7. Ernst von Hesse-Wartegg, *Travels on the Lower Mississippi, 1879–1880*, trans. and ed. Frederic Trautmann (Columbia: University of Missouri Press, 1990), 156.
8. Max O'rell and Jack Allyn, *Jonathan and His Continent: Rambles Through American Society*, trans. Madame Paul Blouet (Bristol: J. W. Arrowsmith, 1889), 33. Paul Bourget also referred to "the interminable succession of luxurious mansions which line Fifth Avenue." Paul Bourget, *Outre-Mer: Impressions of America* (London: T. Fisher Unwin, 1895), 24.
9. J. J. Aubertin, *A Fight with Distances: The States, the Hawaiian Islands, Canada, British Columbia, Cuba, the Bahamas* (London: Kegan Paul, Trench & Co., 1888), 259.
10. Iza Duffus Hardy would make the same mistake in San Francisco when she described it as "cosmopolitan rather than American." Iza Duffus Hardy, *Between Two Oceans: Or, Sketches of American Travel* (London: Hurst and Blackett, 1884), 141.

11. Oscar Wilde, "American Women," in *The Works of Oscar Wilde*, 8–9; Lady Duffus Hardy, 64. Wilde noted of New York that "though one can dine in New York one could not dwell there." Oscar Wilde, "Americans in London," in *The Essays of Oscar Wilde* [1916], ed. Albert and Charles Boni (Bonibooks, 1935), 198. Alexandra Gripenberg also observed that strewn around New York's sidewalks were "rubbish containers, broken china, straw-filled wooden crates, and discarded household goods." Alexandra Gripenberg, *A Half Year in the New World: Miscellaneous Sketches of Travel in the United States* [1889], trans. and ed. Ernest J. Moyne (Newark: University of Delaware Press, 1954), 3.

12. Thomas J. Schlereth, *Victorian America: Transformations in Everyday Life, 1976–1915* (New York: Harper Perennial, 1992), 20.

13. Macrae, 77.

14. Harold Brydges, *Uncle Sam at Home* (New York: Henry Holt and Co., 1888), 150. W. F. Rae said of New York that "the purity of the air is delicious." Rae, 21. F. Barham Zincke noted that Chicago burned bituminous coal, which had put "a complexion on the buildings something like that of London." F. Barham Zincke, *Last Winter in the United States: Being Table Talk Collected During a Tour Through the Late Southern Confederation, the Far West, the Rocky Mountains, &c.* [1868] (Freeport, NY: Books for Libraries Press, 1970), 185. Referring to clean-burning anthracite coal, Henry Irving said, "What a pity we don't have it in London! Only fancy a smokeless London—what a lovely city?" Irving quoted in Joseph Hatton, *Henry Irving's Impressions of America, Narrated in a Series of Sketches, Chronicles, and Conversations* [1884], v. 1 (New York: Benjamin Blom, 1971), 280. In 1892, Antoní Dvořák also praised New York for "the greatest cleanliness." Dvořák to Dr. Emile Kozánek, Letter of 12 October 1892, in Otakar Šourek, *Antonín Dvořák: Letters and Reminiscences,* trans. Roberta Finlayson Samsour (Prague: Artia 1954*),* 149. When he was in New York in 1899, William Archer referred to that city's "keen, sweet, limpid air that one drank in eagerly, like sparkling wine." William Archer, *America To-Day: Observations and Reflections* [1899] (New York: Arno Press, 1974), 44.

15. George Augustus Sala, *America Revisited: From the Bay of New York to the Gulf of Mexico and From Lake Michigan to the Pacific* (London: Vizetelly & Co., n.d.), 76.

16. Anonymous, "Some American Notes," *MacMillan's Magazine* 53 (November 1885), 47.

17. Wilde, "Americans in London," 198; Wilde, "American Women," 5.

18. Lady Duffus Hardy, 283; O'rell and Allyn, 41.

19. Macrae, 91.

20. Wilde, "Americans in London," 197; Marie Therese de Solms Blanc, *The Condition of Woman in the United States: A Traveller's Notes,* trans. Abby Langdon [1895] (New York: Arno Press, 1972), 91.

21. Brydges, 36.

22. E. Catherine Bates, *A Year in the Great Republic,* v. 1 (London: Ward & Downey, 1887), 46.

23. Hübner, 180, 23.

24. William Saunders, *Through the Light Continent, or, The United States in 1877–78* [1879] (New York: Arno Press, 1974), 89, 88.

25. Henry Latham, *Black and White: A Journal of a Three Months' Tour in the United States* [1867] (New York: Negro Universities Press, 1969), 59; Sarah Bernhardt, *Memories of my Life* [1907] (Grosse Pointe, MI: Scholarly Press, 1968), 447.

26. Archer, 69; Élisée Reclus, *The Earth and its Inhabitants. North America: v. 3, The United States* (New York: D. Appleton and Co. 1893), 448. Even W. E. Adams, who struggled to say something nice about Washington, could not be unqualified in his praise: "The site chosen for the seat of government was well adapted for the purpose, though some of the lower ground is said to be conducive to malaria." W. E. Adams, *Our American Cousins: Being Personal Impressions of the People and Institutions of the United States* (London: Walter Scott, 1883), 31.

27. Peter Tchaikovsky, *The Diaries of Tchaikovsky*, trans. Wladimir Lakond (New York: W. W. Norton, 1945), 326; William H. Davies, *The Autobiography of a Super-Tramp* (New York: Alfred A. Knopf, 1917), 108, 109.

28. Bates, v. 1, 278. George Augustus Sala called Baltimore "one of the comeliest, the most sociable, the most refined, and the most hospitable cities of the United States." Sala, 101.

29. Zincke, 32–33.

30. O'rell and Allyn, 13.

31. George Jacob Holyoake, "A Stranger in America," *The Nineteenth Century* 8, no. 41 (July 1880), 70; Lady Duffus Hardy, 223.

32. W. E. Adams, 24. Hamilton Aïdé observed of his time in the United States that "the love of privacy, so prominent a feature in the English character, is unknown: the privilege of exclusion, so rigidly enforced in the walls and fences of our gardens, the closed doors of our withdrawing-rooms on the first floor, is rarely enforced here." Hamilton Aïdé, "Social Aspects of American Life," *The Nineteenth Century* 29, no. 172 (June 1891), 898.

33. W. E. Adams, 25. John Douglas Argyll also noted that New York had "trees at the side of every street." John Campbell Argyll, *A Trip to the Tropics and Home Through America* (London: Hurst and Blackett, 1867), 172.

34. James Fullarton Muirhead, *The Land of Contrasts: A Briton's View of his American Kin* (London: Lamson, Wolffe and Co., 1898), 44; W. E. Adams, 26. Adams added that walking through Milwaukee was like "strolling through a public park." Ibid., 27. J. W. Boddam-Whetham said of Buffalo, New York, that, "The Buffalo people are apparently very fond of trees; two and sometimes three rows of elms and other trees line either side of many of the streets; and as they are constantly adding row to row, some parts of the city appear as if built in a forest." J. W. Boddam-Whetham, *Western Wanderings: A Record of Travel in the Evening Land* (London: Richard Bentley and Son, 1874), 19.

35. One exception, as identified by Paul Bourget, was that by the 1890s the number of cable cars in New York had proliferated to such an extent that horses had become a rarity—making this aspect of the city distinctly different from its European counterparts. Bourget, 21. Street railway cars were rapidly electrified. Forty-one cities had electric street railway lines in 1890. Five years later there were 850 lines in operation. Schlereth, 24.

36. Archer, 53, 56.

37. See Carl Abbott, *How Cities Won the West: Four Centuries of Urban Change in Western North America* (Albuquerque: University of New Mexico Press, 2008), 32.

38. William A. Bell, *New Tracks in North America: A Journal of Travel and Adventure Whilst Engaged in the Survey for a Southern Railroad to the Pacific Ocean During 1867–8* [1870] (Albuquerque: Horn and Wallace, 1965), 6.

39. Hesse-Wartegg, *Travels on the Lower Mississippi*, 21.

40. Charles E. Rosenberg, *The Cholera Years: The United States in 1832, 1849, and 1866* (Chicago: University of Chicago Press, 1987), 135, 115.

41. William Hepworth Dixon, *New America* (Philadelphia: J. B. Lippincott, 1869),11; Charles Wentworth Dilke, *Greater Britain: A Record of Travel in English-Speaking Countries* (London: Macmillan and Co., 1890), 67.

42. Bernhardt, 420.

43. Bates, v. 2, 16, 7–8.

44. Giacosa quoted in Ben Lawton, "Giuseppe Giacosa, 1847–1906," in *Abroad in America: Visitors to the New Nation, 1776–1914* (Reading, MA: Addison-Wesley, 1976), 251. For an excellent overview of Chicago, see William Cronon, *Nature's Metropolis: Chicago and the Great West* (New York: W. W. Norton, 1991).

45. Aubertin, 55. W. G. Marshall observed that "people *do* rush about Chicago as if they were mad. I never saw such racing." W. G. Marshall, *Through America: Nine Months in the United States* (London: Sampson, Low, Marston, Searle & Rivington, 1881), 101.

46. Thomas Hughes, "A Week in the West," pt. 3, *Macmillan's Magazine* 25, no. 41 (November 1871), 4.

47. W. E. Adams, 208. Of house moving in Chicago, Alexander Craib noted that when one read of such things in England, they were considered exaggerations. In the "'go-ahead city'" of Chicago, however, "they are of frequent occurrence." Alexander Craib, *America and the Americans: A Tour in the United States and Canada, With Chapters on American Home Life* (London: Alexander Gardner, 1892), 63.

48. Hübner, 49. When he was in Chicago, J. W. Boddam-Whetham and his companions "were greatly amused one day by suddenly coming upon a good-sized three-storied house, standing dejectedly in the middle of a street, as if it did not know where to settle down. The next day, and for two or three following ones, we were continually meeting this same house, and always at different places." Boddam-Whetham, 33.

49. Zincke, 197.

50. W. E. Adams, 45.

51. Reclus, 449.

52. Hughes, pt. 4, 151; Anonymous, "Some American Notes," 52.

53. Bourget, 117.

54. Giacosa quoted in Lawton, 251.

55. S. C. de Soissons, *A Parisian in America* (Boston: Estes and Lauriat, 1896), 171; Rudyard Kipling, *American Notes* [1891] (Norman: University of Oklahoma Press, 1981), 139. Oscar Wilde referred to Chicago as a "monster-shop, full of bustle and bores." Wilde, "Americans in London," 197.

56. Quoted in Beatrice Webb, *Beatrice Webb's American Diary* (Madison: University of Wisconsin Press, 1963), 105; Henry Trueman Wood, "Chicago and Its Exhibition," *The Nineteenth Century* 31, no. 180 (February 1892), 556.

57. Marshall, 89.

58. O'rell and Allyn, 44.

59. Phil Robinson, *Sinners and Saints: A Tour Across the States, and Round Them; with Three Months Among the Mormons* (Boston: Roberts Brothers, 1883), 14, 15.

60. Boddam-Whetham, 34.

61. Kipling, 149. Harry Kessler noted that Chicago's slaughterhouse operations provided "disgusting impressions for the eyes, nose, and ears," but Kessler also found "a vibrant life as the framework for death—a wonderful drama." Harry Kessler, *Journey to the Abyss: The Diaries of Count Harry Kessler, 1880–1918*, trans. and ed. Laird Easton (New York: Knopf, 2011), 164.

62. Lepel Henry Griffin, *The Great Republic* [1884] (New York: Arno Press, 1974), 22. W. E. Adams said of Chicago's slaughterhouse operations that "it is a sight to be seen once, and only once." W. E. Adams, 47.

63. Davies, 119.

64. Ibid., 120.

65. William T. Stead, *If Christ Came to Chicago!: A Plea for the Union of All Who Love in the Service of All Who Suffer* [1894] (Chicago: Press of the Eight-Hour Herald, n.d.), 245, 231.

66. For a lengthy examination of Stead, See Robert Frankel, *Observing America: The Commentary of British Visitors to the United States, 1890–1950* (Madison: University of Wisconsin Press, 2007), 17–75.

67. Hesse-Wartegg, *Travels on the Lower Mississippi*, 151.

68. Marshall, 262; Kipling, 19; See Emily Faithfull, *Three Visits to America* (New York: Fowler & Wells, 1884), 247; Isabella L. Bird, *A Lady's Life in the Rocky Mountains* (Norman: University of Oklahoma Press, 1969), 3–4; Marshall, 272.

69. Wilde, "Impressions of America," 257. Harry Kessler described San Francisco's Chinatown as "the most depraved and shameless collection of people that I know of and yet I had the sensation of a strange beauty." Kessler, *Journey to the Abyss*, 74.

Marring the beauty of San Francisco was the coal that was burned there. In 1869 W. F. Rae reported being surprised "to see the greater part of the lower town enveloped in a dense cloud of smoke." Rae, 269.

70. Marshall, 269; Kevin Starr, *Americans and the California Dream, 1850–1915* (New York: Oxford University Press, 1973), 133. J. W. Boddam-Whetham said of the hoodlums of San Francisco that they "are rapidly becoming a formidable element in the population." Boddam-Whetham, 158.

71. Faithfull, 228, 229.

72. Quoted in Starr, 240.

73. Lady Duffus Hardy, 136; Marshall, 269.

74. Boddam-Whetham, 174–175.

75. Robinson, 295.

76. Marshall, 164.

77. Marshall, 165; Faithfull, 177; Theodora Guest, *A Round Trip in North America* (London: Edward Stanford, 1895), 81.

78. Marshall, 181. When William Hepworth Dixon was in Salt Lake City, he described "pretty Swiss cottages, like many in St. John's Wood, as to gable, roof, and paint; these are the dwellings of different wives." Dixon, 137. Iza Duffus Hardy took note of "little cottages, each with its own door and solitary window, the number of such divisions publishing to all passersby the number of wives with which the owner was blessed." Iza Hardy, 127.

79. Of the public areas of Salt Lake City, William Hepworth Dixon said that "the hotels have no bars; the streets have no betting-houses, no gaming-tables, no brothels, no drinking-places." Dixon, 136–137. But he did refer to that city's "secret slums," where teamsters who had spent ninety days crossing the plains and mountains assembled for "a week's debauchery." Ibid., 112.

80. Marshall, 403.

81. Robinson, 58.

82. Dixon, 94; Bird, 137, 139.

83. Faithfull, 136; In New York's Central Park in 1881, William Howard Russell also "beheld cockades in the hats of honest Republican 'helps,' and armorial bearings on the panels of democratic broughams." William Howard Russell, *Hesperothen, Notes from the West: A Record of a Ramble in the United States and Canada in the Spring and Summer of 1881*, v. 1 (London: S. Low, Marston, Searle & Rivington, 1882), 25.

84. Ibid, v. 2, 94.

85. Abbott, *How Cities Won the West*, 36.

86. Giuseppe Giacosa claimed that the ugliness of American architecture was "so absolute that nothing can mitigate the disgust." Quoted in Andrew J. Torrielli, *Italian Opinion on America, As Revealed by Italian Travelers, 1850–1900* (Cambridge, MA: Harvard University Press, 1941), 239. Quote trans. from Italian by Pietro Bonomi.

87. James Bryce, *The American Commonwealth*, v. 2 (New York: The Commonwealth Publishing Co., 1908), 771. Lepel Henry Griffin stated flatly that the "monotony" of most American towns was "depressing to the last degree." Griffin, 41.

88. Zincke, 180, 179. William A. Bell believed that this system had been borrowed from Philadelphia. Referring to St. Louis, Bell noted that "the streets, which run parallel to the river, are all named, as in Philadelphia, 1st, 2nd, 3rd, &c., from the quay inland; while the familiar names of Chestnut, Walnut, Spruce, and Pine meet him at every corner, since these avenues (also according to Philadelphian rule) cut the numbered streets at right angles." Bell, 5. George Augustus Sala claimed that the great exception to this system of naming streets was New Orleans, where street names included "Annunciation, Bacchus, Bagatelle, Bolivar, Dauphine, Morales, Lafayette, Izardi, Dryades, [and] Duels." Sala, 283.

89. Horace Annesley Vachell, *Life and Sport on the Pacific Slope* (New York: Dodd, Mead and Co., 1901), 229. As one traveler expressed it, "poor sophisticated Europeans, with their acquired standard of neatness, are saddened by the ragged, untidy look of the country—the gaps between cultivation and the timber-houses in all the rawness of modern erection." Anonymous, "Some Remarks on Travelling in America," *The Cornhill Magazine* 19 (March 1869), 329. One feature of even the smallest of American communities that was noted by European travelers was the early establishment of a well-tended cemetery. Phil Robinson called this provision "for the dead that are to come" a "beautiful touch of national character," while H. Hussey Vivian claimed that "nothing can exceed the beauty of American cemeteries." Robinson, 20, 21; H. Hussey Vivian, *Notes of a Tour in America from August 7th to November 17th, 1877* (London: Edward Stanford, 1878), 48.

90. Abbott, *How Cities Won the West*, 48.

91. See Bell, 17–19.

92. Ibid., 30.

93. Dilke, 68.

94. Hughes, pt. 5, 380.

95. Saunders, 49, 50.

96. Ibid., 60. Lady Duffus Hardy noted that "for any one who is not professionally interested in agricultural progress, there is no temptation to stay in Kansas City." Lady Duffus Hardy, 264.

97. R. H. Inglis Synnot, "The Pacific Express," *The Contemporary Review* 17 (June 1871), 433.

98. Lady Duffus Hardy, 80; Kipling, 136. See also Marshall, 114.

99. Robinson, 22. Henry M. Stanley believed that no town on the Missouri River was more afflicted by swirling clouds of dust than Omaha. Henry M. Stanley, *My Early Travels and Adventures in America* [1895] (Lincoln: University of Nebraska Press, 1982), 192.

100. Kipling, 67–68. E. Catherine Bates described the Portland of 1886 as "busy, thriving and perfectly uninteresting." Bates, v. 2, 154.

101. Kipling, 70. Los Angeles was not a town deemed worthy of a visit by most tourists. E. Catherine Bates called it "flat, dusty and uninteresting," while W. Henry Barneby described it as "not a pretty place." Barneby, however, held out hope for Southern California "if water can be obtained." Bates, v. 2, 76; W. Henry Barneby, *Life and Labor in the Far, Far West: Being Notes of a Tour in the Western States, British Columbia, Manitoba, and the North-West Territory* (London: Cassell & Co., 1884), 78, 80.

102. Kipling, 73. W. Henry Barneby also used the word "sleepy" to describe Victoria. Barneby, 151.

103. Boddam-Whetham, 290.

104. Russell, v. 1, 172.

105. Harry Kessler, "The Kessler Diaries," manuscript trans. and ed. Laird Easton, 12.

106. Kessler, *Journey to the Abyss*, 60–61; Vivian, 17.

107. Lady Duffus Hardy, 45.

108. Dilke, 48. F. Barham Zincke claimed that "the American is the hardest worker in the world, never sparing himself, but always toiling on, in the faith that he will soon be able to bring all things right; and he generally succeeds in doing so. These are not yet the characteristics of the inhabitants of Upper Canada." Zincke, 273. The British hunter Parker Gillmore described Canada as possessing "a partially disaffected and tainted population," and predicted that Canada would soon be annexed by the United States. Parker Gillmore, *A Hunter's Adventures in the Great West* (London: Hurst and Blackett, 1871), 284.

109. Holyoake, 82.

110. Bird, 22.

111. Ibid., 197.
112. Ibid., 34–35.
113. Ibid., 4.
114. See David Lavender, *The Great West* (Boston: Houghton Mifflin, 1965), 421–422. By 1880, Leadville was America's largest silver/lead smelting center, with thirty-seven blast furnaces and fifteen smelters. See Abbott, *How Cities Won the West*, 103.
115. Marshall, 405.
116. James Bryce, who was in Leadville the year after Wilde, noted that tree stumps were left in the streets because the city government could not be bothered to cut or burn them. Bryce, v. 2, 784; Russell, v. 2, 103.
117. Wilde, "Impressions," 258.
118. Lloyd Lewis and Henry Justin Smith, *Oscar Wilde Discovers America* [1936] (New York: Benjamin Blom, 1967), 314.
119. Wilde, "Impressions," 259.
120. Lewis and Smith, 318.
121. Wilde, "Impressions," 259.
122. Lewis and Smith, 317.
123. Wilde, "Impressions," 260. Lepel Henry Griffin agreed, claiming that "the average miner is a pleasant fellow enough, and there are many quarters of London, Paris or New York more dangerous to a well-dressed stranger than the wildest mining town in the Western States." Griffin, 146.
124. Edmonds quoted in Wolfgang Schivelbusch, *The Culture of Defeat: On National Trauma, Mourning, and Recovery* (New York: Harper Perennial, 1992), 82.
125. Quoted in Henry Nash Smith, *Virgin Land: The American West as Symbol and Myth* (Cambridge, MA: Harvard University Press, 1950), 185.
126. David M. Wrobel, *Promised Lands: Promotion, Memory, and the Creation of the American West* (Lawrence: University Press of Kansas, 2002), 20.
127. Quoted in ibid., 21.
128. Quoted in ibid., 40.
129. Hesse-Wartegg, *Travels on the Lower Mississippi*, 35.
130. Kipling, 52.
131. Kipling, 82. The editors of the *Mendocino Democrat* in California flatly stated that "the duty of a local paper is to build up, defend, and advance the interest, good name and prosperity of the place in which it has support and being, and not to decry it, and bring it into bad repute." Quoted in Barbara Cloud, *The Coming of the Frontier Press: How the West was Really won* (Evanston, IL: Northwestern University Press, 2008), 70.
132. Kipling, 68.
133. Aubertin, 77; Brydges, 115. When William Francis Butler arrived in Duluth in 1870, it was barely eighteen months old, but already residents were telling Butler that, "It was to be the great grain emporium of the North-west; it was to kill St. Paul, Milwaukie, Chicago, and half-a-dozen other thriving towns." William Francis Butler, *The Great Lone Land: A Narrative of Travel and Adventure in the North-West of America* [1872] (Rutland, VT: Charles E. Tuttle, 1968), 61–62. Butler's own assessment of Duluth was less upbeat: "the sorriest spectacle of city that eye of man could look upon." Ibid., 70–71.
134. Kipling, 77. As Phil Robinson put it, "presuming for instance that an American understands the real meaning of the word 'city,' what gross and ridiculous notions of self-importance second-class villages must acquire by hearing themselves spoken of as 'cities.'" Robinson, 47.
135. Quoted in Bryce, v. 2, 789. Another Bismarck booster, discounting that city's vulnerability to blizzards, claimed that "pioneering in this country is divested of its rougher features. There are no obstacles of nature to overcome." Quoted in Abbott, *How Cities Won the West*, 8.
136. Aubertin, 83.

137. See Abbott, *How Cities Won the West*, 47.

138. Rae, 185.

139. Hughes, pt. 4, 156–157.

140. Vivian, 28.

141. Abbott, *How Cities Won the West*, 75.

142. Sala, 242.

143. A. Maurice Low, *The American People: A Study in National Psychology*, v. 2 (Boston: Houghton Mifflin, 1909), 75.

144. Kessler, *Journey to the Abyss*, 54.

145. O'rell and Allyn, 34.

146. Quoted in Daniel J. Boorstin, *The Americans: The National Experience* (New York: Random House, 1965), 122.

147. Boorstin, 296. Historian Carl Abbott claims that the booster pamphlet was "the twin of the Fourth of July oration. Independence Day rhetoric reiterated the republican virtues of the nation. Urban boosters reaffirmed the commercial mission of its people." Carl Abbott, *Boosters and Businessmen: Popular Economic Thought and Urban Growth in the Antebellum Middle West* (Westport, CN: Greenwood Press, 1981), 207–208.

148. Macrae, 414.

149. José De Onis, *The United States as Seen by Spanish American Writers (1776–1890)* (New York: Hispanic Institute in the United States, 1952), 171.

150. Anthony Trollope, *North America* (New York: Alfred A. Knopf, 1951), 483.

151. See Boorstin, 135. Boorstin referred to "hotel buildings ridiculously disproportionate to their surroundings—hotels built not to serve cities but to create them." Ibid., 142.

152. While the Northeast boasted the most hotels per square mile, the West had more hotels per capita because of its smaller population. The South had the fewest number of hotels because this was mostly a rural region with undeveloped railroads. Between 1870 and 1880, the number of American hotel clerks grew from roughly 5,000 to 11,000, while the number of other hotel workers grew from roughly 23,000 to 77,000. See A. K. Sandoval-Strausz, *Hotel: An American History* (New Haven: Yale University Press, 2007), 103–104. By the 1870s, American luxury hotels were employing as many as two workers for every three guests. And while most European travelers stayed at luxury American hotels (and most of the literature is focused on these establishments), there was a broad spectrum of hotel types. In addition to luxury hotels, American hotel types included commercial hotels, middle-class hotels, marginal hotels, resort hotels, railroad hotels, and settlement hotels. Subgroups included temperance hotels and ethnic hotels. Ibid., 179, 81–99.

153. Robert Somers, *The Southern States Since the War, 1870–71* [1871] (Tuscaloosa: University of Alabama Press, 1965), 94.

154. Tchaikovsky, 315. American hotels were incubators for the latest technologies. The Eastern Exchange Hotel in Boston was the first American public building that was heated with steam (in 1846), while Holt's Hotel in New York had a steam-powered elevator by 1833. The Hotel Everett in New York was the first hotel with electric light in 1882, while the first hotel with room phones and a private switchboard was New York's Hotel Netherland. See Boorstin, 137–138.

155. Brydges, 146. Henry Irving concluded that American hotels were larger and more complete than the ones in Britain. See Hatton, v. 1, 129. The excellence of American hotels was lacking in Canada. W. Henry Barneby, who traveled both in America and in Canada in 1883, found only a single decent hotel in Canada, and concluded that the Canadians could learn something from how Americans ran their hotels. Barneby, 116.

156. Russell, v. 2, 46.

157. Henry Sienkiewicz, *Portrait of America: Letters of Henry Sienkiewicz*, trans. and ed. Charles Morley (New York: Columbia University Press, 1959), 50.

158. O'rell and Allyn, 278.

159. Sienkiewicz, 3; Lady Duffus Hardy, 57.

160. Vivian, 32.

161. W. E. Adams, 214.

162. Zincke, 81. According to Zincke, the cost of bed and board at these hotels ranged between $3.50 and $5.00 per day.

163. Rae, 19.

164. Anne Farrar Hyde, *An American Vision: Far Western Landscape and National Culture, 1820–1920* (New York: New York University Press, 1990).

165. Edward A. Freeman, *Some Impressions of the United States* (London: Longmans, Green, and Co., 1883), 236.

166. Aubertin, 63. See also Zincke, 73, and W. E. Adams, 225.

167. Aubertin, 64.

168. Robert G. Athearn, *Westward the Briton* (Lincoln: University of Nebraska Press, 1953), 27–28.

169. Hatton, v. 1, 252.

170. Latham, 74–75.

171. O'rell and Allyn, 276; Hatton, v. 1, 75.

172. At the hotel where he stayed in Jackson, Mississippi, Ernst von Hesse-Wartegg observed some people paying two dollars for their lodging and some paying three. When Hesse-Wartegg tried to pay two, the clerk looked at him and said, "'*Are you a drummer, sir?* Another dollar!'" [original emphasis] Hesse-Wartegg, *Travels on the Lower Mississippi*, 75.

173. Macrae, 390

174. Faithfull, 343; Dilke, 175. Also staying at American hotels, according F. Barham Zincke, were "multitudes of men in business, keeping only a counting-house or a store in the city." Zincke, 287.

175. A. S. Northcote, "American Life Through English Spectacles," *The Nineteenth Century* 34, no. 199 (September 1893), 482.

176. Oscar Wilde, "The American Man," in *The Collected Oscar Wilde* (New York: Barnes and Noble Classics, 2007), 308.

177. Macrae, 390. Robert Somers claimed that "the secret of the 'big hotels' in America is that they are designed in a very subordinate degree for travellers, and that they place their main chance on town boarders, to whose convenience they conform all their arrangements. The system of boarding in hotels prevails largely in the cities of the North, and I am sorry to note its rapid introduction into the Southern States." Somers, 96.

178. Stephen Buckland, "Eating and Drinking in America—A Stroll Among the Saloons of New York," in *MacMillan's Magazine* 16 (May, 1867–October, 1867), 453. Shortly thereafter, Buckland discovered his American guide "G." cleaning and polishing his own boots, and was informed that American gentlemen "invariably performed this operation for themselves as a matter of course." Ibid. 454.

179. Marshall, 267. Lepel Henry Griffin complained that anyone staying at an American hotel "will find it difficult to get his boots blacked unless he descended into the nether regions and have them polished on his feet." Griffin, 182.

180. Zincke, 117. J. J. Aubertin related a joke he had heard about boot cleaning when he was in America: "In one case, on a visitor asking whether he could leave his boots outside his door, he was surprised by the unexpected answer—'Oh yes, sir; nobody will touch them.'" Aubertin, 68.

But another traveler told F. Barham Zincke that he had once put his boots outside the door of his hotel room, "and never saw them again." Zincke, 159.

181. Macrae, 56. Because this chore was not the domestic duty of any American, what followed was the creation and proliferation of outdoor shoeshine stands. See Lady Duffus Hardy, 135.

182. Athearn, 26.

183. Bird, 9. William Hepworth Dixon was likewise startled by a pistol shot outside his hotel room in Denver: "on looking out, I saw a man writhing on the ground." Dixon, 102.

184. Bird, 141.

185. Stanley, 90.

186. Zincke, 228.

187. Hesse-Wartegg, *Travels on the Lower Mississippi*, 25.

188. Barneby, 4; Brydges, 149.

189. Somers, 214; Macrae, 408.

190. Macrae, 408–409. Adding spice to a trip up the Mississippi was what Macrae called "the insatiable desire of every Mississippi captain and pilot to beat every other" in a race. Macrae, 412.

191. Somers, 214. As Henry M. Stanley expressed it, "The countless shody steams which have been blown up and sunk in the capacious bosom of the Father of Waters, have contributed in a great measure to retard travelling in this manner." Stanley, 100.

192. Macrae, 417.

193. Freeman, 225; Saunders, 334.

194. Griffin, 42.

195. Macrae, 419.

196. According to Henry M. Stanley, the Hancock expedition of 1867 found five bags of mail and one sack of books in Plum Creek near Fort Larned. Stanley, 49.

197. Dilke, 9.

198. Bell, 459. This could happen even for railroad passengers. When Ernst von Hesse-Wartegg was traveling on a train in Mississippi in 1879, he and his fellow passengers were obliged to get out and push the train when it stalled on a steep grade. Hesse-Wartegg, *Travels on the Lower Mississippi*, 73.

199. Guest, 50. One exception to the bad road rule was the one that ran along the western side of Mobile Bay. It was paved with oyster shells, and made for what Henry Latham called "the smoothest of turnpike roads." Latham, 145.

200. Vivian, 52.

201. Brydges, 141.

202. Hatton, v. 1, 47. W. E. Adams described the streets of New York City as "almost disgusting." W. E. Adams, 137.

203. Latham, 8.

204. Lady Duffus Hardy, 60.

205. Lillie Langtry, *The Days I Knew* (New York: George H. Doran, 1925), 180.

206. O'rell and Allyn, 30.

207. Sienkiewicz, 7.

208. Zincke, 143; Hesse-Wartegg, *Travels on the Lower Mississippi*, 49.

209. Hesse-Wartegg, *Travels on the Lower Mississippi*, 50.

210. Kessler, *Journey to the Abyss*, 24; Russell, v. 2, 62–63.

211. Robinson, 12; Saunders, 32. Perhaps unnecessarily, Saunders observed that American public opinion "was in favour of low rates and unrepaired roads." Saunders, 18. Marie Therese de Solms Blanc also believed that the "atrocious pavement" of Chicago may have been worse than that of New York. Blanc, 68.

212. Russell, v. 1, 37.

213. See Marshall, 27–28.

214. Jacques Offenbach, *Orpheus in America: Offenbach's Diary of His Journey to the New World*, trans. Lander MacClintock (New York: Greenwood Press, 1969), 55–56. Joseph Hatton sardonically called the American street railway car "a very democratic institution" because there were no limits on the number of passengers and "people crowd it as they please." Hatton, v. 2, 42–43. David Macrae found a more genteel style of street railway travel in New Orleans, noting that "the etiquette is for gentlemen to pay before taking their seats, and for ladies, immediately after taking

their seats, to give their fare to the nearest gentleman, who passes it into the box for them." Macrae, 389.

215. Guest, 19.
216. Offenbach, 56.
217. Brydges, 96.
218. Faithfull, 155.
219. Russell, v. 1, 52–53.
220. Gripenberg, 5.
221. Guest, 45.
222. Quoted in Hyde, 122.
223. Iza Hardy, 149.
224. Marshall, 62.
225. Macrae, 458; Jackson Lears, *Rebirth of a Nation: The Making of Modern America, 1877–1920* (New York: Harper, 2009), 130.
226. Sala, 129. There were occasional power reversals. When he entered a coach on a train that was heading south out of Memphis in 1879, Ernst von Hesse-Wartegg found that "about two dozen ladies and gentlemen of the '*coloured race*' already held places there. Stretched out on the best seats, their dirty laundry and bedrolls piled on the rest, the Negroes—black, ragged, boorish—were masters of the situation. We poor victims of white skins given us by Mother Nature, we crowded into corners " [original emphasis]. Hessee-Wartegg, *Travels on the Lower Mississippi*, 65.
227. Boddam-Whetham, 101.
228. Robert Louis Stevenson, "The Amateur Emigrant," in *From Scotland to Silverado* [1892] (Cambridge, MA: Belknap Press, 1966), 115.
229. Stevenson, 133.
230. Tchaikovsky, 320.
231. Kipling, 77.
232. Stevenson, 116.
233. In 1899, Pullman bought out his last competitor, the Wagner Palace-Car Company. August Mencken, *The Railroad Passenger Car* (Baltimore: Johns Hopkins Press, 1957), 80. At the top of the Pullman hierarchy was the "silver palace car," which one traveler described as "well carpeted, richly cushioned, tastefully ornamented" with "handsome hangings" and rails in "polished silver plate." Craib, 100. Lady Duffus Hardy puzzled over why they were called "silver" cars when they were painted a bright yellow. Lady Duffus Hardy, 123.
234. Hughes, pt. 3, 3.
235. Faithfull, 49, 50.
236. Bird, 23; Rae, 29. Theodora Guest likewise noted that "it is wonderful how well and restfully one sleeps" in such a car. Guest, 58.
237. Isabelle Randall, *A Lady's Ranche Life in Montana* (London: W. H. Allen & Co., 1887), 5.
238. See O'rell and Allyn, 252–253.
239. Deedes quoted in Mencken, 146.
240. Saunders, 125.
241. Muirhead, 17.
242. Offenbach, 146, 145.
243. Butler, 55. British traveler J. J. Aubertin said of Pullman sleepers that "it seemed very strange to me, at first, to be all mixed together, male and female; but an imperative law of nature, such as sleep, very soon puts to flight any conventional artifices, and besides this, there is a vast deal of curtaining." Aubertin, 71–72.
244. Vivian, 11–12.
245. Hughes, pt. 3, 1–2; Bates, v. 2, 35.
246. Barneby, 7.

247. Marshall, 65.
248. Macrae, 456; Kipling, 48.
249. Bates, v. 1, 21.
250. Mother and daughter both weighed in on this subject. See Lady Duffus Hardy, 69–70; Iza Hardy, 70.
251. Barneby, 5–6. For her tour of America, Lillie Langtry had her own sleeper car constructed. Accommodations included quarters for her and her staff, a kitchen, bath and piano. Langtry, 186.
252. Marshall, 127.
253. Faithfull, 52.
254. Marshall, 130. When he was in Sidney in 1877, Ernst von Hesse-Wartegg found "a caravansary of scoundrels, hunters, vagabonds, and a few upright people." Ernst von Hesse-Wartegg, "Across Nebraska by Train in 1877: The Travels of Ernst von Hesse-Wartegg," trans. and ed. Frederic Trautmann, *Nebraska History* 65, no. 3 (Fall 1984), 419.
255. "The sudden departure of the American locomotive," said Robinson, was a "shabby sort of practical joke." Robinson, 3. H. Hussey Vivian noted that "'All aboard' is the American guard's warning, and without waiting for 'wicked man' or anyone else, off the train goes, and woe betide the unready." Vivian, 31.
256. Offenbach, 137, 138.
257. Sienkiewicz, 33.
258. Marshall, 62.
259. Faithfull, 50; Bird, 24.
260. Stevenson, 112.
261. Kipling, 76–77.
262. Ibid., 51.
263. Bryce, v. 2, 784.
264. Bird, 7. Iza Duffus Hardy reported that her train trip east from Sacramento was delayed when a thousand feet of snow sheds were destroyed by an avalanche in the Sierra. Iza Hardy, 212.
265. One who has recently fixed a mordant eye on Western railroad building is Richard White. White claims that "in terms of their politics, finances, labor relations, and environmental consequences, the transcontinental railroads were not only failures but near-disasters, and in this they encapsulated the paradox of the arrival of the modern world in western North America." White suggests that "without the extensive subsidization of a transcontinental railroad network, there might very well have been less waste, less suffering, less environmental degradation, and less catastrophic economic busts in mining, agriculture, and cattle raising. There would have been more time for Indians to adjust to a changing world." Richard White, *Railroaded: The Transcontinentals and the Making of Modern America* (New York: W. W. Norton, 2011), 507–508, 517.
266. Bird, 27.
267. Marshall, 132.
268. Iza Hardy, 134.
269. Brydges, 155; Macrae, 461.
270. Faithfull, 382.
271. Saunders, 24. J. J. Aubertin praised the convenience and "great exactness" of the railway baggage system in America. Aubertin, 55. Conversely, what caused the greatest anxiety among Americans traveling on English railroads was "the apparently defective baggage system" in which no brass check was offered as a receipt for a passenger's baggage. Anonymous, "English and American Railways," *Harper's* 71 (August 1885), 382. One American traveler called the baggage system on English railroads "inexcusably bad," and described the carriages themselves as "small

prison vans." Horace White, "An American's Impression of England," *Eclectic Magazine* 22, no. 5 (New Series, November 1875), 553.
272. Macrae, 456–457.
273. Bird, 25; Stevenson, 119.
274. Marshall, 67.
275. Robinson, 278. William Francis Butler worked himself up into a "moral hatred for this precocious pedlar." Butler, 58.
276. Iza Hardy, 65.
277. Latham, 98.

3

CULTURE

Aesthetics, Music, Language, Humor, and Copyright and Journalism

Aesthetics

European travelers in America going back to Tocqueville's time were in general agreement that the United States was an unaesthetic country.[1] In Jacques Offenbach's words, "neither music, nor painting, nor sculpture has found in America conditions suitable for development."[2] A. Maurice Low claimed that art was a product of "luxury and fashion and idleness, of a certain form of voluptuousness." But because there was little idleness to be found in America, "voluptuousness as a national quality does not exist."[3] Some laid the blame on an oppressive American egalitarianism, and the absence of a leisured class, while others claimed that it was American utilitarianism that had throttled aesthetics in its cradle.[4] But as Harold Brydges observed, complaining of America's inartistic character was "like grumbling because the floor of an iron-foundry is not carpeted."[5]

Many connected the aesthetic with settled conditions and antiquity, and because a new country had different requirements than an old one, F. Barham Zincke concluded that higher culture in America was "for future generations."[6] If beauty issued from "ancientness and permanence," as Matthew Arnold believed, the United States could hardly be expected to be beautiful.[7] Because of the enormity of the challenges facing America—in welding masses of immigrants into a single people, settling frontier regions, converting from an agrarian to an industrial society—the United States had not had the time for what the British actor Henry Irving called "the fringes and ribbons and jewels that belong to an age of rest, and luxury, and art."[8] As the American Henry Adams put it, "merely to make the continent habitable for civilized people would require an immediate outlay that would have bankrupted the world," and added that the Americans "who commanded high pay were as a rule not ornamental."[9]

Of the art that was available in America, theater presentations were the most popular, and what drew the largest crowds to American theaters, according to one European critic, were "comic operas, in which the songs are without rhyme and the plot without reason, [and] 'variety' shows of a depth of inanity unparalleled in Europe."[10] It would be untrue, however, to claim that Americans had no appreciation of the finer things in life. In fact, support could be found for cultural presentations even in America's most out-of-the-way communities. When he was in Helena, Arkansas, Ernst von Hesse-Wartegg encountered Dan Rice's Floating Opera House and Museum. Constructed on a large flatboat, Rice's opera house floated down the Mississippi from St. Louis, giving performances all along the way, until it reached New Orleans. Then the ship was broken up, the cast members scattered, and Rice returned to St. Louis to build another opera house.[11] In small American cities such as Indianapolis and Columbus, substantial numbers turned out for Henry Irving's theatrical presentations (although Irving could not help but notice the popularity of such attractions as "The Fat Lady" and "The Two-headed Pig" when he strolled about these towns).[12]

Irving's success in America was repeated by such European visitors as Sarah Bernhardt, Oscar Wilde, Jacques Offenbach, and others. Charles Dickens toured America in 1868, and despite his apprehensions that the excitement over Andrew Johnson's impeachment would thin out his audiences, large numbers showed up and greeted Dickens' readings enthusiastically.[13] Dickens estimated that his tour netted him £20,000.[14] Even those in the American working class, whose finances precluded attending one of these presentations, could enjoy good art, as F. Barham Zincke discovered when he found the night shift at the hotel where he was staying passing the evening "listening to Mr. Dickens's 'Oliver Twist,' each reading aloud in his turn."[15]

Of the artifacts that travelers found beautiful in America, most had been created unconsciously. Several mentioned the beauty of American structures and machinery.[16] Sarah Bernhardt's reaction to the Brooklyn Bridge in 1880 was that it was "insane, admirable, imposing," and that it made her feel proud to be a human being (Figure 3.1).[17] When he walked over the Brooklyn Bridge in 1893, Paul Bourget was inspired to proclaim that "the engineer is the great artist of our epoch."[18] Another traveler was enraptured by the ice factory in New Orleans ("artistic, and beautiful"), and when Oscar Wilde visited the Chicago water works he reported that the symmetry of the great wheels in motion was "the most beautifully rhythmic thing I have ever seen."[19]

Aesthetics was Oscar Wilde's stock-in-trade, and his 1882 tour of America afforded him numerous opportunities to comment on the state of art in the United States. In his lecture "Decorative Art in America," Wilde contended that even something as simple as a teacup could, and should, be artistically crafted (Figure 3.2). He recalled watching a Chinese laborer in San Francisco who every day drank from a teacup that was "as delicate in texture as the petal of a flower." In contrast, the lavish American hotels where Wilde stayed served him his refreshments

FIGURE 3.1 Sarah Bernhardt (ca. 1880). Library of Congress. LC–USZ62–79105.

"in cups an inch and a quarter thick." Lamented Wilde, "I think I have deserved something nicer."[20] Wilde was also brutal in his condemnation of American homes, and in gruesome detail he described his encounters with "bad wall-papers, horribly designed, and coloured carpets, and that old offender, the horse-hair sofa, whose stolid look of indifference is always so depressing."[21] Wilde's remedy was to inspire American workmen by placing them in surroundings that were beautiful, and to establish school workshops that would dedicate one hour per day to teaching decorative arts.[22]

Wilde judged the West to be the most beautiful part of America ("a paradise of beauty"), but noted that any knowledge of art west of the Rockies was "infinitesimal." As evidence, Wilde repeated the apocryphal story of the American art collector who ordered a plaster cast of the Venus de Milo, and then sued the railroad company because the statue arrived without arms.[23]

Americans themselves found beauty in the large and the vast. "Americans adore immensity," said David Macrae, and James Bryce added that "the physically large is to them the sublime."[24] William Howard Russell called immensity "the American idol."[25] The origin of this national characteristic was probably

FIGURE 3.2 Oscar Wilde (ca. 1882). Library of Congress, LC–DIG–ppmsca–07757.

rooted in geography, a notion endorsed by German geographer Friedrich Ratzel. "The breadth of the land," said Ratzel, "has given to the American spirit something of its own side."[26] William Hepworth Dixon claimed that the overwhelming first impression of America for the traveler was its "stupendous size," with another European visitor confirming that "nature is formed in a larger mold than in other lands."[27] Europeans with experience in the United States insisted that one had to travel in America to gain any appreciation of its magnitude which, said Robert Somers, was "all but overwhelming."[28] Another traveler called it a "sense of vastness which neither linear measurement in miles nor variety in the panorama fully explain."[29]

Because American rivers were huge, the mountains enormous, and the territory vast, "so it must be with everything in the American mind."[30] In a more negative interpretation, A. Maurice Low claimed that the immensity of the continent was "all-sufficient" for Americans, making them insular and intellectually isolated.[31] Indeed, James Bryce argued that Americans were "intoxicated" by the majestic scale of the land.[32] But European travelers experienced the same intoxication. In one example, Theodora Guest found herself at an elevation of 14,000 feet in the Rockies, looking out over "the most enormous landscape I ever saw in my life." Surrounded by snow-capped peaks, she stared below at "the boundless prairie, like a greyish-yellow sea" that "melted away into the sky."[33] As historian Daniel Boorstin wryly observed, "The dwarfs and elves and other tiny people who fill the legends of other countries have somehow not been indigenous to American soil."[34]

S. C. de Soissons said of Americans that "they like exaggeration; everything is 'the most beautiful I ever saw, the most delightful I ever saw, the grandest I ever saw,' etc."[35] It hardly mattered whether something was good or bad, as long as it surpassed all others.[36] In her critique of the overly ambitious goals of the Chautauqua schools, Maria Therese Blanc referred to the American taste "for everything that is sketchy, merely hinted, so long as the design is huge."[37] Another traveler claimed that the American love of the immense even extended to their preference for large hotels over quiet, small hotels.[38] "Bulk" was the standard of beauty and excellence in the United States, said Oscar Wilde, and when the American was in Europe he never tired of telling hotel waiters that "the state of Texas is larger than France and Germany put together."[39]

Music

The one area where one might expect that American culture would impress visiting Europeans would be in popular music. But popular music was not yet popular, at least among the well-heeled Europeans who visited the United States after the Civil War. These travelers were especially dismissive of black-based popular and sacred music in America, condemning it out of hand rather than trying to engage the vitality that made this music so attractive. S. C. de Soissons noted the enthusiasm for both the banjo and the minstrel show in America, and used the opportunity both to condemn the music and to air his own racial views. He called the banjo "very easy, and, as those poor darkies have but very little brain, it is an excellent instrument to satisfy their artistic tastes and musical tendencies."[40] He described the minstrel show as "the nigger's national opera," and could not comprehend its popularity with the American masses.[41] Soissons was at least right about its popularity in the United States—blackface minstrelsy was the dominant expression of popular culture in America from the 1840s to the 1880s.[42]

Less judgmental and more droll was a Parisian who knew more about music than other travelers combined, composer Jacques Offenbach. When he attended a minstrel show in New York, Offenbach noted that the "artists are Negroes; the chorus is Negro; the stagehands are Negroes" as well as the members of the orchestra, who were pointing Offenbach out to each other. When he came back after the intermission, Offenbach found that all the participants were now white. The mystery was solved when Offenbach was informed that the personnel had

FIGURE 3.3 Wm. H. West's Big Minstrel Jubilee (ca. 1900). Library of Congress. LC-USZC4-5698.

not changed but were "false Negroes who blackened or bleached their faces three or four times during an evening according to the needs of the play."[43] John Campbell Argyll also noted the popularity of this art form in America, and repeated the story of what happened when a real black person was taken to hear a musical performance of whites in blackface. "What cussed fools dese white men do make of themselves!" said the observer (Figure 3.3).[44]

The origins of blackface minstrelsy can be traced back to 1832, when Thomas Dartmouth Rice, a former carpenter's apprentice wearing blackface, electrified a Bowery crowd with a peculiar dance step accompanied by singing: "Wheel about and turn about, / And do jis so; / Eb'ry time I weel about, I jump Jim Crow."[45] Rice's dance step was the "cakewalk," which American slaves had developed as a parody of their owners' "sophisticated" dance steps.[46] Like carnivals in Europe, where participants in masks seized the opportunity to at least temporarily invert the power structure between rich and poor, blackface minstrelsy in America received its greatest support among the working class. And while this art form has been condemned for its racist overtones, Leroy Ashby and others have argued for its complexity. Blackface was both an unconscious acknowledgment of black influence, and "a way for lower-class groups to mock social elites."[47] By the postbellum era, this form of entertainment had become more elaborate and now real black persons were being employed. (And one of the ironies of this art form

is that light-skinned blacks had to apply blackface to appear more "authentic."[48])
While this provided opportunities for black musicians, dancers, and comics, the
class critique of early minstrel shows had largely been replaced by nostalgia for a
rural life and the supposedly happy plantation days. There were also "uglier representations of blacks, who increasingly appeared as reprehensible, violent brutes."[49]

Many other styles of music and performance could also be found in America,
thanks to America's mixture of ethnicities and races. In Louisiana, French-
speaking refugees from Canada created cajun and Creoles created zydeco.
Southern blacks from the Mississippi delta contributed blues, black and European
residents of New Orleans crafted jazz, and elements of Spanish and Mexican
music could be found throughout the Southwest. In the hill country of the
South, the Celtic influence on music was unmistakable.[50] These styles intermixed
freely, creating an American musical stew. Musicologists have concluded, for
instance, that the melody of "Jim Crow" is more closely related to Irish and
Scottish tunes than to African-American melodies.[51]

George Augustus Sala called Americans "music mad," and claimed that the
United States was "the paradise of fiddlers."[52] Music could be heard in every
corner of the country. Soldiers on the Great Plains pulled out banjos and fiddles
during their leisure hours and, as Henry M. Stanley put it, "All enjoy it, from the
Major-General to the infantry private."[53] As W. G. Marshall's train pulled out of
Laramie, the residents of his sleeping car fired up the organ in their car (the
"Palmyra") and for the next two hours "we amuse ourselves with singing and
playing, our conductor—who was a bit of a musician in his way—coming and
helping us and treating us to a few songs … In this way we spent a very pleasant
evening."[54] In a hotel in the Yosemite Valley, James Fullarton Muirhead and
other guests were entertained by a young singer from San Francisco. No one,
aside from Muirhead, found it incongruous or amusing that the singer jumped
from "Nearer, My God, to Thee" to "The Man Who Broke the Bank at Monte
Carlo," and "I Know That My Redeemer Liveth" to "Little Annie Rooney."[55]
Around the campfire in the Sierras, Henry Sienkiewicz and his companions were
serenaded by a chiote player and a singer who moved some listeners to tears.[56] In
Santa Fe, a band consisting of a clarinet, a French horn, and three brass instru-
ments entertained an appreciative crowd as "sun-burnt brunettes glide[d] most
gracefully through the languid and suggestive movements of their Spanish
dances."[57]

Music could also be found in American parlors. By the 1890s, organs were
common in the homes of both rural and urban workers, with the piano gradually
replacing the organ in the decades ahead. Friends and family members entertained themselves in their homes with hymns and sentimental ballads, and there
was a brisk trade in sheet music for voice and keyboard.[58] On one notable occasion, the entertainer was none other than Mark Twain who, according to
Alexandra Gripenberg, sat down at the piano and "sang in a worn-out but still
clear tenor voice several Negro songs."[59] But none of this was classical music, and

the Frenchwoman Madame de San Carlos was one among many European travelers who condemned "the musical ignorance of Americans."[60]

It should be emphasized that European travelers to America that had a formal grounding in music—especially classical composers—were not so quick to dismiss American music, and could see something in it of great value. A notable example is composer Frederick Delius. Partly to escape his father in Bradford, Yorkshire, who was trying to steer Delius toward a business career, Delius took up residence at a Florida orange plantation in 1883. Exhibiting little interest in the growing of oranges, Delius instead threw himself into the study of music, procuring both a piano and an accomplished music instructor. Delius also invited black workers to sing hymns to him. Julia Sanks remembered, "I was nothin' but a child, hardly, when we sing to him first—Albert and Eliza and me. Oh we loved to go there. It was a happy place."[61] Delius' *Florida Suite* and especially *Appalachia* would incorporate significant elements of American music in them.

During his time in America in the 1890s, Antoní Dvořák also encountered African-American melodies, which he described as "pathetic, tender, passionate, melancholy, solemn, religious, bold, merry, gay or what you will." He encouraged American composers to draw on the possibilities of their own folk music, and Dvořák himself arranged Stephen Foster's "Swanee River" into a cantata.[62] Eventually, of course, American music—especially black music—would conquer Europe as well. Harold Brydges penetrated to the heart of its appeal when he observed that "their plaintive songs, still tinged with the melancholy of slavery, awake the echoes of the woods, and thrill the listener with that luxurious sadness which so often characterizes the music of a conquered race—like the minor music of the Irish peasantry."[63]

Language and Speech

One traveler noted of New York that "half the languages of Europe" were being spoken by the immigrant populations of that city.[64] The same could be said of any big American city, but despite the large numbers of immigrants in the United States, there was little doubt that the English language dominated and was making rapid inroads into immigrant communities.[65] When he visited German enclaves in America, Baron Hübner noted that when immigrants spoke to their children in German, they were answered in English. He concluded that the third generation was "completely Americanised," except for their taste in music and beer.[66] Henry Sienkiewicz was also somewhat disconcerted that in Chicago's Polish neighborhoods in the 1870s "the English influence was clearly perceptible" in the speech of the children.[67] Of the foreign languages that were spoken in America, Maria Therese Blanc found that German was the most widespread, and that "the majority do not speak French."[68] Both Jacques Offenbach and Peter Tchaikovsky complained that nobody in the United States with whom they had dealt spoke anything but English.[69]

While this might be true, travelers from the British Isles discovered that American English and British English diverged considerably from each other.[70] Part of the difference is that American English has tended to accommodate greater functional changes (such as transforming a word from noun to adjective, from verb to noun, or from adjective to verb) than British English.[71] The American proclivity to turn nouns into verbs was especially striking to the British traveler. David Macrae gave the example of Americans "mailing" letters or "rooming" together, and Joseph Hatton said to Henry Irving, "I will 'interview' you, then, as they say in America."[72] Linguist Albert H. Marckwardt has argued that this tendency was even more prevalent out on the American frontier, where extensive mixing of different races and cultures produced a pidgin language.[73] When William Howard Russell traveled through the Southwest in 1882, he concluded that one of the wonders of that region was "extraordinary variety of dialects" of the Indians.[74] American Indian place names were employed everywhere in the United States (e.g. "Mississippi," "Susquehanna," and twenty-seven of the state names).[75]

Americans also borrowed heavily from immigrant languages, including the words *adobe, bonanza, patio, plaza,* and *savvy* from Spanish, and *kindergarten, loafer, dumb,* and *shyster* from German. From the French language, Americans borrowed the word *salon,* naming their taverns *saloons,* as well as *depot, picayune,* and *shanty.*[76] (George Augustus Sala was struck by the American preference for words such as *elevator, bureau, restaurant, janitor, morgue,* and *casket* over the British equivalents.[77]) If one added to this American figures of speech, the result was, as traveler William Archer put it, a "fantastic extravagance of phrase."[78] In his assessment of American speech, Harold Brydges claimed that Americans were "incomparable" for "originality of metaphor, quaint phrases, rough eloquence, and a manner at once ludicrous and dignified."[79]

American expressions were especially baffling to the traveler. Robert Somers was mystified when he encountered an American who told him to "hunt me up" when Somers got to Atlanta, nor could William Archer decipher the expression, "That cuts no ice with me."[80] In gold country, W. G. Marshall commented on a mining town called "You Bet," an expression he claimed corresponded to the British expression "Rather!" or, "I should think so!" Thus, the typical response when a man out West was asked if he liked whiskey was "'You bet!'—in a manner there is no mistaking."[81] William Hepworth Dixon discovered that the word "boss" was being used for "master," and in Denver, he ran across the phrase "gone up," which had been derived from "gone up a tree," or lynched.[82] F. Barham Zincke took note of a parting expression from one coach driver to another: "'Tom, be good to yourself.'"[83] As a rancher, Horace Annesley Vachell ran across the phrase, "'We bit off more'n we could chew,'" and in *The Last Chronicle of Barset* (1867) Anthony Trollope observed that "an American when he has spent a pleasant day will tell you that he has had 'a good time.'"[84] At least one British writer traced the development of a distinctive language in the United States to "the universal prevalence of the faculty of humour in all parts of America."

This exerted less of an influence on the other side of the Atlantic because "the English, in a lump, are not a humourous people."[85]

William Archer collected a large number of "Americanisms" from his 1899 stint in the United States, including "pretty good" ("a phrase of high commendation")[86] He also encountered regional variations (a man in the Bowery was a "mug" while in Chicago he was a "guy"), and condemned the American use of contractions ("an insidious laxity of pronunciation").[87] Also, in a reminder of how words that today seem totally innocuous were once embroiled in bitter controversy, Archer notes that the American word "scientist" was "received in England at the point of the bayonet," with the *Daily News* denouncing it as a "cheap and vulgar product of transatlantic slang."[88] Among the most prominent of Americanisms was "O.K." While its origins are in dispute, its success is not, and by the late nineteenth century it had commenced its ravages on the English speakers of Britain.[89] Today, it has been incorporated into virtually every language on the planet.[90]

The alarm among the British that American English represents a corrupting force is both a very old phenomenon and a contemporaneous one. David Hume, for instance, objected to Benjamin Franklin's adaptation of the noun "colony" into the verb "colonize," and an English reviewer of *Notes on the State of Virginia* took Thomas Jefferson to task for his use of the word "belittle." It should come as no surprise that Jefferson would later coin the word "Anglophobia."[91] Alexis de Tocqueville, in *Democracy in America*, noted that the educated British of the early nineteenth century complained that Americans were introducing new words into the language, giving new meanings to old English words, and mixing styles "in a singular manner."[92] The grousing continued into the twentieth century. In 1978, a member of the House of Lords used the word "hideous" to describe the American form of English, and in 1995, Prince Charles condemned American English for leading people "to invent all sorts of nouns and verbs, and make words that shouldn't be. I think we have to be a bit careful, otherwise the thing can get rather a mess."[93] While it was the British Empire that spread English around the world up until the late nineteenth century, it has been Americans who have been dominant since then in spreading the English language around the world.[94]

Another aspect of American speech that was noted by many travelers after the Civil War was swearing, which Charles Wentworth Dilke called an enthusiasm for making the air "blue with curses."[95] When his train broke down near Meridian, Mississippi, Robert Somers took note of the long strings of curse words that issued from the engineers who were trying to fix it.[96] W. Henry Barneby also complained that he had never heard such horrible swearing in his life, with Americans cramming into a sentence as many foul expressions as possible rather than being satisfied with one.[97] Describing the language of stagecoach drivers, William Francis Butler observed that it "consists of the smallest possible amount of dictionary words, a few Scriptural names rather irreverently used, a very large intermixture of 'git-ups' and ejaculatory 'hi's,' and a general tendency to blasphemy all round."[98] Ernst von Hesse-Wartegg claimed that the "savage curses" that emanated from the "bullwhackers" he encountered near Sidney, Nebraska, exceeded "even those of the Mississippi-riverboat captain."[99] While swearing offended the ears of the European traveler, James Bonwick admitted that the singular construction of oaths and their suggestion of peculiar ideas made it difficult to "restrain a smile."[100] As in many other areas of American life, there may also have been a class element to swearing, with cursing a way to challenge authority figures.[101]

Drinking in America acquired its own specialized vocabulary. The term that Westerners used for taking a drink, according to Thomas Hughes, was "washing the dust out of their throats."[102] J. W. Boddam-Whetham also ran across the expressions, "'Will you go on a bond?'" and "'Stranger, let's irrigate.'"[103] In the East, the mixing of drinks and the terms to describe them were more highly evolved. Drink names in New York included "cocktail, smash, sling, julep, back straightener, corpse reviver, moral suasion, and bottomless pit."[104] On his American tour in 1868, Charles Dickens was served a "Rocky Mountain sneezer," a concoction that was seemingly "compounded of all the spirits ever heard of in the world."[105]

Rudyard Kipling was especially critical of American speech, going so far as to claim that "the American has no language," but only "dialect, slang, provincialism, accent, and so forth."[106] Harold Brydges, however, emphasized that the English spoken in America was as good as that spoken in England, and that local dialects were less extreme than in Britain.[107] Scots writer "R. L. S." (most likely Robert Louis Stevenson) agreed, claiming that one could travel all over the United States and would "scarce meet with so marked a difference of accent as in the forty miles between Edinburgh and Glasgow, or of dialect as in the hundred miles between Edinburgh and Aberdeen."[108] The British were alternately amused and irritated when Americans called attention to their "English accents." British actor Henry Irving noted that one New York reporter told him that he "was surprised to find that I spoke English as well as he did."[109] On her way back to England after a one-year stay in the United States, E. Catherine Bates had the unsettling experience "of really hearing an 'English accent,' and very affected and artificial it sounded to me after a year's absence from it."[110]

Even words that the two English-speaking nations shared often had a different pronunciation. David Macrae observed that American pronunciations typically substituted the "oo" sound for the British "u" sound. Thus it was "Noo York" and "Noo Orleans" and "giving the devil his 'doo.'"[111] In New York, English traveler Stephen Buckland found that the locals pronounced syrup as "surrup," and maple as "mapple."[112] However, Americans did not drop "h" and "r" sounds from their speech, as did the British, and never pronounced "towards" as "towoards."[113]

In other differences, Americans referred to "stores" rather than shops and "helps" rather than servants. The person who had charge of anything in America was referred to as "Captain." While the Britisher might say "I think" or "I suppose," the American in the North said, "I guess," while the Southerner said, "I reckon."[114] (Charles Wentworth Dilke added that those in the West would most likely "calculate.")[115] Meat in America was "rare" rather than "under done."[116]

Emily Faithfull found that in just one area of vocabulary, train travel, nearly every word was different from the British: "The stations are called *depôts*, the carriages are 'cars,' the line is known as the 'track,' the engine is spoken of as a 'locomotive,' the guards as 'conductors,' the luggage is 'freight,' and the signal for starting is the cry of 'All aboard.'"[117] Theodora Guest added that a train that was "on time" in America was punctual.[118] The British historian Edward A. Freeman, who spent considerable time analyzing the differences between British and American speech, claimed that Americans were still using a great number of English words and phrases that were no longer current in England, but which "ignorant people therefore mistake for American inventions."[119]

A number of language usages revealed the American devotion to money. Paul de Rousiers noted that the standard greeting between two men was, "'How's business?'" It was, said Rousiers, "the first subject they think of speaking about."[120] Henry Sienkiewicz was struck by the American usage of the word "worth" to denote how much money a person had. Thus a person in America was "worth" so many thousands rather than "has" so many thousands.[121]

Humor

Humor is a notoriously slippery concept. The scholar Lawrence E. Mintz, veteran of countless conferences on humor, laments that, "We can't even agree upon a central definition of humor, much less on a universal outline for understanding its significance."[122] That has not stopped people from trying. Like so much else in American culture, humor was originally an English import. The English style of humor, which William Keough calls "genteel," puts a premium on wit and "amuses but does not wound."[123] But something happened to American humor in the nineteenth century, especially on the "edges of civilization." It became, according to Keough, nastier, prone to "violent exaggeration," with a raucous tone "poised a hair's breadth from cosmic grief."[124] Looking at the salient features of American humor in 1866, a British writer found a "strong contempt for humbug, and for 'highfalutin' sentiment," as well as a "dislike for the declaration of lofty abstract principles." Compared to British humor, it was drier, keener, and "often more profane."[125]

James Fullarton Muirhead claimed that humor in the United States contained numerous subtleties. These included "its utter irreverence, its droll extravagance, its dry suggestiveness, its *naiveté* (real or apparent), its affectation of seriousness, its fondness for antithesis and anti-climax."[126] He found a number of similarities between the American and Scottish styles of humor. The English, in comparison, were slow "to take up a joke that is anything less than obvious." (Perhaps the

English sense of humor was retarded by "the tremendous seriousness with which the Englishman takes himself and everything else."[127]) In one example of the "dry suggestiveness" of American humor, Muirhead related the following joke: "Mrs. William Hankins lighted her fire with coal oil on February 28. Her clothes now fit the present Mrs. Hankins to a T." Muirhead claimed that while the Englishman would eventually see the point of such a jest, "the more delicate forms of this allusive style of wit will often escape him altogether."[128]

David Macrae believed that extravagant exaggeration and the American love of the immense, referred to earlier, were essential elements of American humor:

> The trees so tall, that it took two men and a boy to see to the top, the first looking till he was tired, and the next beginning where the first left off … The man who snored so loud that he had to sleep two doors off to keep from awakening himself … The patent hair-renovator, so strong that a little of it rubbed on the door-step brought out a strong crop of bristles, and saved the expense of a door-mat … The horse that ran so fast that its shadow couldn't keep up with it.[129]

In another example of exaggeration in American humor, Muirhead related the joke of the woman who was suddenly overtaken by a tornado. She looked up from her gardening to find "the air black with her intimate friends."[130]

If immensity and exaggeration were essential to the American joke, the dead-pan delivery was also a key element. Until his death in 1867, Artemus Ward (Charles Farrar Browne) was probably the best-known American humorist, both in the United States and in Britain (where he lectured and contributed to *Punch*). While Ward's heavy reliance on dialect has not aged well, his style of delivery, described as "imperturbable gravity of countenance, pleased if you laugh, and doubly pleased if you are credulous enough to be awed," would be characteristic of American humor for the rest of the nineteenth century.[131] Mark Twain would assume the mantle of America's most celebrated humorist, and like Ward, Twain was the master of the understated style. At a dinner in New York, Léon Paul Blouet overheard Twain say, "I was in the war too—for a fortnight—but I found I was on the strong side—so I retired—to make the fight even." The joke was delivered, said Blouet, in Twain's "inimitable drawl."[132] Stephen Buckland found that Americans told their stories "with an air of truth that would, of itself, deceive the most suspicious." In one variant on the fast horse theme, someone told Buckland that when he rode his horse out on the track, the horse was "so fast that the whole time, I saw my back directly before me, and was twice in danger of riding over myself."[133] Oscar Wilde denied the existence of American humor altogether (he claimed that the American was "the most abnormally serious creature who ever existed") but perhaps Wilde, like other visitors, was the victim of the dry-as-dust delivery that characterized the American style of joke telling.[134]

Emily Faithfull cited as examples of American humor the "singular" names miners gave to their settlements: "Red Dog, You Bet, Jackass Gulch, Brandy Flat, Gospel Swamp, Slap Jack, Grizzly Flat, and Poverty Hill."[135] In contrast to Wilde, Faithfull said that she found humor everywhere in America "in the newspapers as well as in the pulpit," and claimed to have seen the Rev. Henry Ward Beecher's congregation "convulsed with laughter" at a comic story that he told.[136] In San Francisco, J. W. Boddam-Whetham encountered an example of American humor that he described as "particularly odd." It was a sign on a street railway car that read, "'No gentleman will occupy more seats than one at a time—unless he be twins.'"[137] In Chicago, Bram Stoker ran across a railing with a sign attached that read: "Wanted. A Loafer to Sit on This Rail." Stoker described American humor as "mainly of a dry kind."[138]

Humor was also a mainstay of American newspapers, whose style Arnot Reid described as "humorous and a little improper."[139] He provided examples in the form of headlines: "Dead Men's Talk" (a story on a spiritualist meeting), "Decorated with Handcuffs" (the arrest of a forger), "Students Seeking Blood" (two students attempting to arrange a duel).[140] There was also the tendency of American newspapers to treat even serious subjects with levity, which James Fullarton Muirhead cited as evidence that Americans did not know when to stop being funny.[141] W. E. Adams suggested that one form of American humor was the "surprise party," an institution not embraced by nations (such as Britain) "where practical jokes are less appreciated than they are in America."[142] During his 1883–84 tour of America, the actor Henry Irving was feted by a number of gentlemen's clubs, and the only difference that Irving could discern between these clubs and the London clubs that he was familiar with was that the American after-dinner speeches were mostly humorous, while the English speeches tended toward the solemn.[143] Alexandra Gripenberg also took note of the proclivity of Americans to mix in "a great many anecdotes, jokes, and comparisons" in their speeches, a practice that the dour Finn condemned as "superficial."[144]

As for the jokes themselves, one that was in wide circulation in the West in the late nineteenth century concerns the funeral of a woman who had long persecuted her husband. As her coffin was being carried into the cemetery, it bumped up against a post. The pall bearers heard a scream from within, the coffin lid was unscrewed, and the woman lived for another three years. When the woman died again, and the coffin was once more being hoisted, the husband solemnly instructed the pall bearers, "Boys—*mind that post.*"[145] In Florida, where steamboats had to be built with extremely light drafts to get over shallow stretches of water, an Englishman remarked to one of the captains, "I understand, captain, that you think nothing of steaming across a meadow where there's been a heavy fall of dew." "Well, I don't know about that," replied the captain, "but it's true we have sometimes to send a man ahead with a watering-pot!"[146]

Sometimes humor combined with civic boosterism. William Saunders claimed that when he was in San Antonio he was told that this was a town where "people never die; very old persons sometimes dry up and are blown away, but cemeteries are unnecessary."[147] A similar tale was told to Charles Wentworth Dilke considering Leavenworth, a town so healthy that when they inaugurated the new cemetery they had to shoot someone on purpose.[148] Indeed, the merging of humor with the language of boosterism has been a constant throughout American history. Benjamin Franklin, for instance, played the role of both humorist and colonial booster when he claimed that "the very tails of the American sheep are so laden with wool that each has a Car or Waggon on four little wheels to support and keep it from trailing on the ground."[149]

Copyright and Journalism

One of the great complaints of European writers was the lack of copyright protection in America. Indeed, copyright law had been a transatlantic issue for virtually the entire nineteenth century. The first American copyright law, passed in 1790, offered no copyright protection for foreign writers. In 1891, the law was expanded to include copyright protection for foreign writers, as long as the works of that author were printed and bound in the United States.[150]

Concerns about copyright arguably ruined Charles Dickens' first visit to America in 1842. Obsessed by American pirating of his books, Dickens in speech after speech raged against copyright infringement. He raised the issue in Boston, and in a speech at Hartford he once again appealed for copyright reform. The local paper responded that "we want no advice upon this subject, and it will be better for Mr. Dickens, if he refrains from introducing the matter hereafter."[151] In New York, his hosts begged Dickens to give up his campaign, but Dickens was undeterred and mentioned it once again. In Washington, he handed over a petition for international copyright reform signed by American writers to the House and Senate.[152] Dickens made an irritating presence of himself, which unleashed an enormous press backlash against him.[153] Striking back not only against the press but also against the America that had disappointed him, Dickens produced the vitriolic *American Notes* (1842), and his savage parody of life in the United States, *Martin Chuzzlewit* (1843–44).

After the war, David Macrae raised the issue of copyright infringement with American poet Henry Wadsworth Longfellow, who told him that the resistance to copyright legislation lay with a "lower class of publishers and booksellers here."[154] When Henry Latham spoke to Longfellow about the same issue, the poet told him that the solution was to make all American copyrights valid in England and all English copyrights valid in America. Oscar Wilde encountered a notable example of copyright infringement on a train trip West. As on every American train, boys circulated through the coaches selling food, magazines and, on this particular trip, editions of Wilde's own poems. They were, according to Wilde, "vilely printed on a kind of grey blotting paper," and sold for ten cents. When Wilde called the boys over and explained that selling copies of his poems without paying him was striking a blow at literature, the boys told Wilde that they were making a profit on it and that was all they cared about.[155]

No less incensed at American copyright violations than Dickens or Wilde was Rudyard Kipling. Kipling had stopped in Japan before he came to America, and had found pirated editions of his books published by the American firm Seaside Publishing Company.[156] But when Kipling interviewed Mark Twain (Kipling's two great American heroes were Twain and Bret Harte), Twain seemed notably unconcerned about the issue of copyright. Twain insisted that no law could make a book thrive or die, and that copyright should be like real estate, to be disposed of however the holder desired.[157] There were also numerous instances of British piracy of American literature. Harold Brydges cites the case of American author Lew Wallace, who discovered that thousands of unauthorized copies of his novel *Ben Hur* were being sold in London. The pirates were not only profiting from Wallace's work, but had changed the subtitle, had inserted their own preface, and had omitted several stories from the book.[158]

Perhaps one unintended good that came out of the lack of copyright protection in America was that it forced American writers out of literature and into journalism, which benefitted the readers of American newspapers.[159] Harold Brydges claimed that American reporters were far better than their British counterparts in providing "bright, sparkling descriptions," and their efforts were supported by the American public, who were ravenous consumers of newspapers.[160] Summing up the American attitude toward newspapers, Henry Sienkiewicz argued that they were as "indispensable as bread itself."[161] David Macrae called America "a world of newspapers," claiming that more dailies were published in the state of New York than in England, Scotland and Ireland put together.[162] A Kansas homesteader noted that he had read articles asserting that people moved West to escape civilization, but he claimed that the opposite was the case for most Westerners. "So eager were we to keep in touch with civilization," he said, "that even when we could not afford a shotgun and ammunition to kill rabbits, we subscribed to newspapers and periodicals, and bought books."[163]

In the United States, 970 metropolitan dailies were being published in 1870. By 1900 there were over 2,200. American newspapers tended to be large (averaging twenty-four to thirty-six pages) with nine to ten editions published daily.[164] Multiple newspapers were published both in medium-sized cities (Memphis had five daily newspapers in 1871) and in small towns. W. G. Marshall found that the remote mining community of Leadville, Colorado, had four daily newspapers in 1879.[165] Cheyenne, Wyoming, which had a population of less than 800 in the late 1860s, could also boast of four newspapers.[166]

But according to James Bryce, one consequence of the American appetite for news and the keen journalistic competition was that writers were disposed to "take their chance" as far as the accuracy of the information they had acquired.[167] Charles Dickens complained of newspaper stories in the United States in which, "I say all sorts of things that I never said, go to all sorts of places that I never saw or heard of, and have done all manner of things (in some previous state of existence I suppose) that have quite escaped my memory."[168] There was also the aggressive behavior of reporters toward their subjects, which William Howard Russell referred to as being "accosted in the most familiar way by persons whom they have never seen in their lives."[169] When the story finally appeared, what was revealed, according to Russell, was not an accurate summation of the facts but a display of the journalist's "astonishing powers of imagination."[170] Knut Hamsun called American journalists "powdered-blackened pirates," and Oscar Wilde claimed that journalism in the United States had been taken to its "grossest and most brutal extreme."[171] The American newspaper's emphasis on the sensational, the frivolous, and lies, were almost single-handedly responsible for killing what Matthew Arnold called "the feeling for what is elevated."[172]

It is doubtful that many newspaper readers in the United States yearned after the elevation that Arnold promoted simply because it was so dull in its unadulterated form. Instead, Americans preferred the combination of "wit, humour, and buffoonery with more serious matter" that was the hallmark of American journalism.[173] Another characteristic of the American press was its appetite for murder and mayhem. James Fullarton Muirhead observed that if restraint was a sign of power, "then the American press is weak indeed."[174] One newspaper writer told Horace Annesley Vachell that his editor had instructed him to include at least one murder or suicide in fifteen of the paper's sixteen pages. Such an approach was not deemed necessary for the sixteenth page because it was devoted to editorials, which nobody read anyway.[175] Another staple of American papers, according to J. W. Boddam-Whetham, was the exaggerated retelling of any scandal that happened in England.[176] The one factor that mitigated journalism's destructive potential, according to Harold Brydges, was that even though everyone in America read the newspapers, nobody believed them.[177]

It was not that European newspapers were greatly better. Jacques Offenbach claimed that while the editors of American newspapers were tyrannized by religious sects and political parties, editors in Europe were oppressed by the government.[178] From an earlier era, Tocqueville had expressed his ambivalence about the American free press, admitting that he loved it "out of consideration for the evils that it prevents far more than for the good that it does."[179] James Bryce had similar feelings. He complained that American journalists often played fast and loose with the facts, but admitted that they provided a service in exposing evil-doers, who otherwise might escape under the standards of more rigorous evidence.[180]

One feature of American newspapers that often surprised Europeans was the extensive coverage of European news. Englishman Arnot Reid believed that there were two reasons for this. First, because of the large numbers of immigrants in America, there was a great deal of interest—especially among the Irish and the Germans—in developments in Europe. In addition, it was easier to deliver such items to American newspaper readers because of the time difference between Europe and America. News of events in Europe could be picked up over the wire in time to print in American morning editions.[181] In contrast, said Reid, "British newspapers tell us next to nothing of the life of America," and as a consequence the English were able to maintain "a wonderful ignorance of and carelessness regarding things American."[182] Frenchman Léon Paul Blouet also found much to admire in American journalism. He condemned English newspapers because their only virtue was "facts in all their aridity," and French papers because they took their cue from the provincial French public and served up "nothing but French dishes."[183] In contrast, American journalism was "spicy, lively, bright," and if the facts presented were not exact, "so much the worse for the facts."[184]

Notes

1. Tocqueville said of the world's civilized nations that "few have made less progress in the higher sciences or produced a smaller number of great artists, illustrious poets, and celebrated writers than the United States." Alexis de Tocqueville, *Democracy in America* [1835], trans. Arthur Goldhammer (New York: Library of America, 2004), 516. Tocqueville called Americans "the portion of the English people charged with exploiting the forests of the New World, while the rest of the nation, granted more leisure and less preoccupied with life's material cares, can indulge in thought and develop the human mind in every way possible." Ibid., 517.
2. Jacques Offenbach, *Orpheus in America: Offenbach's Diary of His Journey to the New World*, trans. Lander MacClintock (New York: Greenwood Press, 1969), 70.
3. A. Maurice Low, *The American People: A Study in National Psychology*, v.1 (Boston: Houghton Mifflin, 1909), 37.
4. Lepel Henry Griffin, *The Great Republic* [1884] (New York: Arno Press, 1974), 95–96; 97; Harold Brydges, *Uncle Sam at Home* (New York: Henry Holt and Co., 1888), 150.
5. Brydges, 150, 152.
6. F. Barham Zincke, *Last Winter in the United States: Being Table Talk Collected During a Tour Through the Late Southern Confederation, the Far West, the Rocky Mountains, &c.* [1868] (Freeport, NY: Books for Libraries Press, 1970), 167.
7. Matthew Arnold, "Civilization in the United States," in *Civilization in the United States: First and Last Impressions of America* [1888] (Freeport, NY: Books for Libraries Press, 1972), 172, 173. Henry James summarized what he saw as the deficiencies of American civilization in his 1879 biography of Hawthorne: "No sovereign, no court, no personal loyalty, no aristocracy, no church, no clergy, no army, no diplomatic service, no country gentlemen, no palaces, no castles, nor manors, nor old country-houses, nor parsonages, nor thatched cottages, nor ivied ruins; no cathedrals, nor abbeys, nor little Norman churches, no great Universities nor public schools—no Oxford, nor Eton, nor Harrow; no literature, no novels, no museums, no pictures, no political society, no sporting class—no Epsom nor Ascot." Quoted in Christopher Mulvey, *Transatlantic Manners: Social Patterns in Nineteenth-Century Anglo-American Travel Literature* (Cambridge: Cambridge University Press, 1990), 214.
8. Quoted in Joseph Hatton, *Henry Irving's Impressions of America, Narrated in a Series of Sketches, Chronicles, and Conversations* [1884], v. 2 (New York: Benjamin Blom, 1971), 106, 107. E. Catherine Bates argued that "it is only within the last fifty years that America has had time to turn round and think of a literature or art on her own account at all." E. Catherine Bates, *A Year in the Great Republic*, v. 1 (London: Ward & Downey, 1887), 90.
9. Henry Adams, *The Education of Henry Adams* [1907] (Boston: Houghton Mifflin, 1961), 239, 238.

10. Hamilton Aïdé, "Social Aspects of American Life," *The Nineteenth Century* 29, no. 172 (June 1891), 900–901.

11. Ernst von Hesse-Wartegg, *Travels on the Lower Mississippi, 1879–1880*, trans. and ed. Frederic Trautmann (Columbia: University of Missouri Press, 1990), 89–91.

12. Quoted in Hatton, v. 2, 122–123.

13. From Boston, Dickens reported, "They took it so tremendously last night that I was stopped every five minutes. One poor young girl in mourning burst into a passion of grief about Tiny Tim, and was taken out." Charles Dickens to Miss Georgina Hogarth, 27 and 28 February 1868. Charles Dickens, *The Letters of Charles Dickens*, v. 3, ed. Graham Storey (Oxford: Clarendon Press, 2002), 61–62.

14. Charles Dickens to W. C. Macready, 21 March 1868. *The Letters of Charles Dickens*, 82.

15. Zincke, 63.

16. Jacques Offenbach took note of the American "machines whose perfection and power astound the imagination." Offenbach, 69.

17. Sarah Bernhardt, *Memories of my Life* [1907] (Gross Pointe, MI: Scholarly Press, 1968), 389. Giuseppe Giacosa called the bridge "the most artistic of the mechanical endeavors accomplished by man." Quoted in Andrew J. Torrielli, *Italian Opinion on America, As Revealed by Italian Travelers, 1850–1900*, trans. from Italian by Pietro Bonomi (Cambridge, MA: Harvard University Press, 1941), 238. W. E. Adams referred to the Brooklyn Bridge as "one of the wonders of America." W. E. Adams, *Our American Cousins: Being Personal Impressions of the People and Institutions of the United States* (London: Walter Scott, 1883), 210.

18. Paul Bourget, *Outre-Mer: Impressions of America* (London: T. Fisher Unwin, 1895), 30.

19. Robert Somers, *The Southern States Since the War, 1870–71* [1871] (Tuscaloosa: University of Alabama Press, 1965), 235; Oscar Wilde, "Impressions of America," in Oscar Wilde, *The Works of Oscar Wilde* (New York: AMS Press, 1972), 252–253.

20. Oscar Wilde, *Decorative Art in America: A Lecture by Oscar Wilde Together with Letters, Reviews and Interviews*, ed. Richard Butler Glaenzer (New York: Brentano's, 1906), 14,

21. Wilde, *Decorative Art*, 5. Wilde also found "meaningless chandeliers and machine-made furniture, generally of rosewood, which creaked dismally under the weight of the ubiquitous interviewer," and concluded that American homes were "ill designed, decorated shabbily and in bad taste." Ibid., 5, 181n. 1.

22. Wilde, *Decorative Art*, 6, 14. The results, promised Wilde, would be nothing short of millennarian: "you would soon raise up a race of handicraftsmen who would transform the face of your country." Art, according to Wilde, would "create a new brotherhood among men" and "under its beneficent influences war might pass away." Ibid., 14–15, 13. In another lecture, "The English Renaissance of Art," Wilde held out hope that America could make a significant contribution to aestheticism, and that the very absence of tradition in the United States might be a strength rather than a weakness. Oscar Wilde, "The English Renaissance of Art," in Oscar Wilde, *The Essays of Oscar Wilde* [1916], ed. Albert and Charles Boni (Bonibooks, 1935), 468.

23. Oscar Wilde, "American Women," in Oscar Wilde, *The Works of Oscar Wilde* (New York: AMS Press, 1972), 7; Oscar Wilde, "Impressions of America," 254, 260.

24. David Macrae, *The Americans at Home* [1870] (New York: E. P. Dutton, 1952), 16; James Bryce, *The American Commonwealth*, v.2 (New York: The Commonwealth Publishing Co., 1908), 732.

25. William Howard Russell, *Hesperothen, Notes from the West: A Record of a Ramble in the United States and Canada in the Spring and Summer of 1881*, v. 2 (London: S. Low, Marston, Searle & Rivington, 1882), 46.

26. Ratzel quoted in "A German Appraisal of the United States," *Atlantic Monthly* 75, no. 447 (January 1895), 125.

27. William Hepworth Dixon, *New America* (Philadelphia: J. B. Lippincott, 1869), 249; Windham Thomas Wyndham-Quin, *The Great Divide: Travels in the Upper Yellowstone in the Summer of 1874* (London: Chatto and Windus, 1876), 2.
28. Somers, 180.
29. Phil Robinson, *Sinners and Saints: A Tour Across the States, and Round Them; with Three Months Among the Mormons* (Boston: Roberts Brothers, 1883), 330. Robinson referred to the "prodigious widths of land" he had traveled through and insisted that "the mere fact of traversing so much space had fascinations." Ibid., 303.
30. S. C. de Soissons, *A Parisian in America* (Boston: Estes and Lauriat, 1896), 46. See also Macrae, 15.
31. Low, v. 2, 506.
32. Bryce, v. 2, 786.
33. Theodora Guest, *A Round Trip in North America* (London: Edward Stanford, 1895), 68.
34. Daniel J. Boorstin, *The Americans: The National Experience* (New York: Random House, 1965), 295.
35. Soissons, 45.
36. Macrae, 16; Harold Brydges observed that the American "delights in bulk … He is proud to have had the greatest fires, and the biggest swindles. The greatest war, the longest railroad, the highest statue, the largest rivers, the biggest herds of swine, the highest tariff and the biggest piles of grain—all are classified under one head." Brydges, 7, 8.
37. Marie Therese de Solms Blanc, *The Condition of Woman in the United States: A Traveller's Notes*, trans. Abby Langdon Alger [1895] (New York: Arno Press, 1972), 223.
38. "He must have something large, enormous, immense. He is inclined to judge everything by its size," said Blouet. Max O'rell and Jack Allyn, *Jonathan and His Continent: Rambles Through American Society*, trans. Madame Paul Blouet (Bristol: J. W. Arrowsmith, 1889), 278.
39. Oscar Wilde, "The American Man," in Oscar Wilde, *The Collected Oscar Wilde* (New York: Barnes and Noble Classics, 2007), 306.
40. Soissons, 186.
41. Ibid., 187.
42. Larry Starr and Christopher Waterman, *Popular Music: From Minstrelsy to MP3* (New York: Oxford University Press, 2010), 24.
43. Offenbach, 67, 68.
44. John Campbell Argyll, *A Trip to the Tropics and Home Through America* (London: Hurst and Blackett, 1867), 208.
45. Quoted in Leroy Ashby, *With Amusement for All: A History of American Popular Culture Since 1830* (Lexington: University Press of Kentucky, 2006), 11.
46. Starr and Waterman, 21.
47. Ashby, 13.
48. Starr and Waterman, 25.
49. Ashby, 87–88. As the twentieth century began, Eddie Cantor and Al Jolson, two Jews with Eastern European roots, were performing in blackface while real black performers were limited to the old roles of buffoons speaking in dialect. The popularity of blackface continued well into the middle of the century. *Amos 'n' Andy*, in which two black characters were played by two white actors, was one of the most popular radio shows in American history. As late as World War II, Bing Crosby did two blackface turns in the films *Holiday Inn* (1942) and *Dixie* (1943). See Ashby, 124, 254–255 and Kenneth D. Rose, *Myth and the Greatest Generation: A Social History of Americans in World War II* (New York: Routledge, 2008), 130.
50. This gave the English traveler another opportunity to condemn the Irish and other Celts. William Howard Russell, for instance, saw Southerners dancing what he called "an Irish jig" while a fiddle and banjo player "played uncouth music." Russell quoted

in Grady McWhiney, *Cracker Culture: Celtic Ways in the Old South* (Tuscaloosa: University of Alabama Press, 1988), 118. An Englishwoman described this music as "most defective." Ibid., 123. Russell, however, praised the "great sweetness" and "extraordinary melodies" of the black workers that he heard singing in a Richmond tobacco warehouse. Russell, v. 1, 97.

51. Starr and Waterman, 24.

52. George Augustus Sala, *America Revisited: From the Bay of New York to the Gulf of Mexico and From Lake Michigan to the Pacific* (London: Vizetelly & Co., n.d.), 174.

53. Henry M. Stanley, *My Early Travels and Adventures in America* [1895] (Lincoln: University of Nebraska Press, 1982), 56.

54. W. G. Marshall, *Through America: Nine Months in the United States* (London: Sampson, Low, Marston, Searle & Rivington, 1881), 136.

55. James Fullarton Muirhead, *The Land of Contrasts: A Briton's View of his American Kin* (London: Lamson, Wolffe and Co., 1898), 22.

56. Henry Sienkiewicz, *Portrait of America: Letters of Henry Sienkiewicz*, trans. and ed. Charles Morley (New York: Columbia University Press, 1959), 202–203.

57. William A. Bell, *New Tracks in North America: A Journal of Travel and Adventure Whilst Engaged in the Survey for a Southern Railroad to the Pacific Ocean During 1867–8* [1870] (Albuquerque: Horn and Wallace, 1965), 149, 150.

58. Thomas J. Schlereth, *Victorian America: Transformations in Everyday Life, 1876–1915* (New York: Harper Perennial, 1992), 211.

59. Alexandra Gripenberg, *A Half Year in the New World: Miscellaneous Sketches of Travel in the United States* [1889], trans. and ed. Ernest J. Moyne (Newark: University of Delaware Press, 1954), 71. Of this gathering, Gripenberg noted that Twain "talked on until a late hour, humorously, modestly, pleasantly, and brilliantly. The whole while it seemed as though one could hear under his words the beating of his great, warm heart, just as his large, warm hand seemed always ready secretly to put money into the hand of the whole world." Ibid., 72.

60. Madame de San Carlos, "Americans at Home," *Review of Reviews* 1, no. 6 (June 1890), 487.

61. Lionel Carley, "1862–1888: From Bradford to Leipzig," in *Delius: A Life in Letters, 1862–1908*, ed. Lionel Carley (Cambridge, MA: Harvard University Press, 1983), 5.

62. See Ludmilla Bradová, "Antoní Dvořák, 1841–1904," in *Abroad in America: Visitors to the New Nation, 1776–1914* (Reading: MA: Addison-Wesley, 1976), 233, 235.

63. Brydges, 85.

64. W. F. Rae, *Westward by Rail: The New Route to the East* [1871] (New York: Promontory Press, 1974), 20.

65. Bill Bryson has argued that English tended to dominate over immigrant languages because the extreme mobility of Americans, and the intermingling of disparate groups, forced immigrants to adopt a form of communication that all could understand. In addition, "the desire for a common national identity encouraged people to settle on a single way of speaking." Bill Bryson, *The Mother Tongue: English and How It Got That Way* (New York: William Morrow, 1990), 169.

66. Baron Hübner, *A Ramble Round the World, 1871*, trans. Lady Elizabeth Herbert (London: MacMillan and Co., 1878), 43.

67. Sienkiewicz, 278. Sienkiewicz noted that "English expressions soon force their way into these linguistic gaps and fissures, and the decay of the native speech inevitably sets in. One might say that the English language is wafted in the wind and somehow is inhaled involuntarily by those who arrive from Europe." Ibid., 288–289.

68. Blanc, 215. One exception was New Orleans, where as late as 1892 Harry Kessler observed that "one hardly hears a word of English." Harry Kessler, *Journey to the Abyss: The Diaries of Count Harry Kessler, 1880–1918*, trans. and ed. Laird Easton (New York: Knopf, 2011), 68. F. Barham Zincke observed that in New Orleans the French

language was used extensively: "In the street cars one is almost sure to hear it, coming often from the mouths of coloured people." Zincke, 134.

69. Offenbach, 46–47; Peter Tchaikovsky, *The Diaries of Tchaikovsky*, trans. Wladimir Lakond (New York: W. W. Norton, 1945), 325.

70. In his essay "Concerning the American Language," Mark Twain claimed that "I didn't speak English at all,—I only spoke American." Mark Twain, "Concerning the American Language," [1882] in *Collected Tales, Sketches, Speeches and Essays*, v. 1 (New York: Library of America, 1992), 830.

71. Albert H. Marckwardt, *American English* (New York: Oxford University Press, 1980), 92.

72. Macrae, 555; Hatton, v. 1, 22.

73. Marckwardt, 93. Marckwardt argues that "the frontiersman had to cope daily with many languages, Indian and European, and strange-sounding, half-understood words were an important part of his linguistic experience. Furthermore, groups now known to have been present on the frontier, like Black trappers and cowboys, had elaborate oral traditions of their own." Ibid., 112.

74. Russell, v. 2, 13.

75. Boorstin, 300–301.

76. Ibid., 288, 297, 287.

77. Sala, 22.

78. William Archer, *America To-Day: Observations and Reflections* [1899] (New York: Arno Press, 1974), 246.

79. Brydges, 22. Frenchman Paul Bourget also claimed that "the habitual excess of metaphor" was an "American instinct." Bourget, 39.

80. Somers, 95; Archer, 250.

81. Marshall, 252. Variations on this expression, as identified by J. W. Boddam-Whetham, included "bet your life," and "bet your boots." The latter expression, according to Boddam-Whetham, "extends all through the West, and, I am sorry to say, up into British Columbia." J. W. Boddam-Whetham, *Western Wanderings: A Record of Travel in the Evening Land* (London: Richard Bentley and Son, 1874), 199.

82. Dixon, 435, 97.

83. Zincke, 163.

84. Horace Annesley Vachell, *Life and Sport on the Pacific Slope* (New York: Dodd, Mead and Co., 1901), 123; Anthony Trollope, *The Last Chronicle of Barset* [1867] (New York: Penguin Books, 2002), 534.

85. Anonymous, "The Great American Language," *The Cornhill Magazine* 11 (New Series, October 1888), 376.

86. Archer, 35.

87. Ibid., 251, 234.

88. Ibid., 240.

89. Boorstin, 287.

90. See Bryson, 164–166.

91. Boorstin, 280; Bryson, 172–173.

92. Tocqueville, 547.

93. Prince Charles quoted in Mordecai Richler, "Introduction," to Mark Twain, *The Innocents Abroad* (New York: Oxford University Press, 1996), xlv.

94. Bill Bryson has claimed that "without America's contribution English today would enjoy a global importance about on a par with Portuguese." Bryson, 174–175.

95. Charles Wentworth Dilke, *Greater Britain: A Record of Travel in English-Speaking Countries* (London: Macmillan and Co., 1890), 132.

96. Somers, 149–150.

97. W. Henry Barneby, *Life and Labor in the Far, Far West: Being Notes of a Tour in the Western States, British Columbia, Manitoba, and the North-West* (London: Cassell & Co., 1884), 169, 174.

98. William Francis Butler, *The Great Lone Land: A Narrative of Travel and Adventure in the North-West of America* [1872] (Rutland, VT: Charles E. Tuttle, 1968), 76.

99. Ernst von Hesse-Wartegg, "Across Nebraska by Train in 1877: The Travels of Ernst von Hesse-Wartegg," trans. and ed. Frederic Trautmann, *Nebraska History* 65, no. 3 (Fall 1984), 419–420.

100. Quoted in Robert G. Athearn, *Westward the Briton* (Lincoln: University of Nebraska Press, 1953), 70.

101. See John C. Burnham, *Bad Habits: Drinking, Smoking, Taking Drugs, Gambling, Sexual Misbehavior, and Swearing in American History* (New York: New York University Press, 1993), 214–215.

102. Thomas Hughes, "A Week in the West," part 5, *MacMillan's Magazine* 25 (January 1872), 380.

103. Boddam-Whetham, 253.

104. Stephen Buckland, "Eating and Drinking In America:—A Stroll Among the Saloons of New York," *MacMillan's Magazine* 16 (October 1867), 458.

105. Charles Dickens to Charles Fechter, 24 February 1868, *The Letters of Charles Dickens*, 57.

106. Rudyard Kipling, *American Notes* [1891] (Norman: University of Oklahoma Press, 1981), 20.

107. Brydges, 218.

108. R. L. S., "The Foreigner at Home," *The Cornhill Magazine* 45 (May 1882), 534.

109. Irving quoted in Hatton, v. 1, 134.

110. Bates, 315.

111. Macrae, 553.

112. Buckland, 454, 461.

113. Anonymous, "The Great American Language," 365.

114. Macrae, 554.

115. Dilke, 4.

116. Argyll, 205.

117. Emily Faithfull, *Three Visits to America* (New York: Fowler & Wells, 1884), 48.

118. Guest, 241.

119. Edward A. Freeman, *Some Impressions of the United States* (London: Longmans, Green, and Co., 1883), 89.

120. Paul de Rousiers, *American Life*, trans. A. J. Herbertson (New York: Firmin-Didot, 1892), 13.

121. See Sienkiewicz, 19.

122. Lawrence E. Mintz, "Introduction," to *Humor in America: A Research Guide to Genres and Topics*, ed. Lawrence E. Mintz (New York: Greenwood Press, 1988), ix. In perhaps the most ambitious attempt to discover what it is that's funny, Dr. Richard Wiseman of the University of Herfordshire organized a project called Laugh Lab in 2001. The experiment encouraged people to submit their own jokes via the internet (there were 10,000 entries) and to vote on the funniest joke (some 100,000 voted). Along the way, significant differences emerged between what men and women thought was funny, as well as key national variations in humor. Like so many who have tried, Laugh Lab researchers could come to no definitive conclusions about humor, although they did identify what was voted as the world's funniest joke:

> Sherlock Holmes and Dr. Watson go camping, and pitch their tent under the stars. During the night, Holmes wakes his companion and says: 'Watson, look up at the stars, and tell me what you deduce.'
> Watson says: 'I see millions of stars, and even if a few of those have planets, it's quite likely there are some planets like Earth, and if there a few planets like Earth out there, there might also be life.'

'Watson, you idiot. Somebody stole our tent.'

Polly Stewart, "Scientists Name World's Funniest Joke. Really." *Sacramento Bee*, 21 December 2001.

123. William Keough, *Punchlines: The Violence of American Humor* (New York: Paragon House, 1990), 3.
124. Ibid., 4–9.
125. Anonymous, "American Humour," *The Cornhill Magazine* 13 (January 1866), 35. One who struggled with the origins and elements of what he called "tall talk" was historian Daniel Boorstin. He found so many elements of ambiguity in tall talk that in the end he could only ask, "Was it or was it not humor?" Boorstin, 290.
126. Muirhead, 134.
127. Ibid., 130, 139. In a warning to his son, Lord Chesterfield said that "frequent laughter is the characteristic of ill manner in which the mob express their silly joy in silly things." Quoted in Keough, 3.
128. Muirhead, 137–138.
129. Macrae, 17.
130. Muirhead, 137.
131. Anonymous, "American Humour," 36.
132. O'rell, 103.
133. Buckland, 458.
134. Wilde, "American Man," 308–309. W. E. Adams, who visited America in the same year as Wilde, said that "Americans generally have so much of the humorous element in their character and composition that it bubbles out in almost all they say or write." W. E. Adams, 93.
135. Faithfull, 215. William A. Bell compared the names of American miners' camps, such as "Gulcher Diggins," "Buckskin Joe," "Hooked Man's Prairie," etc. with Hispanic place names ("Santa Domingo," "Spirito Sancto," "Socorro" trail, etc.) and concluded that this demonstrated the contrast between "the rough manly Saxon pioneer and the indolent, superstitious Mexican." Bell, 145.
136. Faithfull, 367. F. Barham Zincke also attended one of Beecher's sermons, and reported the following: "In speaking of excessive drinking, he [Beecher] said 'that the American had not the excuse which the Englishman had, for the latter had so much water outside, that there was a reason for his never taking any inside.' This was received by the congregation with great laughter, as were some other sallies contained in the sermon." Zincke, 21.
137. Boddam-Whetham, 185.
138. Bram Stoker, "A Glimpse of America" [1886] in *Bram Stoker's A Glimpse of America and Other Lectures, Interviews and Essays* (Westcliff-on-Sea, UK: 2002), 27.
139. Arnot Reid, "The English and the American Press," *The Nineteenth Century* 22, no. 125 (July 1867), 224.
140. Ibid., 225.
141. See Muirhead, 151–152. George Augustus Sala also called attention to the American press' "persistent and seemingly incurable drollery." Sala, 374. In one example of over-the-top humor, Mark Twain wrote a story for the *Virginia City Enterprise* called the "Empire City Massacre" that described the murder of a woman and her nine children by a man named Hopkins. The outlandish details clearly revealed that this story was a hoax ("Hopkins dashed into Carson on horseback, with his throat cut from ear to ear, and bearing in his hand a reeking scalp from which the warm, smoking blood was still dripping") but a number of major newspapers were taken in and reprinted the story as fact. See Keough, 22–23.
142. W. E. Adams, 223. Hamilton Aïdé called the American surprise party "another strange diversion, according to our English ideas." Aïdé, 897.

143. Hatton, v. 1, 233. Léon Paul Blouet also noted that "the clubs, in large English towns, are sad and solemn; those in the American cities are bright and gay." O'rell, 48.

144. Gripenberg, 11.

145. Related by Horace Annesley Vachell, 59.

146. Related by William Archer, 83.

147. William Saunders, *Through the Light Continent, or, The United States in 1877–78* [1879] (New York: Arno Press, 1974), 63.

148. Dilke, 68, 69. This joke was not terribly original. J. W. Boddam-Whetham heard the same joke told in regards to Stockton, and at several other places. Boddam-Whetham, 143. While in Denver, Dilke was told that the temperature in jails was kept so low that when prisoners were given their choice of immediate hanging or being hanged in a week, they elected the former because "otherwise they would catch their deaths of cold." Dilke, 115.

149. Nancy Pogel and Paul P. Somers, Jr., "Literary Humor," in *Humor in America: A Research Guide to Genres and Topics*, ed. Lawrence E. Mintz (New York: Greenwood Press, 1988), 1. There were social taboos that made certain subjects off limits to jokes. When he was in the South, William Hepworth Dixon observed that while "Americans are not squeamish as to jokes," jests about interracial relations "excites the wildest rage." Dixon, 473, 472.

150. Rudyard Kipling, "Introduction," in *American Notes* [1891] (Norman: University of Oklahoma Press, 1981), x.

151. Charles Dickens, *The Speeches of Charles Dickens*, ed. K. J. Fielding (Hemel Hempstead, Hertfordshire: Harvester Wheatsheaf, 1988), 25, 27.

152. Ibid., 26, 28, 32.

153. See *Abroad in America*, 86.

154. Macrae, 469.

155. Wilde, "Impressions," 255. On his train between New York and Newport, Paul Bourget saw boys selling copies of Alphonse Daudet's *Sappho*. Bourget noticed that someone had added a second title: "*Or, Lured by a Bad Woman's Fatal Beauty!*" Bourget, 40.

156. Kipling, "Introduction," viii. The enraged Kipling put a curse on all Americans: "Your women shall scream like peacocks when they talk, and your men neigh like horses when they laugh. You shall be governed by the Irishman and the German, the vendor of drinks and the keeper of vile dens, that your streets may be filthy in your midst and your sewage arrangements filthier ... You shall prostitute and pervert the English language, till an Englishman has neither power nor desire to understand anymore. You shall be cursed State by State, Territory by Territory, with a provincialism beyond the provincialism of an English country town. " Ibid., ix.

157. Rudyard Kipling, "An Interview with Mark Twain," in *American Notes* [1891] (Norman: University of Oklahoma Press, 1981), 164.

158. Brydges, 220–221.

159. Henry Adams noted that "the press was an inferior pulpit; an anonymous schoolmaster; a cheap boarding-school; but it was still the nearest approach to a career for the literary survivor of a wrecked education." Henry Adams, 211.

160. Brydges, 137, 139; Joseph Hatton agreed, noting that the lack of a copyright law between Britain and America "forces native writers, who otherwise would be writing books, into the newspaper press." Hatton, v. 2, 92.

161. Sienkiewicz, 10.

162. Macrae, 582. According to one count, there were 140 newspapers being sold on the streets of San Francisco in 1880, including twenty-four foreign language papers. See Barbara Cloud, *The Coming of the Frontier Press: How the West was Really Won* (Evanston, IL: Northwestern University Press, 2008), 73.

163. Quoted in J. Valerie Fifer, *American Progress: The Growth of the Transport, Tourist, and Information Industries in the Nineteenth-Century West* (Chester, CN: Globe Pequot Press, 1988), 194.
164. Schlereth, 182.
165. Somers, 264; Marshall, 405.
166. Boorstin, 131.
167. Bryce, v. 2, 288.
168. Charles Dickens to Charles Fechter, 8 March 1868, *The Letters of Charles Dickens*, 68.
169. Russell, v. 1, 20–21.
170. Ibid., v. 2, 52.
171. Hamsun, 25; Oscar Wilde, "Soul of Man Under Socialism," in *The Essays of Oscar Wilde* [1916], ed. Albert & Charles Boni (Bonibooks, 1935), 39. S. C. de Soissons claimed that American newspapers respected nothing and attacked "everything and everybody." Soissons, 116, 121.
172. Arnold, 178, 177. Arnold was no doubt piqued that a Chicago newspaper described him in the following manner: "He has harsh features, supercilious manners, parts his hair down the middle, wears a single eye-glass and ill-fitting clothes." Ibid., 179–180. Herbert Spencer also referred to American journalism's "moral trespassing" and "recklessness of statement." Herbert Spencer "Report of Mr. Spencer's Interview," in Edward Youmans, *Herbert Spencer on the Americans and the Americans on Herbert Spencer: Being a Full Report of his Interview, and of the Proceedings of the Farewell Banquet of Nov. 11, 1882* (New York: D. Appleton, 1883), 18, 10.
173. Reid, 232.
174. Muirhead, 152.
175. Vachell, 215.
176. Boddam-Whetham, 182.
177. Brydges, 124, 132. When W. E. Adams asked an American why no one sued newspapers for libel, he was told, "Oh, nobody here pays any attention to newspapers." Quoted in W. E. Adams, 161.
178. Offenbach, 111.
179. Tocqueville, 205.
180. Bryce, v. 2, 289. Marvin Olasky has traced at least three phases in journalism in Europe and America. The *official story*, dominant until the eighteenth century, was based on the presumption that those in power knew best. The *corruption story*, which persisted well into the nineteenth century, emphasized the frailty of humans and the tendency of those in power toward corruption. By the late nineteenth century, the *oppression story* came into play, which posited that humans were basically good but were tyrannized by oppressive social systems. Marvin Olasky, *Central Ideas in the Development of American Journalism: A Narrative History* (Hillsdale, NJ: Lawrence Erlbaum Associates, 1991), 1–2.
181. Reid, 220–221.
182. Ibid., 222, 223.
183. O'rell, 127, 129.
184. Ibid., 121, 120.

4

PERSONAL HABITS

Dining, Drinking, Tobacco Chewing, and Gun Use

European travelers were amused by some of the personal habits of Americans, and horrified by others. In the former category was the American practice of sitting with feet elevated. In Philadelphia, Jacques Offenbach saw outdoor cafes with rows of men stretched out with feet resting above their heads.[1] William Saunders also took note of this practice in Chicago, where a person would "throw back his chair, put his feet on the writing desk, and 'guess there are many things in Chicago to astonish a Britisher.'"[2] In the House of Representatives, members joked, read newspapers, wrote letters and leaned back in their chairs "with their feet elevated on the desks before them."[3] While Europeans found this behavior bizarre, at least it was not grossly offensive.

The American personal habits that produced the most venom from European commentators centered on dining (they were repelled by the low quality of American cuisine, and by the rapidity with which Americans devoured this dismal fare), drinking and the free flow of alcohol, and the American habit of spitting tobacco juice everywhere. Also disturbing to Europeans was the wide dissemination of firearms in America and the casualness of gun use.

Dining

Before the Civil War, most Americans were probably suffering from some dietary deficiency, either because of lack of access to fresh foods and milk, or lack of funds to purchase them.[4] Especially in the South and West, a diet of "hog and hominy" dominated.[5] (David T. Courtwright even argues that the bow-leggedness of cowboys may have been as much a consequence of a calcium-deficient diet as it was of spending hours in the saddle.[6]) As in so many other areas of American life, the post-war railroad boom became an agent of change, in this case for the American diet. In the 1870s, railroads opened up the grasslands of the Great Plains to meat production, and in the decades ahead refrigerated railroad cars allowed for shipments of both dressed meat and fruits and vegetables over long distances. The distribution of food was now national, rather than regional.[7] Better nutrition, the pasteurization of milk, and the acceptance of the germ theory of disease significantly increased life expectancy in the United States, from age 40 in 1850 to age 48 by 1900.[8]

As for the *style* of dining in America, most foreign travelers agreed that it consisted of large quantities of bad food rapidly consumed. Lepel Henry Griffin called the plentitude of the American table "the Homeric abundance of quartered oxen and sheep roasting whole on the spit."[9] At restaurants, all courses (and there could be fifteen or so of them) were served at the same time in what was called a "medley dinner." The ability of Americans to rapidly ingest these huge portions was a source of wonderment to European travelers.[10] Knut Hamsun even provided a statistical table that he claimed proved that the American was eating almost three times as much food as the European.[11] In both East and West, and among all classes, Americans feasted as if they were trying to set a speed record.[12] At New York's upscale Astor House, W. G. Marshall witnessed a "rapid bolting of food," but the same was true for that city's more modest boarding houses. Stephen Buckland noted that if you did not take your place at the boarding-house table immediately after the ringing of the bell, you ran the risk of there being nothing left to eat.[13] French traveler Lucien Biart said that while he had seen electricity and steam perform marvels of speed, "they are surpassed by the rapidity with which an American will gulp down a meal; it is legerdemain applied to gastronomy."[14]

Eating for Americans was serious work, with no time for idle chit-chat. On a steamer plying the waters of the West, one traveler witnessed passengers rushing the table, gorging themselves on a dozen different kinds of food, and finishing in ten minutes. At the St. Vrain Hotel in Colorado, Isabella Bird observed that all the unmarried men of Longmont "came in and fed silently and rapidly."[15] At other lodgings, she saw twenty men in work clothes enter, sit down, eat rapidly, and leave, without anybody speaking.[16] Referring to the awe-inspiring ability of Americans to chew quickly through enormous portions of food, Paul Bourget claimed that this was characteristic of "a predatory race," whose teeth had "become as important as talons to the vulture or claws to the lion."[17]

American fare consistently conformed to a low culinary standard, which Henry Sienkiewicz bluntly judged to be "the worst on earth."[18] Dining horrors included the dinner William A. Bell was served in a Salina, Kansas, hotel: "fried fish, fried mutton, fried eggs, fried mush (a great luxury), fried potatoes, and fried pudding—all swimming in grease."[19] At one point in his travels, John Campbell Argyll was presented with "a speck of blood and gristle supposed to represent a beefsteak," while in Vallejo, California, Robert Louis Stevenson had the misfortune of eating at what he called a typical "two-bit house," whose enticements included huge portions of vile food and "rough, coatless men devouring it in silence."[20] The food served at railroad stations was especially grim, but what most appalled E. Catherine Bates was that this mess was all served on one plate, degrading the diner "to the level of a pig and its trough."[21]

The consensus among Europeans was that an American cuisine did not exist. Jacques Offenbach dined in French, Swiss and German restaurants in New York, where he found the food acceptable, but claimed that in America it was impossible to find an American meal.[22] Offenbach was roughly correct, and throughout much of the nineteenth century the wealthy of the United States showed a preoccupation with French cuisine.[23]

But travelers did make some culinary finds that were distinctly American. The Italian General Bartolomeo Galletti, who accompanied tragedienne Adelaide Ristori on her American tour of 1875, identified four things about America that he considered outstanding: women, apples, oysters, and white bread.[24] In San Francisco, J. J. Aubertin encountered a dish that was new to him called "clam chowder." But he decided not to order it when he observed the reaction of a nearby Englishwoman who had sampled a clam: "'Oh, dear me—very nasty, very nasty indeed!'"[25] Canvasback duck was much sought after in Baltimore (as late as the 1870s, professional hunters were killing 15,000 ducks a day on the Chesapeake.)[26] In Washington, D.C., William Howard Russell and his party were presented with a dish of frog legs. The waiter assured this group that frog legs were good to eat, and to further highlight the virtues of this dish he sprinkled some salt on the legs "which immediately were agitated with convulsive twitches, amounting in several instances to vigorous kicks." According to Russell, "we overcame our repugnance so far as to order a dish, and found it very excellent indeed."[27]

In New York, the natives were wild for turtle soup (Theodora Guest described terrapin as "the great and costly luxury of the States").[28] When Peter Tchaikovsky was served turtle in New York, he was surprised enough to put three exclamation marks into his diary ("a sauce of small turtles [!!!]").[29] But to describe other dining experiences in America, Tchaikovsky twice used the word "repugnant."[30] The turtle soup competition was fierce, and one restaurant, according to Stephen Buckland, took the unusual step of tying up a live turtle in front with a sign on his back announcing that "he will be served up on such a day in the shape of soup, and promising a rich treat by the words 'I am very fat.'"[31] Only oysters could command the same reverie among New York diners. Harold Brydges estimated that New Yorkers consumed 810 million oysters per year, or some 660 per inhabitant.[32] It was also in New York that George Augustus Sala encountered baked Alaska, a dish that began as a warm cream *soufflé* "till you come, with somewhat painful suddenness, on the row of ice."[33]

More than most travelers, Stephen Buckland explored the United States through the medium of his stomach. Buckland discovered both the buckwheat hot cake and milk toast, and was enthusiastic about the former (especially since there was no extra charge for the syrup and butter), but condemned the latter as fit only for infants.[34] There was also the extraordinary popularity of pie in America, the mere sight of which was enough to make Buckland faintly bilious. In one window display he observed stacks of pie forming a series of pastry columns, a monument, said Buckland, to the American stomach's extraordinary digestive powers.[35] David Macrae also acknowledged the centrality of pie to American culture, and theorized that while Americans might accept the prohibition of alcohol, any attempt to prohibit pie would cause a revolution.[36] In a similar vein, George Augustus Sala called pie "the Transatlantic incubus," while J. W. Boddam-Whetham speculated that "the number of victims of intemperance in pie-eating must be enormous in America."[37]

Frenchmen were especially eager to weigh in on the subject of American dining since, as the world recognizes, they are authorities on both food and women. S. C. de Soissons called cooking America's worst feature, and his countryman Hugues Le Roux described American food as "bad, unpalatable and unwholesome."[38] Frenchwoman Marie Therese Blanc also found that there were many American dining habits that would "astonish a foreigner," including "the abuse of icewater" and "heresies in the matter of wines."[39] Yet it was an Englishwoman who delivered up the most withering critique of American cooking. In her list of American culinary sins, Emily Faithfull included "indigestible hot breads, tough beefsteaks hardly warmed through, greasy potatoes—considered an indispensable breakfast dish in America—to say nothing of wonderful and fearful inventions in the shape of pastry cakes." Faithfull's conclusion was that "a sense of taste is probably one of the last and highest stages of civilization."[40] One wonders what Faithfull would have made of the American Indian feast hosted by Spotted Tail, chief of the Brules, and served to Henry M. Stanley on the Great Plains. The *pièce de résistance*, as described by Stanley, was "three dogs, of a dropsical appearance, the hair merely scorched, which had been roasted entire, intestines and all. Over this Indian delicacy was poured the gravy, dog's grease. The dripping had been collected in bone dishes."[41]

There was one American dining tradition that was almost universally praised by Europeans. Jacques Offenbach called it the places "where *you eat for nothing*" [Offenbach's emphasis], namely the saloons and hotel bars where for the price of a drink a patron acquired access to the buffet. Offenbach was so impressed with this arrangement that he reproduced the buffet menu.[42] (Given Offenbach's dismissiveness of American food, his enthusiasm brings to mind the old joke about the food being terrible, and in such small quantities.) Harold Brydges was also enraptured by the wide variety of free fare at saloons, as was Rudyard Kipling, who claimed that in the saloons of San Francisco one could dine sumptuously for less than a rupee.[43]

Drinking

Drinking in America shared at least one characteristic with dining—it was done with prompt dispatch. Travelers noted that while Americans liked to take a drink, they did not linger over it. They stepped briskly up to the bar, tossed down their drinks in a single swallow ("like a wineglassful of water," as W. G. Marshall put it) and left.[44] Giuseppe Giacosa theorized that Americans drank in silence because "they enjoy being drunk more than drinking."[45] All classes frequented drinking venues with a casual openness, and while bars in most places were supposed to be closed on Sundays, those who knew the system never had a problem finding a drink.[46] The serving of drinks was also important in the private home. When Hugues Le Roux attended a dinner party at a wealthy Fifth Avenue address, the host himself mixed the cocktails rather than trusting such a duty to a servant.[47] Another French commentator, Léon Paul Blouet, observed that one thing New York and London had in common were hundreds of churches and hundreds of saloons—the "Anglo-Saxon mixture of bible and beer, of the spiritual and the spirituous."[48]

Europeans were divided over how much Americans drank, and whether it was more than Europeans themselves were drinking. W. E. Adams claimed to have seen more drunks on the streets of Newcastle during a Bank Holiday than he saw in seven weeks in America (weeks that included Decoration Day and the Fourth of July).[49] This impression was confirmed by another Briton who said that one could encounter more intoxicated men and women on the streets of London in a single day "than those of any city of the United States in six months."[50] There did seem to be more public drinking among women in the U.K. than in the United States. An American visiting England claimed that "the spectacle of women who are not harlots drinking raw gin at a public bar, has a staggering effect upon an American tourist."[51]

But other European travelers, especially those of the reforming stripe, were agitated by what they saw as a lack of moderation in American drinking habits. Emily Faithfull insisted that in America, people tended to be either total abstainers or hard drinkers or, as Paul de Rousiers put it, "water-drinkers or drunkards."[52] (Rousiers endorsed the pleasing French myth that wine drinking did not lead to alcoholism, and that what America needed was not prohibition "but vine-growers."[53]) Other visitors included the fondness for drink in the United States as part of their overall critique of Americans. According to J. W. Boddam-Whetham, for instance, it was "whisky, high wages, and universal suffrage" that were the primary enemies of the American people.[54]

Liquor was widely available everywhere in the United States, and was the cause, according to Isabella Bird, of most shootings in Western mining camps.[55] Heavy drinking did seem to be part of the culture of such places. In Sonora, California, for instance, one visitor estimated that every other structure in the town was a saloon of some sort.[56] Leadville, Colorado, had 249 saloons in 1880 doing $4 million worth of business a year. Only banking and mining exceeded that total. Well into the 1890s Montana averaged one saloon for every eighty inhabitants.[57] Horace Annesley Vachell observed that while the drunkards of England were confined to a certain class, "the drunkards of the West are ubiquitous."[58]

The extent to which America was a nation of heavy drinkers in the second half of the nineteenth century—British traveler W. F. Rae claimed that "the custom of the country is to drink as often as possible"—was the subject of heated debate during that era (and among scholars in our own time).[59] Alcohol consumption had peaked in 1830 to a little over seven gallons of absolute alcohol per year per the drinking-age population. Thanks to a vigorous temperance movement, by the decade of the 1870s it had been reduced to the lowest level in American history: 1.72 gallons per year. In addition, American drinkers were beginning to shift their allegiance from distilled spirits to the more healthful beer.[60] What fueled the prohibition movement after the Civil War is probably related to the proliferation of saloons. In the early 1870s there were about 100,000 saloons in the country (one for every 400 persons). By 1900 there were 300,000—one for every 250 persons, with especially large concentrations in American cities.[61]

One characteristic of drinking in the United States was that Americans added ice to nearly all of their beverages.[62] W. E. Adams contended that the ice harvest in the United States was as important as any fruit crop, and mentioned huge structures erected along the banks of the Hudson for storing it.[63] Demand for ice was no less intense in the South than it was in the North, despite the obvious fact that the South was not an ice-producing region. If we use New Orleans as an example, we find that on the eve of the Civil War, the residents of that city were consuming 28,000 tons of ice per year.[64] Visiting New Orleans immediately after the war, David Macrae discovered that every office, store and house provided iced water.[65] Technology was soon applied to the production of ice, making it no longer necessary to harvest it from northern lakes. By 1879, there were thirty-five commercial ice plants in the United States, two hundred plants ten years later, with the numbers increasing exponentially thereafter. These plants provided ice for both businesses and for iceboxes in American homes, and greatly reduced the cost of ice.[66] Ice had previously been brought to New Orleans from Northern ice importers at the cost of 40 to 60 dollars per ton. The ice factory in New Orleans cut the price to 15 dollars a ton.[67]

Even on trains, "the supply of ice was liberal and unfailing," and one traveler observed that whenever the train stopped at a major station, the train attendants grappled with large blocks of ice which they stored in an ice reservoir.[68] Regardless of the season, Americans were constantly drinking water with "ice floating in it."[69] W. E. Adams even discovered that during the hottest months of the summer "an agreeable beverage is prepared by pouring hot tea upon a lump of ice."[70] Theodora Guest had her first experience with a grapefruit in the United States, and noted that it, "like everything else, including the tea, comes up iced."[71] Worse yet, Dario Papa found Americans putting ice in their wine, a practice he called "a sacrilege."[72] One visitor even condemned the use of ice on temperance grounds because ice made cocktails more "palatable."[73] In American restaurants, meals typically began by a waiter bringing a large glass of iced water to the diner, and in contrast to the European model, most Americans did not drink wine with their meals but preferred iced water, tea or milk.[74] Jacques Offenbach insisted that if you went into an American restaurant and saw someone with beer or wine in front of them, that person would almost certainly be a European.[75]

Tobacco Chewing

That America was a nation of tobacco chewers had been documented from an early date, most notably by Frances Trollope, whose tirades against this vice date from the 1820s. Indeed, of the many deficiencies of American culture identified by Mrs. Trollope (and they are legion) it was this one in particular that most exercised her. In an 1833 letter to the Cincinnati *Mirror*, Trollope noted that if a lady took a stroll with a gentleman on an evening when there was a slight breeze, she would likely discover the following day that her skirt was "completely bespattered and besprinkled, as if she had been caught in a shower of tobacco juice."[76] Trollope confirms the universality of this habit in Congress ("nearly all, spitting to an excess that decency forbids me to describe"), in theatres ("the spitting was incessant") and at virtually every other social venue.[77]

This habit continued to be a part of American life in the postbellum period, and while smoking tobacco was rising in popularity, in terms of pounds of tobacco sold, smoking tobacco did not move past chewing tobacco until 1908.[78] In the mid-1860s, David Macrae concluded that the spitting of tobacco was to be found everywhere in the country, and by the late 1870s William Saunders was calling the chewing of tobacco "the greatest scourge of American life."[79] In Chicago, Saunders found the floor of the Exchange "entirely covered, and quite slippery, with discharged mucous and saliva," while at public meetings he often found himself the recipient of "a stream of saliva pouring down close to my coat from the lips of a bystander."[80] According to Lady Duffus Hardy, the sidewalks of San Francisco in 1881 were in a "disgusting condition" from tobacco juice, forcing the lady to gather up her skirts and still running the risk "of having a quid squirted over her as she passes along."[81] At New York's fashionable Astor House, W. G. Marshall took note of a crowded hall covered with the detritus from scores of tobacco chewers and smokers. The American spitting habit he said was "one of the most serious drawbacks to one's comfort during a visit to the United States."[82] Even as late as 1891, Alexander Craib insisted that "this objectionable habit—so foul and impure—is among all classes almost universal."[83]

On railroad cars one spittoon was provided for every two passengers and they were sorely needed because, as Isabella Bird put it, these cars were "full of chewing, spitting Yankees."[84] Elsewhere, there were reeking spittoons on staircases, in bedrooms, and in bars, and one traveler spied spittoons even in churches.[85] "No apartment," said Joseph Hatton, "is sacred enough in this free country to keep out the spittoon."[86] Léon Paul Blouet called the spittoon "the most indispensable, most conspicuous, piece of furniture in America."[87]

In Washington, one visitor described the steps of the Capitol as "splashed and blotted with tobacco stains."[88] Inside, Emily Faithfull observed that each member of Congress was in possession of his own elaborately ornamented spittoon.[89] (A detail that was especially revolting was that the aim of the Congressmen was not terribly accurate, and tobacco juice splattered on the hot brass coverings over the heating flues.[90]) Faithfull was amused that while national courtesy required that a man remove his hat if a woman entered an elevator, it allowed him "to spit in front of her before they reach the next landing."[91] Paul de Rousiers claimed that American women were chewers as well, not of tobacco but of "a gum expressly made for the purpose. Their teeth are in constant motion, and an apparent swelling appears, moving about and deforming their cheeks."[92] As James Fullarton Muirhead put it, nothing so "robs the human countenance of the divine spark of intelligence" as chewing.[93]

Gun use

The history of gun rights in America and in Europe is long and extremely complicated, yet something needs to be said about it as it has been the subject of mutual incomprehension between Americans and Europeans since colonial days. Historically, gun ownership had been relatively rare in Europe, and fairly common in America, for a number of reasons. Hunting was a privilege largely reserved to the aristocracy in Europe, which was never the case in America, nor did Europeans have to deal with Indian conflicts. For much of the colonial era, the British ruled their colonies with what Edmund Burke called "salutary neglect," a style much favored by Americans who preferred running their own affairs.[94] This changed at the conclusion of the French and Indian War, when the British made two decisions which, in hindsight, would prove to be disastrous to their empire. First, large numbers of British troops were permanently stationed in the colonies rather than going home. With the threat of the French eliminated, Americans viewed the presence of these troops not as guarantors of their liberties, but as oppressors.[95] To add insult to injury, Americans would be paying for the upkeep of the British military through the Sugar and Stamp Acts.[96]

There was no denying the heavy symbolism of this occupying force as American colonists began to clash with their colonial masters—and to contemplate independence. By 1774, George III stopped all shipments of arms and ammunition to the colonies, and in the following year British troops began seizing stockpiles of arms and ammunition maintained by local militias.[97] The previous century, another monarch, the Catholic James II, had tried to disarm Protestants through the Militia Act of 1664 and the Game Act of 1671. The Glorious Revolution toppled James, and the English Bill of Rights restored gun rights to the English.[98] Now it was time for a different revolution, at the conclusion of which Americans created their own Bill of Rights, which included a provision that guaranteed the right of citizens to bear arms as a counterweight to any future army of occupation.[99] Colonial history also helps explain American resistance to a large standing army (with the Civil War years being an important exception) during most of the nineteenth century.[100] For instance, in debate over the creation of a police force for Washington, D.C., Senator Ambrose Sevier of Arkansas condemned the police bill as "nothing more nor less than a proposition to establish a little standing army."[101]

Not surprisingly, the American national government has tended to trust private citizens with the possession of firearms, while those in power in Europe have reacted with alarm at any hints of an armed citizenry.[102] When rioters in Paris grabbed some 30,000 firearms during the French Revolution, authorities throughout Europe moved quickly to disarm the public.[103] By the end of the eighteenth century, the French government was denying access to guns by individual French citizens, and much the same was accomplished in England when Parliament passed the "Six Acts" of 1819. A more repressive piece of legislation could hardly be imagined. In addition to authorizing searches for arms in private homes, the acts greatly curtailed freedom of assembly and speech in Britain. Wellington believed that the British example would do some good in France and Germany, and expressed the hope that "the whole world will escape the universal revolution which seems to menace us all."[104] If nothing else, the Six Acts confirmed the good judgment of Americans in fomenting their own revolution and separating from Great Britain. While many of these restrictions in France and England were rescinded by the 1880s, ordinary European citizens no longer felt the need or inclination to arm themselves.[105] An American soldier in Yellowstone penetrated to the heart of the gun divide between America and England in a conversation with Rudyard Kipling: "'in England a man aren't allowed to play with no firearms. He's got to be taught all that when he enlists. I didn't want much teaching how to shoot straight 'fore I served Uncle Sam. And that's just where it is.'"[106]

The legend of the pistol-packing American had been established in Europe from an early date (Figure 4.1), and with the conclusion of the Civil War, gun ownership in the United States increased dramatically. Millions of men had been trained in the use of firearms during the war, huge numbers of weapons had been produced for the war effort, and once the war was over these guns were dumped on the civilian market.[107] Weapons were also available via mail order, with Sears doing a brisk $3 million business annually in revolvers.[108]

In the South, as numerous foreign travelers testified, the disarmament of the Confederate Army after the Civil War apparently did not extend to individual residents.[109] In one example of the ubiquity of firearms in the South, F. Barham Zincke was on a train traveling in the vicinity of Jackson, Mississippi, when a cow was mangled underneath one of the cars, but remained alive. When the conductor asked the passengers for the loan of a pistol to put the cow out of its misery, "in an instant almost from every window on that side of the train a hand was extended offering the desired instrument." Zincke remarked to the passenger next to him on the extraordinary number of firearms, and the passenger told

FIGURE 4.1 Virginia City, Nevada, 1865: "Home for the boys." Library of Congress. LCUSZ62-61322. *Harper's* 31 (June 1865), 5.

Zincke that Zincke was probably the only unarmed man on the train. Because of "apprehension of the blacks," the passenger explained, "no one ever thought of moving without his six-shooter."[110]

Southerners seemed willing to pull out their guns on the slightest of pretexts. Charles Wentworth Dilke was on a steamboat that was cruising on Virginia's James River when an eagle alighted on a nearby tree. Travelers on all three decks shot off their pistols against the bird, which flew off unharmed.[111] In another incident along the James, this time in a canal boat, John Campbell Argyll reported that "whole broadsides of pistol shots were discharged at every unfortunate big green-headed bull-frog or water-snake" on the shore.[112] In Louisiana, both Henry Latham and Robert Somers noted that passengers on their trains fired off their revolvers at flocks of ducks.[113] Latham also noticed that when he passed tailors' shops in New Orleans the trousers that were hanging up had a special pocket on the hip for a gun or knife.[114] The gun also seemed to be an ordinary item of dress in Vicksburg, with Ernst von Hesse-Wartegg observing of the residents that they "carry revolvers as a matter of habit, as they might pencils or toothpicks."[115]

David Macrae declared that in parts of the South "it seemed to me that almost everybody carried some murderous weapon about with him," but he found little in the way of gun carrying in New England or in the more settled northern states.[116] Jacques Offenbach, however, who spent most of his time in America in large northern cities, referred to the "prominent bulge" under men's frock coats indicative of a concealed weapon.[117] On his train from New York to Albany, Frenchman Lucien Biart was taken aback when "several of my travelling companions shouldered their guns to fire past me from the carriage at an unfortunate crow."[118] There was also the American tradition of firing pistols into the air to celebrate the Fourth of July. W. E. Adams was in New York for the Fourth in 1882, and noted that the *New York Herald* on the following day reported that the previous evening had produced twelve victims from random gunfire.[119]

It was in the unsettled West, however, where guns were most prominent. In the Nevada desert, Charles Wentworth Dilke and his companions ran into a group of prospectors with whom they traded pleasantries until someone spotted a rattlesnake. Whereupon "every revolver discharged with a shout, all hailing the successful shot with a 'Bully for you; thet hit him whar he lives.'"[120] In California, James Fullarton Muirhead watched the engineer on his train shoot rabbits from the locomotive while the fireman jumped down, picked them up, and hoisted himself back onto the still moving train.[121] Even in civilized San Francisco, Rudyard Kipling estimated that fifty percent of the men in saloons carried pistols.[122]

For Europeans, the prospect of traveling among an armed populace was both frightening and titillating. When he was in Julesburg, Colorado, in 1867 (shortly after its founding), the unarmed Henry M. Stanley (who would later gain considerable notoriety as an African explorer) expressed dismay at the town's violence and depravity, and noted that even local prostitutes glided through its streets "carrying fancy derringers slung to their waists."[123] A little more than ten years later W. G. Marshall also passed through Julesburg, but, unlike Stanley, Marshall had provided himself with a pistol and was clearly thrilled at the prospect of some gun play as his train pulled into what he called the "wickedest town in America." The train had been robbed here a few days earlier, but Marshall's train passed through Julesburg without incident, and a disappointed-sounding Marshall noted that, "As yet we had had no occasion to use our revolvers."[124] Actress Sarah Bernhardt always carried a pistol with her ("a very prettily chased revolver, ornamented with cats' eyes") and on her tour of America came closer to using her firearm than Marshall.[125] Bernhardt traveled with a valuable cache of jewelry, and en route between St. Louis and Cincinnati robbers plotted to steal the jewelry by derailing Bernhardt's train. The robbers, however, mistakenly derailed the train just in front of Bernhardt's, and when Bernhardt and company came upon the scene, robbers and railroad detectives had just finished an intense gun fight.[126]

For many Americans, a firearm was simply a necessary tool that one always kept close by. In contrast to Bernhardt, Isabella Bird carried no gun as she traveled through the wilds of Colorado, and when she revealed this fact to "Mountain Jim" Nugent, he expressed astonishment, "and adjured me to get a revolver at once."[127] Europeans who spent considerable time in the West generally saw things Nugent's way. Henry Sienkiewicz encountered a cougar in the Mariposa wilderness when he was unarmed, and vowed that henceforward he would "never be so foolish as to go into a thicket without my knife and loaded rifle."[128] When William A. Bell's party was threatened by Arapahos just north of the New Mexico border in 1867, it happened on the one day that Bell had decided to leave his gun behind. He declared that "I took good care that it should be the last."[129] Another Englishman who had worked on a sheep ranch in the early 1880s condemned what he called the "cant" that proclaimed that not carrying a firearm was the best policy for foreign travelers in America. "All I can say," said the sheep herder, "is that the men who preach this have either never been out west at all, or have only stayed there a very short time."[130] Even on social occasions, guns were within easy reach. The English couple Isabelle and Jem Randall were hosting a luncheon for their English friends at their Montana ranch when a flock of geese flew over the house. The group rushed out with their firearms and a volley of gunfire brought down a twenty pound Canada goose.[131]

There is also evidence that Americans carried guns when they deemed it necessary, but were willing to abandon them when the necessity had passed. On the train from Colorado Springs to Denver in the early 1880s, Iza Duffus Hardy took note of the "liberal assortment of deadly weapons" carried by the male passengers. At the Denver hotel where she stayed, however, she saw some of the same men checking their guns with the hotel clerk before going in to dinner. The clerk explained to Hardy that when the men found themselves in a peaceable community, they were willing to dispense with their firearms.[132]

While America certainly seemed to be a land of gun carriers after the Civil War, was the United States a "gunfighter nation," as historian Richard Slotkin has suggested?[133] As we have seen, this was certainly the image of America that many European travelers brought with them, but opinion among historians is divided on this issue. Richard White has suggested that what he calls "personal violence" in the American West was only a small part of a wide spectrum of violence that included range wars, vigilante actions, clashes between races, industrial and class conflicts, social banditry, and Indian hunting.[134] Because young men are more prone toward violent acts, and because demographically there was a greater percentage of young men living in frontier regions, David T. Courtwright claims that the West produced a greater incidence of violence than in more settled areas.[135] In contrast, Richard Hofstadter argued against the proposition that violence in America should be attributed to America's frontier history, not only because a small number of Americans at any one time lived on the frontier, but also because "most American domestic violence has been urban."[136] Clare V. McKanna, Jr., however, claims that there were "high lethal-violence levels in the American West."[137]

One convincing argument for the *lack* of extensive gun violence in the West, put forward by Robert R. Dykstra, is that it was simply bad for business. As Dykstra puts it, "entrepreneurial motives" "provided a powerful impetus for the suppression of violence."[138] Of all the parts of the West, it was the cattle towns of Ellsworth, Dodge City, Wichita, Abilene, and Caldwell that garnered the greatest reputation for being wild and lawless, and with the male-to-female ratio in western Kansas standing at roughly 77:1 in 1870, these towns should theoretically have had extremely high levels of violence.[139] While city businessmen wanted the cattle trade, what they did not want was cowboys shooting up their towns. What followed were local ordinances forbidding the carrying of firearms, concealed or otherwise, within city limits. Guns were checked in with the city marshal, for which the gun owner received a metal token.

Dykstra claimed that this strategy was a great success, with the average number of killings per cattle town during the season standing at a modest 1.5 per year.[140] David Courtland and Clare McKanna criticize Dykstra for not using the standard measurement of homicides per 100,000, but this would seem to be an instance in which rigid adherence to a statistical norm obscures more than it illuminates.[141] A single murder in a town of 100, for instance, would create the horrific murder rate of 1,000 per 100,000 population, and leave the impression that here was an extremely violent community indeed.

Gun control actually worked. Dykstra notes that when Wild Bill Hickok was marshal of Abilene, he killed just two men (one by mistake). Wyatt Earp, during his tenure as lawman in Wichita and Dodge City, "may have mortally wounded one law violator." William B. ("Bat") Masterson killed no one in the years that he resided in and around Dodge.[142] This is not to say that the lot of a cow town lawman was an easy one, and among the most onerous of his duties was bringing drunken cowboys to heel. (Wyatt Earp's preferred technique was "buffaloing" the unruly—that is, a blow to the head with a gun barrel.[143]) But according to Dykstra, impressive numbers of violent deaths in the United States occurred not on the streets of Western towns, but in the vicinity of trains, where in the single year 1893 some 433 men died in railroad accidents.[144] The beloved set piece of the Western film, the shootout, was extremely rare, and it's often forgotten that at the heart of the most famous shootout in American history—the gunfight at the O.K. Corral—was an attempt to enforce an ordinance against the carrying of deadly weapons.[145] It is also possible to argue that the very wide dispersal of weapons in the United States may have inhibited their use as a way of settling arguments. F. Barham Zincke claimed that no people were "more careful about giving offence than Americans" because from an early date in the United States "the pistol had always been simultaneous with the offence."[146]

Notes

1. Jacques Offenbach, *Orpheus in America: Offenbach's Diary of His Journey to the New World*, trans. Lander MacClintock (New York: Greenwood Press, 1969), 130.
2. William Saunders, *Through the Light Continent, or, The United States in 1877–78* [1879] (New York: Arno Press, 1974), 32. Henry M. Stanley observed "drummers" (commercial travelers) lounging "with their feet elevated to the level and altitude of their heads," and F. Barham Zincke was even introduced to a governor (of which state Zincke declines to say) who was conducting official business with "his feet on the table." Henry M. Stanley, *My Early Travels and Adventures in America* [1895] (Lincoln: University of Nebraska Press, 1982), 103; F. Barham Zincke, *Last Winter in the United States: Being Table Talk Collected During a Tour Through the Late Southern Confederation, the Far West, the Rocky Mountains, &c.* [1868] (Freeport, NY: Books for Libraries Press, 1970), 40.
3. W. E. Adams, *Our American Cousins: Being Personal Impressions of the People and Institutions of the United States* (London: Walter Scott, 1883), 114. See also David Macrae, *The Americans at Home* [1870] (New York: E. P. Dutton, 1952), 396. Researchers at Columbia and Harvard have concluded that if people were placed in postures of power, such as "feet on the desk, fingers interlaced behind the head, elbows expansive," they secreted more testosterone. John Cloud, "Strike A Pose," *Time*, November 29, 2010, 61.
4. Elaine N. McIntosh, *American Food Habits in Historical Perspective* (Westport, CN: Praeger, 1995), 94–95.
5. Ibid., 91. Grady McWhiney has noted that meals in the antebellum South "almost always included some form of pork, cornbread, and sour milk. Sometimes wild game, beef, chicken, sweet potatoes, field peas, rice, and greens either substituted for or supplemented the usual fare." Rare in the South but abundant in the North was "wheat bread, fresh meat, butter, cheese, and what Southerners called 'sweet milk.'" Grady McWhiney, *Cracker Culture: Celtic Ways in the Old South* (Tuscaloosa: University of Alabama Press, 1988), 81, 83.
6. David T. Courtwright, *Violent Land: Single Men and Social Disorder from the Frontier to the Inner City* (Cambridge, MA: Harvard University Press, 1996), 94.
7. See Alfred F. Smith, *Eating History: 30 Turning Points in the Making of American Cuisine* (New York: Columbia University Press, 2009), 85–90. By 1903, a strain of lettuce that was able to travel long distances ("iceberg") was being shipped from California. Thomas J. Schlereth, *Victorian America: Transformations in Everyday Life, 1876–1915* (New York: Harper Perennial, 1992), 125.
8. See Joseph E. Illick, *American Childhoods* (Philadelphia: University of Pennsylvania Press, 2002), 63–64.
9. Lepel Henry Griffin, *The Great Republic* [1884] (New York: Arno Press, 1974), 83. Horace Annesley Vachell, a Briton who was a rancher in California, also referred to "Homeric feasts" (barbecues) "whereat the meat was hung upon long willow spits, roasted over glowing wood-coals, and eaten with a sauce cunningly compounded of tomatoes, onions, and chiles." Horace Annesley Vachell, *Life and Sport on the Pacific Slope* (New York: Dodd, Mead and Co., 1901), 117.
10. See George Augustus Sala, *America Revisited: From the Bay of New York to the Gulf of Mexico and From Lake Michigan to the Pacific* (London: Vizetelly & Co., n.d.), 150.
11. See W. G. Marshall, *Through America: Nine Months in the United States* (London: Sampson, Low, Marston, Searle & Rivington, 1881), 99; Offenbach, 74; Knut Hamsun, *The Cultural Life of Modern America* [1889] (Cambridge, MA: Harvard University Press, 1969), 11, 12.
12. J. J. Aubertin said of American diners that "they do not understand intervals." J. J. Aubertin, *A Fight with Distances: The States, the Hawaiian Islands, Canada, British Columbia, Cuba, the Bahamas* (London: Kegan Paul, Tranch & Co., 1888), 66. Lady

Duffus Hardy found the same phenomenon in Canada where, she said, "people did not eat, they *bolted*; flung their food into their mouths, and sent their knives after it to see that it was all right" [original emphasis]. Lady Duffus Hardy, *Through Cities and Prairie Lands: Sketches of an American Tour* (London: Chapman and Hall, 1881), 15.

13. Marshall, 38; Stephen Buckland, "Eating and Drinking In America:—A Stroll Among the Saloons of New York," *MacMillan's Magazine* 16 (October 1867), 464.

14. Lucien Biart, *My Rambles in the New World* [1876], trans. Mary de Hauteville (London: Sampson, Low, Marston, Searle, & Rivington, 1877), 71.

15. Isabella L. Bird, *A Lady's Life in the Rocky Mountains* (Norman: University of Oklahoma Press, 1969), 72.

16. Ibid., 32.

17. Paul Bourget, *Outre-Mer: Impressions of America* (London: T. Fisher Unwin, 1895), 11.

18. Henry Sienkiewicz, *Portrait of America: Letters of Henry Sienkiewicz*, trans. and ed. Charles Morley (New York: Columbia University Press, 1959), 4.

19. William A. Bell, *New Tracks in North America: A Journal of Travel and Adventure Whilst Engaged in the Survey for a Southern Railroad to the Pacific Ocean During 1867–8* [1870] (Albuquerque: Horn and Wallace, 1965), 20.

20. John Campbell Argyll, *A Trip to the Tropics and Home Through America* (London: Hurst and Blackett, 1867), 329; Robert Louis Stevenson, "The Silverado Squatters," in *From Scotland to Silverado* [1892] (Cambridge, MA: Belknap Press, 1966), 193.

21. E. Catherine Bates, *A Year in the Great Republic*, v. 2 (London: Ward & Downey, 1887), 6. On her train trip west, Lady Duffus Hardy claimed that only the stations at Cheyenne, Humboldt, and Laramie had decent food. Lady Duffus Hardy, 90.

22. Offenbach, 74, 75. Referring to Delmonico's in New York, William Howard Russell claimed that "every dish was a culinary triumph." William Howard Russell, *Hesperothen, Notes from the West: A Record of a Ramble in the United States and Canada in the Spring and Summer of 1881*, v. 1 (London: S. Low, Marston, Searle & Rivington, 1882), 45.

23. McIntosh, 9.

24. Andrew J. Torrielli, *Italian Opinion on America, As Revealed by Italian Travelers, 1859–1900* (Cambridge, MA: Harvard University Press, 1941), 29, n. 70.

25. Aubertin, 156. J. W. Boddam-Whetham described clams as "an acquired taste," and noted that when he first ate them "I thought them like india rubber boiled in brine." J. W. Boddam-Whetham, *Western Wanderings: A Record of Travel in the Evening Land* (London: Richard Bentley and Son, 1874), 10.

26. Lee Kennett and James LaVerne Anderson, *The Gun in America: The Origins of a National Dilemma* (Westport, CN: Greenwood Press, 1975), 135.

27. William Howard Russell, v. 1, 101, 102.

28. Joseph Hatton, *Henry Irving's Impressions of America, Narrated in a Series of Sketches, Chronicles, and Conversations* [1884], v. 1 (New York: Benjamin Blom, 1971), 205; Theodora Guest, *A Round Trip in North America* (London: Edward Stanford, 1895), 28.

29. Peter Tchaikovsky, *The Diaries of Tchaikovsky*, trans. Wladimir Lakond (New York: W. W. Norton, 1945), 302.

30. Ibid., 314, 316.

31. Buckland, 456.

32. Harold Brydges, *Uncle Sam at Home* (New York: Henry Holt and Co., 1888), 148.

33. Sala, 78.

34. Buckland, 454, 455. According to J. J. Aubertin, "against the buckwheat cake, with its butter and syrup, nothing can be said." Aubertin, 234.

35. Buckland, 462.

36. Macrae, 41.

37. Sala, 92.

38. S. C. de Soissons, *A Parisian in America* (Boston: Estes and Lauriat, 1896), 48; Hugues Le Roux, *Business and Love* (New York: Dodd, Mead and Co., 1903), 173. French

actress Sarah Bernhardt agreed, calling American food "unspeakably awful." Sarah Bernhardt, *Memories of my Life* [1907] (Grosse Pointe, MI: Scholarly Press, 1968), 393.

39. Marie Therese de Solms Blanc, *The Condition of Woman in the United States: A Traveller's Notes* [1895], trans. Abby Langdon Alger (New York: Arno Press, 1972), 131, 132.

40. Emily Faithfull, *Three Visits to America* (New York: Fowler & Wells, 1884), 53. From an early date, travelers noted that the food that was available in California mining towns was of an exceptionally high quality. When Charles Wentworth Dilke was in Placerville in 1866, a restaurant was offering "baked rock-cod à la Buena Vista, broiled Californian quail with Russian River bacon, Sacramento snipes on toast, Oregon ham with champagne sauce, and a dozen other toothsome things." Charles Wentworth Dilke, *Greater Britain: A Record of Travel in English-Speaking Countries* (London: Macmillan and Co., 1890), 155. In Austin, California, in 1868, William A. Bell and his companions dined on "fresh oysters from San Francisco, large salmon-trout from the Humboldt River, and a variety of dishes beautifully cooked and served. We drank Perrier Jouet of the best quality, and claret which is not to be despised." Bell, 460. J. J. Aubertin praised a California Zinfandel for its "honest quality and honest price," and W. F. Rae was also impressed by the "excellent California wine" he encountered. Aubertin, 67; W. F. Rae, *Westward by Rail: The New Route to the East* [1871] (New York: Promontory Press, 1974), 59.

41. Stanley, 283. When he was on the Plains, J. W. Boddam-Whetham dined on prairie dogs, "and found them excellent—quite as good as rabbits." Boddam-Whetham, 62.

42. Offenbach, 75–76.

43. Brydges, 28. Rudyard Kipling, *American Notes* [1891] (Norman: University of Oklahoma Press, 1981), 19. Taking a dimmer view was Stephen Buckland, who complained of the saltiness of saloon lunches. Buckland, 456.

44. Marshall, 41; See also Buckland, 458, and Macrae, 532.

45. Quoted in Ben Lawton, "Giuseppe Giacosa, 1847–1906," in *Abroad in America: Visitors to the New Nation, 1776–1914* (Reading, MA: Addison-Wesley, 1976), 251.

46. Macrae, 531. In New York, for instance, if one pushed through the bar's "family entrance" on a Sunday he could find a drink and numerous patrons to keep him company. Marshall, 42. Another tactic included "purchasing alcohol disguised as stomachics and cordials at the drug stores." Sala, 320.

47. Le Roux, 17. The quality of liquor in the United States varied widely. Le Roux was no doubt served the best alcohol, but Robert Somers described the effects of the whiskey he encountered in Jonesborough, Tennessee, as an "aching void of brain and stomach," followed closely by "general despair." Robert Somers, *The Southern States Since the War, 1870–71* [1871] (Tuscaloosa: University of Alabama Press, 1965), 133.

48. Max O'rell and Jack Allyn, *Jonathan and His Continent: Rambles Through American Society*, trans. Madame Paul Blouet (Bristol: J. W. Arrowsmith, 1889), 33. Blouet also noted that, "In France, we have men who swear and men who sing hymns. The Anglo-Saxon race alone furnishes men who do both with equal gusto." Ibid., 12.

49. Adams, 64.

50. W. C. M., "American Traits," *Eclectic Magazine* 16, no. 1 (New Series, July 1872), 57.

51. Horace White, "An American's Impression of England," *Eclectic Magazine* 22, no. 5 (New Series, November 1875), 555.

52. Faithfull, 98; Paul de Rousiers, *American Life*, trans. A. J. Herbertson (New York: Firmin-Didot, 1892). 318.

53. Ibid., 321.

54. Boddam-Whetham, 157.

55. Bird, 182.

56. Marshall, 335.

57. Elliott West, *The Saloon on the Rocky Mountain Mining Frontier* (Lincoln: University of Nebraska Press, 1979), xv.

58. Vachell, 67.

59. Rae, 231.

60. Merton M. Hyman et al., *Drinkers, Drinking, and Alcohol-Related Mortality and Hospitalizations* (New Brunswick, NY: Rutgers University Center of Alcohol Studies Publications Division, 1980), 3.

61. See Kenneth D. Rose, *American Women and the Repeal of Prohibition* (New York: New York University Press, 1996), 17.

62. William Howard Russell claimed that "the rudest miner is accustomed to it; iced drinks are consumed by classes in America far below the social level of those who never taste them in this country" (Britain). William Howard Russell, v. 2, 168.

63. Adams, 219.

64. Daniel J. Boorstin, *The Americans: The National Experience* (New York: Random House, 1965), 11.

65. Macrae, 392.

66. The mechanical refrigerator came into use in the 1920s. Daniel J. Boorstin, *The Americans: The Democratic Experience* (New York: Random House, 1973), 330.

67. See Somers, 235. William Saunders visited this New Orleans plant in the late 1870s. His description of the ice-making process was that "water flows down a series of perpendicular iron pipes cooled by ether, and ice forms on these pipes about a foot thick in two days." The plant was producing 70 tons a day. Saunders, 68.

68. William Howard Russell, v. 2, 115.

69. Zincke, 66.

70. Adams, 219; W. G. Marshall also commented on iced tea. Marshall, 98.

71. Guest, 163.

72. Quoted in Torrielli, translated from the Italian by Pietro Bonomi, n. 53, 233.

73. Aubertin, 65.

74. See Buckland, 455; Marshall, 65. When Henry Irving was served oysters on the half shell, he was struck by the fact that "they were lying on a bed of crushed ice." Irving quoted in Hatton, v. 1, 203. The light-bodied lager beer that Americans preferred also dictated that it be served cooler than other beers. At breweries it was stored in huge cellars at near freezing temperatures because it would not stand up to the heat as did other beers. See W. Henry Barneby, who toured such a brewery in St. Louis. W. Henry Barneby, *Life and Labor in the Far, Far West: Being Notes of a Tour in the Western States, British Columbia, Manitoba, and the North-West Territory* (London: Cassell & Co., 1884), 10.

75. Offenbach, 47. J. J. Aubertin also said of American restaurants that "if you happen to catch sight of a bottle or two here and there, you may be next to certain that there are foreigners dining there." Aubertin, 64–65. Paul de Rousiers observed that, "A man must be German or French to ask for beer or wine." Rousiers, 318.

76. Frances Trollope, *Domestic Manners of the Americans* [1832] (New York: Alfred A. Knopf, 1949), 58, n. 4.

77. Ibid., 226, 234.

78. John C. Burnham, *Bad Habits: Drinking, Smoking, Taking Drugs, Gambling, Sexual Misbehavior, and Swearing in American History* (New York: New York University Press, 1993), 88.

79. Macrae, 400; Saunders, 378.

80. Saunders, 377.

81. Lady Duffus Hardy, 140.

82. Marshall, 39.

83. Alexander Craib, *America and the Americans: A Tour in the United States and Canada, With Chapters on American Home Life* (London: Alexander Gardner, 1892), 156. The popularity of tobacco chewing probably peaked in the 1890s. Per capita consumption of chewing tobacco in 1890 was 2.8 pounds per capita. By 1937 it had declined to 0.53 pounds. See Burnham, 89.

84. Bird, 30; Barneby, 36.

85. Kipling, 18; Buckland, 463.

86. Hatton, v. 2, 18. In American hotels, spittoons were "dotted over the floor of the hall; they are disposed in rows along the corridors; they are placed in corners on the staircases; and no bed-room is considered furnished without at least one of them." Adams, 75.

87. O'rell and Allyn, 50.

88. Adams, 74.

89. Faithfull, 37.

90. Aubertin, 279.

91. Faithfull, 344.

92. Rousiers, 332.

93. James Fullarton Muirhead, *The Land of Contrasts: A Briton's View of his American Kin* (London: Lamson, Wolffe and Co., 1898), 11.

94. Burke quoted in Fred Anderson, *The War that Made America: A Short History of the French and Indian War* (New York: Penguin, 2005), 243.

95. William R. Nester notes that, "King George III led the faction determined to maintain an army in the American colonies. The purpose was not just to protect the colonists against potential attacks from the Indians and other European powers, but to distribute office commissions as patronage to followers and, perhaps most importantly, to intimidate the Americans against increasing their already considerable autonomy." William R. Nester, *The First Global War: Britain, France, and the Fate of North America, 1756–1775* (Westport, CN: Praeger, 2000), 244.

96. Ibid., 247.

97. See ibid., 254–255.

98. See Adam Winkler, *Gunfight: The Battle over the Right to Bear Arms in America* (New York: W. W. Norton, 2011), 100–103.

99. Richard Hofstadter traced the roots of this attitude to "the classic radical Whig conviction that a standing army, along with the potential Caesars and Cromwells who command it, is one of the greatest dangers to free government, while an armed populace is one of freedom's primary safeguards." Richard Hofstadter, "Reflections on Violence in the United States," in *American Violence, A Documentary History*, ed. Richard Hofstadter and Michael Wallace (New York: Alfred A. Knopf, 1970), 24.

100. Before the Civil War, the size of the army was roughly 16,000. It swelled to one million during the war, then declined to 29,000 once the war was over. See *The Oxford Companion to American Military History*, s.v. Army, U.S., ed. John Whiteclay Chambers II (Oxford: Oxford University Press, 1999).

101. In New York City in 1854, police officers objected to the wearing of uniforms, and viewed the creation of a uniformed police force as "the commencement of the establishment in the City of a standing Army." Quoted in Eric H. Monkkonen, *Police in Urban America, 1860–1920* (Cambridge: Cambridge University Press, 1981), 45.

102. Richard Hofstadter noted that "the United States long exhibited the interesting spectacle of an armed population juxtaposed to feeble police and military establishments, a remarkable testimony to public confidence in the loyalty of the citizens and in their disposition, if they were to use their arms at all, to use them only against each other and not against civil authority." Hofstadter, 25.

103. Kennett and Anderson, 30.

104. See Frederick B. Artz, *Revolution and Reaction: 1814–1832* (New York: Harper & Brothers, 1945), 125–126.

105. See Kennett and Anderson, 30–33.

106. Kipling, 105.

107. Kennett and Anderson, 153.

108. Courtwright, 43.

109. The terms put forward by U.S. Grant for Robert E. Lee's surrender at Appomattox included the following provisions: "The arms, artillery and public property to be

parked and stacked, and turned over to the officers appointed by me to receive them. This will not embrace the side-arms of the officers, nor their private horses or baggage." Quoted in Bruce Catton, *Grant Takes Command* (Boston: Little, Brown and Co., 1983), 465.

110. Zincke, 149. In the South, Radical Reconstruction leaders created black militias at the same time as whites were arming themselves in their own militias. Clashes between these groups took place all over the South, until black militias were dissolved when Reconstruction ended in 1877. See Hofstadter, 16.

111. Dilke, 8.

112. Argyll, 315.

113. Henry Latham, *Black and White: A Journal of a Three Months' Tour in the United States* [1867] (New York: Negro Universities Press, 1969), 144–145; Somers, 190.

114. Latham commented that "the argument is strong for carrying arms in a country where the majority go armed, but stronger still for putting a forcible end to the custom altogether." Ibid., 161.

115. Ernst von Hesse-Wartegg, *Travels on the Lower Mississippi, 1879–1880*, trans. and ed. Frederic Trautmann (Columbia: University of Missouri Press, 1990), 77.

116. Macrae, 403.

117. Offenbach, 110. In 1896, Bertrand Russell and his American wife visited New Jersey and spent time with an acquaintance named Edith Thomas, who told Russell that "she always carried a revolver, saying one could never know when it would come in handy." Thomas had literary aspirations, and after a trip to Europe, where she received no encouragement to continue writing, she returned to America and "after placing her husband's love letters over her heart, she had shot herself through them with the revolver." Bertrand Russell, *The Autobiography of Bertrand Russell, 1872–1914* (Boston: Atlantic Monthly Press, 1967), 193.

118. Biart, 68.

119. Adams, 237. As late as 1898, Beatrice Webb reported that the youth of San Francisco fired pistols in celebration of the Fourth of July. Beatrice Webb, *Beatrice Webb's American Diary* (Madison: University of Wisconsin Press, 1963), 136.

120. Dilke, 152.

121. Muirhead, 20.

122. Kipling, 41. Iza Duffus Hardy claimed that for the San Francisco male, the revolver "is as much a finishing touch to a gentleman's toilette as his watch." Iza Duffus Hardy, *Between Two Oceans: Or, Sketches of American Travel* (London: Hurst and Blackett, 1884), 190.

123. Stanley, 166.

124. Marshall, 128–129.

125. Bernhardt, 422.

126. Bernhardt, 426. Because of the Bernhardt incident, the railroad officials on Henry Irving's touring train were armed. See Hatton, v. 2, 69. Lillie Langtry said that in her discussions with Bernhardt, "I have heard her speak enthusiastically of the people of the United States, and of the luxury and bohemianism of travelling in America." Lillie Langtry, *The Days I Knew* (New York: George H. Doran, 1925), 119.

127. Bird, 93.

128. Sienkiewicz, 223.

129. Bell, 98.

130. Anonymous, "Ranche Life in the Far West," *MacMillan's Magazine* 48 (August 1883), 298.

131. Isabelle Randall, *A Lady's Ranche Life in Montana* (London: W. H. Allen & Co., 1887), 24–25.

132. Iza Duffus Hardy, 242.

133. See Richard Slotkin, *Gunfighter Nation: The Myth of the Frontier in Twentieth-Century America* (New York: Atheneum, 1992).

134. See Richard White, *"It's Your Misfortune and None of My Own": A History of the American West* (Norman: University of Oklahoma Press, 1991), 328–351.

135. Courtwright, 46, 58.

136. Hofstadter, 11–12.

137. Clare V. McKanna, Jr., *Homicide, Race and Justice in the American West, 1880–1920* (Tucson: University of Arizona Press, 1997), 155. McKanna claimed that the typical perpetrator of a murder in the American West was an intoxicated male, either in a saloon or out in the street late at night, who had a dispute with an acquaintance, and who resolved the dispute with a handgun. Ibid., 17.

138. Robert R. Dykstra, *The Cattle Towns* (New York: Alfred A. Knopf, 1968), 115.

139. Courtwright, 96.

140. Dykstra, *The Cattle Towns*, 121–122, 146.

141. Courtland, 58; McKanna, 200, n. 14.

142. Dykstra, *The Cattle Towns*, 143.

143. See Jeff Guinn, *The Last Gunfight: The Real Story of the Shootout at the O.K. Corral—and How It Changed the American West* (Simon and Schuster, 2011), 34–39. Earp's other duties at Wichita included enforcing building codes, repairing sidewalks, collecting license fees from saloons and whore houses, and picking up dead animals from the streets. Ibid., 35–36.

144. Robert R. Dykstra, "Postscript: Overdosing on Dodge City," in *Major Problems in the History of the American West*, ed. Clyde A. Milner II et al. (Boston: Houghton Mifflin, 1997), 221. Richard White observes that while Bodie, California, was one town with a high murder rate (twenty-nine killings in its peak years), it was mostly bad men killing other bad men. For most Bodie residents, "everyday public life remained secure." White, 331–332.

145. See Guinn. Adam Winkler concludes that, "The Shootout at the O.K. Corral, then, is not only a story about America's gun culture. It is also a tale about America's gun *control* culture" [Winkler's emphasis]. Winkler, 173.

146. Zincke, 175. Baille-Grohman also noted that because men in the West "deem life too valuable to jeopardize it for some pettifogging meanness, or verbal affront, or slander, they are, as a rule, careful of their words and actions." William A. Baille-Grohman, *Camps in the Rockies: Being a Narrative of Life on the Frontier, and Sport in the Rocky Mountains, with an Account of the Cattle Ranches of the West* (New York: Charles Scribner's Sons, 1884), 29.

5

DOMESTIC RELATIONS

Women, Men, and Children and Their Education

Relations between the sexes in America were notably different from the European norm. Travelers from Europe were struck by the paradox that women and men in the United States shared more in their personal lives, but were separated more in their social lives. Also in contrast to Europe, child rearing in America was characterized by a laissez-faire approach that produced, according to one's viewpoint, either children that were more independent and mature, or children that were extremely rude and aggressive. Furthermore, when these children were old enough, they were typically educated together rather than separately—a novelty to Europeans who both praised and condemned the notion that the two sexes might prosper in the same classroom.

Women

Europeans were nearly united in praising American women—especially young American women—for their charm, independence, and lack of social snobbery.[1] Due to American women's "independent thought and action … they associated with whomsoever they pleased."[2] Summarizing the American woman's approach to life, Horace Annesley Vachell put it even more bluntly: "She obeys no law save that of her own sweet will."[3]

The independence of women in the United States was reflected in what Oscar Wilde called a "frank, fearless candour" and a rejection of "the subtle evasion and graceful mendacities of high life in Europe."[4] Indeed, in their observations of American women we can see the heavy weariness of these travelers with European social conventions, or "petty restraints" as Bram Stoker characterized them.[5] Léon Paul Blouet claimed that the American woman had grown "tired of the old formula, 'A lady cannot do that—it would be improper.'"[6] Women in the United

States, observed Emily Faithfull, were "happily not yet hampered by the arbitrary red-tape regulation" which weighed down her European sisters, and French scholar S. C. de Soissons believed that American women did not know social snobbery, which he described as "that moral sickness of all time."[7] For James Fullarton Muirhead, the great virtue of American women was that they lacked "the brutality of condescension" and "the meanness of toadyism."[8]

There was little doubt that there was greater freedom between the sexes in America than in Europe. Indeed, Paul de Rousiers claimed that a stranger's first impression of America was that "there are no sexes in the United States."[9] American boys and girls were more often than not educated in the same class-room and there was a free mixing of the two sexes on social occasions. Because American girls were "thrown into such free and ample relations" with American boys from an early age, a spirit of comradeship was developed with little "of the unknown or the mysterious about the opposite sex."[10] This created a number of positive outcomes later in life that were missing from the European social realm. A young American woman could laugh and talk and express herself, according to E. Catherine Bates, "without this depressing consciousness of peril to her future prospects."[11] (Bates makes a withering reference to "the pruning knife of English etiquette."[12]) There also seemed to be more respect shown to women by American men. Observing that a woman in America could walk by herself along Broadway and that no one would annoy her, Henry Latham asked, "Can as much be said for Regent Street or the Boulevards?"[13]

The confidence of American women and their disdain for European conventionality was expressed in a number of ways. Alexander Craib, for instance, was surprised by the number of American women who drove their own carriages.[14] When he was in Yosemite, J. W. Boddam-Whetham made the startling discovery that "strong-minded ladies here ride astride, and declare that it is easier and more comfortable than the orthodox mode." The disapproving Boddam-Whetham described one such lady as "a grim Amazon."[15] Paul de Rousiers claimed that the freedom given to American girls "would be disastrous in France," but "the decency of American manners" made it possible in the United States.[16] American women were granted a wide latitude in behavior because, as Oscar Wilde put it, "the worship of women is the national religion."[17] Every woman was a queen in America, exercising a charming, though despotic, rule over American men, and reveled in the confidence that nothing was too good for her.[18] And when she was in Europe, "'I am an American girl' is answer enough to any timid old-world bigot," said Wilde.[19]

Through a combination of naturalness, physical beauty, and conversational skill, American women ruled supreme. William Howard Russell was struck by what he called "an exquisite abandon and naturalness," while others were captivated by their beauty.[20] David Macrae cited "eyes radiant with intelligence, a light, graceful, often fragile form," and Harry Kessler referred to "tall, slender apparitions with dark eyes and a complexion like milk and roses."[21] (In a reminder of how standards of beauty change from era to era, Macrae claimed that every American girl knew her weight to within a few ounces, and that "every ounce of increase is hailed with delight."[22] Indeed, one of Marie Therese Blanc's criticisms of young American women was "too much thinness."[23]) Certainly, there was an element of women in the United States basking in their own beauty. Francesco Varvaro claimed that they did not so much want others to look at them as "they want to look at themselves." And, he added, "they know how to do it well."[24]

From an early date, American women had the reputation of being gifted conversationalists. Tocqueville confessed himself to be "surprised and almost frightened by the singular skill and pleasing audacity with which young American girls marshal thoughts and words while deftly negotiating the shoals of a sprightly conversation."[25] Part of this facility was no doubt related to the truncated childhood that prevailed in America. "The child is never a child in America," said Hamilton Aïdé, and as a consequence when a girl entered society "she is already an accomplished little woman of the world, quite able to take care of herself" and "to hold her own in verbal fence with young men and old."[26] Harry Kessler observed that young American girls were included in conversations from which they would have been excluded in Europe. Even more surprising, Kessler discovered that these girls often led the conversation, lending to the proceedings "something comradely" and allowing the stranger to become better acquainted with a girl in an evening than was possible in a week in Europe.[27] One European described young American women as possessing a "French verve and force about them, but there is also a Teutonic truthfulness."[28]

Léon Paul Blouet found that rather than being forced to exchange nothing but tiresome commonplaces as was the case in conversations with young French girls, with the American girl he could "chat away with as little embarrassment as I would with a young brother-officer of my regiment."[29] Another Frenchman, Paul Bourget, referred to a "picturesque speech which, when mingled with gaiety, produces an original and novel 'humor.'"[30] There was some doubt that American women actually knew what they were talking about (Oscar Wilde claimed that their success was based on never talking seriously "except about amusements").[31] But David Macrae added that "their general intelligence and vivacity make them very delightful companions."[32] Among the most important of their charms, according to "J. W. C.," was their lack of pretentiousness: "They are simply natural."[33]

American women not only reigned over their own country, but over the rest of the world as well. E. Catherine Bates called American girls "more companionable, brighter, more simple and less self-conscious" than English girls.[34] Even the French were conquered by the American female. Parisian Jacques Offenbach said that American women were the most "seductive women in the world" and that "many more of them are beautiful than in Paris."[35] S. C. de Soissons allowed that "a modern American woman is charming and almost superior to the majority of European women."[36]

Of the factors that had created what he called London's "social revolution," Oscar Wilde argued that the most important was the invasion of American women.[37] They "shine in our salons, and delight our dinner-parties; our guardsmen are taken captive by their brilliant complexions, and our beauties made jealous by their clever wit."[38] A similar state of affairs prevailed in Paris. Léon Paul Blouet said that when the American girl visited Paris "men seek her for her gaiety, wit, or beauty; mothers look favourably upon her for her dollars. The younger women tear her to shreds; nothing is wanting to her success."[39] M. E. W. Sherwood (Mrs. John Sherwood) also took note of this feminine triumph, claiming that "the march over England and the Continent by the American girl is a triumphant one. It is a great story of conquest."[40] The young American woman was not without her critics. Anne Clough, sister of the English poet, complained of American girls that they were too willing to engage in general conversation and talk of matters of which they had no expert knowledge.[41] Another Briton objected to the American girl's pronunciation ("unmusical and unpleasant to us") and to her "absence of that delicate reserve, that fragrance of propriety." Most galling of all, "we do not like your air of success, your air of appropriating everything." Sherwood shot back, "perhaps they do not altogether like the fact of success."[42]

Most American women, of course, did not have the luxury of spending their days being charming. There was broad agreement among European travelers that the women who were financially obliged to become part of the labor force found more kinds of work open for them in the United States than in Europe. Alexander Craib claimed that American women were employed in government offices to a much greater extent than women in Britain, and by 1900, one-third of clerical positions in the United States were filled by women.[43] Another area of white-collar employment for women in the United States was teaching—a profession that was increasingly feminized as the century wore on. At the lower economic end, women in America did needlework (one of the most poorly compensated jobs), and performed various others kinds of sweatshop work (rolling cigars, making paper collars and artificial flowers).[44] There was also mill work which, despite the twelve to thirteen hour days, was popular with young New England women because no other occupation paid as much.[45] One exception to the employment rule was bar maid, an occupation that Americans viewed "as degrading as the field-work of French and German women."[46]

The largest single category of work for women in 1890 was domestic and personal service (42.6 percent) with manufacturing and industry the next largest category (26.3 percent).[47] Domestic service in the United States was dominated by Irish immigrant women because, as historian Hasia Diner has noted, native-born Protestant girls found this labor "so odious, so demanding, so beneath their sense of self" that they would take poorer-paid jobs elsewhere rather than suffer the indignity of working in another woman's home.[48] In one example, an American woman who had taken on a well-paying job as a domestic quit because, she said, "'The cook and the waitress were just common, uneducated Irish, and I had to room with one and stand the personal habits of both.'"[49] The supposed hopelessness of Irish "Bridgets" became a stock joke among their middle-class employers (e.g. the Bridget who answered the door by yelling through the key-hole, or the Bridget who crawled down stairways on hands and knees).[50]

The strong American work ethic dictated that even financially prosperous women be willing to do rough work when it was necessary. In one example, Alexandra Gripenberg went to visit a young woman "with a fortune of several hundred thousand dollars" and discovered her shaking the carpets and sweeping the floors on her maid's day off. According to Gripenberg, the woman "didn't even explain the reason for my finding her on her knees on the floor, broom in hand."[51]

Men

At a banquet attended by Hugues Le Roux, General Horace Parker told his audience that "'in the United States we men are governed by our wives, and our wives are governed by our daughters. So the country is run by the young girls!'"[52] Parker was exaggerating for humorous effect, but not by much, and there were few doubts that women totally dominated middle- and upper-class society in America. As Joseph Hatton expressed it, the American male was content to accept "a happy form of petticoat government."[53] Rudyard Kipling noted that, "Nothing is too good for an American's daughter," and Hugues Le Roux claimed that he had never seen anything to compare with the luxuries that the American father bestowed upon his daughter.[54] In his summation of the status of American women, James Bryce put it simply: "The world is at their feet."[55]

Picking up the tab for the American female's social ascendency was the American male. Primogeniture, which in Europe typically meant that the eldest son inherited the estate, was absent in both practice and law in America. (At least one traveler claimed that this eliminated the dissension and unhappiness that were so characteristic of British families.[56]) Instead, it was the wishes and education of girls that received first priority among the American middle class, while most boys abandoned their studies at age fifteen or earlier, rushing into work as "a greyhound to rush after the hare." They received little or no help from their fathers.[57] It was a long, grim haul for the sons, taking on "the overwhelming burden of business the day the father, killed by overwork, shall fail his family."[58] American men made a point of not acquainting female family members with the crushing financial burdens under which they labored and, as a consequence, "often the divinity is the last to learn that the worshipper who has decked her with diamonds is on the eve of bankruptcy."[59]

The extent to which the American woman appreciated the sacrifices that were being made for her cannot be known, but Léon Paul Blouet had the impression that she "does not render to man a hundredth part of the adoration he renders to her."[60] As for the American man, "His lot is a lonely one," said Rudyard Kipling.

"The women get the ha'pence; the kicks are all his own."[61] As he traveled along Broadway in New York, H. Hussey Vivian could see clear evidence of how the money, "made by the sweat of men's brows in the south, is wasted by their gentle mates in the northern end of the same street."[62]

With American girls groomed to be charming and American boys groomed for work, it is not surprising that there was a gap in social accomplishments. Emily Faithfull claimed that American girls were more clever than boys, and Oscar Wilde found young American women "pretty and charming" and American men "entirely given to business."[63] While men were chained to their jobs, American women were learning French and German, reading the latest books, and widening the gulf between themselves and their men.[64] Business, said Rose G. Kingsley, was "the haunting demon of America," while Mrs. E. H. Carbutt referred to the "dreadful" hours that American men spent on the job: "There can be no social life or interest in music, literature, politics, or science when men are at their office twelve hours a day."[65] The consequence, as noted by Harry Kessler, was that American women were "fully responsible for society" in the United States because the devotion of American men to their jobs meant that they were unable to sparkle either socially or intellectually.[66] "It is by woman and for woman," said Paul Bourget, "that these social circles exist."[67]

During the daylight hours, women and men were effectively segregated from each other. When Italian visitor Giuseppe Giacosa was in America in 1891, he took note of a phenomenon that was rare in Italy: the separation of the workplace and the home. Without the "mitigating influence of the home," said Giacosa, the American male was able to "arm himself for business with a harsh, thankless selfishness."[68] When she was in the United States in 1894, Marie Therese Blanc became acquainted with many American women's clubs (which, of course, had an exclusively female membership). Blanc was bewildered by the absence of men, observing that "nothing could be more foreign to French habits."[69] Emily Faithfull also could not help but notice that at afternoon receptions there was an absence of men, who could not attend because they could not sacrifice to society their working hours.[70] As Madame de San Carlos put it, "for the American woman life is pleasure taken seriously; for the men it is work, which becomes the only pleasure."[71] At the end of the day, men staggered home from their jobs to find that their lack of polish made them unfit for women's company.[72] Foreigners frequently commented that at an American dinner "the men sit silent, and are talked to and entertained by their fair neighbours."[73]

Remarkably, American men responded to this gender disparity not with resentment, but with chivalry. Harold Brydges claimed that the men of America were "more chivalrous than those of any other nation."[74] "Even the purgatorial fires of matrimony," said Alexandra Gripenberg, could not destroy the attentiveness that American men bestowed on women.[75] This was an impression held both by those who admired America and those who hated it. William H. Davies, who held American society in high regard, claimed that the most pleasing trait of

American males was the great esteem in which they held women.[76] Lepel Henry Griffin, who found little to like in America, seconded Davies' opinion, concluding that nothing placed the country "in a brighter or more honourable light, than the universal respect publicly paid to women by men of all degrees."[77] Like Griffin, French traveler Lucien Biart was "no admirer of Americans; they are rough, ill-bred, and their brusqueness is proverbial." Still, the respect for women in America "makes me envy this quality for my countrymen."[78]

On her ocean voyage to America, Iza Duffus Hardy could not help but notice that there was one male aboard who was always assisting women who were trying to navigate the heaving deck. He turned out to be an American and, as Hardy put it, a "credit to the reputed chivalry of his nation."[79] Likewise, on her ship from France to America, Marie Therese Blanc noted with approval the respect shown by American men even to women with whom they were unacquainted.[80] Once in the United States, Blanc herself would be the recipient of an act of chivalry when an "ill-dressed man, who looked like a vagabond" politely assisted her off the platform of a street railway car.[81] Italian Dario Papa describes an incident that speaks both to the American drive to make money and to the chivalrous regard of the fair sex. In New York there was an elevated railway accident in which the structure was damaged and the passengers had to be evacuated through the homes that adjoined the tracks. The homeowners charged each male passenger twenty-five cents for the privilege of climbing through their houses, but charged the female passengers nothing.[82]

Certainly, this deference to women was not the custom elsewhere in the world. Hugues Le Roux was standing in line at a post office in a Western American town and was astonished to see that the men let the women pass before them, and that the women accepted this courtesy "as though it were the most natural privilege."[83] Men were also expected to take their hats off to women in elevators ("there is a flounce in and a flounce out—'Hats off; we're here,'" as one traveler put it).[84] In his condemnation of American society, Knut Hamsun berated this custom, as well as the practice of giving women the inside of the sidewalk, offering women seats on a crowded streetcar, and immediately apologizing if one forgot oneself and swore in front of a woman.[85]

The custom of American men surrendering their seats on public transportation to women was especially irritating to European males. J. J. Aubertin called it "absurd obsequiousness, for the women care not how crowded a car is when they know they can make others move for them."[86] Baron Hübner reported riding on a tram and being roused from his meditations by "a tap of a parasol … I see standing right in front of me a young woman, who looks at me from head to foot, with an imperious, haughty, and even angry expression." Hübner hastily surrendered his seat, "which she takes at once, without deigning to thank me, even by a look or a smile."[87] In San Francisco, Horace Annesley Vachell was a witness to an amusing tableau in which an English tourist refused to give up his seat to a woman on a cable car. With the full attention of the car upon him, the Englishman blustered, "'You're all looking at me,' he said angrily; 'and you think I ought to give up my seat. Well, I'm not going to do it. And if the men of this country had more sense they'd keep what they've paid for, and then the cable companies would provide seats enough to go around.'" According to Vachell, the gentleman "was scarlet in the face before he finished, and everybody laughed."[88] Gallantry toward women was no more the rule in Italy than it was in England. Francesco Carega di Muricce concluded that American men were more courteous toward women from all classes than Italian men were toward upper-class women, and noted that the general term of address found throughout America— "Ladies and Gentlemen"—was in inverse order in Latin countries.[89]

Nowhere was the American male's chivalry more dramatically illustrated than in his treatment of women traveling alone. William Saunders said that "it is the pride of Americans" that an unaccompanied woman could travel from coast to coast "without being subject to any unpleasantness or to a vestige of impertinence."[90] Emily Faithfull made just such a trip, and noted that she had received "every kindness and consideration" while praising "the polite deference shown by American gentlemen."[91] As David Macrae put it, "a lady in America may traverse the whole continent alone without the slightest fear of insult or annoyance, and will find special accommodation awaiting her at every point."[92] (One such accommodation, the "Ladies' Drawing Room" in hotels, had the advantage of admitting only gentlemen who were willing to "temporarily forego the delights of tobacco." Hotel clerks also checked women into their rooms before men.)[93] On her trip west, Lady Duffus Hardy was struck by the kind regard that men gave to female passengers, and especially by the great care that they bestowed on a young girl traveling by herself from Boston to Arizona. "Indeed," said Hardy, "to thoroughly enjoy travelling in perfect comfort and freedom from anxiety, one must be an unprotected female."[94] Lucien Biart contrasted the American example with that of France, where the unescorted female traveler was forced to endure "the insolent looks or the vulgar compliments which are so common among French people."[95]

Marriage and Divorce

It was somewhat of a contradiction that Europeans often viewed America both as a country where the prospects for a happy marriage were greater and as a place where the severance of a marriage was overly easy. A number of observers noted that young American women and men spent much more time together, and on a freer basis, than was the case in Europe. In England, said one traveler, "a man often knows next to nothing of the girl he is engaged to," while the girl "has even fewer opportunities of judging what a young man is worth." But in America, "it is generally a man's or a girl's own fault if he or she does not succeed in making out pretty well what the other is good for."[96] Indeed, the very concept of marriage in the United States was different from the European norm. As Paul de Rousiers noted, marriage in America was a union of two people, rather than an alliance of two families.[97]

On the other side of the marital coin, travelers were scandalized by the easy divorce laws that prevailed in the United States.[98] There is little doubt that divorce carried less of a stigma in the United States than it did in Europe. As E. Catherine Bates put it, "*Here*, when the chain begins to gall, it can be cut with far less risk to their social status" (original emphasis). Emily Faithfull devoted an entire chapter to the subject of divorce, and in a peculiar choice of words, condemned what she called the "alluring" divorce court that would willingly "set the captive free."[99] She was especially disturbed by the divorce rate in California, an appalling 10 percent.[100] When Iza Duffus Hardy and her companion attended a dinner party of fourteen in San Francisco, they made a passing reference to divorce and immediately became conscious that it was a subject to avoid. When Hardy later asked her American friend why they had received warning glances, she was told that these were second marriages for each of the couples.[101]

Marriage and divorce in America was the province of individual states, and those fleeing marriages in the East generally found that the further west one went the looser were the divorce laws. The most liberal states could grant divorces on whatever grounds the court deemed proper. Long before the Civil War, Indianapolis was a Mecca for divorce, until the Indiana legislature passed a law in 1873 that tightened up the requirements for marital separation.[102] Chicago also enjoyed a reputation as a place where a marriage could easily be dissolved (Scottish visitor David Macrae condemned that city not only for its ease of divorce but for its prevalence of abortion).[103] One perhaps apocryphal story then in circulation was that when railway conductors announced that the train would soon be arriving in Chicago, they would add, "'Twenty minutes for divorce.'"[104] Further west, both North Dakota and South Dakota established a thriving business in migratory divorce beginning in the 1880s.[105] What peeved Knut Hamsun about divorce in America was that it was easier for a woman to get a divorce than a man.[106] Not surprisingly, Oscar Wilde was the one European traveler to put a positive spin on American-style divorce, which he claimed added an element of "romantic uncertainty" to marriage.[107]

Children

Historian Steven Mintz has emphasized that the Civil War's impact on family life included "huge numbers of orphans and impoverished fatherless families." Eight states opened institutions for the orphans of dead soldiers, and the war and the ongoing poverty of immigrant families pushed lower-class children to the brink.[108] Mintz also sees two contradictory trends emerging in how Americans formulated childhood: The "useful childhood," in which children worked to contribute to the family economy, and the "protected childhood," in which children were sheltered from the responsibilities of adulthood.[109]

European travelers observed both types of childhood in the United States, but one thing that seemed nearly universal among American children was that they matured quickly and asserted their independence from an early age. Tocqueville had already concluded in the 1830s that adolescence had been eliminated in America, with persons moving directly from childhood to adulthood.[110] This impression was confirmed by later travelers, with one Englishman claiming that children in the United States "aim to be little men and women as soon as they can walk and speak."[111] Why this was so was the subject of some debate. Horace Annesley Vachell believed that it was related to a gradual withdrawal of maternal love as the child grew older, while others theorized that "a little republicanism" had passed from the nation into the private home, endowing children with an independence and equality seldom found among European children.[112] According to A. Maurice Low, American parents regarded freedom as essential to a child's development, and rebellion was seen as sign of good character.[113] The roots of this attitude, he said, could be traced to an American contempt for the law, fed by "the fetish of individualism" and disdain for "artificial conventions."[114] The end result, as Charles Wentworth Dilke bluntly asserted, was that American children were "'forward,' ill-mannered, and immoral."[115]

Children in the United States grew up early in part because their labor was often essential to the survival of their families. By 1890, close to 20 percent of American children between the ages of 10 and 15 (some 1.5 million) were classified by the U.S. Census as "gainful workers."[116] In one case, a school teacher in frontier California expressed frustration about one of his fifteen-year-old students who was often absent from school. But this teacher also had great admiration for the heavy, adult responsibilities this student shouldered, including driving his father's wagon loaded with produce some 150 miles across the Sierra mountains and selling the produce to miners, while simultaneously maintaining his livestock and wagon, and looking out for hostile Indians.[117] Children in mining communities were also forced to mature quickly, entering the mines as soon as they were able to supplement the family's meager income.[118]

But most European travelers could only see the negative aspects of the early maturation of American children. From her observations in the West, Isabella Bird concluded that childhood had been eliminated, and installed in its place "debased imitations of men and women." After being nurtured in an atmosphere of profanity, greed and godlessness, these children, according to Bird, asserted and gained independence from their parents at the age of ten.[119] During his travels, William A. Baille-Grohman met a boy of fourteen whom he described as "a genuine Western-raised child." He admired the boy for his maturity, but felt hampered in his communication with the boy because of the boy's "astonishing flow of bad language and the constant application to his plug."[120] Another visitor, who had the misfortune of being guided through Yellowstone by a teamster and his son, advised future travelers that they "never allow a boy to accompany a party of this kind, and, least of all, a western frontier boy. The patience with which an American will submit to insolence from an ill-conditioned young cub of this kind is truly marvellous, and utterly passes the comprehension of an Englishman."[121] "Parental authority," said German traveler Baron Hübner, "is *nil*."[122] The upper-class society of New York created a similar result in a totally different social milieu. Beginning at the age of seven or eight, society children were sent to "dancing schools" where they were thrown in contact with the opposite sex, and turned into what European commentators saw as grotesque caricatures of men and women.[123]

Outside this charmed circle, conditions for children were considerably grimmer. In Boston alone, some 6,000 children were living on the streets in 1865, and conditions in New York were considerably worse. When American social reformer Charles Loring Brace published his landmark study *The Dangerous Classes of New York* in 1872, he estimated that in that city alone there were some 20,000–30,000 homeless children.[124]

"Spoilt, capricious, precocious little old men and women" were the words that E. Catherine Bates used to describe American children (or at least the middle-class children she encountered), and she believed that an important factor in producing this crop of young monsters was hotel life. Children raised in hotels were always in the company of elders and non-family members, and parents were all too willing to acquiesce to children's demands to avoid embarrassment in front of strangers.[125] "The effects of hotel life on the lives and manners of young people," said J. W. Boddam-Whetham, "are but too evident."[126]

But while the good manners of these children were often lacking, American society as a whole continued to both indulge and respect the young and to listen to them despite their youth.[127] Bates saw this tendency at its worst at a hotel in Las Vegas, where she and some other travelers relaxing in the drawing room became a captive audience to a play put on by some of the guests' children. The play "dragged its weary length along" for some two hours, said Bates, with the parents seemingly oblivious to the intense boredom of the majority.[128] George Augustus Sala summed up the feelings of many Europeans when he said that "close and frequent acquaintance with small juveniles in an American hotel is apt to induce the conviction that, all things considered, you would like the American child best in a pie."[129]

Surely one element in the European condemnation of American child rearing was that this approach was so alien to European practice. Paul de Rousiers related an anecdote from a transatlantic voyage that illustrated this difference. While on deck, Rousiers observed an American four-year-old girl climb up on the railing and lean out over the water. As Rousiers readied himself to rescue the child, her mother came by and asked her if she was enjoying herself—then walked to the other end of the deck. Rousiers noted that a French mother would have panicked under similar circumstances, but because the American mother believed that everyone should be able to look after themselves, "she naturally applies it to her child." While younger American children were sometimes "imprudent," said

Rousiers, as youths they were "bold and enterprising." In contrast, French children—raised to be obedient and cautious—"lack initiative" as youths.[130]

Other defenders of the American style of child rearing included Finnish traveler Alexandra Gripenberg, who confirmed that Americans took their children everywhere with them, seldom punished them, and talked to them like adults. As a consequence, said Gripenberg, American children were imbued with strong characters at an early age, while Finnish children "seem to be nothing but small animals which eat and sleep."[131] For James Fullarton Muirhead, the best measure of child rearing was in the adults that resulted, and in the United States, by some "moral miracle," "the horrid little minx blossoms out into a charming and womanly girl," and "the cross and dyspeptic little boy becomes a courteous and amiable man."[132]

Education

David Macrae found that "nothing in America excited my admiration more than the system of common schools."[133] This view was echoed by most European travelers, with one calling the establishment of public schools the "proudest distinction" of the Republic.[134] Even those who expressed some skepticism found much to like in the American educational system. James Fraser, who was dispatched to the United States by Parliament in 1865 to report on the American common school system, did not find schooling in America to be universally good. But Fraser admitted that Americans were "if not the most highly educated, yet certainly the most generally educated and intelligent people on the earth."[135]

Among the impressive aspects of American education was that the children of the wealthy went to the same schools as poor children, that textbooks were provided at public expense, and that there was no corporal punishment in the classroom.[136] Some European travelers even held out hope that the American educational system could bring to heel the savage immigrant populations. When British clergyman F. Barham Zincke visited a school in New York, he noted with approval that the children of "the lowest and most vicious part of the Irish and German population of the city" were being educated.[137] Even in remote frontier areas, the establishment of schools was a priority. In rural Kansas, schools "spring up like mushrooms" wherever there were a dozen houses grouped together, while rough mining towns had free schools where the poorest person could send his child.[138] This translated into a high literacy rate and, according to James Bryce, "a vast multitude of intelligent, cultivated, and curious readers."[139] In 1876, 80 per cent of Americans were literate, and by 1915 the literacy rate had risen to 94 per cent.[140] While schooling tended to be spotty in the American West (in 1910, 25 percent of schools in Montana were open for only four months while the school term in rural Arizona averaged 105 days), even here John Fox was impressed by the overall literacy rate, and amazed "to find cowmen who liked to read even ancient histories."[141]

A common criticism of the American educational systems was its provincialism. F. Barham Zincke found that while American geography was carefully taught in the schools, "the geography of the rest of the world was almost ignored."[142] Alexandra Gripenberg referred to the "sublime Anglo-Saxon ignorance of everything Scandinavian" in America.[143] Knut Hamsun was equally miffed at the emphasis that American schools placed on American subjects, and was additionally peeved that Americans referred to all Scandinavians as "Swedes."[144] But what really set Hamsun off was a teacher's professed amazement when Hamsun told him that Norway also had the telegraph.[145] But provincial or not, the American, according to one British traveler, knew more about his country than the average Englishman knew about his.[146]

As in many other areas of American life, the South was the exception to general trends in education. In much of the antebellum South it had been illegal to teach a slave how to read, and Southern whites had not fared much better than Southern blacks in gaining an education. Before the Civil War only Kentucky and North Carolina offered free public education. The result had been predictably low literacy rates: in 1850, 20 percent of Southern whites could not read or write (compared to 0.42 percent in New England).[147]

In the postbellum South there continued to be little in the way of community support for the education of black children. The editor of the *Alabama Christian Advocate*, for instance, called such concerns a "form of negrophilism" influenced by "Yankee fanaticism."[148] Also, the idea of educating different classes and different races together was, according to David Macrae, especially "abhorrent to Southern ideas."[149] The problem was compounded by a deficient number of teachers, with few in the South entering into the teaching profession. When he was in Mississippi in 1871, Robert Somers reported that there was a great shortage of both white and black teachers.[150] Still, during Reconstruction, tax-supported schools were established in every state in the South, although in race-segregated classrooms.[151] The end of Reconstruction adversely affected education for both blacks and whites. Louisiana is the most doleful example. Between 1880 and 1900, it had the dubious distinction of being the only state in the Union in which the percentage of whites able to read and write actually decreased.[152]

Immigration had a huge impact on education in America. In America's large cities with teeming immigrant populations, schools were bursting at the seams and large numbers of students were denied admission to classrooms simply because there was no room for them. New York City, for instance, turned away 9,000 students in 1881.[153] The amount of education a child received in America was often determined by his or her ethnic group. Among Jewish, Italian, and Polish immigrants, boys were more likely to stay in school longer. Among Irish, Swedish, and German immigrants (and among native-born whites), it was girls who most typically received extended educations.[154]

German immigration was a special case, with German immigrants tending to settle in rural areas and medium-sized cities rather than in large cities.

When William Saunders visited Grand Island, Nebraska, in the late 1870s, the local school teacher told him there were some twenty school-aged children in the vicinity, but only three, on average, attended. The reason, said the teacher, was that most area farmers were Germans, who "kept their children at home."[155] While this would seem to be aberrant behavior from a culture that highly valued education, Germans often withheld their children from American schools because from an early date American educators tried to "Americanize" (or from the German perspective, "deculturalize") German-speaking children by substituting English for German in classroom instruction. The Germans pushed back, and succeeded in gaining classes conducted in German in cities that included Cincinnati, St. Louis, Indianapolis, Louisville, and St. Paul.[156]

In a departure from the European norm, girls and boys were taught in the same classroom in American schools. This approach started in the West, where it was financially impossible to maintain two separate school systems. Coeducation rapidly made inroads in the East as well, and was additionally adopted in high schools and colleges. European visitors to American classrooms were somewhat surprised to discover that this style of learning benefitted both sexes, with the male students better behaved and the female students having "no difficulty in holding their own." Hoping to institute a similar system in England, Dudley Campbell assured Britons that "the minds of the women seemed to remain essentially feminine."[157]

As a profession, teaching in America was rapidly feminized, a process that began as early as the 1830s, when school districts discovered they could get away with paying female teachers some 60 percent less than male teachers.[158] When F. Barham Zincke visited a school with 600 students in Cincinnati, he noted that the entire teaching staff, except one, was female.[159] The rising number of states with mandatory school attendance laws also made teaching an expanding profession.[160]

Hugues Le Roux, who spent a great deal of energy investigating the American education system, was disconcerted to find in the United States a spectacle that existed nowhere else on the planet: "a nation where the women taken as a whole are more learned than the men."[161] Most boys abandoned their studies around the age of fifteen, then rushed into business or the trades.[162] Girls tended to stay in school longer than boys (more girls than boys were enrolled in secondary schools), and when they went to universities or normal schools for teacher training, they were able to flourish.[163] When Le Roux asked one young woman at a college if she was not anxiously waiting for the end of her studies so that she could marry, she answered that on the contrary,

> 'We would like to lengthen the days and add years upon years.'
> 'It is not only the study that we love, but it's the discussion, the passionate discussion and defence of our own ideas, our own enthusiasms.'
> 'Where will we find as interesting and as cultured a surrounding again?'[164]

With American males "absorbed in business," continued the student, it was easy to understand why "almost none of us are impatient to marry, and why a great many of the more serious of us have decided not to marry at all."[165]

Such attitudes, and the creation of what Le Roux calls "the third sex" (women who had chosen a career over raising children) were extremely disturbing to this French visitor. Women, claimed Le Roux, were "destined by God and by Nature to live for others, as a young girl for her parents, as a married woman for her husband, as a mother for her children, as a grandmother for her descendants."[166] And despite testimony from young women themselves (in her travels in the United States, Emily Faithfull noted that "several mothers complained to me that daughters are always asking 'to spend another year at Vassar'"), Le Roux concluded that women's college studies "are beyond the capacity of their sex, they impair their chances of fulfilling their part in the divine plan upon earth."[167] While Paul Bourget was less judgmental about women who chose careers (he observed one female typist who possessed what he called a "serenity of conscience, a calm will, a dignity"), the weight of French views was generally against higher education and careers for women.[168] When Marie Therese Blanc was invited to an American club for female college graduates, she expressed fears that these women were "overloaded with learning," and could not help asking herself, "What use is all this in the home?"[169] Certainly, the view that biology is destiny was not unique to the French. For instance, as late as 1914, Los Angeles Schools Superintendent John Haywood Francis declared that "the study of algebra had caused many a girl to lose her soul."[170]

Notes

1. Southern women, according to David Macrae, were less emancipated because "the South preserves a higher standard of female virtue, perhaps I should say white virtue." David Macrae, *The Americans at Home* [1870] (New York: E. P. Dutton, 1952). 273.
2. William Saunders, *Through the Light Continent, or, The United States in 1877–78* [1879] (New York: Arno Press, 1974), 4–6. Lucien Biart described a fellow passenger on a ship as "a true American woman, and did just what she liked." Lucien Biart, *My Rambles in the New World* [1876], trans. Mary de Hauteville (London: Sampson, Low, Marston, Searle, & Rivington, 1877), 63.
3. Horace Annesley Vachell, *Life and Sport on the Pacific Slope* (New York: Dodd, Mead and Co., 1901), 51. Referring to American women, Kipling said, "they understand; they can take care of themselves; they are superbly independent." Rudyard Kipling, *American Notes* [1891] (Norman: University of Oklahoma Press, 1981), 38. James Bryce claimed that American custom allowed women a "greater measure of freedom in doing what they will and going where they please" than in any nation, with the possible exception of Russia. James Bryce, *The American Commonwealth*, v. 2 (New York: The Commonwealth Publishing Co., 1908), 682.
4. Oscar Wilde, "American Women," in Oscar Wilde, *The Works of Oscar Wilde* (New York: AMS Press, 1972), 12.
5. Bram Stoker, "A Glimpse of America" [1886] in *Bram Stoker's A Glimpse of America and Other Lectures, Interviews and Essays*, ed. Richard Dalby (Westcliff-on-Sea, UK: Desert Island Books, 2002), 19.

6. Max O'rell and Jack Allyn, *Jonathan and His Continent: Rambles Through American Society*, trans. Madame Paul Blouet (Bristol: J. W. Arrowsmith, 1889), 66.

7. Emily Faithfull, *Three Visits to America* (New York: Fowler & Wells, 1884), 338; S. C. de Soissons, *A Parisian in America* (Boston: Estes and Lauriat, 1896), 13–14.

8. James Fullarton Muirhead, *The Land of Contrasts: A Briton's View of his American Kin* (London: Lamson, Wolffe and Co., 1898), 53.

9. Paul de Rousiers, *American Life*, trans. A. J. Herbertson (New York: Firmin-Didot, 1892), 265.

10. Muirhead, 33.

11. E. Catherine Bates, *A Year in the Great Republic*, v. 1 (London: Ward & Downey, 1887), 49. Madame de San Carlos argued that the American woman respected merit without troubling about birth or wealth. Madame de San Carlos, "Americans at Home," *Review of Reviews* 1, no. 6 (June 1890), 487. Not everyone was so enthusiastic. Referring to the women of New York, Antonio Gallenga claimed that "she is an equal, and more often an aggravating, overbearing confederate!" Quoted in Andrew J. Torrielli, *Italian Opinion on America, As Revealed by Italian Travelers, 1859–1900* (Cambridge, MA: Harvard University Press, 1941), n. 2, 170.

12. Bates, v. 1, 53.

13. Henry Latham, *Black and White: A Journal of a Three Months' Tour in the United States* [1867] (New York: Negro Universities Press, 1969), 251. An anonymous writer for *Cornhill Magazine* also observed of the American woman that, "She may go on foot or in the horse-cars through the streets of a city without being exposed to remark, much less to impertinence." Anonymous, "On Some Peculiarities of Society in America," *The Cornhill Magazine* 26 (December 1872), 707.

14. Alexander Craib, *America and the Americans: A Tour in the United States and Canada, With Chapters on American Home Life* (London: Alexander Gardner, 1892), 99.

15. J. W. Boddam-Whetham, *Western Wanderings: A Record of Travel in the Evening Land* (London: Richard Bentley and Son, 1874), 124.

16. Rousiers, 269.

17. Wilde, "American Women," 7.

18. Wilde, "American Women," 7, 6; Oscar Wilde, "The American Man," in Oscar Wilde, *The Collected Oscar Wilde* (New York: Barnes and Noble Classics, 2007), 307–308.

19. Wilde claimed that "this phrase expresses at once dignity, courage, self-respect and the independence of the emancipated republican." Wilde, "American Women," 11.

20. William Howard Russell, *Hesperothen, Notes from the West: A Record of a Ramble in the United States and Canada in the Spring and Summer of 1881*, v. 1 (London: S. Low, Marston, Searle & Rivington, 1882), 167.

21. Macrae called the American woman "nearer the popular idea of an angel than any being I ever beheld out of dream-land." Macrae, 40; Harry Kessler, *Journey to the Abyss: The Diaries of Count Harry Kessler, 1880–1918*, trans. and ed. Laird Easton (New York: Knopf, 2011), 63.

22. Macrae, 40, 41.

23. Marie Therese de Solms Blanc, *The Condition of Woman in the United States: A Traveller's Notes* [1895], trans. Abby Langdon Alger (New York: Arno Press, 1972), 26.

24. Quoted in Torrielli, 188. Translated from the Italian by Pietro Bonomi.

25. Alexis de Tocqueville, *Democracy in America* [1835], trans. Arthur Goldhammer (New York: Library of America, 2004), 693.

26. Hamilton Aïdé, "Social Aspects of American Life," *The Nineteenth Century* 29, no. 172 (June 1891), 891.

27. Kessler, 53.

28. Anonymous, "On Some Peculiarities of Society in America," 711.

29. O'rell and Allyn, 67, 68.

30. Paul Bourget, *Outre-Mer: Impressions of America* (London: T. Fisher Unwin, 1895), 68.
31. Oscar Wilde, "Americans in London," in Oscar Wilde, *The Essays of Oscar Wilde* [1916], ed. Albert & Charles Boni (Bonibooks, 1935), 200.
32. Macrae, 42.
33. J. W. C., "Social New York," *MacMillan's Magazine* 26 (June 1872), 121–122.
34. Bates, v. 1, 15.
35. Jacques Offenbach, *Orpheus in America: Offenbach's Diary of His Journey to the New World* [1877], trans. Lander MacClintock (New York: Greenwood Press, 1969), 82.
36. "She is more amusing, more frank, more funny,—and has infinite variety; she is more serious also." Soissons, 8.
37. Wilde, "Americans in London," 202–203.
38. Wilde, "American Man," 305. Matthew Arnold noted that "a perfectly natural manner is as rare among Englishwomen of the middle classes as it is general among American women of like condition with them." Matthew Arnold, "Civilization in the United States," in Matthew Arnold, *Civilization in the United States: First and Last Impressions of America* [1888] (Freeport, NY: Books for Libraries Press, 1972), 168.
39. O'rell and Allyn, 68.
40. M. E. W. Sherwood, "American Girls in Europe," *North American Review* 403 (June 1890), 689.
41. Christopher Mulvey, *Transatlantic Manners: Social Patterns in Nineteenth-Century Anglo-American Travel Literature* (Cambridge: Cambridge University Press, 1990), 184.
42. Sherwood, 684.
43. Craib, 129; Thomas J. Schlereth, *Victorian America: Transformations in Everyday Life, 1876–1915* (New York: Harper Perennial, 1992), 67.
44. See Hasia Diner, *Erin's Daughters in America: Irish Immigrant Women in the Nineteenth Century* (Baltimore: Johns Hopkins University Press, 1983), 74–80.
45. Grady McWhiney observes that while school teachers received slightly higher wages than mill workers, they were only paid for part of the year. Grady McWhiney, *Southerners and Other Americans* (New York: Basic Books, 1973), 13–14.
46. Harold Brydges, *Uncle Sam at Home* (New York: Henry Holt and Co., 1888), 52. Maria Therese Blanc observed that "the European custom of permitting women to work in the fields like beasts of burden seems to Americans barbarous." Blanc, 257. In Milwaukee, W. E. Adams found that most people waiting on tables were female, while black men dominated the ranks of waiters in Washington, and Irish men made up the majority of waiters in New York. W. E. Adams, *Our American Cousins: Being Personal Impressions of the People and Institutions of the United States* (London: Walter Scott, 1883), 212.
47. See Émile Levasseur, *The American Workman*, trans. Thomas S. Adams (Baltimore: Johns Hopkins University, 1900), 352.
48. Diner, 81. Diner adds that Italian women and Jewish women also rejected domestic service "as a result of the dictates of their own cultures and opted for other kinds of jobs that they defined as more harmonious with their values." Ibid., 83. In 1900, over 60 per cent of Irish female wage earners in America were domestics. Schlereth, 73.
49. Quoted in Levasseur, 354.
50. Schlereth, 72.
51. Alexandra Gripenberg, *A Half Year in the New World: Miscellaneous Sketches of Travel in the United States* [1899], trans. and ed. Ernest J. Moyne (Newark: University of Delaware Press, 1954), 201.
52. Quoted in Hugues Le Roux, *Business and Love* (New York: Dodd, Mead and Co., 1903), 75.
53. Joseph Hatton, *Henry Irving's Impressions of America, Narrated in a Series of Sketches, Chronicles, and Conversations* [1884], v. 1 (New York: Benjamin Blom, 1971), 287.
54. Kipling, 39; Le Roux, 108.

55. Bryce, v. 2, 684.

56. W. C. M., "American Traits," *Eclectic Magazine* 16, no. 1 (New Series, July 1872), 55. An American traveling in Britain observed that "the social arrangement which selects one child out of a family to be the exclusive recipient of the honors and estate, and discriminates against girls, is held in profound disfavor, and could by no possibility be made to take root among us." Horace White, "An American's Impressions of England," *Eclectic Magazine* 22, no. 5 (New Series, November 1875), 555.

57. J. W. C., 119; Le Roux, 74, 71; Saunders, 400. Madame de San Carlos also noted of young American men that they started in business without assistance from their families. San Carlos, v. 1, no. 6, 487. Paul de Rousiers cites an experience in which he dined with a millionaire brewer and his family one evening, then toured the brewery the following day with the owner. When they went into the cooper's shop, the owner asked Rousier if there was anyone there he recognized. There was—the brewer's son that Rousier had dined with the previous evening, but who now had blackened hands and was wearing workman's clothing. Rousiers, 258.

58. Le Roux, 103.

59. Vachell, 54–55. Vachell claimed that this pampering of daughters cut across class lines: "Upon a hundred ranches I have seen mothers cooking, washing, sewing, while the daughters of the house were reading novels or playing the piano. I have known a mother make her own underclothing out of flour sacks, where her little girl was wearing silk." Ibid., 74. A. Maurice Low noted that, "It came to be accepted as a canon of so-called chivalry that men must keep their wives in ignorance of their business, because knowledge would harass and annoy them; and it was proof of wifely loyalty to accept the gifts that the male god provided in the shape of horses and carriages, jewels and frocks, but to seek no reason why the conjugal heaven rained manna." A. Maurice Low, *The American People: A Study in National Psychology*, v. 2 (Boston: Houghton Mifflin, 1909), 95–96. Baron Hübner claimed that it was the woman who suffered the most from this arrangement because "she cannot lighten his burden or share his labour, anxiety, and cares, for she knows nothing of his business, or, for want of time, there has been little or no interchange of thought between them." Baron Hübner, *A Ramble Round the World, 1871*, trans. Lady Elizabeth Herbert (London: MacMillan and Co., 1878), 56.

60. O'rell and Allyn, 82.

61. Kipling, 39.

62. H. Hussey Vivian, *Notes of a Tour in America from August 7th to November 17th, 1877* (London: Edward Stanford, 1878), 50.

63. Faithfull, 342; Oscar Wilde, "Impressions of America," in Oscar Wilde, *The Works of Oscar Wilde* (New York: AMS Press, 1972), 261.

64. Vachell, 53. Harold Brydges also found American men to be accomplished at business, but "in the gentle arts which make up the brightness of life," they were inferior to their sisters or wives. Brydges, 39.

65. Rose G. Kingsley, *South by West, or Winter in the Rocky Mountains and Spring in Mexico* (London: W. Isbinster and Co., 1874), 54; Mrs. E. H. Carbutt, *Five Months' Fine Weather in Canada, Western U.S., and Mexico* (London: Sampson, Low, Marston, Searle, and Rivington, 1889), 29.

66. Kessler, 53.

67. Bourget, 73.

68. Quoted in Ben Lawton, "Giuseppe Giacosa, 1847–1906," in *Abroad in America: Visitors to the New Nation, 1776–1914* (Reading, MA: Addison-Wesley, 1976), 250.

69. Blanc, 107.

70. Faithfull, 117. Paul Bourget found this to be the case even when American "society" was vacationing in Newport. Because the American upper class was drawn almost exclusively from businessmen, these men were "absent several days in the week, occupied in making the money which it is the function of their wives to display." Bourget, 56.

71. San Carlos, v. 1, no. 5, 399. Hugues Le Roux quotes one American who describes his father as "'a brilliant success in his business, and it's all owing to his own merit too. He's a self-made man.'" He was president of his club, a person others sought for advice, but "'the minute he leaves his office or the club, he becomes absolutely silent. At meals he carves for us without saying a word. It's my sisters and my mother who do the talking.'" Le Roux, 91.

72. Quoted in Torrielli, 193.

73. A. S. Northcote, "American Life Through English Spectacles," *The Nineteenth Century* 34, no. 199 (September 1893), 486.

74. Brydges, 42.

75. Gripenberg, 212.

76. William H. Davies, *The Autobiography of a Super-Tramp* (New York: Alfred A. Knopf, 1917), 25.

77. Lepel Henry Griffin, *The Great Republic* [1884] (New York: Arno Press, 1974), 61. W. E. Adams also found that "deference to the fair sex is universal in America." Adams, 85. Oscar Wilde noted that the American man's "reverence for the [female] sex has a touch of compulsory chivalry about it." Wilde, "American Man," 307–308.

78. Biart, 63. James Fullarton Muirhead believed that one test of the state of civilization of a country was in "the character of its roads, its minimising of noise, and the position of its women." While Muirhead found the United States wanting in the first two categories, "its name assuredly leads all the rest in the third." Muirhead, 59.

79. Iza Duffus Hardy, *Between Two Oceans: or, Sketches of American Travel* (London: Hurst and Blackett, 1884), 6.

80. Blanc, 30.

81. Ibid., 52–53.

82. Torrielli, n. 43, 194–195.

83. Le Roux, 202. In some of the larger American post offices, there were separate areas for men and women. F. Barham Zincke, *Last Winter in the United States: Being Table Talk Collected During a Tour Through the Late Southern Confederation, the Far West, the Rocky Mountains, &c* [1868] (Freeport, NY: Books for Libraries Press, 1970), 198.

84. J. J. Aubertin, *A Fight with Distances: The States, the Hawaiian Islands, Canada, British Columbia, Cuba, the Bahamas* (London: Kegan Paul, Trench & Co., 1888), 244.

85. Knut Hamsun, *The Cultural Life of Modern America* [1889] (Cambridge, MA: Harvard University Press, 1969), 126. Harold Brydges felt it necessary to inform Englishmen who intended to visit America that "it is the custom to remove the hat in any building where ladies are. This applies especially to an elevator, and the passages and halls of a hotel." Brydges, 121.

86. Aubertin, 243.

87. Hübner, 56–57.

88. Vachell, 28–29. British travelers in the first half of the nineteenth century also complained that American women reacted to the courtesies extended to them with haughty entitlement. See Christopher Mulvey, 70–72.

89. Torrielli, 185.

90. Saunders, 401.

91. Faithfull, 344.

92. Macrae, 511; See Bryce, v. 2, 682, 686.

93. Muirhead, 49–50; Hübner, 32–33.

94. Lady Duffus Hardy, *Through Cities and Prairie Lands: Sketches of an American Tour* (London: Chapman and Hall, 1881), 87.

95. Biart, 63.

96. Anonymous, "On Some Peculiarities of Society in America," 714.

97. Rousiers, 276.

98. F. Barham Zincke took note of "the numerous divorces which so much astonish those who look into the social conditions of American life." Zincke, 294. See also Lepel Henry Griffin, who complained of "a too facile divorce law." Griffin, 63.

99. Faithfull, 289.

100. Ibid., 228.

101. Iza Duffus Hardy, 181–182.

102. Daniel J. Boorstin, *The Americans: The Democratic Experience* (New York: Random House, 1973), 68–69.

103. Torrielli, 196; Macrae, 440, 441. F. Barham Zincke referred to a "large establishment in the most fashionable street in the city of New York, from whence the great high priestess of this evil system dispenses her drugs and advice, and where also she receives those who need her direct assistance." Zincke, 294.

104. Brydges, 112. One joke in circulation in the 1880s posited that the only cure for love was marriage and that the only cure for marriage was divorce, and that those seeking divorce should, "Beware of imitations; none genuine without the word 'Chicago' blown on the bottle." Quoted in Hatton, v. 1, 236. Léon Paul Blouet repeated the joke about the announcement on the train, except it was "'Indianapolis—twenty minutes for divorce!'" O'rell and Allyn, 192.

105. Boorstin, 69. Boorstin notes that South Dakota toughened up its divorce laws after an Episcopal bishop launched a campaign in 1893 against what he called "consecutive polygamy." Boorstin observes that "this pattern—an early period of liberal divorce laws, followed by scandals, a conservative campaign for reform, and the tightening of laws, thereby spoiling the divorce—was repeated all over the West." Ibid., 70.

106. Hamsun, 127.

107. Wilde, "American Man," 307, 308.

108. Steven Mintz, *Huck's Raft: A History of American Childhood* (Cambridge, MA: Belknap Press of Harvard University Press, 2004), 131–132.

109. Ibid., 152.

110. Tocqueville, 685.

111. Anonymous, "An Englishman in Vermont," *Eclectic Magazine* 18, no. 2 (New Series, August 1873), 245.

112. Vachell, 61; Zincke, 70, 71. William Howard Russell claimed that the "want of reverence on the part of children towards their parents" emanated from the school system, which taught the young "to mock at any authority but that of the schoolmaster." Russell, v. 2, 155–156. Historian Elliott West also emphasizes the upside to a childhood in the West, claiming that the virtues of the Western child included "a resilient strength, a self-reliance and sense of worth, and a tested understanding that hard times can be endured." Elliott West, "Children and the Frontier," in *Major Problems in the History of the American West*, ed. Clyde A. Milner, et al. (Boston: Houghton Mifflin, 1997), 254.

113. Low, v. 2, 346–347.

114. Ibid., 346.

115. Charles Wentworth Dilke, *Greater Britain: A Record of Travel in English-Speaking Countries* (London: Macmillan and Co., 1890), 175; a satirical article by Frank R. Stockton called "On the Training of Parents" proclaims that if "parental training is begun early enough, the child will find its task an easy one." However, "When it becomes necessary to punish a parent, no child should forget the importance of tempering severity with mercy." When the child has successfully "reduced its parents to a condition of docile obedience, and sees them day by day, and year by year, pursuing a path of cheerful subservience, it can scarcely fail to appreciate what will be expected of it when it shall itself have become a parent." Frank R. Stockton, "On the Training of Parents," *The Century Magazine* 28, no. 1 (May 1884), 124, 125, 126.

116. U.S. Department of Commerce, Bureau of the Census, *Historical Statistics of the United States: Colonial Times to 1957* (Washington, D.C.: GPO, 1961), 72, 10.

117. See A. R. Cólon and P. A. Cólon, *A History of Children: A Socio-Cultural Survey Across Millennia* (Westwood, CN: Greenwood Press, 2001), 423. Steven Mintz observes that while "a frontier childhood encouraged a youth of self-reliance, inner-directedness, and early independence, many western children experienced youths of withering poverty, dispiriting routine, and personal entrapment." Mintz, 151.

118. Steven Mintz notes that one state survey in the late nineteenth century estimated that a minimum income of $754 a year was needed to sustain a family of five. The miners of eastern Pennsylvania made less than $450 per year. Mintz, 145.

119. Isabella L. Bird, *A Lady's Life in the Rocky Mountains* (Norman: University of Oklahoma Press, 1969), 67.

120. William A. Baille-Grohman, *Camps in the Rockies: Being a Narrative of Life on the Frontier, and Sport in the Rocky Mountains, with an Account of the Cattle Ranches of the West* (New York: Charles Scribner's Sons, 1884), 378.

121. F. Francis, "The Yellowstone Geysers," *The Nineteenth Century* 11, no. 61 (March 1882), 372.

122. Hübner, 55.

123. J. W. C., 120, 119.

124. Mintz, 131; Charles Loring Brace, *The Dangerous Classes of New York, and Twenty Years' Work Among Them* [1872] (Washington, D.C.: National Association of Social Workers, n.d.), 31.

125. Bates, v. 1, 52.

126. Boddam-Whetham, 38.

127. See Griffin, 80; Soissons, 36–37. Emily Faithfull also noted that "Young America" did not "sit at the master's feet and worship" but expressed its opinions "with the bold confidence born of youthful inexperience and immaturity." Faithfull, 95. S. C. de Soissons called this appreciation of youth "one of the secrets of the great development of a country." Soissons, 38.

128. Bates, v. 2, 21.

129. George Augustus Sala, *America Revisited: From the Bay of New York to the Gulf of Mexico and From Lake Michigan to the Pacific* (London: Vizetelly & Co., n.d.), 344–345.

130. Rousiers, 254, 255.

131. Gripenberg, 205, 206.

132. Muirhead, 70.

133. Macrae, 597.

134. Anonymous, "An Englishman in Vermont," 248.

135. Fraser quoted in Anonymous, "The Education of the People in England and America," *Blackwood's Edinburgh Magazine* 627, no. 103 (January 1868), 114.

136. Craib, 75. Bates claimed that "the best families" of Boston "send their girls to such schools; in fact, only delicate or rather stupid girls seem to go to private schools here." Bates, v. 1, 114, 115.

137. Zincke, 14.

138. William A. Bell, *New Tracks in North America: A Journal of Travel and Adventure Whilst Engaged in the Survey for a Southern Railroad to the Pacific Ocean During 1867–8* [1870] (Albuquerque: Horn and Wallace, 1965), 15. The typical child was in school for five years, with most working-class children leaving the classroom at age twelve or thirteen because their families needed their income. See Joseph E. Illick, *American Childhoods* (Philadelphia: University of Pennsylvania Press, 2002), 90–93. School attendance tended to be higher in rural areas than urban areas. Priscilla Ferguson Clement, "The City and the Child, 1860–1885," in *American Childhood: A Research Guide and Historical Handbook*, ed. Joseph M. Hawes and N. Ray Hiner (Westport, CN: Greenwood Press, 1985), 238–239.

139. Bryce acknowledged that a majority of men "read little but newspapers, and many of the women little but novels. Yet there remains a number to be counted by millions who enjoy and are moved by the higher products of thought and imagination."

Bryce, v. 2, 819. Henry Sienkiewicz claimed that because of the excellent educational system in the United States, there was hardly anyone from the younger generation "who cannot read, write, or calculate, who does not understand politics, and who, in short, is not more or less prepared for his duties as a citizen." Henry Sienkiewicz, *Portrait of America: Letters of Henry Sienkiewicz*, trans. and ed. Charles Morley (New York: Columbia University Press, 1959), 24. See also W. G. Marshall, *Through America: Nine Months in the United States* (London: Sampson, Low, Marston, Searle & Rivington, 1881), 400.

140. Schlereth, 253.
141. Mintz, 151; Fox quoted in Robert G. Athearn, *Westward the Briton* (Lincoln: University of Nebraska Press, 1953), 98.
142. Zincke, 177.
143. Gripenberg, 63.
144. Hamsun, 10.
145. Ibid., 9. The incident about the telegraph so incensed Hamsun that he mentioned it twice. Ibid., 114.
146. Edward A. Freeman, *Some Impressions of the United States* (London: Longmans, Green, and Co., 1883), 42. James Bryce also claimed that Americans knew the history of their country better than the English knew theirs. Bryce, v. 1, 5. William Howard Russell emphasized the mutual incomprehension of Americans and British of certain aspects of each other's culture: "To millions of Americans the exact status of a Duke is as great a mystery as the rank of a Jam or of a Thakoor is to the mass of Englishmen out of India ... But, after all, how many Englishmen are there who could give an exact account of the workings of the Electoral College in the election of one of the most potential of sovereigns, or who could define the differences between a Republican and a Democrat?" Russell, v. 1, 28.
147. See Grady McWhiney, *Cracker Culture: Celtic Ways in the Old South* (Tuscaloosa: University of Alabama Press, 1988), 197, 196.
148. Quoted in Winthrop S. Hudson, *Religion in America: An Historical Account of the Development of American Religious Life* (New York: Macmillan, 1987), 209.
149. Macrae, 27.
150. Robert Somers, *The Southern States Since the War, 1870–71* [1871] (Tuscaloosa: University of Alabama Press, 1965), 156.
151. Eric Foner, *Forever Free: The Story of Emancipation and Reconstruction* (New York: Alfred A. Knopf, 2005), 162.
152. Ibid., 201.
153. Clement, 242.
154. See Mintz, 205.
155. Saunders, 39.
156. See Roger Daniels, *Coming to America: A History of Immigration and Ethnicity in American Life* (New York: Perennial, 2002), 159–164, and Clement, 244–245.
157. Dudley Campbell, "Mixed Education of Boys and Girls," *The Contemporary Review* 22 (July 1873), 262.
158. See David Nasaw, *Schooled to Order: A Social History of Public Schooling in the United States* (New York: Oxford University Press, 1981), 62.
159. Zincke, 178. One professor told Hugues Le Roux that, in 1898, 70 percent of the teachers in the United States were female. Le Roux, 70.
160. Only six states had mandatory school attendance laws in 1871. By 1900, virtually every state in the North and West had such laws. See Robert H. Wiebe, *The Search for Order, 1877–1920* (New York: Hill and Wang, 1987), 119.
161. Le Roux, 74–75.
162. Ibid., 74, 71.
163. See Illick, 74.
164. Le Roux, 57.

165. Ibid., 57, 58.
166. Ibid., 245–246.
167. Faithfull, 74; Le Roux, 143.
168. "Must we believe," asked Bourget, "that the active independence of such a woman necessarily results in a relocation of family ties?" Bourget, 38–39.
169. Blanc, 166. Blanc partially answered this question herself. As she watched young women "delicately torturing a frog or a lobster" in a biology class at Bryn Mawr, Blanc received reassurances from an instructor that biology could teach these students "many natural things in a scientific and hence a healthy fashion." Blanc thought to herself "that in France, on the contrary, mothers and teachers bend all their efforts to hiding certain natural things from their daughters until the day when marriage throws an unexpected light upon them." Ibid., 174, 175.
170. Quoted in Nasaw, 142.

6

RACE, IMMIGRATION, AND RELIGION

Of all the regions of the United States, it was probably the South that struck Europeans as the most exotic because of its large black population. With the conclusion of the Civil War, millions of former slaves had been emancipated, and Europeans were enthralled as they watched the country struggle to fashion a role for these new citizens in the national scheme. Also novel to the European experience were the huge numbers of immigrants that were now crowding into the United States. Indeed, Europeans would not be faced with the task of integrating significant numbers of racial and ethnic minorities into their own societies until the late twentieth and early twenty-first centuries. Further disorienting to foreign visitors was the proliferation of religious sects in America—and the absence of a state church.

Race and the South

David Macrae and Charles Wentworth Dilke were two European travelers who visited the South in the immediate aftermath of the Civil War, talking to both whites and blacks. Macrae and Dilke both had thoughtful observations to make and came to many of the same conclusions. One former planter told Macrae that blacks were "happier in slavery. Many of them would like it back."[1] In contrast, a former slave told Macrae, "'No, sah; we are all better off now. They cannot sell us now. They cannot whip us now. They cannot put us in prison now. Some of our people are poor, but they would rather be poor, sah, and be free.'"[2] When Charles Wentworth Dilke arrived at Norfolk in 1866, he found large gangs of black workers laboring in the hot sun removing the carcasses of sunken ships. Shortly thereafter, a white patron at one of Norfolk's hotel bars told Dilke that blacks would not work as long as the Yanks fed them. Dilke deemed it unwise to point out that a large number of blacks were laboring 100 yards away.[3] Like Macrae, Dilke quickly learned that in the South, "believe nothing you are told" because the "facts" varied so radically depending on to whom one talked.[4]

Dilke encountered a chronic inability on the part of Southern planters to engage the reality of freed blacks. Instead they ridiculed any misstep made by blacks in their freedom, and complained that blacks would not work without compulsion.[5] Dilke pointed out, however, that the same could be said of any European, and believed that American blacks, who had made the best of every opportunity given them, could have hope for the future.[6] The impact of slavery on the slave was horrendous, but many travelers concluded that its effects on the master were even worse.[7] Sifting through the ruins of Southern culture in the years immediately following the Civil War, David Macrae argued that slavery had sapped the energy and enterprise of the South, and had produced an "omnipresent class of loafers" whom, because they were white, considered themselves gentlemen, and because they were gentlemen would not work, and because they would not work "remained in a state of poverty and dependence."[8] The removal of the slave system also had a physical impact on the Southern landscape, with the large estates that had dominated Southern agriculture before the war now "abandoned and allowed to return to wood."[9]

In the 1870s, Robert Somers and William Saunders also visited the region. In his many discussions with white employers of black workers, Somers found that nearly all expressed satisfaction that slavery had been eliminated.[10] Saunders also found this to be the case, and was struck by the fact that despite their past views, no one in the South would admit that they had previously been wrong on the slavery issue.[11] Whites did gain one advantage with the abolishment of slavery, according to Saunders. Formerly, slaves had to be taken care of when they were sick, but, now "if one man does not suit he can be changed for another."[12]

Even the most thoughtful European travelers found it difficult to move beyond the stereotypes of Southern blacks. Descriptions of blacks as being "more like children than grown people" or possessing an "indolence of mind" were extremely common.[13] F. Barham Zincke, who was in the South in 1867, called blacks "constitutionally lazy," and fit only for low-skilled positions.[14] But Zincke also judged a black person to be the most knowledgeable speaker he heard in the United States, which forced him into some racial gymnastics. Zincke first looked for evidence that the speaker had some white blood in his skin color (he could detect none) and finally emphasized that this person "had most completely the head and features of the European."[15] Others, such as J. J. Aubertin, also encountered highly intelligent blacks in America, but could not praise them without being condescending ("a great many of them seem to have imbibed some of the mental energies which belong to the white race").[16]

Racial amalgamation in the South had never been a possibility, and David Macrae found that "the dread that lies deepest in the Southern heart, and gave most fury to its opposition," was inter-racial marriage.[17] The consequences to those who contemplated such a marriage were made clear to Ernst von Hesse-Wartegg when he visited the town of Grenada, Mississippi, in 1879. On the street he encountered "a Negress somewhat less than clothed. Her face, arms, legs, shoulders, and nape of the neck had been whitewashed; she looked like a female Punchinello." When Hesse-Wartegg inquired as to what had happened, he was told that a white man and a black woman had announced their intention of getting married, and the locals (both black and white) had responded by white-washing the woman. As Hesse-Wartegg noted, had a black man tried to marry a white woman, he might well have been lynched.[18] Most European visitors to the United States were no more tolerant on racial issues than the natives. F. Barham Zincke, for instance, rejected what he called a "fusion" of the two races because "the most richly endowed race of the human family," would be "sunk and degraded by admixture with the lowest race of all."[19] Another British writer, who claimed to have supported the emancipation of blacks, intoned that, "We who wished honestly to see the nigger free, hated him as the cause of the troubles, and as our English or 'Anglo-Saxon' breed always hates an inferior race."[20]

The Jim Crow system, where separate facilities were established in the South for blacks and whites, gained momentum after the end of Reconstruction in 1877. As historian C. Van Woodward expressed it, this was abetted by "the withdrawal of federal troops from the South, the abandonment of the Negro as a ward of the nation, the giving up of the attempt to guarantee the freedman his civil and political equality, and the acquiescence of the rest of the country in the South's demand that the whole problem be left to the disposition of the dominant Southern white people."[21] There was also the nationwide depression of the 1870s during which, according to Eric Foner, "economic recovery replaced Reconstruction as the main focus of national and local political debates."[22]

In the decades following the Civil War, American blacks not only lost their rights but even the purpose for which the war had been fought. Gradually, the abolition of slavery and the preservation of the Union was replaced by a rapprochement between white veterans of the North and South that emphasized a common valor on the battlefield. Frederick Douglass, in an 1878 speech, pleaded that "there was a right side and a wrong side in the late war, which no sentiment ought to cause us to forget," but he was swimming against the cultural tide.[23] By 1913, when Civil War veterans gathered for a reunion at Gettysburg, the chairman of the reunion, Colonel J. M. Schoonmaker, claimed that, "'It matters little to you or to me now what the causes were that provoked the War of the States in the Sixties.'"[24]

Jim Crow was not only endorsed by the majority of Americans, but by European travelers as well. William Archer, for instance, referred to the "fatal blunder" of allowing blacks to vote in the South, and noted with approval the establishment of literacy tests at polling places where an official could "admit or exclude a man at his discretion."[25] It was not that the North was much better. When he visited the main Union cemetery in Arlington in 1881, William

Howard Russell could not help but notice that "even in death the white and the black are divided—the former buried near Arlington House, the coloured men's remains lie half a mile or more away."[26]

The separation of blacks and whites would be nearly total. Just one year after the end of Reconstruction, William Saunders observed that the two races did not share religious observances, that black children were educated apart from whites, and that the children of the two races did not even play together.[27] Jacques Offenbach noted that public transportation was forbidden to blacks, that they could not attend the theater, and that they were only admitted to restaurants "if they are serving there."[28] Likewise, Robert Somers found that while white passengers on riverboats were served a "choice dinner" in the saloon with good claret, black passengers had their meal under an awning on the deck.[29] One British writer took Jim Crow a step further, suggesting that blacks, "like the Red Indians, might not advantageously be set apart in reserves."[30] The outlook for blacks in America was undeniably bleak, and F. Barham Zincke called their "extermination by moral and economical causes" "inevitable."[31]

Many travelers focused on the physical traits of black Americans as evidence of their innate inferiority. W. G. Marshall, who witnessed a parade of black troops on Decoration Day, took note of their "rare and unique collection of noses, the breadth of some of them was really too ridiculous."[32] The ugliness and the personal nature of these racial attacks are appalling. When she encountered a black child, Therese Yelverton struggled over whether to describe it as a "gigantic fly" or an organ grinder's monkey.[33] After referring to "that dark Frankenstein of the South" and accusing blacks of widespread infanticide, Yelverton hit her stride with the following assessment:

> They possess the mimicry of the monkey, the sagacity of the dog, the stealthiness of the cat, perversity in exact ratio with that of the mule, uncleanliness proportionate to the swine, laziness intense as that of the sloth, arrogance emulating that of the barn-door fowl, and vanity which outvies the peacock's.[34]

No less vile in his expressions of racial hatred was Lepel Henry Griffin. He claimed that the black person was "as fit for the franchise as the monkey he closely resembles," and raised fears about unchecked population growth among blacks. Griffin concluded that blacks could "be happy on the simple elements of sunshine and sweet potatoes."[35] Also weighing in was Phil Robinson, who described a group of blacks (near Dallas) who were dressed up in their Sunday best as looking "like gorillas masquerading." Robinson called American blacks "the most deplorable libel on the human race that I have ever encountered."[36] Even the more thoughtful Rudyard Kipling expressed doubts that the black race could be uplifted by education "because black blood is much more adhesive than white, and throws back with annoying persistence."[37]

In 1870, Robert Somers had observed the "marks of servility" that character-ized relations between blacks and whites in the South.[38] But by the 1890s, William H. Davies detected a distinct difference between the old and new gen-erations of blacks, contrasting former slaves who still raised their hats "to any seedy looking white man" with "the half defiant gloom of the free, young gen-erations."[39] Among Southern whites, however, old attitudes persisted, putting the lives of blacks in the South, especially those accused of crimes, in peril. In one Southern community (not identified by Davies) there was a horrifying incident. Davies encountered a group of some one hundred armed men marching through town, and followed out of curiosity. The group halted in front of the jail, where-upon the sheriff surrendered his keys without protest. The mob pulled a scream-ing black man from his cell, took him to a nearby tree, put a rope around his neck, and hanged him. Even this was not enough, and "all these men shouldered their guns, fired one volley, and in a second the body was hanging lifeless with a hundred shots."[40] Between 1889 and 1918, over 2,400 blacks would be lynched by whites in the South.[41]

Perhaps even worse for Southern blacks than race hatred was their ongoing poverty which, as in our own day, was most dramatically brought to the fore by natural disasters. During her American tour of 1880–81, Sarah Bernhardt and her troupe arrived in New Orleans in the midst of a terrible flood. Because black residents were forced to live in the cheapest (and lowest) parts of the city, the flood's impact on the black community was especially dire. From elevated side-walks Bernhardt saw water snakes glide by, along with the wrecked cabins of black residents that had fallen into the water. According to a shocked Bernhardt, hundreds "squatted upon these moving wrecks, with eyes burning from fever, their white teeth chattering" while near them dead bodies floated past, bumping into the wooden piles.[42]

Immigration

A number of travelers were impressed by the transforming impact of America on the immigrant. Byørnstjerne Bjørnson called the rebirth of the Norwegian peas-ant into both a citizen of the United States and a valued member of the com-munity a "beautiful sight." But even more inspiring was "to see his grandson as an American gentleman."[43] A. Maurice Low acknowledged America's "extraor-dinary and only partially explained power of absorbing alien people" into its social and political system. Even the immigrant who was most resistant to assim-ilation, according to Émile Boutmy, became a good citizen once he embraced the American dream, which Boutmy defined as "to be free to choose your path, to see victory before you with no artificial barrier blocking its approaches, to move forward with the certainty of reaching it."[44]

It was often the case that the immigrant himself did not realize how pro-foundly he had changed until he returned to his country of origin.[45] During his visit to the United States, Baron Hübner had the opportunity of talking to a number of Italian immigrants who had made their fortunes in the American West. Twenty-four of them returned to Italy, but all but three of them came back to the United States because, as one put it, "we can't associate with the gentry in Europe, and we can't live with our equals there, because, without knowing it, we have raised ourselves far above them."[46] Another commentator claimed that America had taken the "human slag from the mines of monarchical Europe," and created precious metal from it.[47]

Most European travelers, however, maintained that this alloy would only have sufficient strength if it was a "fusion of the Caucasian race" from northern and western Europe.[48] In 1868, Charles Dickens described the British and American peoples as "essentially one, and that it rests with them jointly to uphold the great Anglo-Saxon race."[49] Other races introduced into the mix—such as the Hispanic residents of Monterey that Lady Duffus Hardy described as "a dark, swarthy, lazy-looking race," who "scarcely seem to have energy enough to keep themselves awake"—would be both unassimilable and doomed to domination by whites.[50] From his travels in America in 1866, William Hepworth Dixon identified the four prominent races in America—whites, blacks, Indians, and Chinese—and designated a single person to represent each race (Figure 6.1).[51] Not surprisingly, Dixon claimed that the white race was dominant because it was "master in every zone."[52]

By the 1880s, second-wave immigrants from eastern and southern Europe were flooding into America. Facilitating this process were extremely cheap steamship tickets (by 1900, a ticket in steerage from Naples to New York cost just $15).[53] Increasingly, there was less confidence and more anxiety among European observers about this new racial and ethnic landscape. Harold Brydges was adamant in stressing the deleterious impact of immigration on American life, claiming that immigrants were the major inhabitants of prisons and workhouses, that they controlled the liquor traffic in the United States, and that they dominated the rolls of the anarchists and secret societies.[54] For James Bryce, the new immigrants ("largely of Slavonic race") were likely to be less influenced by mainstream American culture and might "retain their own low standard of decency and comfort."[55] Alexandra Gripenberg claimed that the "large number of immigrants and ignorant Negroes" who had the vote could only be offset by the enfranchisement of American women.[56]

Other European travelers feared that a low Anglo birth rate would surrender the United States to the "inferior immigrant and his progeny."[57] James Bryce predicted the reversal of natural selection, with fewer children being born to the well-to-do and more children "born to the physically weak and morally untrained."[58] Someone who knew something about natural selection, Herbert Spencer, held out hope that a "mixture of the allied varieties of the Aryan race" in America would produce "a finer type of man."[59]

It must be noted that the blithe assumptions of Anglo-Saxon superiority (and the readiness to condemn those who could not claim such a status) dominated the

THE FOUR RACES.

FIGURE 6.1 The Four Races. From William Hepworth Dixon, *New America*, p. 254.

thinking of the American middle class as well. Historian Eric Foner argues that by the late nineteenth century the issue of race "had assumed a central place in American public life, more central, in fact, than during the days of slavery." Now the term "race" was being applied not just to blacks, but also to immigrant groups such as Jews, Italians, and Slavs, in juxtaposition to the "Anglo-Saxon" race.[60]

Racism, of course, was nothing new in America, but as historian Jackson Lears has emphasized, late nineteenth-century racism "was more self-conscious, more systematic, more determined to assert scientific legitimacy."[61] The racial/ethnic/ religious subcurrents in the United States were complex, and there is no better example of this complexity than the largest lynching incident in American history, which took place in New Orleans in 1891. Those lynched were not a group of blacks, but a group of eleven Sicilian Catholic immigrants who had been seized by an angry mob after a jury had found them not guilty in the murder of the city's police chief. Prominent among the lynchers were Germans, Irish, French, and even Italians, who had defended slavery in the antebellum period, then had established segregated parishes in the postbellum South.[62]

It was often the very class of Americans who professed to have the immigrant's best interest in mind that was the most virulently nativist. American social reformer Charles Loring Brace cited one instance of "the demoralizing influence of emigration" as that "so large a proportion of the female criminal class should be Irish-born."[63] In another example, Frances Willard, revered leader of the Woman's Christian Temperance Union, declared that, "I am first a Christian, then I am a Saxon, then I am an American." As for immigrants, Willard called upon Congress to "enact a stringent immigration law prohibiting the influx into our land of more of the scum of the Old World, until we have educated those who are here."[64] Often, even the desperate poverty of the immigrant was attributed to the deficiencies of the immigrant himself. Observing the wretchedness of life in lower Manhattan, English traveler W. E. Adams put the blame on "the dissipated and improvident habits of the persons who endure the misery."[65]

It is doubtful that the European travelers who found immigrants in America so contemptible spent much time with them. One happy exception was Robert Louis Stevenson. The Scotsman saw himself as an emigrant, mingling with steerage passengers on the voyage from Scotland to the United States, traveling with them on an "emigrant train" from the East Coast to the West, and socializing with them in California.[66] He described the immigrants on his ship as "quiet, orderly, obedient citizens, family men broken by adversity, elderly youths who had failed to place themselves in life, and people who had seen better days."[67] All were "full of hope for the future."[68] Stevenson, however, found that a strange logic dominated their thinking. The immigrant was confident he could get on anywhere, but "Why," asked Stevenson, "could he not do the same in Scotland?"[69]

Once in America, there was the terrible yearning for the land the immigrant had left behind. On Stevenson's train to the West, a cornet player was playing tunes to which nobody paid attention until he played "Home, Sweet Home." All conversation ceased, "and the faces began to lengthen."[70] Finally settling in at Monterey, Stevenson often found himself in the midst of a multicultural stew that included a Frenchman, two Portuguese, an Italian, a Mexican, and an Indian, as well as persons from China, Switzerland, and Germany. As Stevenson put it, "each race contributes something of its own."[71]

Stevenson's sympathy for immigrants, however, was the exception. Most foreign travelers in America were dismissive of the immigrants they encountered. Germans, for instance, were either reviled because they were Jewish (Kipling makes a reference to "German Jew all over a man's face and nose") or because they were consumers of beer ("in quantities sufficient to float a navy," as Stephen Buckland put it).[72] But the traveler who actually took the time to converse with an immigrant often came away with a different impression. Horace Annesley Vachell noted that if you asked a German that "you have contemptuously stigmatised as a beer-swiller" what he had read, you would often find that he had mastered Schiller, Goethe, and Heine, and could talk intelligently about history and metaphysics.[73] While German immigrants came in for rough treatment at the hands of European travelers, the two groups that excited the most contempt were the Irish and the Chinese.

It is not surprising, given Britain's troubled history with Ireland (E. Catherine Bates called it "that terrible British blister"), that the British would be especially critical of the Irish in the United States, who dominated not only American political machines but domestic service as well.[74] These attacks were often quite personal, which can be seen in William A. Bell's comparison of the Irish and Mexicans. Bell observed that while both groups were Catholic and both were "indolent by nature," the Mexicans were preferable because their homes were neat, while in the case of the Irish domicile "you instinctively hold your nose, and back out."[75] The issue of race and religion was never far below the surface. Charles Wentworth Dilke described the Irish as a danger to "our race," while Lepel Henry Griffin credited the success of the "mostly illiterate" Irish in New York's political machine to the "absolute rule of the priests," who told them how to vote.[76] These visitors, like their American counterparts, combined nativism and hostility toward Catholicism in a very straightforward manner. For instance, when W. E. Adams commented upon the competition between parochial schools and public schools in America, he worried that a "foreign element" might undermine the public schools system.[77]

As for Irish domestics, they were, according to David Macrae, both ignorant and unskilled, with just enough knowledge of republican notions of equality "to make them disagreeable."[78] Maria Therese Blanc said that there was nothing like an encounter with "the dirty, ignorant, familiar Irish maid-servant" in America to make one appreciate the maids of France, and even Emily Faithfull, social reformer and the great champion of working women, referred to "Bridget's ignorance and wastefulness."[79] Almost alone among British travelers in expressing any sympathy for the Irish in America, at least the agricultural Irish, was William Saunders. He speculated on the feelings of the Irish immigrant who received a grant of free land under the Homestead Act, which in Ireland would have been "a handsome fortune." Saunders also contrasts the oppressive government of Ireland with the "friendly" American government, which would not "assist his landlord to extort rent."[80] The British were not the only travelers who rained down condemnation on the Irish in America. Henry Sienkiewicz also endorsed the conventional British line that the Irish were slaves to their vices and their priests, and that they constituted "a very dangerous" threat to the republic.[81]

It should be emphasized that the Irish themselves nurtured a variety of racial and ethnic resentments against other groups in America. They clashed with the Chinese in California, and one of the chronic problems plaguing the Butte Miners' Union in Montana was tensions between Irish and Cornish miners.[82] There was also the long-running race grudge between Irish and blacks in the United States, with the two groups competing for the same menial, labor-intensive jobs. American society often lumped the two groups together (Figure 6.2),

FIGURE 6.2 The Ignorant Vote—Honors are easy (1876). Wood engraving after Thomas Nast. Library of Congress. LC-USZ62-57340.

and one of the few distinctions the Irish could claim was that they were white. This helps explain the overwhelming opposition of the Irish not only to abolitionism, but also to any form of anti-slavery.[83] The hostility of the Irish toward blacks continued after the Civil War. David Macrae noted of Irish servants that "they hate the 'nigger,' with an ineradicable hatred," and that a black servant who worked in the same house with an Irish servant "leads the life of a dog." In one place that Macrae stayed, the Irish servants would not allow a black servant to eat with them.[84]

In his book *The American People: A Study in National Psychology*, A. Maurice Low illuminates one of the ironies of immigration by quoting from a lecture by S. S. McClure. "Yearly hundreds of thousands of immigrants come into this country who are of such a low breed that they will degrade the average of the breed in this country," said McClure. As we have seen, there was nothing remarkable about such sentiments, but what *was* remarkable is that McClure himself was born in Ireland and seemed oblivious to the fact that the same thing was said about the Irish.[85]

The situation for the Chinese (a majority of whom were in California) was even more dire than it was for the Irish, and it is not stretching a point to claim that the Chinese received roughly the same treatment as blacks in the South.[86] Charles Wentworth Dilke, for instance, was brought up short by a newspaper story in California that described a disturbance in which "one man and a Chinaman" was killed.[87] In another incident, a young Chinese man who was an army prisoner being transported by train, jumped off the train in an escape attempt and was horribly mutilated. Baron Hübner, who witnessed this tragedy, was appalled by the indifference of the other passengers. "At any rate he was a man!" said Hübner. "No, no," was the reply, "he was a Chinese!"[88] When W. F. Rae was in San Francisco in 1869, he noticed that the Chinese were not allowed to sit inside street cars, but were compelled to cling to the outside.[89] Things had not changed much by 1882 when Iza Duffus Hardy was in that city. She reported that when she entered a street car in which all the seats were taken, the conductor "took the nearest Chinaman by the collar, and coolly dragged him out of the car without a word."[90]

If anything, travelers from the British Isles were even more contemptuous of the Chinese they encountered in America than they were of the Irish. Indeed, cultural sensitivity was no more a hallmark of the British traveler than it was of most American residents. When Emily Faithfull visited a joss house, she found one man "muttering prayers before some ugly-looking idol, another is consulting the Josh by balancing bamboo splints, and a third is prostrating himself on the ground before a tinsel image." Faithfull was gratified to learn that active missionary work was underway to counter such paganism.[91] Aside from the joss house visit, standard Chinatown attractions included taking in a performance of the Chinese opera and, for the most intrepid, a visit to an opium den. When she attended the Chinese opera, Emily Faithfull judged the acrobatics to be "simply marvelous," but added that a short stay at one of these performances was "quite sufficient for the most stage-struck English playgoer."[92] Like Faithfull, W. G. Marshall ranked the acrobatics as "first rate" but called the overall performance "a hideous Chinese nightmare."[93] Theodora Guest also could not get past the "horrible, deafening, music."[94] When he visited the Chinese opera, Henry Sienkiewicz was struck by the sound of cracking beechnuts which the audience consumed throughout the performance, and the noise of an occasional scuffle between white hoodlums and Chinese.[95]

W. Henry Barneby turned down the opportunity to visit an opium den, judging it to be "better imagined than seen," but others were less squeamish.[96] Observing the effects of the drug on the habitués of one opium den, J. J. Aubertin found that some were enjoying themselves while others were "doubled up like shrivelled rabbits in a hutch."[97] W. G. Marshall condemned opium smokers for "indulging in so filthy and degrading a luxury," but amusingly, Marshall and his companions tried some opium themselves, and found that it was both "savoury and agreeable," and that "the more one indulged in it the more one liked it."[98]

E. Catherine Bates was perhaps typical when she expressed the "hopelessness" of trying to redeem the Chinese from their "purely animal life."[99] Even those who praised the Chinese seldom did so without qualification. Rudyard Kipling, for instance, admired the fire-proof brick buildings that the Chinese lived in, but said that the large numbers crammed into such buildings produced "filth and squalor" whose only parallel could be found in the slums of India.[100] Emily Faithfull also called San Francisco's Chinatown "a filthy place," but noted that the Chinese themselves were "very clean in their own persons."[101] Praising the Chinese servant, H. Hussey Vivian called him "as docile as a poodle, and moves about his work as quietly as a tame cat."[102]

Still, the consensus was that differences between the Chinese and Anglo-Saxons meant that these were "races that will never assimilate."[103] One traveler even predicted a labor war "between the races which feed on beef and the races which thrive on rice."[104] Finally, in a statement that looks forward to the Holocaust and ethnic cleansing, British historian Edward A. Freeman insisted that "every nation has a right to get rid of strangers who prove a nuisance, whether they are Chinese in America, or Jews in Russia, Servia, Hungary, and Roumania."[105] Certainly, the British were not the only Europeans with such views of the Chinese in America. When she was in San Francisco, Finnish traveler Alexandra Gripenberg noted of the Chinese that they "crawl out of their corners and, as night approaches, they become active just as do some vermin and insects."[106]

Summing up attitudes toward the Chinese, the almost uniquely sympathetic Robert Louis Stevenson observed that they were considered to be stupid because of their imperfect mastery of English, and base because their frugality and dexterity enabled them to underbid lazy Caucasians. Nativism, it seems, was as fluid and as shifting as immigration itself: "A while ago it was the Irish, now it is the Chinese that must go."[107] As historian Patricia Nelson Limerick has noted, hatred of the Chinese in California was the one sentiment that provided "unity to an otherwise diverse state," with divisions between Protestants and Catholics temporarily put aside, and even the stigmatized Irish joining the majority that stigmatized them.[108] There would be mob actions against the Chinese all over the West, with immigrants themselves often taking the lead.[109] The most serious incident took place in Rock Springs, Wyoming in 1885. Some fifty Chinese were killed in a mining dispute, and as Richard White has noted, "The murderers were English, Scots, Welsh, Swedes, Danes, Irish, and, in smaller numbers, Poles, Bohemians, and Hungarians. Their victims were Chinese."[110] Even in advertisements, anti-Chinese sentiment was ubiquitous (Figure 6.3).

European travelers not only held the Chinese in contempt, but virtually every other immigrant group and racial minority they came across in America. In most European descriptions of blacks, immigrants (and Indians), there is the almost complete absence of compassion for these people. The very fact that these travelers could afford extended stays in the United States meant that they were highly placed in their societies, yet their attacks on those they saw as outside elements in America were virulent and, for the most part, unadorned. John Campbell Argyll observed that Southerners viewed blacks in much the same way that many English viewed the "low Irish": "they are nuisances, and no one troubles himself much as to what is to become of them."[111] Edward A. Freeman was quite blunt in his view that "an Aryan land might do better still without any negro vote, [and] that a Teutonic might do better still without any Irish vote." He observed that, "Very many approved when I suggested that the best remedy for whatever was amiss would be if every Irishman should kill a negro and be hanged for it."[112] Later, he chided his Irish critics for not getting the "joke."[113]

The variety of races and ethnicities in America astounded European visitors. William Hepworth Dixon found that one could sit down to dinner in a miner's house with guests that might include "a Polish Jew, an Italian count, a Choctaw chief, a Mexican rancher, a Confederate soldier (there called a 'whitewashed reb'), a Mormon bishop, a Sandwich Island sailor, a Parsee merchant, a Boston bagman, a Missouri boss."[114] From New Orleans, Ernst von Hesse-Wartegg was dumbstruck by the variety of life in the streets: "What a mingling of peoples! Americans and Brazilians; West Indians, Spanish and French; Germans, Creoles, quadroons, mulattoes, Chinese, and Negroes surge past us."[115] Paul Bourget reported with some amazement that, "I have seen living, side by side, blacks and whites, Germans and Irish, Chinamen and Scandinavians, Italians and Anglo-Saxons."[116] Still, Bourget described the possibility that there might be a similar mingling of different races in Europe a "menace of barbarism," and took pains to contrast the virtuous native-born American workingmen with the "ignorant" workers "of foreign origin."[117] This lack of empathy for fellow human beings may be partially explained by noting that many European travelers were from relatively homogenous nations, and they were confronted by a multicultural society for the first time when they visited America. But in the final analysis, all one can do is to fall back on the melancholy truism that every culture is ethnocentric, and that the strong pull of European culture precluded any sympathetic feelings

FIGURE 6.3 Bock beer (ca. 1879). Library of Congress. LC-USZ62-16984.

for those who were unlike themselves. At least one Frenchman, Paul de Rousiers, could see what others could not: that immigration to America was not a threat but a national necessity. "America will cease to be America," said Rousiers, "the day that European immigration ceases."[118]

Religion

It is virtually impossible to make any definitive statement about religion in America in this era (and in our own) because the American religious experience has been so varied. From early in the century Tocqueville had taken note of the "wild spiritualism" and "bizarre sects" that were common in the United States but rare in Europe.[119] "Nowhere in the world and never in history," said historian Martin E. Marty, "had Christians been divided into so many conflicting groups as in America."[120] Put another way, Léon Paul Blouet observed that "in America, religion is served up with sauces to suit all palates."[121]

The spectacular growth of the Roman Catholic Church in the United States, mirroring the influx of immigrants, was the most important religious development in America after the Civil War. There were four million Catholics in America in 1870. By 1900 there were twelve million.[122] In the East, mainstream Protestant churches coexisted uneasily with Catholic immigrant churches, while revivalism was a frequent visitor to rural frontier areas where, as William Hepworth Dixon expressed it, "religious passion breaks out, like a fever, in the hottest places and in the wildest parts" of America.[123] There were also the religious fads that occasionally surfaced in American culture. When she was in Boston in 1894, Marie Therese Blanc took note of the enthusiasm for "Mozoomdar, the Hindoo reformer."[124] At the same time, utopian communities founded by groups such as the Shakers, Mormons and many others were flourishing. Indeed, by the 1890s Paul Bourget had concluded that any discussion of religion in America was "impossible" because "absolute freedom has so multiplied sects, and shades of difference in the sects."[125]

As in so many other areas of American life, the Civil War had an impact on religion. Historian Drew Gilpin Faust observes that the massive killing of the war "could not help but raise disturbing questions about God's benevolence and agency." At the same time, religion was one of the few resources to which one could turn for comfort.[126] The main Southern Protestant denominations—Methodist, Presbyterian, and Baptist—had seceded from their Northern brethren in the 1840s. These churches spent much of the pre-war period fending off attacks against slavery (the Presbyterian J. H. Thornwell claimed that "the Scriptures not only fail to condemn slavery, they as distinctly sanction it as any other social condition of man"). They spent the post-war period trying to explain the South's defeat.[127] One approach was to compare Southern defeat to the trials of Job (historian Wolfgang Schivelbusch calls this "a perennial favorite among vanquished nations") in which Job's suffering was a sign of God's favor.[128] Many Americans after the war turned away from mainstream churches altogether and sought to communicate with the dead through spiritualism. Interest in spiritualism had been increasing since the 1840s, but there is little doubt that the Civil War unleashed an intense yearning in America to make contact with those who had died. Even Mary Lincoln attempted to speak to her dead son through seances held at the White House.[129] The American enthusiasm for spiritualism was not unique, and the mechanized slaughter of World War I would create a similar spiritualist fervor in Britain.[130]

A number of European travelers to the United States after the Civil War took note of the American susceptibility to mediums, fortune tellers, and clairvoyants.

In Boston and New York, E. Catherine Bates attended various seances which brought forth "an old Egyptian," Joan of Arc, and other less renowned spirits.[131] A child spirit appeared at a seance attended by Alexandra Gripenberg in Philadelphia, and delivered a message from the Other Side with mangled spelling. Gripenberg drily observed that, "Perhaps the spirit could have spelled better if it had not left school so young."[132] In Denver, William Hepworth Dixon met Madame Mortimer, a "claivoyant physician," who created portraits of a woman's future husband or a man's future wife for the sum of two dollars.[133] James Bryce found advertisements for eighteen such practitioners in a single issue of a San Francisco newspaper, and Charles Wentworth Dilke pronounced the success of astrology and spiritualism in the United States as "amazing."[134] Indeed, according to Alexandra Gripenberg revelations of "the grossest frauds" did not seem to dampen the enthusiasm of American spiritualists.[135]

The splintering and resplintering of religion in America acquired some of the feverish energy of the American people themselves, and became entangled with questions of nativism, imperialism and race theory. Here the views of American Protestant leaders reveal a strange mixture of supreme confidence and haunting anxiety, and there is no better example than Josiah Strong. Strong was a representative of both the American Home Missionary Society and the American Evangelical Alliance, and in 1886 he published *Our Country: Its Possible Future and Its Present Crisis*. It went on to become one of America's all-time best sellers.[136] "Surely, to be a Christian and an Anglo-Saxon and an American in this generation is to stand on the mountain-top of privilege," exulted Strong.[137] But Strong also worried about the impact of the immigrant on American life, referring to the immigrant's "meager or false" moral training, his criminal inclinations, and his contributions to "the liquor power."[138] There was also the menace of "Romanism," with its rapidly growing number of adherents acting "as one man in obedience to the will of a foreign potentate and in disregard of the laws of the land."[139] Ultimately, however, Strong believed in the inevitability of "the extinction of inferior races before the advancing Anglo-Saxon."[140] Certainly, the views of Strong and other American Protestants differed little from those of Anglo-Saxon visitors to America. A non-Anglo-Saxon visitor, Frenchwoman Maria Therese Blanc, perhaps put it best when she called Protestantism "the proud religion of those who have never sinned."[141]

Strong predicted that "the star of empire" would settle over the American West, but European travelers found that religion in the West was often conspicuous by its absence.[142] Of her time in Colorado, Isabella Bird noted that the Sabbath was spent in one of three ways: "one, to make it a day for visiting, hunting, and fishing; another, to spend it in sleeping and abstinence from work; and the third, to continue all the usual occupations."[143] Westerners seemed to be singularly irreligious, with Bird complaining that "the blasphemous use of our Savior's name is peculiarly revolting."[144] A Texas cattle dealer observed that "the average cowboy does not bother himself about religion. The creeds and isms that worry civilization are a sealed book to the ranger, who is distinctively a fatalist."[145] Horace Annesley Vachell found that church attendance in the West was largely female and that ministers were chronically underpaid. This, said Vachell, was a reflection of the reality that in a new land, "the interpreters of the spiritual lie beneath the heel of the material."[146] On the frontier, according to historian William A. Clebsch, there was the unmistakable tendency of religion "to demand morality and to settle for good manners."[147]

Many travelers agreed with S. C. de Soissons that America's one great contribution to world religion was its separation of church and state, with religion being "entirely free from State control and support."[148] Edward A. Freeman was struck by the "perfect equality" of all religious sects, and James Bryce was impressed that, "No Established Church looks down scornfully upon Dissenters."[149] This attitude was also found at the grass-roots level, where Americans were devoted to their own religious tenets, but granted "complete freedom to those who think differently."[150] William Howard Russell noted with some wonderment that "there is neither dissension nor controversy among the congregations," and contrasted the state of affairs in America with the friction between church-goers of different denominations in Ireland and England.[151] American travelers to Britain were no less impressed by the very different system that prevailed on that side of the Atlantic, with one such visitor observing that "the union of Church and State is a most conspicuous headland to every American sojourner in England."[152]

But American freedom *of* religion was not the same as freedom *from* religion. James Fullarton Muirhead referred to a sign put up by the management of a mill in Lawrence, Massachusetts, that read "'regular attendance at some place of worship and a proper observance of the Sabbath will be expected of every person employed.'"[153] Others, such as Henry Sienkiewicz, believed that American church attendance was driven more by custom than piety because the emphasis on business left no time for serious transcendental contemplation. But Sienkiewicz also found that Americans considered religious freedom "the jewel in the Constitution."[154] There were two great exceptions to this philosophy of religious toleration: the Protestant condemnation of Catholicism (based as much on the perceived *foreignness* of the Catholic church as on its religious precepts), and a society-wide detestation of Mormonism (Figure 6.4).

Mormons

A special mention must be made of the Mormons because of all the utopian sects that flourished in nineteenth-century America—Quakers, Shakers, Mennonites, Amish, Rappites, Millerites and countless others—none were more notorious to Americans, or to Europeans, than the Mormons. That notoriety was almost exclusively due to the establishment of polygamy as a religious principle by founder Joseph Smith. In the words of historian Patrick Q. Mason, polygamy "doomed Mormons to the basest representations in the popular imagination."[155]

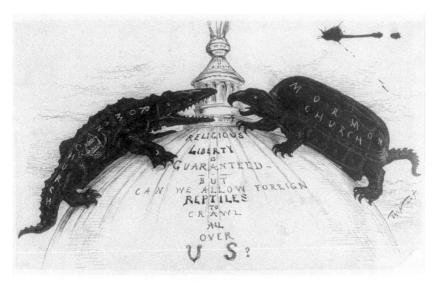

FIGURE 6.4 "Religious liberty is guaranteed: but can we allow foreign reptiles to crawl all over us?" Thomas Nast drawing (ca. 1860–1902). Library of Congress. LC-USZ62-50658.

At first the idea of polygamy was repugnant, even to many at the top of the Mormon hierarchy. When Brigham Young was instructed to take another wife, for instance, he reportedly wished for death. (Young overcame his initial reservations, and by 1846 had thirty-five wives—eight of whom were the widows of Joseph Smith.[156]) As Young put it, "We must gird up our loins and fulfill this, just as we would any other duty"[157] (Figure 6.5).

Interest in the Mormons was especially keen in Britain where, as historian Anne F. Hyde has noted, Mormon missionaries had been hugely successful in finding converts in "the fading rural villages and harsh industrial towns of England and Wales ... Nearly sixty thousand Britons responded to the critique of the 'Babylon' that industrialization had created in England."[158] More than any other person, it was Richard Burton who brought Mormons to the attention of people outside the United States, and who made Salt Lake City an important destination for Europeans traveling in America. Burton spent three weeks in that Mormon community in 1860, and in 1861 published an account of his visit called *City of the Saints*. Famous as an outsider who had penetrated the mysteries of Mecca and Harar, and renowned as the first European to identify Lake Tanganyika, Burton combined the explorer's gifts of endurance and tenacity with the erudition of an ethnographer and linguist. His examination of the religion and folkways of the Mormons was no less thorough, and in *City of the Saints* Burton produced what Fawn Brodie called "the best book on Mormons published during the nineteenth century."[159]

FIGURE 6.5 Brigham Young (1854). Wood engraving. Library of Congress.
LC-USZ62-50426.

What separates Burton's account of the Mormons from others is his willingness to engage Mormons on their own terms and his *un*willingness to be judgmental. Burton's objectivity in regards to the Mormons, he said, was based on
avoiding "looking at them from the fancied vantage-ground of an English point
of view." Burton, it was safe to say, was one of the few foreign visitors who had
actually studied polygamous societies elsewhere in the world, and he found a
rational basis for polygamy among the Mormons ("polygamy is the rule where
population is required").[160] While Burton detected little in the way of romance
in Mormon polygamous marriages, what he found instead was "household comfort, affection, circumspect friendship, and domestic discipline."[161] He was also
impressed with the intellect of many Mormons, especially Brigham Young.
When the Mormon leader received Burton and asked him where his recent
African explorations had taken him, Burton replied that he had been about ten
degrees north of the Zambesi. One of Young's associates rose and pointed to a

spot on a map of Africa that was some one hundred miles off, and Brigham Young corrected him. Burton observed that there were many educated people in England who could not have done as well, including an editor at the *London Review* who seemed to have only a vague notion of the geography of Africa.[162]

Some five years after Burton was in Salt Lake City, Charles Wentworth Dilke and William Hepworth Dixon spent fifteen days with the Mormons. On their way to Utah they had come upon a large group of Mormons in the Rockies where "men and women were seated round the campfires praying and singing hymns." A Mormon bishop and his two wives fed Dilke and Dixon and provided forage for their horses, leaving these English travelers "inclined to look favourably on polygamy."[163] At the nearby Mormon community of Coalville, Dixon gazed in wonder at "the courage, industry, [and] fanaticism" that had wrested a thriving agricultural community from a desolate valley.[164]

Once in Salt Lake City, Dixon took note of the absence of drunks and beggars in the streets. No one appeared poor, and in contrast to other Western towns, the people were "quiet and civil."[165] As for polygamy, Mormon historian George A. Smith (cousin of Joseph) told Dixon that there were some 500 bishops and elders living in polygamy in the Salt Lake vicinity in 1866, with an average of four wives and fifteen children each.[166]

Dixon refused to say that this system degraded the Mormon woman, but he did say it "lowers her."[167] When Dixon visited a Mormon household, the women in the family were brought out "as children are with us," and after being introduced they promptly disappeared.[168] (This was confirmed by William A. Bell, who claimed that a Mormon man always used the term "his women" rather than his wives, and that the dinner guests at a Mormon's table were almost always men, with the wives waiting on table.[169]) Dixon's companion, Charles Wentworth Dilke, found in Mormon women an "unconscious melancholy," with the "same sad eye" that he had encountered only once before—at the Shaker community at New Lebanon.[170]

Those who spent the most time with Mormons and those who had been exposed to cultures very different from their own tended to be the most sympathetic observers of Mormon society. Like Richard Burton, Phil Robinson was extremely well traveled, having spent time in India, Burma, Ceylon, and parts of Africa.[171] He also spent a full three months among the Mormons and came away impressed by Mormon society's lack of poverty and by the industriousness of its members.[172] When Robinson arrived in Salt Lake City in 1882, the Edmunds Anti-Polygamy Act, which made polygamy a felony, had just been passed.[173] That seemed to have no immediate effect on polygamy in Utah, and Robinson himself was the guest of a Mormon polygamist. Robinson called the Mormons "kind-hearted, simple, [and] hard-working," but like others he condemned the impact of polygamy on Mormon women. "In polygamy the highest happiness of woman is contentment," said Robinson. But contentment was not the same thing as happiness, but was rather "the lame sister of happiness, the deaf-mute in the family of joy."[174]

Burton, Dixon, Dilke, and Robinson were the exceptions, however, and travelers who approached Mormon society with the even-handedness of these men were few indeed. Most had already formed opinions about Mormonism, and they reveled in the shocking details about Mormon life with which they were provided. For instance, we can contrast Burton's description of Brigham Young as an able, highly intelligent person, with W. F. Rae's description of Young's "sensual expression" and "fondness for a ritual which, by consecrating polygamy, gives free scope for indulging in every whim and freak of passion."[175] When someone pointed out to W. G. Marshall one of Brigham Young's grand-sons, he told Marshall that, "This man had married his aunt! Another man was shown us who had married a couple of sisters!"[176] Polygamy, said Marshall, must be "speedily suppressed."[177] W. Henry Barneby also visited Salt Lake City, and after praising the prosperous and well-cultivated landscape, he insisted that Mormonism must be abolished because it was "a disgrace" to a civilized country like the United States.[178]

Both Marshall and Emily Faithfull used the word "degradation" to describe the condition of Mormon women. Iza Duffus Hardy went further, referring to the "heart's crucifixion in the daily martyrdom of a Mormon marriage."[179] J. W. Boddam-Whetham observed the "dead-alive" look of Mormon women, and contrasted it with the "jolly and free" look of Mormon men, who "appeared to leave the burden of the 'cross,' about which they talk a good deal, to be borne by their wives."[180] John Mortimer Murphy confirmed that "Mormon sisters moved along in subdued groups, as if it were a sin or a crime to be joyous."[181]

Travelers also tried to make a connection between the abject status of Mormon women and their physical appearance. Rudyard Kipling called Mormon women "not lovely," Oscar Wilde referred to Mormons as "wholly deficient in personal beauty," and Isabella Bird flatly stated that "the women were ugly." (Both Kipling and Bird described the dresses worn by Mormon women as "hide-ous.")[182] Lady Duffus Hardy took note of "antiquated millinery and quaint com-bination of colours," while her daughter Iza chose the damning-with-faint-praise route in her statement that "we saw very few well-dressed ladies, but many sweet, good, womanly faces."[183]

Some indication of how mainstream Americans viewed Mormons can be gleaned from the reaction to a play by James B. Runnion called *One Hundred Wives*. The subject of the play was Mormonism, which a *New York Times* review described as "the flagrant evil which is allowed to thrive, weed-like, in our free land."[184] William Howard Russell attended a performance of this play in Toledo in 1881, and was struck by "the vigorous and sustained applause which greeted any situation or sentiment in which the Mormon leaders and their teachings were held up to contempt and hatred." As the curtain came down, the audience cheered loudly as "half-a-dozen soldiers, in the uniform of the United States infantry, appeared to execute justice and to establish the predominance of the United States Constitution in the land of the Saints."[185]

Notes

1. David Macrae, *The Americans at Home* [1870] (New York: E. P. Dutton, 1952), 132.
2. Ibid., 133.
3. Charles Wentworth Dilke, *Greater Britain: A Record of Travel in English-Speaking Countries* (London: Macmillan and Co., 1890), 4, 5.
4. Ibid., 15.
5. Ibid., 14, 18.
6. Ibid., 17.
7. Ibid., 16.
8. Macrae, 275.
9. F. Barham Zincke, *Last Winter in the United States: Being Table Talk Collected During a Tour Through the Late Southern Confederation, the Far West, the Rocky Mountains, &c.* [1868] (Freeport, NY: Books for Libraries Press, 1970), 69. Zincke contrasts this with what he saw in the North, where "all the way from Philadelphia to Baltimore I found the country sown with houses. This arises from the fact that every 100 or 150 acres belong to a separate proprietor (large estates being unknown) who has his house upon his small farm, which he cultivates with his own hands and the assistance of his family." Ibid., 31.
10. Robert Somers, *The Southern States Since the War* [1871] (Tuscaloosa: University of Alabama Press, 1965), 280.
11. William Saunders, *Through the Light Continent, or, The United States in 1877–78* [1879] (New York: Arno Press, 1974), 73, 82; George Augustus Sala reported that, "Not once have I spoken with a Southerner who has defended slavery in the abstract." George Augustus Sala, *America Revisited: From the Bay of New York to the Gulf of Mexico and From Lake Michigan to the Pacific* (London: Vizetelly & Co., n.d.), 199.
12. Saunders, 74. Saunders praised Southern whites for "restoring order and local government" (or, more accurately, depriving blacks of their rights). Ibid., 73.
13. Somers, 84; Macrae, 342.
14. Zincke, 58.
15. Ibid., 123, 124.
16. J. J. Aubertin, *A Fight with Distances: The States, the Hawaiian Islands, Canada, British Columbia, Cuba, the Bahamas* (London: Kegan Paul, Trench & Co., 1888), 70. Almost alone in his positive view of American blacks was Alexander Craib. Craib had been impressed by the intelligence of three black students he had met on the train between Detroit and Chicago, and observed, "We are accustomed to talk and think of 'the black men' of the world as so far behind the white men, as less intelligent and less able to deal with intellectual problems, but if the three above referred to be a fair sample, they will, with our advantages as a people, rival us any day." Alexander Craib, *America and the Americans: A Tour in the United States and Canada, With Chapters on American Home Life* (London: Alexander Gardner, 1892), 53.
17. Macrae, 297.
18. Ernst von Hesse-Wartegg, *Travels on the Lower Mississippi, 1879–1880*, trans. and ed. Frederic Trautmann (Columbia: University of Missouri Press, 1990), 70–71.
19. Zincke, 107. A rare exception to the European distaste for interracial amalgamation was Tocqueville's traveling companion Gustave de Beaumont. Beaumont returned to France and wrote an anti-racist novel called *Marie*. While popular in France, this novel did not appear in the United States until 1958, probably because it dealt with interracial marriage. See Daniel Walker Howe, *What Hath God Wrought: The Transformation of America, 1815–1848* (Oxford: Oxford University Press, 2007), 307.
20. Anonymous, "American Humour," *The Cornhill Magazine* 13 (January 1866), 36.
21. C. Van Woodward, *The Strange Career of Jim Crow* (Oxford: Oxford University Press, 1966), 6. Woodward notes that "the origin of the term 'Jim Crow' applied to Negroes is lost in obscurity. Thomas D. Rice wrote a song and dance called 'Jim Crow' in 1832, and the term had become an adjective by 1838." Ibid., 7.

22. Eric Foner, *Forever Free: The Story of Emancipation and Reconstruction* (New York: Alfred A. Knopf, 2005), 192.
23. Douglass quoted in Thomas J. Brown, "Rituals of Remembrance," in Thomas J. Brown, *The Public Art of Civil War Commemoration: A Brief History with Documents* (Boston: Bedford/St. Martin's, 2004), 42–43.
24. Quoted in Cecilia Elizabeth O'Leary, "'Blood Brotherhood': The Racialization of Patriotism, 1865–1918," in *Bonds of Affection: Americans Define Their Patriotism*, ed. John Bodnar (Princeton: Princeton University Press, 1996), 78.
25. William Archer, *America To-Day: Observations and Reflections* [1899] (New York: Arno Press, 1974), 135, 136. "Thus," said Archer, "illiterate whites are not necessarily deprived of the suffrage … At any rate (it is argued), the illiterate white is a totally different man from the illiterate negro." Ibid., 136–137.
26. William Howard Russell, *Hesperothen, Notes from the West: A Record of a Ramble in the United States and Canada in the Spring and Summer of 1881*, v. 1 (London: S. Low, Marston, Searle & Rivington, 1882), 103–104.
27. Saunders, 77, 78.
28. Jacques Offenbach, *Orpheus in America: Offenbach's Diary of His Journey to the New World* [1877], trans. Lander MacClintock (New York: Greenwood Press, 1969), 94–95. Summing up the situation, one traveler put it this way: "The black man is despised as of old, and no one hails him as a brother. His children must go to separate schools—he must travel by separate cars on the railway. Will it be so always with these six millions of free citizens of the American Republic?" Anonymous, "Some American Notes," *MacMillan's Magazine* 53 (November 1885), 50.
29. Somers, 216.
30. Anonymous, "The Antagonism of Race and Colour; or, White, Red, Black, and Yellow in America," *Blackwood's Edinburgh Magazine* 653, no. 107 (March 1870), 326.
31. Zincke, 105.
32. W. G. Marshall, *Through America: Nine Months in the United States* (London: Sampson, Low, Marston, Searle & Rivington, 1881), 51.
33. Therese Yelverton, *Teresina in America*, v.1 (London: Richard Bentley and Son, 1875), 61.
34. Ibid., 47, 66, 71.
35. Lepel Henry Griffin, *The Great Republic* [1884] (New York: Arno Press, 1974), 140, 129.
36. Phil Robinson, *Sinners and Saints: A Tour Across the States, and Round Them; with Three Months Among the Mormons* (Boston: Roberts Brothers, 1883), 350.
37. Rudyard Kipling, *American Notes* [1891] (Norman: University of Oklahoma Press, 1981), 42. With the social and economic deck stacked against American blacks, Kipling came to the obvious conclusion: "it is not good to be a negro in the land of the free and the home of the brave." Ibid., 43. James Bryce found that "thoughtful observers" in the South "expect that for many years to come the negroes, naturally a good-natured and easy-going race, will be content with the position of an inferior caste, doing the hard work, and especially the field work, of the country." James Bryce, *The American Commonwealth*, v. 2 (New York: The Commonwealth Publishing Co., 1908), 813.
38. Somers, 130.
39. William H. Davies, *The Autobiography of a Super-Tramp* (New York: Alfred A. Knopf, 1917), 138, 139.
40. Ibid., 142.
41. Clare V. McKanna, Jr., *Homicide, Race and Justice in the American West, 1880–1920* (Tucson: University of Arizona Press, 1997), 49. See also David W. Blight, *Race and Reunion: The Civil War in American Memory* (Cambridge, MA: Belknap Press, 2001), 344.
42. Sarah Bernhardt, *Memories of my Life* [1907] (Grosse Pointe, MI: Scholarly Press, 1968), 430, 431.
43. Quoted in Sigmund Skard, "Bjørnstjerne Bjørnson, 1832–1910," in *Abroad in America: Visitors to the New Nation, 1776–1914* (Reading, MA: Addison-Wesley, 1976), 195.

44. Boutmy quoted in Denis Lecorne, *Religion in America: A Political History* (New York: Columbia University Press, 2011), 90.

45. A. Maurice Low, *The American People: A Study in National Psychology*, v. 2 (Boston: Houghton Mifflin, 1909), 23.

46. Baron Hübner, *A Ramble Round the World, 1871*, trans. Lady Elizabeth Herbert (London: MacMillan and Co., 1878), 46–47.

47. Quoted in Skard, 201. William Saunders also praised the spectacle of people from all nations "welded into a harmonious whole." Saunders, 225–226. Another observed that "a generation or two, at most, seems to suffice to stretch the fat placid German and to sober the excitable Irishman into the lean, eager, and self-restrained Yankee." Anonymous, "American Humor," 28.

48. William Francis Butler, *The Great Lone Land: A Narrative of Travel and Adventure in the North-West of America* [1872] (Rutland, VT: Charles E. Tuttle, 1968), 54.

49. Charles Dickens, *The Speeches of Charles Dickens*, ed. K. J. Fielding (Hemel Hempstead, Hertfordshire: Harvester Wheatsheaf, 1988), 382.

50. Lady Duffus Hardy, *Through Cities and Prairie Lands: Sketches of an American Tour* (London: Chapman and Hall, 1881), 211.

51. William Hepworth Dixon, *New America* (Philadelphia: J. B. Lippincott, 1869), 260.

52. Ibid., 256. Blacks, according to Dixon, shrank from any contact with northern climes and were but a "local fact" in the sunny lands of the South. Indians had likewise been pushed into a single region between the prairies and the Rockies, where they made their home "with the wolf, the rattlesnake, the buffalo, and the elk." The Chinese, most of whom lived in the West, were described by Dixon as "harmless" and as "weak and useful." Ibid., 257, 258, 259. Tocqueville, who wrote *Democracy in America* before significant Chinese immigration, identified the three races of America as white, black, and Indian: "Among these diverse men, the first to attract the eye, the first in enlightenment, power, and happiness, is the white man, the European, man par excellence. Below him appear the Negro and the Indian." Alexis de Tocqueville, *Democracy in America* [1835], trans. Arthur Goldhammer (New York: Library of America, 2004), 366.

53. Thomas J. Schlereth, *Victorian America: Transformations in Everyday Life, 1876–1915* (New York: Harper Perennial, 1992), 10.

54. Harold Brydges, *Uncle Sam at Home* (New York: Henry Holt and Co., 1888), 184–185. The Frenchman Hugues Le Roux described America as "made up of such sundry and diverse elements, constantly modified by immigration, and prevented, for this reason, from becoming a 'race'." Le Roux suggested that Americans might consider, as a leavening agent, something resembling the French Catholic education. Hugues Le Roux, *Business and Love* (New York: Dodd, Mead and Co., 1903), 44, 45.

55. Bryce, v. 2, 815.

56. Alexandra Gripenberg, *A Half Year in the New World: Miscellaneous Sketches of Travel in the United States* [1889], trans. and ed. Ernest J. Moyne (Newark: University of Delaware Press, 1954), 9, 10. Gripenberg was an observer at the Republican Convention in Chicago in 1888, as was Susan B. Anthony. They had a brief meeting with a black delegate from the South, and Gripenberg commented, "It seemed strange to look at Miss Anthony, distinguished, brilliant, a very refined woman, next to that ignorant and pompous Negro. The former did not have the right to vote; the latter arrogantly made a show of his right to cast a ballot. America gives such lessons at every step." Ibid., 94.

57. Archer, 96. Theodore Roosevelt was among those who called upon Anglo-Saxon women to have more babies. He called it "the warfare of the cradle." Quoted in Evan Thomas, *The War Lovers: Roosevelt, Lodge, Hearst, and the Rush to Empire, 1898* (New York: Back Bay Books, 2010), 44.

58. Bryce, v. 2, 816. Bryce did acknowledge "the amazing solvent power which American institutions, habits, and ideas exercise upon new-comers of all races." Ibid., v. 2, 814.

59. Herbert Spencer, "Report of Mr. Spencer's Interview," in Edward Youmans, *Herbert Spencer on the Americans and the Americans on Herbert Spencer: Being a Full Report of his*

Interview, and of the Proceedings of the Farewell Banquet of Nov. 11, 1882 (New York: D. Appleton, 1883), 19.

60. Foner, 209.

61. Jackson Lears, *Rebirth of a Nation: The Making of Modern America, 1877–1920* (New York: Harper, 2009), 93.

62. See Patrick Q. Mason, *Mormon Menace: Violence and Anti-Mormonism in the Postbellum South* (Oxford: Oxford University Press, 2011), 180–182. Mason adds that while "anti-Catholicism was present at all levels of southern society and arguably even intensified from the 1890s to 1910s, it was usually manifest as fear of the international, not local, Catholic menace. Good will toward local Catholics and fear of the shadowy Roman conspiracy often operated simultaneously in southern communities." Ibid., 185.

63. Charles Loring Brace, *The Dangerous Classes of New York, and Twenty Years' Work Among Them* [1872] (Washington, D.C.: National Association of Social Workers, n.d.), 36.

64. Willard quoted in Kenneth D. Rose, *American Women and the Repeal of Prohibition* (New York: New York University Press, 1996), 26. William Archer also called for immigration restrictions, claiming that it was of crucial importance not only for America but also for the world at large that the United States should be "peopled by 'white men' in every sense of the word." Archer, 96.

65. W. E. Adams, *Our American Cousins: Being Personal Impressions of the People and Institutions of the United States* (London: Walter Scott, 1883), 300. Alexander Craib claimed that "among the French, German, and Irish we found 'drink' to be an abounding evil prevailing here as elsewhere." Craib, 143. See also Paul Boyer, *Urban Masses and Moral Order in America, 1820–1920* (Cambridge, MA: Harvard University Press, 1978), 146.

66. While there were no classes on American trains, emigrant trains, which were slower and offered reduced fares, were for all intents and purposes second-class trains. See W. Henry Barneby, *Life and Labor in the Far, Far West: Being Notes of a Tour in the Western States, British Columbia, Manitoba, and the North-West Territory* (London: Cassell & Co., 1884), 5.

67. Robert Louis Stevenson, "The Amateur Emigrant," in *From Scotland to Silverado* [1892] (Cambridge, MA: Belknap Press, 1966), 11.

68. Ibid., 12.

69. Ibid., 22, 33.

70. Ibid., 118.

71. Robert Louis Stevenson, "The Old and New Pacific Capitals," in *From Scotland to Silverado* [1892] (Cambridge, MA: Belknap Press, 1966), 161–162.

72. Kipling, 86; Stephen Buckland, "Eating and Drinking In America—A Stroll Among the Saloons of New York," *MacMillan's Magazine* 16 (October 1867), 460. Tchaikovsky also makes slighting references to Jews who tried to sell him souvenirs at Niagara, and to an "Odessa Jew" in Philadelphia who hit him up for money. Peter Tchaikovsky, *The Diaries of Tchaikovsky*, trans. Wladimir Lakond (New York: W. W. Norton, 1945), 321, 330.

73. Horace Annesley Vachell, *Life and Sport on the Pacific Slope* (New York: Dodd, Mead and Co., 1901), 144. W. E. Adams found that Germans in America did love their beer gardens, but he praised their decorum and the German workman's willingness to share his leisure time with his wife and children. Adams, 226. Ernst von Hesse-Wartegg, himself a German Austrian, said of the St. Louis German that "his irrepressible conviviality, active societies, thriving clubs, cultivation of art and music, and diligent, able press are to be remarked even by comparison to the Anglo-Saxon life that surrounds his." Hesse-Wartegg, 19–20.

74. E. Catherine Bates, *A Year in the Great Republic*, v. 1 (London: Ward & Downey, 1887), xviii.

75. William A. Bell, *New Tracks in North America: A Journal of Travel and Adventure Whilst Engaged in the Survey for a Southern Railroad to the Pacific Ocean During 1867–8* [1870] (Albuquerque: Horn and Wallace, 1965), 242.

76. Dilke, 31. Dilke also claimed that the Irish were the core of America's "criminal and pauper class." Ibid., 210. Griffin, 132, 131. From San Francisco, Kipling sneeringly spoke of the Irish "saloon Parliament," from which blocs of voters could be summoned to vote for or against anything. Kipling, 33.

77. Adams, 288. By 1890, less than half of Catholic children were enrolled in parochial schools, and of those most were in primary grades. Priscilla Ferguson Clement, "The City and the Child, 1869–1885," in *American Childhood: A Research Guide and Historical Handbook*, ed. Joseph M. Hawes and N. Ray Hiner (Westport, CN: Greenwood Press, 1985), 240.

78. Macrae, 57.

79. Marie Therese de Solms Blanc, *The Condition of Woman in the United States: A Traveller's Notes* [1895], trans. Abby Langdon Algber (New York: Arno Press, 1972), 248; Emily Faithfull, *Three Visits to America* (New York: Fowler & Wells, 1884), 53.

80. Saunders, 293.

81. Henry Sienkiewicz, *Portrait of America: Letters of Henry Sienkiewicz*, trans. and ed. Charles Morley (New York: Columbia University Press, 1959), 13–15.

82. See Patricia Nelson Limerick, *The Legacy of Conquest: The Unbroken Past of the American West* (New York: W. W. Norton, 1988), 117.

83. See Kevin Kenny, *The American Irish: A History* (Harlow, England: Pearson, 2000), 119.

84. Macrae, 59. When she was in Galesburg, Illinois, Maria Theresa Blanc also took note of "the refusal of Irish and Swedish servants to eat at the same table with negroes." Blanc, 203.

85. Low, v. 2, 389.

86. The Chinese constituted one-fifth of the population of California by the late 1870s. Between 1850 and 1882, 332,000 Chinese came to California. See Lears, 113.

87. Dilke, 182.

88. Hübner, 130.

89. W. F. Rae, *Westward by Rail: The New Route to the East* [1871] (New York: Promontory Press, 1974), 304. Indians in the West were allowed to ride on the outside of freight cars, paying no money for their passage. Iza Duffus Hardy saw the Paiutes clinging to the outside of freight cars, and J. W. Boddam-Whetham saw the Pawnees riding in a similar fashion. Iza Duffus Hardy, *Between Two Oceans: Or, Sketches of American Travel* (London: Hurst and Blackett, 1884), 220; J. W. Boddam-Whetham, *Western Wanderings: A Record of Travel in the Evening Land* (London: Richard Bentley and Son, 1874), 54.

90. Iza Hardy, 187.

91. Faithfull, 221.

92. Ibid., 222.

93. Marshall, 300.

94. Theodora Guest, *A Round Trip in North America* (London: Edward Stanford, 1895), 99.

95. Sienkiewicz, 252.

96. Barneby, 41.

97. Aubertin, 134, 135.

98. Marshall, 304, 303. Dorothea Guest also found the sight of a Chinese man under the thrall of opium "rather horrible," though she judged him to be less degraded than "that of the ordinary European drunkard." Guest, 98.

99. Bates, v. 2, 140.

100. Kipling, 28.

101. Faithfull, 222.

102. H. Hussey Vivian, *Notes of a Tour in America from August 7th to November 17th, 1877* (London: Edward Stanford, 1878), 135.

103. Marshall, 288.

104. Dixon, 260.

105. Edward A. Freeman, *Some Impressions of the United States* (London: Longmans, Green, and Co., 1883), 153.

106. Gripenberg, 143.

107. Stevenson, "Amateur," 139.

108. Limerick, 263.

109. See Richard White, *"It's Your Misfortune and None of My Own": A History of the American West* (Norman: University of Oklahoma Press, 1991), 340–344.
110. Richard White, *Railroaded: The Transcontinentals and the Making of Modern America* (New York: W. W. Norton, 2011), 311.
111. John Campbell Argyll, *A Trip to the Tropics and Home Through America* (London: Hurst and Blackett, 1867), 264.
112. Freeman, 138. Freeman added, "The position held by the Irish and the negroes made me feel more and more strongly the danger of that hasty and indiscriminate bestowal of citizenship which has become the practice, and rather the pride, of the United States." Ibid., 157.
113. Ibid., 258–259.
114. Dixon, 255. In his description of "cosmopolitan" San Francisco, William A. Bell noted with some astonishment that, "Every morning I had my boots blacked by an African, my chin shaved by a European, and my bed made by an Asiatic; a Frenchman cooked my dinner, an Englishman showed me to my seat, an Irishman changed my plate, a Chinaman washed my table-napkin, and a German handed me my bill." Bell, 401.
115. Hesse-Wartegg, 161.
116. Paul Bourget, *Outre-Mer: Impressions of America* (London: T. Fisher Unwin, 1895), 415.
117. Bourget, 6, 215–216.
118. Paul de Rousiers, *American Life*, trans. A. J. Herbertson (New York: Firmin-Didot, 1892), 223.
119. Tocqueville, 623.
120. Martin E. Marty, *Pilgrims in their Own Land: 500 Years of Religion in America* (New York: Penguin, 1986), 341. Taking note of this phenomenon was Scottish visitor Robert Somers, who found religious sects in America to be more numerous "than in any other part of the Christian world." Somers, 67.
121. Max O'rell and Jack Allyn, *Jonathan and His Continent: Rambles Through American Society*, trans. Madame Paul Blouet (Bristol: J. W. Arrowsmith, 1889), 160.
122. See Winthrop S. Hudson, *Religion in America: An Historical Account of the Development of American Religious Life* (New York: Macmillan, 1987), 232–233.
123. Dixon, 343. Baron Hübner referred to revivals as "those great meetings in the forests and prairies of the Far West, where a sudden thirst for spiritual consolation bursts out with extraordinary violence, seizing upon the masses like an epidemic and producing the most fantastic scenes, now tragic, now comic." Hübner, 20. Almost alone among Europeans in departing from the purple descriptions of American revivals was Élisée Reclus, who emphasized the social and recreational aspects of such meetings: "Impelled by the need of change and excitement ingrained in all Americans, and especially by the love of society, the farmers, living mostly in isolation, feel from time to time a yearning for a 'revival,' which is itself a relaxation from the routine of daily existence and a stimulus for future work." Revivals, said Reclus, "are really holidays combining pleasure with religion." Élisée Reclus, *The Earth and its Inhabitants. North America: v. 3, the United States* (New York: D. Appleton and Co., 1893), 477.
124. Blanc, 160.
125. Bourget, 70.
126. Drew Gilpin Faust, *This Republic of Suffering: Death and the American Civil War* (New York: Alfred A. Knopf, 2008), 174.
127. Thornwell quoted in Hudson, 200, n. 1.
128. Wolfgang Schivelbusch, *The Culture of Defeat: On National Trauma, Mourning, and Recovery* (New York: Picador, 2003), 67–69. Schivelbusch notes that "the Northern and Southern Methodist churches were reunited in 1939, their Presbyterian equivalents only in 1983. The Southern and Northern Baptist churches remain separate to this day." Ibid., 67.
129. See Faust, 180–188.

130. Arthur Conan Doyle, creator of Sherlock Holmes, lost a son in the Great War, and began attending seances with others who sought to communicate with the dead. Doyle and his wife would become leaders of the post-World War I spiritualist movement, and in 1926 Doyle published a two-volume set called *The History of Spiritualism*. In it, Doyle denounces as "a clumsy lie" the claims of his critics that his grief had overwhelmed his critical faculties. Arthur Conan Doyle, *The History of Spiritualism*, v. 2 (New York: George H. Doran Company, 1926), 225.
131. See Bates, v. 1, 194–232.
132. Gripenberg, 48.
133. Dixon, 93.
134. Bryce, v. 2, 785, Dilke, 113. Horace Annesley Vachell observed that "the number of mediums, clairvoyants, astrologers, and palmists in San Francisco alone is most significant." Vachell, 193.
135. Gripenberg, 55. Spiritualism in America arguably began in 1848 when the sisters Maggie and Katie Fox produced "rappings" that were supposedly evidence of communication with the dead. The sisters confessed that they had perpetrated a hoax in 1888. See Hudson, 187. Gripenberg also ran afoul of a family of Christian Scientists with whom she was staying in Chicago. When Gripenberg mentioned feeling weary and faintly ill, it seemed that "everyone was taken aback because I admitted such a humiliating thing." While Gripenberg judged that there was a great deal of "humbug" in Christian Science, its one redeeming feature was the impact it had had on hypochrondriacs. Gripenberg, 98, 108.
136. Marty, 339–340, 338.
137. Strong quoted in Marty, 338.
138. Josiah Strong, *Our Country: Its Possible Future and Its Present Crisis* [1885] (Cambridge, MA: Belknap, 1963), 53–55.
139. Ibid., 65.
140. Ibid., 215.
141. Blanc, 234.
142. Strong, 40.
143. Isabella L. Bird, *A Lady's Life in the Rocky Mountains* (Norman: University of Oklahoma Press, 1969). 70.
144. Ibid., 188.
145. Quoted in Richard W. Slatta, *Cowboys of the Americas* (New Haven: Yale University Press, 1990), 227.
146. Vachell, 236, 235.
147. William A. Clebsch, *From Sacred to Profane America: The Role of Religion in American History* (New York: Harper & Row, 1968), 161.
148. S. C. de Soissons, *A Parisian in America* (Boston: Estres and Lauriat, 1896), 199.
149. Freeman, 158; Bryce, v. 2, 763.
150. Gripenberg, 214.
151. Russell, v. 2, 132–133. H. Hussey Vivian said, "I suspect that denominationalism is not half so strong a sentiment in America as it is with us." Vivian, 247.
152. Horace White, "An American's Impression of England," *Eclectic Magazine* 22, no. 5 (New Series, November 1875), 550.
153. Quoted in James Fullarton Muirhead, *The Land of Contrasts: A Briton's View of his American Kin* (London: Lamson, Wolffe and Co., 1898), 11.
154. Sienkiewicz, 29.
155. Mason, 7.
156. Marty, 203.
157. Young quoted in Daniel Boorstin, *The Americans: The National Experience* (New York: Random House, 1965), 64.
158. Anne F. Hyde, *Empires, Nations, and Families: A History of the North American West, 1800–1860* (Lincoln: University of Nebraska Press, 2011), 363. Hyde finds similarities

between Mormons and Indian societies: "like many Native nations, the Mormons traveled in family groups, did business almost exclusively with their kin, and took great pleasure in refusing to do things the 'American way.'" Ibid., 358.

159. Fawn Brodie, "Editor's Introduction," in Richard F. Burton, *The City of the Saints and Across the Rocky Mountains to California* (New York: Alfred A. Knopf, 1963), vii.

160. Richard F. Burton, *The City of the Saints and Across the Rocky Mountains to California* (New York: Alfred A. Knopf, 1963), 480.

161. Ibid., 481.

162. Ibid., 271. While the Mormon faith was open to virtually everyone, Brigham Young told William Hepworth Dixon that the one exception was the Negro, who, according to Young, "is a descendant of Cain, the first murderer, and his darkness is a curse put on his skin by God." Dixon, 189.

163. Dilke, 97.

164. Dixon, 129.

165. Ibid., 140. Referring to the Mormons, Dixon concluded that "many people in the United States would be able to endure them a little better if they would only behave themselves a good deal worse." Ibid., 171.

166. Ibid., 220.

167. Ibid., 233.

168. Ibid., 234.

169. Bell, 462.

170. Dilke, 99, 100, 105. Baron Hübner also described Mormon women as having "a sad, timid look." Hübner, 109.

171. Referring to Burton, Robinson noted that "there has not been a single trustworthy book written about Mormonism since 1862." Robinson, 86.

172. As Robinson put it, "There are no pauper Mormons, for there are no idle ones. In the daytime there are no loafers in the streets, for every man is afield or at his work, and soon after nine at night the whole city seems to be gone to bed ... the pervading stillness and the emptiness of the streets is dispiriting to rowdyism, and so the Gentile damns the place as being 'dull.'" Ibid., 71.

173. Robinson, referring to the Mormon reaction to the Edmunds Act, predicted that "they will simply ignore the Bill as long as it ignores them, and that when it is put in force against them, they will accept the penalty without complaint." Ibid., 83–84. In 1889, when Rudyard Kipling visited Salt Lake City, he expressed doubts that the law was being very rigorously enforced because most of the local police were Mormons. Kipling hated Mormonism, calling it "that amazing creed and fantastic jumble of Mahometanism, the Mosaic law, and imperfectly comprehended fragments of Freemasonry, [that] calls to its aid all the powers of a hell conceived and elaborated by coarse-minded hedgers and ditchers." Kipling, 116, 117. In 1890, Mormon President Wilford Wodruff had a revelation that proscribed plural marriage. Utah was not admitted as a state until 1896. See Boorstin, 65.

174. Robinson, 269, 96. Robinson elaborated that "polygamy is wrong in itself and a cardinal crime against the possibilities of a woman's heart." Ibid., 97.

175. Rae, 107. In no uncertain terms, Rae condemned both Burton's and Dixon's portrayals of the Mormons. The former he described as "an awkward joke or an elaborated paradox," while the latter was "apparently designed to breed doubts and excite suspicions." Ibid., xi.

176. Marshall, 177.

177. Ibid., 179.

178. Barneby, 35.

179. Marshall, 185, 186; Faithfull, 160; Iza Hardy, 130. Hardy believed that there was only one class of women who could thrive under Mormonism—"those who are by nature mothers more than wives." Ibid., 129.

180. Boddam-Whetham, 80, 75.

181. John Mortimer Murphy, *Rambles in North-Western America, from the Pacific Ocean to the Rocky Mountains* (London: Chapman and Hall, 1879), 237.

182. Kipling, 120; Oscar Wilde, "American Women," in Oscar Wilde, *The Works of Oscar Wilde* (New York: AMS Press, 1972), 8; Bird, 24. W. F. Rae claimed that "the wives of the Saints are not over-burdened with good looks." Rae, 109. Carlo Gardini also tried to link what he saw as the physically unattractive Mormon woman to the morality of her religion. Andrew J. Torrielli, *Italian Opinion on America, As Revealed by Italian Travelers, 1859–1900* (Cambridge, MA: Harvard University Press, 1941), 196.

183. Lady Duffus Hardy, 119; Iza Hardy, 123.

184. *New York Times*, 15 February 1881.

185. Russell, v. 1, 169–170.

7

WAR, POLITICS, AND PATRIOTISM

War

As the greatest catastrophe in American history, the impact of the Civil War would reverberate for decades. Approximately 620,000 soldiers (by some counts, 750,000) died in the war, and 470,000 were wounded. Ten percent of able-bodied men in the North and almost 25 percent of able-bodied men in the South were dead or wounded at the end of the war.[1] As historian David W. Blight has noted, "The most immediate legacy of the war was its slaughter and how to remember it."[2] Writing in the *Atlantic Monthly* in 1869, the American James Russell Lowell claimed that before the war, Americans were viewed by Europeans as a "mob of adventurers and shop-keepers." To fight such an enormously bloody war for an abstraction that had nothing to do with dollars and cents should have, in Lowell's view, modified these views.[3] Indeed, in the estimation of Élisée Reclus, the Civil War "revealed prodigious resources in physical energy and the solid qualities of endurance and courage" among the millions of Americans who had participated.[4]

Certainly, visitors in the immediate aftermath of the war were sobered by the extent of the destruction. John Campbell Argyll commented on the ragged holes from shot and shell that marred the houses of Fredericksburg, and as Charles Wentworth Dilke's ship cruised up Virginia's James River in 1866, he observed "rows of iron skeletons, the frameworks of the wheels of sunken steamers."[5] On shore, at Dutch Gap, there were "forests of crosses of unpainted wood" on virtually every piece of flat ground.[6] Richmond was a city of broken columns, blackened walls, and empty streets (Figure 7.1). The predominant dress of the residents was black for mourning.[7] David Macrae was also shocked by the devastation of the city, and the gloom that had settled on the inhabitants.[8]

FIGURE 7.1 Ruins on the Canal Basin, Richmond, VA (1863, printed later). Library of Congress. LC-USZC4-7935.

Things were arguably worse further south. In Charleston, Therese Yelverton referred to "roofless houses" and "paneless windows."[9] For F. Barham Zincke, Charleston was a "city of the dead," sunk under "abject and irrecoverable poverty." He found a similar state of affairs in Mississippi and Louisiana.[10] In the Tennessee Valley, there was lingering evidence of the Civil War in the form of "burnt-up gin-houses, ruined bridges, mills, and factories."[11] Even as late as 1881, William Howard Russell described Harper's Ferry as having "an indelible mark of wreck and ruin about it."[12] The human costs were even more terrible. In the first year of peace, the state of Mississippi spent one-fifth of its revenue on artificial legs and arms for returning veterans.[13] As for a revival of the rebellion, Charles Wentworth Dilke could find no Southerner willing to entertain such a notion. It seemed that only foreign travelers such as himself were asking whether the South would fight again.[14]

In the North, specialty shops catered to the grim harvest of war. By 1863, New York's Lord & Taylor had opened up a mourning department, while grievers in Philadelphia could go to Besson & Son, Mourning Store.[15] When John Campbell Argyll visited New York in 1866, he could not help but notice the large number of advertisements for wooden arms and legs.[16] In the same year, the suffering of the war was brought home to Charles Wentworth Dilke in dramatic fashion when he attended Harvard's graduation ceremonies. Former graduating classes processed in as groups, and when the classes of 1859, 1860 and the war years passed through, Dilke observed "many an empty sleeve."[17] Harvard would build the Memorial Hall to commemorate those from the university who had lost their lives during the Civil War, and E. Catherine Bates found that "it was very depressing to walk through the long corridor lined with small tablets bearing the names of so many young men cut off in the very flower of their youth."[18]

North and South mourned their dead separately. At Cold Harbor in 1866, John Campbell Argyll encountered a "national" cemetery where the bodies of over two thousand Union troops had been collected and buried, while "Confederate dead were allowed to lie where they fell."[19] This was not an isolated incident. When John Trowbridge, a writer for *Atlantic Monthly*, stumbled over some unburied bodies at the Wilderness in 1865, his companion examined the buttons on the uniforms and remarked, "'They were No'th Carolinians; that's why they didn't bury 'em'"[20] (Figure 7.2). John Cook brought the first group of British travelers to America in 1866, and when they toured the battlefields in the vicinity of Richmond, Virginia, they seemed fascinated by the "skulls, arms, legs, etc., all bleaching in the sun."[21] The work of collecting the Union dead was done all over the country, and at its completion in 1871, over 303,000 Union soldiers had been reinterred in seventy-four cemeteries, at a cost of $4 million.[22]

FIGURE 7.2 A burial party on the battlefield at Cold Harbor, April 1865. Photograph by John Reekie. NARA 165-SB-94.

At the behest of the Union veterans' organization, the Grand Army of the Republic, a day was set aside to mourn the Union dead called Decoration Day. The first Decoration Day was held on May 30, 1868 (a date chosen to coincide with the appearance of spring flowers) at Arlington cemetery and at 183 other cemeteries across the country.[23] While there were several hundred Confederate dead buried at Arlington, Southern mourners were barred from the ceremony.[24] The South set aside its own day to mourn its dead called Memorial Day, and it was not until after World War I that a single day was designated to include all Americans killed in battle.[25] Especially in the immediate aftermath of the war, the differences in funding for burial of the dead in North and South was striking, resulting in decrepit burial places in the South and well-tended cemeteries in the North.

Primarily responsible for mobilizing mourners—both North and South— were women's organizations. In the North, this work was done by the Northern Women's Relief Corps, which by 1890 had a membership of some 100,000.[26] In the South, a number of women's groups became involved in the repatriation to the South of Confederate war dead that remained in the North. The Ladies Hollywood Memorial Association of Richmond brought back some 3,000 of Virginia's war dead from Gettysburg in 1871, and eighty-nine Confederate dead from Arlington the following year.[27] In Vicksburg, the Ladies Confederate Cemetery Association reinterred the bodies of some 1,600 Confederate soldiers, and similar work was done at Chattanooga, Atlanta, and elsewhere. When a local Unionist in Marietta suggested burying the Union and Confederate dead together, local women were horrified, and insisted that the Confederate dead be "protected from a promiscuous mingling with the remains of their enemies."[28] As historian Drew Gilpin Faust has observed, these Civil War cemeteries were unlike anything ever seen in America, with "row after row of humble identical markers, hundreds of thousands of men, known and unknown, who represented not so much the sorrow or particularity of a lost loved one as the enormous and all but unfathomable cost of the war."[29]

The importance of these days of commemoration was obvious even to European travelers, with one counting Decoration Day as among the four great American holidays.[30] In Atlanta, Iza Duffus Hardy witnessed a Memorial Day commemoration where crowds gathered at a cemetery around a marble obelisk dedicated to the Confederate dead. War widows were given a place of honor on the steps leading to the obelisk, and Hardy observed that most of the officials at the ceremony were "maimed or crippled in some way; some have lost a leg, some an arm, others only a few fingers."[31] The memorial obelisk became a feature of virtually every Southern town of any size. George Augustus Sala noted of the obelisk in Augusta that it was dedicated "to those who fell for the Honour of Georgia, for the Rights of the States, for the Liberty of the People, and for the Principles of the Union as handed down to his Children by the Father of a Common Country."[32] Indeed, it was devotion to the cause, rather than the hope of eternal life, that was the dominant sentiment of Confederate epitaphs. Examining the tombstones in New Orleans, F. Barham Zincke found that the inscriptions were related to the deceased having "died in the discharge of his duty, or in defence of the rights of his country ... [but] no inscriptions that had any direct reference in any way to what Christians believe."[33] Nor was reconciliation with the former enemy a prominent theme. A memorial that was erected in Alexandria, Virginia, features a Confederate soldier looking south toward the old Confederate capital, with his back pointedly turned away from Washington, D.C.[34] Assessing the impact of the war on Southerners in 1872, Therese Yelverton claimed that "it was impossible to ignore the hold it had on them."[35]

Passions ran high in the North as well. In New York, David Macrae mentions women carrying baskets of flowers to decorate soldiers' graves on Decoration Day and a huge parade staged by the Grand Army of the Republic.[36] In 1877, William Saunders also witnessed a parade of Union veterans in Boston that included a number of "Confederate prisoners" who marched under a large banner and whom seemed proud of the role that they played. A Boston newspaper pointed out that the number of Confederate participants was fewer than hoped for because they were too poor to pay traveling expenses and too proud to accept assistance.[37]

There were a few Europeans who failed to grasp the serious meaning that the Civil War had for Americans. The facile Knut Hamsun proclaimed that the Civil War had nothing to do with morality or the emancipation of the slaves, but was instead waged "for extermination of the Southern aristocracy."[38] His conclusion was that there was no other point to a parade of Civil War veterans than "an attention-getting march through the streets."[39] Of the display in Niagara to commemorate the Civil War, the glib Lady Theodora Guest sniffed, "Better forgotten, I should have thought."[40]

For decades the long shadow of the war would intrude into virtually every aspect of American life. R. W. Dale claimed that the war had had "a great effect on national manners," and that the "self-control and orderliness" that he found to be characteristic of the American people could be traced to "the discipline, the serious work, and the perils and sufferings of those terrible years."[41] The impact of the war was especially marked in the realm of politics, where the military hero was glorified, the army vote became a powerful bloc, and military service acted as "the quickest road to civil preferment."[42] Indeed, William Howard Russell reported that as he and his party were leaving the White House in 1881, they encountered "a delegation of one-armed and one-legged veterans" entering with a petition demanding that veterans receive preferential treatment for federal job appointments.[43] While the war could never be forgotten by those who participated in it, by the mid-1870s Decoration Day speeches had become more conciliatory, emphasizing the valor that was common to both Union and Confederate soldiers.[44] According to historian Thomas J. Brown, another reason for conciliation was to celebrate "the integrity of the United States at a time when many northerners worried that the influx of immigration imperiled American identity."[45]

It was obvious, however, that Southerners continued to feel more connected to the war than Northerners. Northerners had victory, after all, and as George Augustus Sala observed, they were "quite content with the triumphant end, as well they may be, and do not care to inquire about the means by which that end was brought about."[46] All Southerners had was the "Lost Cause," which historian Wolfgang Schivelbusch calls "the South's central myth after the collapse of the Confederacy."[47] Elements of the Lost Cause included an identification with the Scottish clans (especially in Walter Scott novels) who fought valiantly in a losing effort against "coldly mercantilist England," as well as the conviction that the North had not waged a fair fight but had overwhelmed the South through sheer numbers and a cowardly strategy of "scorched earth."[48] For Southerners, reconciliation with such an enemy was clearly going to be difficult. In 1883, Iza Duffus Hardy contrasted the differences in attitudes toward the war in New York, where it was so seldom mentioned there might never have been a war, and in Richmond, where she immediately felt she was "living on the very morrow of the war."[49]

But by the end of the century some of the wounds were beginning to heal, and, ironically, it was a new war, and new wounds, that facilitated the healing process. William Archer was in Washington in April 1899 when President McKinley presided over a special ceremony at Arlington Cemetery to commemorate the dead of the Spanish–American War. Archer reported that the significance of both Northerners and Southerners killed fighting for the same cause was widely commented on in the North.[50] Also in 1899, McKinley traveled to Atlanta with former Confederate General "Fighting Joe" Wheeler to drum up support for the Treaty of Paris, which ended hostilities between Spain and the United States and authorized the payment of $20 million for the Philippines. Speaking before the Georgia legislature, McKinley emphasized that, "Sectional feeling no longer holds back the love we feel for each other." His promise that the federal government would care for neglected Confederate graves in the North was greeted with wild applause.[51]

The Spanish–American War also helped to reconcile Americans with their British cousins, with race solidarity an important ingredient. A British military attaché who reached the top of Kettle Hill in Cuba with American troops proclaimed, "It's a great day for us Anglo-Saxons."[52] William Archer believed that "the sympathy with which England regarded America's determination to 'take up the white man's burden'" in the wake of the Spanish–American War was key to the rapprochement of the two nations.[53] As one British writer put it, it had been "race energy and race aptitudes" that had made the United States and Great Britain commercial powerhouses, and he looked forward to the day when British and American Anglo-Saxonism would wield a decisive influence on "the less advanced peoples."[54]

Even so, William Archer detected among Southern Civil War veterans an "aloofness from the national jubilation over the Spanish War."[55] While the Spanish–American War may have softened "the harsh outlines of the fratricidal struggle," the Civil War would be an essential part of Southern consciousness well into the twentieth century.[56] Ernest B. Furgurson, who grew up in Danville, Virginia, in the 1930s, said, "It's hard to explain how close 1865 was to us, how reminders of that war still surrounded us so long after Appomattox."[57]

Politics

There was a good deal of debate among Europeans about the basic structure of American government. Lord T. B. Macaulay, whose views were widely discussed on both sides of the Atlantic, predicted the inevitable demise of the American republic. Arguing that supreme authority in a nation should never be placed in the hands of a majority of citizens ("the poorest and most ignorant part of society"), Macaulay claimed that the American government "will never be able to restrain a distressed and discontented majority."[58] Ultimately, said Macaulay, there would be chaos, and order in the United States would either be restored by a dictator, or the nation would be "fearfully plundered and laid waste by barbarians."[59] Henry Hussey Vivian, who visited the United States in 1877, helpfully suggested that Americans create an aristocracy ("there are fortunes amply large enough to support hereditary rank") and "transform their Senate into a House of Peers."[60]

Matthew Arnold responded negatively to both Macaulay and Vivian. Arnold claimed that what Macaulay had forgotten was that the United States lacked what "accentuates the division between rich and poor—the distinction of classes."[61] As for American political institutions, Arnold found the American mixture of national, state, and city governments "thoroughly suited" to the nation, and used the analogy of "a suit of clothes which fits him to perfection, leaving all his movements unimpeded and easy."[62] In contrast to Vivian, Arnold suggested that the British remake the House of Lords along the lines of the U.S. Senate.[63]

While there was some disagreement about political structure in America, European travelers were mostly united in condemning American political campaigns as appallingly vicious. "Passions are let loose; intrigues are on foot; the most odious calumnies are circulated," as one traveler put it.[64] Therese Yelverton referred to the "villainous machinations, deceits, egotism, peculations, frauds, briberies, &c." of American politics.[65] Knut Hamsun expressed it more simply: "people fight until the blood flows."[66] Playing a leading role in the brutality of politics was the press, serving up "condiments of exaggeration, scandal, lies and bad jokes" about the candidates.[67] After the ordeal of a campaign, the country finally submitted to a winner who, according to Emily Faithfull, had been accused "of every possible offence against law and morality"[68] (Figure 7.3).

Visitors found that both houses of Congress were fairly raucous. In the Senate, there was the constant clapping of hands as Senators summoned messenger boys, and J. J. Aubertin was surprised that Senators read their speeches (a practice "utterly inadmissible" in England).[69] In the House of Representatives (which

THE JUDGE.

"TO BEGIN WITH, 'I'LL PAINT THE TOWN RED'."

FIGURE 7.3 The Democratic Party as the devil, with a paintbrush in which appears a caricature of Grover Cleveland. Chronograph by Grant E. Hamilton. Library of Congress. LC-DIG-ppmsca-10484.

William Saunders called "a kind of Exchange where members transact private business") bedlam ruled (Edward A. Freeman called it a "scene of mere hubbub").[70] During House speeches, members wrote, read the newspaper, dozed, and chatted amiably.[71] Saunders claimed that no one in the House who spoke was listened to or expected to be heard, and that if a representative was saying something of which members of the press were actually interested, reporters would leave their seats and gather around the speaker to take notes.[72] The House of Representatives' "want of dignity," said H. Hussey Vivian, "impressed me most disagreeably."[73]

Whatever unfavorable impressions European visitors had of Congress were offset by how easily accessible public officials were, starting with the president. Several mentioned the lack of barriers at the White House. William Howard Russell was surprised that there were "no sentries, not even a policeman on duty" and Alexander Craib found that "a stranger may enter without obstruction or questions."[74] William Saunders was passing the White House one day when he saw a large number of what he called "shabbily-dressed" Americans ring the bell and ask the porter if they could see President Rutherford B. Hayes. Saunders attached himself to this group and they were immediately ushered in to the president. According to Saunders, a black girl was holding a jam pot that she presented to the president. "He gave her a specially cordial reception, and as she came out her face was beaming with satisfaction."[75] Italian traveler Carlo Gardini was also impressed by Hayes' friendliness and lack of pretension, and French traveler Léon Paul Blouet's reaction to Grover Cleveland was that he had not "the least suspicion of haughtiness, and you are at your ease with him at once."[76] Other presidents elicited the same reaction. William Howard Russell described President James A. Garfield's welcome to his party as "most kindly," and Joseph Hatton likewise reported that he and his family received a "home-like reception" from President Chester A. Arthur. The president, said Hatton, was "chatting in a pleasant, unconstrained, familiar way, that is characteristic of American manners, and eminently becomes the chief of a great republic."[77]

This ease of accessibility was to be found at every level of government. When William Saunders dropped by the War Department and asked to see General William T. Sherman, Saunders was immediately directed to Sherman's office. The general "entered into conversation in as friendly a manner as if he had known me for twenty years."[78] Even in the lower public offices, Saunders saw "the same civility manifested to each applicant—rich or poor."[79] He contrasted this with the "vulgar indifference" of public officials in London.[80] W. E. Adams also called access to public men in America "exceedingly easy," and added that "to persons who have ever had occasion to call upon a member of the House of Commons, where one has to run the gauntlet of I know not how many policemen, who regard all strangers as 'suspicious characters,' the contrast between Westminster and Washington must appear immense and surprising."[81]

But it was politics at the city level, where bosses and political machines prevailed, that produced the majority of remarks from European travelers. Mostly, they were eager to place the corruption and inefficiency of machine politics at the feet of the immigrant, but with little willingness to analyze the evolution or popularity of this system. Few European travelers could see massive immigration and manhood suffrage as anything other than a threat to the republic—what W. E. Adams called "the great danger from without."[82] Harold Brydges condemned "the German vote, the Irish vote, the liquor vote, a Senate of millionaires," and "the evil influence of millions of illiterate aliens."[83] For Lepel Henry Griffin, the waste and corruption of city political machines could be blamed on "manhood suffrage" and "the surging mass of emigration."[84] Because Americans were "mad about liberty," said George Jacob Holyoake, they were willing to endow every "alien knave" with the franchise "before he has had time to learn the responsibility of freedom."[85]

The immigrant himself had a very different perspective. Those who arrived in American cities after the Civil War faced horrible housing, back-breaking labor, a high crime rate, and unsanitary living conditions. In Buffalo, New York, in

1900, two-fifths of Italian and Polish children did not live to become adults.[86] There was little in the way of government social welfare programs, and the charitable organizations that tried to ameliorate the plight of immigrants were totally overwhelmed by the large numbers of them. Immigrants understood that it was going to be the political machine, and not good government types, who provided deliveries of food or fuel during hard times, or assistance finding work, or even the money to pay for the funeral of a destitute family member (a service that a Tammany boss rendered for the funeral of the father of future New York governor Al Smith). The more thoughtful travelers understood this, and even admitted that bosses were not an American invention. George Jacob Holyoake claimed that their equivalents could be found "in every borough in the kingdom."[87] Even future progressive reformer Theodore Roosevelt conceded that "a machine politician really desirous of doing honest work on behalf of the community is fifty times as useful an ally as is the average philanthropic outsider."[88] At the same time, it was the political machine that opposed the rising nativist hostility that was so much a part of white Anglo-Saxon Protestant (WASP) thinking among Americans and, as we have seen, among their European cousins as well.[89]

Few European travelers, however, could see the human element of political machines, and New York's Tammany Hall came in for especially rough treatment. Alexander Craib even denied that New York was an American city, but was "held and controlled by foreign power."[90] Léon Paul Blouet was more specific, and insisted that "contemporary America is governed by the Irish," and that "New York is the real capital of Ireland."[91] There was more than a little truth to Blouet's claim, as at mid-century it was estimated that one-quarter of the population of New York had been born in Ireland. The Irish exhibited a genius for American urban politics, and between 1871 and 1924 Irish bosses would dominate Tammany Hall.[92]

David Macrae declared that there was no city in the world where "there is so much official jobbery and corruption," and W. E. Adams said that New York was more badly governed than any city on the planet.[93] Macrae and Adams were correct—the machine's powers of corruption were unmatched—but the boss system persisted well into the twentieth century because it actually did something to alleviate the suffering of the urban poor. Martin Lomasney, Boston's South End boss, insisted that, "There's got to be in every ward somebody that any bloke can come to—no matter what he's done—and get help. Help, you understand, none of your law and justice, but help."[94]

There was a general consensus among travelers that, as William Howard Russell expressed it, the "respectable classes" of America held themselves "aloof from politics."[95] Edward A. Freeman argued that the reason for this "divorce" between politics and the respectables was that the latter were focused on making as much money as quickly as possible.[96] And while the upright citizen might be momentarily appalled by a political scandal of unusual audacity, his indignation soon passed and he returned to "making his personal pile bigger and bigger."[97]

Despite the deficiencies of the American political system, A. Maurice Low believed that the greatest triumph of America was that it "gave to the world the first concept of human liberty and encouraged man to seek his freedom."[98] "Of all the great countries in the world," said R. W. Dale, "America contains the smallest number of people that can have any motive for desiring a social revolution."[99] Somewhat surprisingly, Oscar Wilde was among the most impassioned defenders of the American political system. Wilde ended his "Impressions of America" by calling Americans "the best politically educated people in the world. It is well worth one's while to go to a country which can teach us the beauty of the word FREEDOM and the value of the thing LIBERTY" [Wilde's emphasis].[100]

Patriotism

That Americans had a proclivity for making passionate assertions of devotion to their country, what some might call patriotism, was noted by almost every European traveler beginning in the early nineteenth century. Tocqueville referred to the "irritable patriotism of the American" that "wearies even those who honor it."[101] In Charles Dickens' *Martin Chuzzlewit* (1843–1844) it received its most biting parodic treatment. When Mr. La Fayette Kettle gives a speech to the "Watertoast Sympathisers" (a group that had awarded a ceremonial plate to a judge who had ruled "that it was lawful for any white mob to murder any black man"), Kettle ends his address to great acclaim by expressing the wish that "the British Lion have his talons eradicated by the noble bill of the American Eagle, and be taught to play upon the Irish Harp and the Scotch Fiddle that music which is breathed in every empty shell that lies upon the shores of green Co-lumbia."[102] The tiresome patriotism of Americans was a theme in a number of other British novels, including Anthony Trollope's *The American Senator*. Here, the senator in question, Mr. Gotobed, spends a winter's season among England's country aristocracy and makes a considerable nuisance of himself in his denunciations of the British class system and his praise of the United States. At a dinner party, an exasperated Lady Augustus asks Gotobed, "'Suppose we were to allow at once,' she said, 'that everything is better in the United States than anywhere else, shouldn't we get along easier?'"[103]

When Harold Brydges toured America in 1887, he found that while the two political parties might have their differences, there was no difference "as to the general excellence of the United States."[104] Knut Hamsun called American patriotism as "loudmouthed as it is vehement," and Kipling advised travelers that if they wanted to keep Americans quiet, they should praise the United States "unsparingly, and without discrimination."[105] Émile Levasseur also found that one distinctive trait of Americans was their "superb confidence in the superiority of their civilization."[106] On his ship to the United States in 1891, Alexander Craib met an American whom "had much to say on the superiority of America 'to all the nations of the world.'"[107] Craib was amused by this encounter, but for

Matthew Arnold, this insistence on American greatness constituted a national "tic, a mania, which every one notices in them, and which sometimes drives their friends half to despair."[108]

A few European travelers responded positively to American patriotism. Léon Paul Blouet asked, "May not men who have done marvels be permitted a certain amount of self-glorification?"[109] Dutch traveler Charles Boissevain called the "republican pride" of Americans a "delightful vanity. Long live the self-confidence and the vanity of the American nation!"[110] Americans were also willing to put their patriotism into action. Horace Annesley Vachell noted the case of an older, well-to-do member of society who volunteered to serve in the Spanish–American War in any rank. This person's willingness to abandon all that makes life comfortable to serve his country, said Vachell, had a "curious significance to a foreigner."[111]

The differences between patriotism in America and in England were especially dramatic, for a number of reasons. Vachell contended that the English could take their patriotism for granted because they had been English for a thousand years. But in America "is it not common prudence to demand from the Kelt, the Teuton, the Latin, the Slav, an answer to the question, 'Are you truly of us, or merely with us?'"[112] There was also the issue of "ownership," or the stake that people perceived they had in their country. In the late eighteenth century, Hector St. John de Crèvecoeur had asked, "What attachment can a poor European emigrant have for a country where he had nothing?"[113] A hundred years later George Jacob Holyoake argued that expressions of patriotism were rare in England because "the working men, as a rule, have no substantial interest in the national glory … the people do not feel that they own the country."[114] In contrast, the national pride found throughout the United States could be traced to the conviction that "every man in America feels as though he owns the country, because the charm of recognised equality and the golden chances of ownership have entered his mind."[115] Even Rudyard Kipling, despite some reservations, believed that the American set an example for patriotism that could profitably be copied by the Englishman, who seemed to regard his own country "as an abstraction to supply him with policemen and fire-brigades." The American love of country and belief in its future, said Kipling, was a "proud, passionate conviction to which I take off my hat and for which I love them."[116]

By necessity, patriotism played a different role in America from that in Europe because Americans had to forge a nation out of many different elements. Over 13,500,000 immigrants came to America between 1865 and 1900.[117] Without a common national origin or a common religion to link these people together, patriotism was one of the few options available to create an American identity. Indeed, despite numerous setbacks, it can be argued that America has been more successful than any other nation in inculcating in its citizens a "civic nationalism" (based on shared ideas of democracy and egalitarianism) as opposed to the "ethnic nationalism" that has dominated everywhere else.[118] With the nations of Europe now facing similar trials, this old issue in America has gained a new currency across the Atlantic.

Notes

1. Shelby Foote, *The Civil War, A Narrative: Red River to Appomattox* (New York: Random House, 1974), 1040. Historian J. David Hacker has recently suggested that the standard estimate of casualties from the Civil War is too low. Hacker puts the number killed in the conflict at approximately 750,000. Guy Gugliotta, "New Estimate Raises Civil War Death Toll," *New York Times*, April 3, 2012.
2. David W. Blight, *Race and Reunion: The Civil War in American Memory* (Cambridge, MA: Belknap Press, 2001), 64.
3. J. R. Lowell, "On a Certain Condescension in Foreigners," *Atlantic Monthly* 23 (January 1869), 92.
4. Élisée Reclus, *The Earth and its Inhabitants. North America: v. 3, the United States* (New York: D. Appleton and Co., 1893), 451.
5. John Campbell Argyll, *A Trip to the Tropics and Home Through America* (London: Hurst and Blackett, 1867), 261; Charles Wentworth Dilke, *Greater Britain: A Record of Travel in English-Speaking Countries* (London: Macmillan and Co., 1890), 7.
6. Dilke, 8.
7. William Hepworth Dixon, *New America* (Philadelphia: J. B. Lippincott, 1869), 489; Argyll, 262. Drew Gilpin Faust notes that when Union forces first moved into Richmond in April 1865, a reporter that accompanied them observed that "'the women are nearly all dressed in mourning.'" Drew Gilpin Faust, *This Republic of Suffering: Death and the American Civil War* (New York: Alfred A. Knopf, 2008), 149.
8. David Macrae, *The Americans at Home* [1870] (New York: E. P. Dutton, 1952), 135.
9. Therese Yelverton, *Teresina in America*, v. 1 (London: Richard Bentley and Son, 1875), 44.
10. F. Barham Zincke, *Last Winter in the United States: Being Table Talk Collected During a Tour Through the Late Southern Confederation, the Far West, the Rocky Mountains, &c.* [1868] (Freeport, NY: Books for Libraries Press, 1970), 117, 97, 98.
11. Robert Somers, *The Southern States Since the War, 1870–71* [1871] (Tuscaloosa: University of Alabama Press, 1965), 114.
12. William Howard Russell, *Hesperothen, Notes from the West: A Record of a Ramble in the United States and Canada in the Spring and Summer of 1881*, v. 1 (London: S. Low, Marston, Searle & Rivington, 1882), 105.
13. Foote, 1041.
14. Dilke, 25. Confederate General Joseph E. Johnston was on the deck of a steamer not long after he surrendered to Union forces when he heard a young man proclaim that the South had been "conquered but not subdued." When Johnston asked him where he had served, the young man told Johnston that unfortunately it had been impossible for him to be in the army. "Well, sir, I was," Johnston told him. "You may not be subdued, but I am." Quoted in Foote, 1048.
15. Faust, 152.
16. Argyll, 183. When he visited New York's Barnum Museum, Argyll found that the biggest attraction was a series of paintings of Civil War battles in which "the stars and stripes were being borne in triumphant over the bodies of Confederates, bayoneted by the victorious soldiers of the Union." Ibid., 173. In his memoir, Henry Latham reprinted the report of the Surgeon-General's Department that said it had supplied "to maimed soldiers 3,981 artificial legs, 2,240 arms, 9 feet, 55 hands, and 125 surgical apparatus" between July of 1862 and July of 1866. Surgeon-General's report quoted in Henry Latham, *Black and White: A Journal of a Three Months' Tour in the United States* [1867] (New York: Negro Universities Press, 1969), 90.
17. Dilke, 41.
18. E. Catherine Bates, *A Year in the Great Republic*, v. 1 (London: Ward & Downey, 1887), 98.
19. Argyll, 277.
20. Quoted in Faust, 237.

21. See Cindy S. Aron, *Working at Play: A History of Vacations in the United States* (New York: Oxford University Press, 1999), 143.

22. Faust, 236.

23. Blight, 71.

24. Robert M. Poole, *On Hallowed Ground: The Story of Arlington National Cemetery* (New York: Walker, 2010), 77, 78.

25. Memorial Day in the deep South was usually held on April 26, the date that Joseph E. Johnston surrendered to William Tecumseh Sherman. In South and North Carolina, May 10 was adopted to mark the anniversary of Stonewall Jackson's death. By 1916, ten Southern states were holding Memorial Day on June 3, Jefferson Davis' birthday. See Blight, 77.

26. Ibid., 71.

27. In 1883, 100 Confederate dead were moved from Arlington to North Carolina for reburial in Raleigh. Poole, 79.

28. Quoted in Faust, 243. 244.

29. Ibid., 248, 249.

30. The others, according to W. E. Adams, were the Fourth of July, New Year's Day, and Thanksgiving. Christmas was not mentioned. W. E. Adams, *Our American Cousins: Being Personal Impressions of the People and Institutions of the United States* (London: Walter Scott, 1883), 234. Christmas was not celebrated in colonial America, and many credit Charles Dickens and the publication of *A Christmas Carol* in 1843 with creating "an event that had never existed." Christmas, with its central figure Santa Claus, became a holiday for children in the second half of the nineteenth century. See Joseph E. Illick, *American Childhoods* (Philadelphia: University of Pennsylvania Press, 2002), 66–67. Thomas Nast helped create the physical appearance of Santa Claus—rotund, white beard, jolly—in a series of illustrations for *Harper's* in 1863. Daniel J. Boorstin, *The Americans: The Democratic Experience* (New York: Random House, 1973), 160.

31. Iza Duffus Hardy, *Between Two Oceans: Or, Sketches of American Travel* (London: Hurst and Blackett, 1884), 319.

32. George Augustus Sala, *America Revisited: From the Bay of New York to the Gulf of Mexico and From Lake Michigan to the Pacific* (London: Vizetelly & Co., n.d.), 248. Ernest B. Furgurson described the obelisk at Danville, Virginia: "It was decorated with bronze bas-relief images of Robert E. Lee and Stonewall Jackson, and words chosen by the Ladies' Memorial Association, which raised $2,000 to erect it in 1878: 'Patriots!' it said. 'Know that these fell in the effort to establish just government and perpetuate constitutional liberty. Who thus die will live in lofty example.' And on another side: 'They died as men who nobly contend for the cause of truth and right.' 'They softly lie and sweetly sleep.'" Ernest B. Furgurson, "Hallowed Ground," *Smithsonian* 41, no. 9 (January 2011), 15.

33. Zincke, 138.

34. Cecilia Elizabeth O'Leary, "'Blood Brotherhood': The Racialization of Patriotism, 1865–1918," in *Bonds of Affection: Americans Define Their Patriotism*, ed. John Bodnar (Princeton: Princeton University Press, 1996), 72.

35. Yelverton, 47.

36. W. G. Marshall, *Through America: Nine Months in the United States* (London: Sampson, Low, Marston, Searle & Rivington, 1881), 49.

37. William Saunders, *Through the Light Continent, or, The United States in 1877–78* [1879] (New York: Arno Press, 1974), 7, 8. One foreign visitor in Detroit in 1891 witnessed the annual convention of the Grand Army of the Republic and was impressed by the well-behaved crowds and surprised that these same crowds went wherever they pleased because there were no cordons to protect officials and guests. Anonymous "The Grand Army of the Republic," *Macmillan's Magazine* 65 (December 1891), 131, 132. The Grand Army of the Republic had a membership of 350,000 by 1890—one-third of the surviving Union veterans. The United Confederate Veterans would reach a membership of 80,000, somewhere between one-fourth and one-third of surviving

members. Thomas J. Brown, "Introduction: American Commemoration and the Civil War," in Thomas J. Brown, *The Public Art of Civil War Commemoration: A Brief History with Documents* (Boston: Bedford/St. Martin's, 2004), 4.

38. Knut Hamsun, *The Cultural Life of Modern America* [1889] (Cambridge, MA: Harvard University Press, 1969), 131.

39. Ibid., 7.

40. Theodora Guest, *A Round Trip in North America* (London: Edward Stanford, 1895), 190.

41. R. W. Dale, "Impressions of America," pt. 1, *Eclectic Magazine* 27, no. 6 (New Series, June 1878), 671.

42. A. Maurice Low, *The American People: A Study in National Psychology*, v. 2 (Boston: Houghton Mifflin, 1909), 507.

43. Russell, v. 1, 79.

44. See Blight, 86–97.

45. Brown, "Introduction," 10.

46. Sala, 43.

47. Wolfgang Schivelbusch, *The Culture of Defeat: On National Trauma, Mourning, and Recovery* (New York: Picador, 2003), 51–52.

48. Ibid., 50, 61. Confederate General Jubal Early claimed that the South's armies "had been gradually worn down by the combined agencies of numbers, steam-power, railroads, mechanism, and all the resources of physical science." Quoted in Thomas J. Brown, "Robert E. Lee and the Lost Cause," in Brown, 81–83.

49. Iza Duffus Hardy, 268.

50. William Archer, *America To-Day: Observations and Reflections* [1899] (New York: Arno Press, 1974), 129–130.

51. See Poole, 112–113. During the Spanish-American War McKinley had awarded major general commissions to both Wheeler and Fitzhugh Lee of Virginia. See O'Leary, 72–73.

52. Quoted in Evan Thomas, *The War Lovers: Roosevelt, Lodge, Hearst, and the Rush to Empire, 1898* (New York: Back Bay Books, 2010), 337.

53. Archer, 165.

54. G. S. Clarke, "England and America," *The Nineteenth Century* 44, no. 258 (August 1898), 194. The Briton A. V. Dicey also suggested that "the prosperity not only of the whole English people, but also of the civilized world, depends on the maintenance of cordial friendship between the two great divisions of the Anglo-Saxon race." A. V. Dicey, "England and America," *Atlantic Monthly* 82, no. 492 (October 1898), 444.

55. Archer, 141.

56. Ibid., 139.

57. Furgurson, 15.

58. "Letter of Lord T. B. Macaulay to Henry S. Randall," *Harper's* 54, no. 321 (February 1877), 460, 461.

59. Ibid., 461.

60. H. Hussey Vivian, *Notes of a Tour in America from August 7th to November 17th, 1877* (London: Edward Stanford, 1878), 233.

61. Matthew Arnold, "A Word More About America," in Matthew Arnold, *Civilization in the United States: First and Last Impressions of America* [1888] (Freeport, NY: Books for Libraries Press, 1972), 121.

62. Ibid., 115, 116.

63. Ibid., 143–144.

64. Max O'rell and Jack Allyn, *Jonathan and His Continent: Rambles Through American Society*, trans. Madame Paul Blouet (Bristol: J. W. Arrowsmith, 1889), 208.

65. Yelverton, 10.

66. Hamsun, 30.

67. Harold Brydges, *Uncle Sam at Home* (New York: Henry Holt and Co., 1888), 173. Brydges claimed that "the silver question and the tariff" were the only issues in which people took any interest in Congress. Ibid., 110. For the most part, American

politicians paid little attention to base journalistic conduct, deeming it not worth their time to appeal to the law. Adams, 118.

68. Emily Faithfull, *Three Visits to America* (New York: Fowler & Wells, 1884), 7.

69. Guest, 33; J. J. Aubertin, *A Fight with Distances: The States, the Hawaiian Islands, Canada, British Columbia, Cuba, the Bahamas* (London: Kegan Paul, Trench & Co., 1888), 277.

70. Edward A. Freeman, *Some Impressions of the United States* (London: Longmans, Green, and Co., 1883), 117.

71. Lady Duffus Hardy, *Through Cities and Prairie Lands: Sketches of an American Tour* (London: Chapman and Hall, 1881), 270–271. See also Baron Hübner, *A Ramble Round the World, 1871*, trans. Lady Elizabeth Herbert (London: MacMillan and Co., 1878), 24.

72. Saunders, 94, 93. F. Barham Zincke was unimpressed by the quality of speeches in Congress, and theorized that the style of speaking had been formed "by the practice of canvassing-speeches and mob-oratory." Zincke, 44. Iza Duffus Hardy was surprised that the visitors' gallery at the House of Representatives was large and spacious (compared to what she called "the little grated prison" of the Ladies Gallery at the House of Commons) and that entrance was not barred by any formalities. Iza Duffus Hardy, 260.

73. Vivian, 203.

74. Russell, v. 1, 76; Alexander Craib, *America and the Americans: A Tour in the United States and Canada, With Chapters on American Home Life* (London: Alexander Gardner, 1892), 129.

75. Saunders, 100–103. When German traveler Harry Kessler met President Benjamin Harrison in 1892, he was part of a White House crowd that he described as "men from the West, with large cowboy hats, fat store owners their fleshy fingers covered in rings and wet umbrellas, little middle-class girls giggling in the corners of the large hall; an assembly such as one generally sees in a bus station." Harry Kessler, *Journey to the Abyss: The Diaries of Count Harry Kessler, 1880–1918*, trans. and ed. Laird Easton (New York: Knopf, 2011), 57.

76. Andrew Torrielli, *Italian Opinion on America, As Revealed by Italian Travelers, 1850–1900* (Cambridge, MA: Harvard University Press, 1941), 100; O'rell and Allyn, 196.

77. Russell, v. 1, 77; Joseph Hatton, *Henry Irving's Impressions of America, Narrated in a Series of Sketches, Chronicles, and Conversations* [1884], v. 2 (New York: Benjamin Blom, 1971), 185.

78. Saunders, 99. F. Barham Zincke, who had become acquainted with Sherman ten years earlier, called him "one of the kindliest and friendliest men" he had ever met. Zincke, 166. Lieutenant General Sherman commanded the Division of the Missouri, and directed military affairs east of the continental divide. Philip Weeks, *Farewell, My Nation: The American Indian and the United States, 1820–1890* (Arlington Heights, IL: Harlan Davidson, 1990), 112.

79. Saunders, 384.

80. Ibid., 385.

81. Adams, 110, 112. Like Saunders and Adams, David Macrae concluded that American government officials made themselves much more available to the public than their counterparts in Britain, and that the courtesy of these officials "continually astonished me." Macrae, 397.

82. Adams, 319.

83. Brydges, 176. David Macrae took note of the Democratic Party's appeal to "the lower classes of Irish voters, who seem everywhere in America to have an ineradicable hatred to the 'nigger.'" Macrae, 493.

84. Lepel Henry Griffin, *The Great Republic* [1884] (New York: Arno Press, 1974), 119, 120. Matthew Arnold said of Griffin, who was an administrator in India, "In politics I do not much trust Sir Lepel Griffin. I hope that he administers in India some district where a profound insight into the being and working of institutions is not requisite." Arnold, "A Word More About America," 152. James Fullarton Muirhead referred to Griffin's "supercilious Philistinism, aggravated no doubt by his many years' experience as a ruler of submissive Orientals." James Fullarton Muirhead, *The Land of Contrasts: A Briton's View of his American Kin* (London: Lamson, Wolffe and Co., 1898), 80.

85. George Jacob Holyoake, "American and Canadian Notes," *The Nineteenth Century* 14, no. 77 (July 1883), 292. Élisée Reclus mentions the arrival of second-wave immigrants and the fears expressed by the American "educated classes" of "ignorant electors exercising their right of suffrage in a blind or venal way." Reclus, 451.

86. See Steven Mintz, *Huck's Raft: A History of American Childhood* (Cambridge, MA: Belknap Press of Harvard University, 2004), 202.

87. Holyoake, "American and Canadian Notes," 296.

88. Theodore Roosevelt, "Machine Politics in New York City," *The Century Magazine* 33, no. 1 (November 1886), 74.

89. See Charles N. Glabb and Theodore Brown, *A History of Urban America* (New York: Macmillan, 1976), 205–207.

90. Craib, 171.

91. O'rell and Allyn, 204.

92. See Kevin Kenny, *The American Irish: A History* (Harlow, England: Pearson, 2000), 120, 160–163.

93. Macrae, 76; Adams, 136.

94. Quoted in Howard P. Chudacoff, *The Evolution of American Urban Society* (Englewood Cliff, NJ: 1981), 161.

95. Russell, v. 2, 137.

96. Freeman, 200; Griffin, 120. Emily Faithfull argued that "political life in America is at a low ebb, owing to the disinclination of the best section of society to have anything to do with it." Faithfull, 10. As early as the 1830s, Tocqueville seemed to predict the rise of political machines. He found that "the citizens who work do not choose to turn their minds to the public's business." The possible consequence was that if "a shrewd and ambitious man happens to seize power, he will find nothing standing between him and every imaginable kind of usurpation." Alexis De Tocqueville, *Democracy in America*, [1835] trans. Arthur Goldhammer (New York: Library of America, 2004), 630.

97. Brydges, 74, 75. What kept the boss system in place, according to Herbert Spencer, was the "lack of certain moral sentiments." Herbert Spencer, "Report of Mr. Spencer's Interview," in Edward Youmans, *Herbert Spencer on the Americans and the Americans on Herbert Spencer: Being a Full Report of his Interview, and of the Proceedings of the Farewell Banquet of Nov. 11, 1882* (New York: D. Appleton, 1883), 16.

98. Low, v. 2, 13.

99. Dale, pt. 1, 672.

100. Oscar Wilde, "Impressions of America," in Oscar Wilde, *The Works of Oscar Wilde* (New York: AMS Press, 1972), 262.

101. Tocqueville, 271, 719. Tocqueville explained that "men who live in democracies love their country in the same way that they love themselves, and they carry the habits of their private vanity over into their national vanity." Ibid., 720.

102. Charles Dickens, *Martin Chuzzlewit* [1843–1844] (New York: Penguin Books, 1995), 427, 411. Commenting on what Dickens missed in America, G. K. Chesterton observed that, "A man may smile and smile and be a villain; but a man may also make us smile and not be a villain. He may make us smile and not even be a fool. He may make us roar with laughter and be an exceedingly wise man. Now that is the paradox of America which Dickens never discovered." G. K. Chesterton, *What I Saw in America* [1922], in *The Collected Works of G. K. Chesterton*, v. 21 (San Francisco: Ignatius Press, 1990), 228.

103. Anthony Trollope, *The American Senator* [1876–77] (Oxford: Oxford University Press, 1991), 88–89.

104. Brydges, 110.

105. Rudyard Kipling, *American Notes* [1891] (Norman: University of Oklahoma Press, 1981), 86.

106. Émile Levasseur, *The American Workman*, trans. Thomas S. Adams (Baltimore: Johns Hopkins University, 1900), 72. William Howard Russell noted that "the attachment

of Americans to the land of their birth or adoption is generally intense." Russell, v. 1, 15.

107. Craib, 10.

108. Matthew Arnold, "General Grant," in Arnold, *Civilization in the United States*, 60–61. Isabella Bird was surprised to discover that the deep, patriotic strain that ran through America could even be found in a remote cabin in the Rockies, which Bird shared with three American men. They entertained each other after dinner by singing songs and Bird noted that "one of the young men sang a Latin student's song and two Negro melodies; the other 'Sweet Spirit, hear my Prayer.' 'Jim' sang one of Moore's melodies in a singular falsetto, and all together sang, 'The Star-spangled Banner' and 'The Red, White, and Blue.'" Isabella L. Bird, *A Lady's Life in the Rocky Mountains* (Norman: University of Oklahoma Press, 1969), 90.

109. O'rell and Allyn, 291.

110. Quoted in A. N. J. den Hollander, "Charles Boissevain, 1842–1927," in *Abroad in America: Visitors to the New Nation, 1776–1914* (Reading, MA: Addison-Wesley, 1976), 194.

111. Horace Annesley Vachell, *Life and Sport on the Pacific Slope* (New York: Dodd, Mead and Co., 1901), 36, 37.

112. Ibid., 38.

113. Hector St. John de Crèvecoeur, "What Is An American," in Hector St. John de Crèvecoeur, *Letters From An American Farmer* [1782] (London: J. M. Dent and Sons, 1926), 43.

114. George Jacob Holyoake, "A Stranger in America," *The Nineteenth Century* 8, no. 41 (July 1880), 69–70.

115. Ibid., 70.

116. Kipling, 152.

117. U.S. Department of Commerce, Bureau of the Census, *Historical Statistics of the United States: Colonial Times to 1957* (Washington, D.C.: GPO, 1961), 56–57.

118. John Bodnar, "The Attractions of Patriotism," in *Bonds of Affection: Americans Define Their Patriotism*, ed. John Bodnar (Princeton: Princeton University Press, 1996), 6, 7.

8

THE WEST

Landscape, Human Inhabitants, and Decline

Landscape

Two distinct motivations dictated why Americans went West and why European travelers went West. As historian Roderick Nash has emphasized, Americans went West for natural resources: fur, gold, timber, and homesteads. European travelers went West for "wilderness appreciation," and even as late as the 1870s, "almost all the nature tourists on the American frontier continued to be foreigners."[1] They encountered a vast landscape unlike anything in their experience, and they struggled to find metaphors for it.

First they had to cross the Great Plains, which James Fenimore Cooper, who exerted such a strong influence on European travelers, described as

> not unlike the ocean, when its restless waters are heaving heavily, after the agitation and fury of the tempest have begun to lessen. There was the same waving and regular surface, the same absence of foreign objects, and the same boundless extent to the view.[2]

European travelers added their own oceanic descriptions, such as "the roll of the prairie as grand as that of the Atlantic," a "boundless sea of grass, a verdant undulating ocean stretching to the far distant horizon" and grasses "rolling in long undulations, like the waves of a sea which had fallen asleep."[3]

There was also the hugeness of the Plains, a spectacle conveying what W. G. Marshall called "an overpowering sense of vastness."[4] Emily Faithfull similarly referred to "those vast, voiceless plains," and Robert Louis Stevenson claimed that one could discern "the whole arch of heaven, this straight, unbroken, prison-line of the horizon."[5] In the face of such immensity, normal concepts of space and time broke down, and European travelers enquiring about distances in

America were perplexed when told that something was "six hours" or "only a day" away. They were also intrigued by the four different times zones through which they traveled from coast to coast.[6] In America, "three or four hundred miles go for nothing," and eventually travelers themselves began casually speaking of distances that in Europe would have been exceptional.[7]

Baron Hübner said of the Plains that, "One seems to breathe a new life in this fresh, elastic, scented air. It is the very type of unlimited liberty."[8] But others found in the Plains something more unsettling. "The limitless desolation of this dead-level seems to crush us," said Iza Duffus Hardy.[9] Windham Thomas Wyndham-Quin said that the Plains conveyed an atmosphere that was "inexpressibly sad and mournful."[10] Others referred to an "awful solitude," "a solitude which no words can paint," and "a mighty loneliness."[11] When he crossed the Plains, Henry Sienkiewicz was mesmerized by the long lines of telegraph poles. With their crossbars at the top they resembled crucifixes, "sad and funereal, as far as the eye could see."[12]

The mountains and the vistas they provided were even more awe-inspiring than the Plains. As he descended into the valley toward Laramie, W. G. Marshall was in raptures: "What a glorious panorama is now before us! What intensity of colour! How clear is the atmosphere, how blue the mountains, how diversified the landscape!"[13] Rivaling this view was the Salt Lake basin as seen from the mountains above, which William Hepworth Dixon called "one of the half-dozen pure and perfect landscapes which the earth can show."[14] To W. F. Rae it was "a dream of fairyland."[15] Even out on the deserts of the Southwest where there were few landmarks, mirages brought forth phantasms in which horses were elongated into giraffes, tents became mountain ranges, and great pillared cities materialized in the distance.[16] When William Howard Russell and his party crossed the Arizona desert, "We saw with delight widespread lakes with fairy islands in the midst; placid seas washing the base of the distant hills."[17]

Some visitors went so far as to express what they were witnessing in religious terms. In Montana, the hunter Parker Gillmore found what he called "a sanctuary" that had "not been contaminated by the presence of man," while in Colorado Emily Faithfull referred to the "glimpses of glory" of the "terrible precipices" of the Rocky Mountains.[18] In the Sierras, Lady Duffus Hardy witnessed a "spiritual sunshine, falling straight from heaven," and Isabella Bird said of her first glimpse of those mountains that "it was one of those glorious surprises in scenery which make one feel as if one must bow down and worship"[19] (Figure 8.1). William A. Baille-Grohman likewise felt something close to worship when he gazed upon the Tetons for the first time. "I wished myself alone," wrote Baille-Grohman, "to do homage to what I then, and still, consider the most striking landscape the eye of a painter ever dreamt of."[20]

Even Lepel Henry Griffin, who found all things in America objectionable, was dumbstruck by the landscape in Colorado, where he saw mountains "aflame with the thousand tints with which autumn in America decorates the forests."[21] Indeed, the colors in America seemed to possess a beauty that was close to savage. Speaking

FIGURE 8.1 Albert Bierstadt, *Among the Sierra Nevada, California,* 1868. Smithsonian American Art Museum, Bequest of Helen Huntington Hull, granddaughter of William Brown Dinsmore, who acquired the painting in 1873 for "The Locusts," the family estate in Dutchess County, New York.

of Western sunsets, Windham Wyndham-Quin insisted that there was something about them that was "startling, barbaric, even savage in their brilliancy of tone, in their profusion of colour, in their great streaks of red and broad flashes of yellow fire."[22] When Rudyard Kipling viewed the Gorge of the Yellowstone, he described "one wild welter of color—crimson, emerald, cobalt, ochre, amber, honey splashed with port-wine, snow-white, vermilion, lemon, and silver-gray, in wide washes."[23]

In these descriptions of the Western landscape, we see the rapturous mixing with something resembling terror. At Yosemite, J. W. Boddam-Whetham encountered "ghostly precipices and solemn Falls," and an "indefinite vastness." The overall effect was a "vague sense of imprisonment and oppression," and a desire to flee Yosemite "into the world once more."[24] Rose G. Kingsley likewise referred to the "prison walls" of a canon that loomed over her in Colorado, and used the word "oppressive" to describe the silence that prevailed.[25] This was not the decorous mingling of nature with the Gothic ruin, but something more sinister.

Nature in the West seemed to embody both spiritual ecstasy and violent disorder. For Isabella Bird, Long's Peak in Colorado was "splintered, pinnacled, lonely, ghastly, imposing."[26] Yellowstone, said one visitor, combined "some of the grandest, [and] some of the most grotesque scenery."[27]

Human Inhabitants: Indians

Few European travelers were able to disguise their terrible disappointment when the romantic stories that they had read about Indians—what William Hepworth

Dixon called "a picture, a poem, a romance"—did not square with reality.[28] Unable to escape race biases and engage Indians on their own terms, foreign travelers were just as dismissive of the Indians they encountered as were most white Americans. And perhaps because their own disappointment was so keen, these same travelers viewed the final passing away of Indians with equanimity.

Charles Wentworth Dilke admitted that before he left London he had elevated the Indian "on a pedestal of nobility."[29] His first disappointment was that Indians were not red, and he was appalled by what he called "their debased condition."[30] The "Indian of romance" could not be found in the "squalid and repulsive outcasts" of real Indians, according to Lepel Henry Griffin—a sentiment echoed by another traveler who complained that the Indians showed "no trace whatever of the war-like red man of romantic story."[31] Likewise, Edward A. Freeman reported that what he had expected to see of Indians were "graceful and statuesque forms," but what reality served up instead was "the dullest and heaviest-looking of mankind."[32] Rose Pender called Indians "an insignificant and ugly race," then delivered what to a British aristocrat must have seemed like the ultimate insult: "A great many had the lowest Irish type of features."[33] What most Europeans saw were "blanket Indians" who loitered around railroad depots and towns begging for coins.[34] As J. W. Boddam-Whetham expressed it, the Indian's "'wild turkey' appearance is pretty in a picture, though not in the reality—at all events, not near a railway station."[35] But few Europeans expressed an interest in meeting Indians on their own ground, nor, for the most part, did they mark cultural differences among individual tribes. Instead, they were content to record whatever first impressions they had. W. G. Marshall, for instance, described the Winabago Indians as "ugly and bloated in appearance," and the Shoshone as "filthy and dirty-looking in the extreme."[36]

Rudyard Kipling said that Americans were "charmingly frank about the Indian. 'Let's get rid of him as soon as possible,' they say. 'We have no use for him.'"[37] This impression was confirmed by Lepel Henry Griffin, who found that settlers looked upon Indians as "'vermin,' to be exterminated as speedily as possible."[38] These attitudes were to be found at the highest levels. Even Ulysses S. Grant, in an uncharacteristic outburst, declared in 1868 that the United States must "clear the plains for the immigrants even if extermination of every Indian tribe is necessary."[39] When Charles Wentworth Dilke asked one American about his views on Indians, he responded, "Well, sir, we can destroy them by the laws of war, or thin 'em out by whisky; but the thinning process is plaguy slow."[40]

"Plague" was the operative word in 1849 when gold seekers on the way to California brought cholera with them as they crossed the Great Plains, claiming the lives of thousands of Plains Indians.[41] Traffic across the Plains slackened somewhat during the Civil War, then picked up again once the war was over—just in time for another cholera epidemic in 1866. Time was not on the side of the Indians. David Macrae emphasized that "people who eat their meals in four minutes and a half, and push railway lines across the prairie at the rate of two miles a day, cannot wait a hundred years to give the Indian time to bury his tomahawk, wash his face, and put on a pair of trousers."[42]

The sheer number of Americans moving into the Great Plains after the Civil War threatened to annihilate the Indian population. Aiding the process of annihilation was the rapid decline of the buffalo, the traditional food source of the Plains Indians.[43] Before the coming of the white man, estimates of the number of these animals ran into the millions, representing what Walter Prescott Webb called "an inexhaustible beef supply, unrivaled by anything elsewhere known to man."[44] But even before the great post-Civil War buffalo kill-off, these herds were already under stress. Great Plains buffalo were competing with some two million horses for the same grasses and water, as well as suffering from drought and bovine diseases. Perhaps most significantly, they were subject to wolf predation, which claimed some one-third of the buffalo annual increase.[45] The Indians themselves occupied the Plains in greater numbers and had become more efficient hunters. Increasingly, they were hunting not only for their own subsistence, but also for the European market. As early as 1846, the Southern Cheyenne chief Yellow Wolf noted that, "We have long since noticed the decrease of the buffalo, and we are well aware it cannot last much longer."[46] By the 1850s, an Indian agent stationed on the upper Arkansas River estimated that the 11,000 Indians under his jurisdiction were killing 112,000 buffalo a year, in addition to 40,000 deer, 7,000 bear, and 3,000 elk—all for the hide trade.[47]

It didn't help that European "sportsmen" took great pride in killing as many buffalo as they could. One of the most notorious examples was the Sir St. George Gore hunting party of 1854–1857. Gore brought along an armory of seventy rifles and thirty miscellaneous firearms, and spent half a million dollars on this expedition to the American West. Determined to see how many buffalo he could kill in a single day, Gore set a rifle on a tripod near a buffalo herd and began blazing away. Every time Gore fired, servants replaced the rifle with one that was loaded. By the end of the day, Gore had dispatched 1,000 buffalo.[48] Gore's final count at the end of his trip was 2,000 buffalo, 1,600 elk and deer, 105 bears, and wolves, coyotes, and mountain sheep by the thousands.[49] Wealthy American hunters were no better. In 1871, "Buffalo Bill" Cody accompanied a hunting party from New York that employed twenty-five wagons carrying items that included carpets for the tents, as well as china, porcelain, and glassware. This group killed 600 buffalo and 200 elk, and left behind a heap of empty bottles that marked the site for years.[50] Shooting buffalo from the train was also a popular amusement of travelers crossing the Great Plains. The train would slow down to match the speed of the herd, passengers would take out their firearms, and begin firing on the herd[51] (Figure 8.2).

With buffalo herds already in decline, the movement of large numbers of white hunters into the region after 1865 tipped the herds toward extinction.

THE FAR WEST.—SHOOTING BUFFALO ON THE LINE OF THE KANSAS-PACIFIC RAILROAD.

FIGURE 8.2 Shooting buffalo on the line of the Kansas-Pacific Railroad (1871). Library of Congress. LC-USZ62-133890.

By the late 1860s, the buffalo of the Central Plains were being killed by the tens of thousands per week, turning the region, in historian Philip Weeks' words, into "a great charnel house: a buffalo graveyard of decaying, putrid, stinking remains."[52] The great herds had disappeared from the Central Plains by 1870, and hunters now turned their attention to the buffalo of the Southern Plains. In a single year, between 1872 and 1873, 1,250,000 buffalo hides were shipped from the Southern Plains to the East.[53] The last big buffalo kill took place in 1883, after which nothing remained but stacks of bones which, as one commentator noted, were "gathered up by poverty-stricken farmers and shipped east for fertilizer or to be used in the making of bone china."[54] "No sight is more common on the plains," said Theodore Roosevelt in 1886, "than that of a bleached buffalo skull."[55] By 1895, fewer than 1,000 buffalo survived in the United States.[56] The traditional way of life of the Plains Indians was doomed, and would soon be overwhelmed by the remorseless march of progress (Figure 8.3).

Even without the extinction of the buffalo, the Indian Wars of the 1860s and 1870s would no doubt have doomed the tribes of the Great Plains. A notable reporter who was posted to the Great Plains to cover these wars was Henry M. Stanley. While Stanley is sometimes referred to as an "American," he was born in Wales, and spent the latter part of his life in England, where he was knighted and served as a member of Parliament for Lambeth North. Stanley is best known for finding the missionary and explorer David Livingstone in Tanzania in 1871, but in 1867 he was a correspondent for an American newspaper assigned

FIGURE 8.3 Across the Continent, "Westward the Course of Empire Takes Its Way." Lithograph by F. (Fanny) Palmer, published by Currier & Ives, ca. 1868. Library of Congress. LC-DIG-ppmsca-03213.

to cover the Indian campaigns of Generals Winfield Scott Hancock and William T. Sherman.

The army was meeting with Great Plains tribes at Medicine Lodge Creek, Kansas, with the goal of convincing them to move to reservations. Stanley took detailed notes on the negotiations. The main complaint of tribal leaders, according to Stanley, concerned the building of roads and railroads through Indian hunting grounds and the subsequent diminishment of game.[57] They also expressed fierce resistance to the idea of relocation. The Kiowa chief Satanta, when told of plans to move his tribe to a reservation near the mountains, said, "I don't want to settle there. I love to roam over the wide prairie, and when I do it I feel free and happy, but when we settle down, we grow pale and die"[58] (Figure 8.4). Comanche chief Ten Bears said, "I want to live and die as I was brought up. I love the open prairie, and I wish you would not insist on putting us on a reservation."[59] General William T. Sherman was equally blunt, emphasizing that the railroads "will be built" and that if there was any interference "you will be swept away." Sherman suggested that Indians "choose your own homes, and live like white men, and we will help you all you want."[60]

There was little sympathy among American whites for Indians in general, and even less for the tribes of the Great Plains because of the horrific practice of

FIGURE 8.4 Kiowa chief Satanta (ca. 1870–1875). Photograph by William S. Soule. Library of Congress. LC–USZ62–13680.

scalping by Plains Indians. Stanley took note of a fight between the U.S. cavalry and a group of Cheyennes in 1867 that left several Indians dead. While inspecting the bodies of the Indians the troops found "the scalp of a woman with long auburn hair attached to it." The soldiers were so angry that they refused to bury the bodies.[61] In Omaha, Stanley met William Thompson, a native of England who had survived a scalping. People crowded into Thompson's room to view his "gory baldness" and to ogle his scalp, which was placed in a pail of water next to him. According to Stanley, the scalp was "somewhat resembling a drowned rat, as it floated, curled up, on the water."[62] *Harper's*, apparently anxious to cut short any sympathy that the public might harbor for Indians, ran a number of illustrations showing Indians torturing whites (Figure 8.5).[63]

LO, THE POOR INDIAN!

FIGURE 8.5 "Lo, the poor Indian!" *Harper's* 35 (July 1867), 149.

Of the few European travelers who expressed sympathy for the Indians, perhaps a majority were hunters who had had significant contact with them. The British hunter Windham Wyndham-Quin referred to "the much-abused, long-suffering, and little-understood Red Indian race ... Their history is one long story of mismanagement, of rights withheld, treaties broken, and promises unfulfilled."[64] The Indian "problem," he said, could be directly traced to "the contaminating influence of white men."[65] Parker Gillmore, a British army veteran of the Crimean War who had hunted in India, China, and Africa as well as North America, called the treatment of the American Indian "without a parallel for inhumanity," and insisted that the "savage son of man is less a savage than his educated brother" the white man.[66] One hunter who was less generous toward Indians was John Mortimer Murphy, whose party of elk hunters was attacked by the Sioux in Wyoming's Wind River Mountains. The Indians captured one of the hunters, who "was scalped in our sight by the howling savages." "Few thinking minds," said Murphy, "will regret the time when Nature has placed them in the lowly cemetery where their rude forefathers sleep."[67]

This view was endorsed by most European travelers. Isabella Bird, for instance, condemned the treatment of Indians by whites, but she found it hard to get past the Indians' physical condition ("hideous and filthy, and swarming with vermin").[68] She concluded that "the Americans will never solve the Indian problem till the

Indian is extinct."[69] Europeans, like their American counterparts, found it easier to justify annihilation of the Indians by first reducing them to subhuman status. Lady Duffus Hardy called Indians "the most revolting specimens of the human race," claimed that their cruelty was "a quality native born," and observed that "the dog, poor brute, cannot help being mad, but it must be got rid of."[70] Indians bore an expression that was closer to that of "a brute rather than that of a human being," said W. F. Rae, and William A. Bell viewed the Apaches of the Southwest as "vastly inferior beings in every respect" (even though they had successfully defended their territory for some 200 years).[71]

Often, Europeans seemed unaware of the inconsistency of their own views. Alexandra Gripenberg said of Indians that "one sought in vain for a conscious, human look" and that they were as "brutal as animals." Gripenberg then condemned the U.S. government because "the redskins have been pursued and killed like beasts of the forests."[72] Others, such as Charles Wentworth Dilke, couched the passing of Indians in terms of biology. The extinction of the "inferior races," said Dilke, was both "a law of nature" and "a blessing to mankind."[73] A British commentator for *Blackwood's* magazine noted of both British and Americans that "wherever they go, they must be kings and lords over all men who have skins of a different colour from their own." The "unsubmissive red man" had been regarded by the white man "as if he were a wolf, to be shot down, hunted down, extirpated," but if the Indian had "consented to be made a slave, he would have been affectionately cared for."[74]

As historian Patrick Brantlinger has emphasized in *Dark Vanishings*, between 1800 and 1930 the view that the "savage races" of the world were doomed to extinction was "rarely contested," and "became a mantra for the advocates of British imperial expansion and American manifest destiny."[75] William T. Sherman certainly put the war against the Plains Indians in this context, calling it "an inevitable conflict of races, one that must occur when a stronger is gradually displacing a weaker."[76] European travelers also looked placidly upon the extermination of the Indian, and none was more chillingly frank than Theodora Guest: "Happily, I think, the tribes are dying out from illnesses and epidemics, and this is surely not to be regretted."[77]

Human Inhabitants: Settlers and Travelers

European observers of the United States generally agreed that a distinctive sort of American was attracted to the frontier areas of the West. William Howard Russell called them "the wild adventurers and daring spirits which society, in the process of formation, throws out as a sort of advanced guard."[78] To James Bryce, they were "the most enterprising and unsettled" of society.[79] Virtually every type and race was represented on the frontier. In communities such as Junction City, Kansas, one could find the Mexican, the Yankee, "the patient phlegmatic Dutchman, the restless and refractory Irishman—the eagle-eyed Israelite, the overbearing southerner, and the independent frontiersman."[80] It was a society in extreme flux, where "no one has any fixed occupation; he is a storekeeper to-day, a ranchman to-morrow, a miner next week."[81] Sometimes the ambitious Westerner practiced a number of disparate professions at the same time, such as the entrepreneur whose store front sign read: "'HOME-MADE BREAD: JOB PRINTING: RUBBER STAMPS.'"[82] In Albuquerque, William A. Bell made the acquaintance of the town's butcher, only to discover the next day that the butcher was also editor of the *Albuquerque Chronicle*.[83]

European travelers who sought out the West had a very different agenda from Americans. Less interested in the entrepreneurial opportunities of the West, Europeans were instead attracted to the possibilities that the West seemed to offer for a life free of conventional restraints. Here, according to William A. Baille-Grohman, one could be "entirely emancipated from the rest of mankind, unrestrained by the fetters and by the exigent demands of civilization … as free as the deer you constantly startle from their covert."[84] "The life of the primal man," said Horace Annesley Vachell, was "an antidote to the fever of modern life."[85] Windham Wyndham-Quin contrasted being able to "inhale a full draught of fresh pure air; with a sense of glorious independence" with the life of the "fashionables" of London, "who pass laborious days panting in the dusty jam of a London summer, and spend perspiring nights struggling on a staircase, inhaling your fellow-creatures, absorbing fat dowagers, breathing men and women!"[86]

The few women who ventured into the wildest parts of the West had much the same reaction. Speaking of the Rockies, Isabella Bird proclaimed that "its unprofaned freshness gives me new life."[87] Isabelle Randall noted of her time as the mistress of a Montana ranch that "I would not exchange my happy, free, busy, healthy life out here, for the weariness and *ennui* that makes so many girls at home miserable."[88] Even the West's most developed city, San Francisco, possessed what Lady Duffus Hardy called a "picturesque lawlessness" which she found refreshing compared to her own society, where "natural impulse is bound down in the straitest of strait-waistcoats."[89]

A number of sources fed the European hunger for the romance of the West, but prominent among them was Buffalo Bill's Wild West Show. Indeed, of all the fabulous characters that emerged from the frontier, none was more synonymous with the wildness of the American West than William F. ("Buffalo Bill") Cody. Without hyperbole, historian Louis S. Warren calls him "the most famous American of his age."[90] Earning his nickname when he was employed by the Kansas Pacific railroad to provide meat for the workers, Buffalo Bill killed 4,200 buffalo in eighteen months.[91] In a contest with another buffalo hunter, Cody killed sixty-nine in a day.[92] During his time on the Plains, Cody served as a Pony Express rider, army scout, Indian fighter, and hunting guide, all of which would have made Cody's career remarkable enough. (He was the subject of some 550 dime novels.[93]) But what really set Cody apart from other legends of the West was his understanding of the entertainment value, and even diplomatic value, of the West.

Cody began to gain some insight into the attractiveness of the West to outsiders when Grand Duke Alexis, son of the Russian Tsar, came to America on a hunting trip in 1871–72. President Grant was especially anxious that Alexis enjoy himself, and instructed General Philip Sheridan to spare no expense. Two companies of infantry, two of cavalry, and even the regimental band were detached to accompany the Russian hunting party, with Cody the front man for this lavish entertainment.[94] Sioux Chief Spotted Tail and a group of Indians were brought in by Cody to, as Cody put it, "give a war dance in honor of the distinguished visitor."[95] (Also included among Alexis' hunting party was George Armstrong Custer, whom Cody reported "carried on a mild flirtation with one of Spotted Tail's daughters.") Cody gave the Duke lessons in hunting buffalo, and when Alexis succeeded in killing a buffalo after some initial disappointment, Cody described him as "very much elated at his success, taking off his cap and waving it vehemently."[96] There is little doubt that the outcome was satisfactory for all concerned. Also in 1872, Cody accompanied Windham Thomas Wyndham-Quin—the Earl of Dunraven—on an elk hunting trip.[97]

For those who could not be brought to the West, Cody would bring the West to them through his Wild West Show, which he established in 1883 (Figure 8.6). Performances at the show included a Pony Express relay race, an Indian "attack" on the Deadwood stagecoach, a reenactment of Custer's Last Stand, and various demonstrations of cowboy skills.[98] The show had remarkable success everywhere, and in 1887 Cody decided to bring the Wild West Show to London. Both Oscar

FIGURE 8.6 Buffalo Bill's Wild West (ca. 1899). Lithograph. Library of Congress. LC-USZC6-57.

Wilde and Henry Irving predicted that it would be a big hit. "It will take the town by storm," said Irving, which turned out to be an understatement.[99] The Prince of Wales and Queen Victoria attended a private performance of the show, and it obviously had an impact on the Queen. She wrote in her journal, "All the different people, wild, painted Red Indians from America, on their wild bare backed horses, of different tribes,—cow boys, Mexicans, &c., all came tearing round at full speed, shrieking & screaming, which had the weirdest effect."[100]

In *Story of the Wild West*, Cody describes two events from the London shows that either did not happen, or did not happen as Cody said they did (and here one is reminded of Oscar Wilde's fanciful descriptions of his Leadville lectures). In the first story, the Prince of Wales arranged for four European kings to attend the show. They were forthwith packed into the Deadwood coach which, of course, was attacked by Indians.[101] Louis S. Warren notes that while witnesses saw the Prince of Wales and the King of Denmark on the coach, the other kings were sitting in the audience.[102] Cody also recorded a remarkable incident at the private performance that was given for Queen Victoria. The show started with a procession of the participants on horseback, one of which carried the American flag. According to Cody, "Her Majesty rose from her seat and bowed deeply and impressively towards the banner. The whole court party rose, the ladies bowed, the generals present saluted, and the English noblemen took off their hats." "For the first time in history," declared Cody, "since the Declaration of Independence, a sovereign of Great Britain had saluted the star spangled banner." It was a sign, he said, of "the extinction of that mutual prejudice" between Britain and America.[103] But according to the British press, the flag appeared in the middle of the show, and it was lowered before the Queen, who "inclined her head twice in recognition of the courtesy." As Warren puts it, "the scene suggests the *reverse* of the famous legend: not the queen honoring the American flag, but the American showmen symbolically recognizing their debt to Her Majesty for attending."[104]

What did the London run of the Wild West Show mean for Americans and what did it mean for the British? For Americans, Cody's outrageous success was something in which they could take pride. During its six-month run in London, some two-and-a-half million people attended Buffalo Bill's Wild West Show.[105] The *Times* of London called the show "irresistible," and proclaimed Cody "the hero of the London season."[106] Americans were pleased to note that salons of the most polished British aristocracy were opened for Cody, and that the female portion of society seemed especially intrigued by Buffalo Bill. But James Fullarton Muirhead, one of our British travelers to America and someone with intimate knowledge of the British class system, knew better. Muirhead noted that the "social recognition given by English duchesses" to Cody occurred precisely because the social gap between the duchesses and Bill was "so irretrievably vast and so universally recognised that the duchesses can afford to amuse themselves cursorily with any eccentricity that offers itself."[107]

The meaning of the Wild West Show was complicated for Britons, who saw the show both as a gratifying display of muscular Anglo-Saxonism, and as "a specter of reverse colonization by racially powerful frontier warriors, the Americans."[108] Historian Joy Kasson believes that the show also carried an imperial meaning: "To the prince and to British aristocrats, the Wild West evoked a world of risk and dominance, of virility and exoticism that formed both the amusement and the serious business of the British Empire."[109]

Cody had many imitators (there were some 116 competing shows) but none were as successful, in part because Cody made sure that the show remained current.[110] He reenacted the Battle of San Juan Hill in 1899, and presented "The Rescue at Pekin" in 1901. The latter depicted the rescue of Americans during the Boxer Rebellion in China, with Indians playing the roles of Chinese.[111] While Cody's theatrical productions played up the romantic appeal of the American frontier, it should be emphasized that the legendary and the actual intermixed freely. Indeed, many who participated in this show at various times, including James Butler "Wild Bill" Hickok, and Cody himself, had played *real* roles in the history of the West. This sometimes produced some rich ironies. Sitting Bull and Black Elk both performed in the Wild West Show (Sitting Bull in 1884 and Black Elk during the London tour in 1887) and both had been at the Little Big Horn when George Armstrong Custer and his troops were killed—which was reenacted in the Show.[112]

Henry M. Stanley was able to meet both Hickok and Custer while they were engaged on the Great Plains in the 1860s. Custer was head of the 7th Cavalry on these expeditions, and Stanley described him as possessing "a certain impetuosity and undoubted courage," both of which would contribute to Custer's doom in 1876.[113] Stanley was able to spend more time with Hickok, who already had a considerable reputation as a gunslinger. When Stanley asked him point blank "'how many white men have you killed,'" Hickok replied, "'I suppose I have killed considerably over a hundred.'"[114] While no doubt an outlandish exaggeration, Hickok's physical abilities should not be underestimated.[115] In the course of the Hancock expedition, Hickok was attacked by a party of six Indians, two of whom he killed while driving the others off (a story confirmed by another scout).[116] And on another occasion, in which Stanley himself was insulted by a ruffian, Hickok "seized the fellow, with long nervous hands, and flung him across a billiard table."[117]

For some Europeans, merely visiting the West was not enough. The enticements were strong enough for many to consider moving to this part of the country. This idea was promoted by William Saunders, who claimed that "with a very small amount of capital a young Englishman might begin as a grazier in the Far West. If he is strong and enterprising he would enjoy life in the saddle, with the boundless prairies for his range."[118] James Aiken encouraged his fellow Scots to take up farming in America, emphasizing that "your hope of a brighter future, your redemptions from a life of profitless toil, lies in the fair and fertile fields of the West."[119] Encouraged by such reports, a number of the more intrepid

Europeans would seek their fortunes in America. Horace Annesley Vachell identified them by types, which included "the family fool," "the parson's son, the fortune-hunter, the moral idiot, the remittance man, and the sportsman."[120] With the exception of the sportsman, Vachell held them all in contempt.

In *Prairie Fever: British Aristocrats in the American West, 1830–1890*, historian Peter Pagnamenta describes British efforts to establish colonies in the West where the younger sons of the aristocracy might find a place for themselves. These settlements included the communities of Victoria and Runnymeade in Kansas, and Le Mars in western Iowa. To make these colonies amenable to young British gentlemen, there were tennis courts, cricket competitions, and riding to hounds. Predictably, attempts to make these communities productive all faltered under the combination of inexperience and a malevolent natural environment.[121]

As these young men found out for themselves, the reality of life in the West was very different from the myth. Nature in the West seemed peculiarly violent, bringing forth drought, hail stones, tornados, prairie fires, blizzards, and hostile wildlife. Of the latter, bears were the most dangerous. On one hunting trip, Parker Gillmore put two bullets into a bear at point-blank range. The bear responded by delivering "a blow that knocked me almost out of time, sending my gun from my hands with the rapidity of electricity." It took two more shots from Gillmore's revolver before the bear finally succumbed.[122] In Colorado, the scout Mountain Jim Nugent was not so lucky. He described to Isabella Bird an encounter with a grizzly bear in which the bear broke his arm, raked him with his claws, tore out one of his eyes, and left him for dead.[123]

Out on the Great Plains, Henry M. Stanley took note of the prevalence of scurvy among the troops serving there, and William Hepworth Dixon reported being surprised by the number of people in the West who had lost either toes or fingers to frostbite.[124] The perils posed to livestock were equally significant. During William A. Bell's exploration of the Southwest, one of his mules slipped off a narrow ledge and was smashed on the rocks below.[125] In addition, a rattlesnake bit two of Bell's horses on the lips as they were grazing along the Rio Grande. One recovered in a week but the other was reduced to "a perfect skeleton" and was not restored to health for three months.[126]

The insects of the West were likewise notorious. Parker Gillmore described having to painstakingly remove ticks from his body, and William Francis Butler noted that during a wet summer, it was not uncommon in Minnesota and Dakota "for oxen and horses to perish from the bites of mosquitoes."[127] Swarms of grasshoppers sometimes descended on the Plains, devouring everything in their path. Their numbers were often large enough to stop a train.[128] An English farmer in Kansas was the victim of one such infestation in which grasshoppers "alighted on houses, people, animals, fences, crops, covering everything, while the ground was strewn several inches thick, so that it was impossible to walk about without killing dozens at each step … Flowers, leaves, silk, corn, ears, all had vanished down their rapacious maws."[129] One writer emphasized that while farmers in

Britain might be filled with envy at "the bounteous increase of cereal crops which rewards their American brethren," the loss to American farmers from infestations of insects amounted to $200 million per year.[130]

Emily Faithfull cautioned that life in the West was "often hard and coarse, and it is the fashion to work hard, spend little, and save something." Those unwilling to submit to such a regime should stay at home.[131] People who had experienced ranch life firsthand found it hard to discern its romantic elements. A good example is "Buffalo Bill" Cody, who could hardly be accused of naivety in regards to conditions in the real West. At one point in his career, Cody invested in a Texas herd, and joined the cowboys who were driving the cattle to Kansas. He was appalled by the brutal conditions and soon quit, explaining that, "There is nothing but hard work on these round-ups. [I could not] possibly find out where the fun came in."[132] George Shafer, who grew up on a ranch (Shafer would later become governor of North Dakota) claimed that almost every cowboy he had come across was a "physical wreck at the age of thirty-five years."[133] Pointing out that the roughness of the life of a stockman might repel someone coming from an "English club existence," William A. Baille-Grohman emphasized that in short order "the effeminate and unmanly" would be weeded out.[134] Horace Annesley Vachell, an Englishman who operated a California cattle ranch for seventeen years, described the life of the rancher as being constantly employed in hard labor, eating the plainest food, sleeping in the hardest bunks, smoking the coarsest tobacco, and wearing canvas overalls, "but you are strong and well."[135]

Likely to be especially galling to the English proprietor of a ranch was the independent cowboy, who would not hesitate to let the ranch owner know that "who is the better man of the two has long been settled in his own mind."[136] Englishwoman Isabaelle Randall, whose husband Jem supervised a ranch in Montana, noted that the ranch hands all took off their hats to her, but did so because she was a woman, and not the wife of their employer. Jem told her that they would never dream of taking their hats off to him, "or showing any other token of respect."[137] Moreton Frewen, a Briton who established a cattle kingdom in Wyoming, complained that the cowboys who worked for him were "the most impracticable, aggressively independent people possible, and I often long to thrash one or two but for the want of dignity in such a proceeding."[138] Describing the cowboys who worked on his ranch, Horace Annesley Vachell observed that, "Drunk, they are dangerous; sober, most capital fellows—cheery, kindly, without fear, hard as nails, and generous to a fault."[139]

One Englishman who was seduced by the prospect of ranch life in America penned an anonymous article for *MacMillan's Magazine* in which he tried to discourage others from this course. In painful detail he describes his first days on the job at a sheep ranch, beginning with furnishing himself a largely worthless set of clothes. This included corduroy trousers and "a huge pair of English riding-boots, imposing in appearance, but calculated to blister horribly the feet of the unfortunate wearer." The "crowning touch" was a Colt revolver that he strapped to his waist. Anxious to try out this weapon, our tenderfoot shot a rabbit that ventured too close. After examining his prize and estimating how far away the rabbit had been when he shot it, he turned his attention back to his sheep. The herd had vanished. An exhausting chase followed, highlighted by "catching my foot in a prairie dog's hole and tumbling head foremost upon a bed of inhospitable cactuses, the thorns of which remained in my hands for hours."[140] While he would stick with the job, this Englishman concluded that "this herding, which *looks* so easy and pleasant, becomes, on actual experience, one of the hardest of the trials of western life" [original emphasis].[141]

Even more enticing than ranch life to would-be European adventurers was the prospect of getting rich quick in the Klondike gold rush of the late 1890s. William H. Davies was perhaps typical in describing his own expectations of the gold region as "childish in the extreme. I thought the rocks were of solid gold."[142] His career as a prospector ended before it began, when he fell from a train he was hopping in Canada and his right foot was severed.[143] A Briton who actually made it to the Klondike was Charles C. Osborne, and his descriptions of the work that was involved in prospecting for gold was served up as a grim, cautionary tale. Osborne found that it sometimes took weeks of hard labor to get through the permanently frozen ground with hot rocks or wood fires, and when bedrock was finally reached, gold was usually not found.[144] Thanks to the mosquitoes ("venomous and irritating") "life was often rendered intolerable," and "the number of deaths from typhoid fever, dysentery, scurvy, and other diseases, was appalling." Throughout the Alaska mining region, said Osborne, one could see once-strong men "now broken, emaciated, and doomed, the ghosts of their former selves."[145]

Women who settled in the West tended to do well, receiving even more chivalrous attention than they did elsewhere in part because of their relative scarcity. In 1870, there were sixteen males for every one female in California, and it was worse elsewhere. In Nevada it was thirty-two to one, and in Idaho it was forty-three to one.[146] Indeed, as an enticement, Wyoming Territory extended the franchise to women in 1869 (Utah followed suit the following year). In short, women were a valuable commodity in the West. Englishwoman Isabelle Randall noted that it was impossible to find female servants for her husband's ranch in Montana because they were quickly married off: "I have seen young girls of thirteen and hideous old girls of fifty snapped up eagerly as soon as they arrived in the country."[147]

James Bryce claimed that there were only two unpardonable sins in the West, "horse-stealing and insults to women," to which Emily Faithfull added, "I believe there is no country which holds woman's honor more sacred than America."[148] A resident of the extremely violent mining town of Bodie, California, insisted that he could not remember a single instance in which a woman there had been insulted or accosted. The reason, he believed, was partly due to "the respect depravity pays to decency," and partly due "to the knowledge that sudden death would follow any other course." Another mining town (Yellowstone City) stipulated death by hanging for insulting a woman.[149] On her train between Colorado

Springs and Denver, Iza Duffus Hardy and her companion were the only women, with the rest an assortment of rough, heavily armed men. Hardy was surprised that the men conversed with each other with a "gentleness of voice and manner," and did not intrude on the privacy of the women other than "offering to open or close the window for us, carrying our bags for us, and helping us up or down the steps."[150]

Like the railroads, women were agents of civilization in the West, and whenever females showed up in a Western town, "oaths were less frequently heard; knives were less frequently drawn, pistols were less frequently fired."[151] As historian David T. Courtwright puts it, "The history of the maturation of frontier towns is the history of women turning them into places actually worth living in."[152] In Butte, Montana, E. Catherine Bates took note of the "softening effect" that women had had on this formerly rough mining town.[153] William A. Baille-Grohman claimed that "the Western woman's word is never disputed. Her dignity, *savoir-faire*, and independence make her the master of the most puzzling situations."[154] When Isabella Bird shared a primitive meal with a group of five men near Fort Collins, Colorado, she expressed amusement at the men for "apologizing to me for being without their coats, as if coats would not be an enormity on the Plains."[155] Even in the case of saloon prostitutes, Henry Stanley claimed that the chivalrous code of the West would not allow them to be abused even by men "whom they may have robbed."[156] Here, Stanley was surely mistaken, as the chivalry lavished on "respectable" women was seldom extended to prostitutes, who daily dealt with the threat of physical violence, as well as wretched pay, alcoholism, and drug addiction.[157]

Decline

When William Hepworth Dixon and Charles Wentworth Dilke traveled from Leavenworth to Salt Lake City in 1866, they were unnerved by crossing hostile Indian territory, but exhilarated by the variety of animal life they encountered. There were antelopes, wolves, and herds of buffalo and, as Dilke put it, "We never seemed to be without a million companions in our loneliness."[158] For Dixon, what most impressed were buffalo by "thousands on thousands, tens of thousands after tens of thousands … thundering in our front."[159] But his companion could not help but notice the huge numbers of buffalo skeletons, "left by the hunters, who take but the skin."[160]

Emily Faithfull was no less astonished when, on her way from Ogden to San Francisco, "droves of antelopes came flying down in such numbers from the mountains that while they crossed the track the train was obliged to come to a full stop."[161] William A. Baille-Grohman reported killing nine elk in two days in the vicinity of Laramie Peak, and noted that he easily could have tripled that number because, without previous contact with humans, the animals had no fear of people.[162] In Colorado, the trout were so numerous that they crowded the streams. Isabella Bird claimed that they were caught "as fast as the hook can be baited … Sometimes two men bring home 60 pounds of trout as the result of one day's winter fishing."[163] Likewise, the oysters were so abundant in the Gulf of Mexico that one traveler saw them hauled into the boats as fast as the men could work their rakes.[164]

There are countless such descriptions, but with the end of the Civil War and the completion of the transcontinental railroad in 1869, settlers were moving westward by the thousands and forever altering this once wild region. In 1870, 150,000 traveled as through- or way-passengers on trains between Omaha and Sacramento. By the end of the decade the number approached one million.[165] It is striking how quickly the West was transformed from a land of few human inhabitants and abundant wildlife to a region of bustling communities and a disappearing natural environment. When W. F. Rae took a train trip West in 1869, he expected a landscape that was "wild and desolate," but instead found one that was "filled with settlers."[166] Windham Wyndham-Quin, who took his first hunting trip to the United States in 1870, noted that by 1874 "the whirr of the thrashing-machine is now heard where last year the silence was broken only by the coughing of deer, the barking of foxes, and the dismal howls of coyotes. I expect I should starve to-day in a place where four years ago I saw, I am sure, more than a thousand wapiti in one week."[167] By 1880, Wyndham-Quin said of the wapiti that "they are hunted with a thoughtless brutality that must shortly lead to their extermination."[168]

California was more rapidly settled—and its wilderness more rapidly despoiled—than any part of the West. A number of travelers noted that the sea-lions near San Francisco's Cliff House had been placed under the protection of the government to keep people from killing them.[169] In the early 1870s, J. W. Boddam-Whetham observed that even though the hunting of deer in California was restricted to five months, the locals flaunted the law and hunted whenever they pleased. Boddam-Whetham predicted that "the merciless and incessant war waged on every wild animal, bird, and fish, at all times and in all places, in season and out of season, will soon render hunting, shooting, and fishing in America sports of the past."[170] By the late 1870s Robert Louis Stevenson was already mourning the passing of California's "two noblest indigenous living things"—Indians and redwoods.[171] Settlers were moving into the vicinity of Yosemite by the early 1880s, and devastating the landscape by burning whatever got in their way. As he and his party approached Yosemite in 1882, William Howard Russell observed the "charred trunks" of trees that lay everywhere among the ferns. Russell condemned what he called this "reckless, wicked waste."[172] The following year, W. Henry Barneby took note of the pall of smoke that hung in the air in the Yosemite region. The smoke was from fires set by settlers, who cut the timber they needed for their homes and fencing, then burned the rest.[173]

The prairie and plains regions were also filling up. Thomas Hughes witnessed emigrants in Iowa "starting for the prairies, in their long covered waggons loaded with lumber for their first houses."[174] Much of the land had been sold off already, forcing the prospective farmer to plod a great distance before reaching soil where no one would "dispute his ownership."[175] William Saunders reported that as early as the mid-1870s, the state of Nebraska had banned the shooting of prairie hens because of their increasing scarcity.[176] Passenger pigeons were in great abundance in America, but they were hunted to extinction, with the last one dying in the Cincinnati Zoo in 1914.[177] Most dramatic was the passing of the buffalo. When his train reached Sydney, Nebraska, in 1876, Henry Sienkiewicz found that the station was adorned with the heads of buffalo "shot from the train."[178] By the early 1880s, the buffalo had disappeared from the Great Plains. When Phil Robinson crossed the Great Plains in 1882, he noted that, "There are no bison now. They cannot stand before the stove-pipe hat."[179]

Humans were changing the landscape in other ways as well. Rudyard Kipling took note of the vandalism that he found at Yellowstone, where young ladies scratched their names around geisers and in the bottom of shallow pools. "Nature fixes the insult indelibly," said Kipling, "and the after-years will learn that 'Hattie,' 'Sadie,' 'Mamie,' 'Sophie,' and so forth, have taken out their hairpins, and scrawled in the face of Old Faithful."[180] When Baron Hübner visited California's giant sequoias in 1871, he reported that "the greater part of these trees are marked by the inscriptions of different celebrated persons. One of them bears the name of Ferdinand de Lesseps."[181] The built environment of the West did not fare much better. Alexandra Gripenberg found that the walls of the original Spanish mission in San Diego were "profaned by the common inscriptions of tourists."[182]

With the rise of the tourist industry in the West, Europeans themselves played a significant role in the taming of a region that they revered for its wildness. As historian Orvar Löfgren observes, inherent in "the institutionalization of vistas, sceneries, and tourists sights" was the risk of them "becoming routinized and trivialized: an old idyll can lose its power to arouse strong emotions in the observer."[183] Guidebooks were attracting both American and European tourists to the West in increasing numbers, and especially influential was George A. Crofutt's *Great Trans-Continental Tourist's Guide*, which first appeared in 1869. By 1871, Crofutt had some two million readers per year, one-quarter of them in Europe.[184] Thomas Cook also helped open up the West to Europeans. Cook had long prospered by arranging tours for British and European travelers in the Old World, and in 1873 he published an American edition of *Cook's Excursionist*. By 1874 he had opened a U.S. branch of Thomas Cook and Son, and began arranging package trips to the West, with an emphasis on California and Colorado. By 1884 Cook was offering excursions to Yellowstone.[185] Other travel companies, such as the American firm Raymond and Whitcomb Travel Agency, would follow, and the funneling of tourists into the resort hotels that were established in the American West was an important element in the settling of the area.[186]

British physician William A. Bell and his American partner William J. Palmer developed the first major Western resort site at Colorado Springs and at nearby Manitou Springs. The two put up a series of hotels in the area (culminating in the opening of the luxury hotel The Antlers in 1883) that were modeled on the style the English preferred.[187] Helping to attract British investment in Colorado was a testimonial from London physician Samuel Solly on the supposed health benefits of the area's mineral springs. Rose G. Kingsley enthused in 1873 that "the English and Canadian incomers are now making a marked portion of the population."[188] Indeed, Colorado Springs acquired the nickname "Li'l Lunnon."[189] Three miles away, at Broadmoor, members of the Cheyenne Mountain Country Club could gamble at a casino, play polo, go pigeon shooting, or ride out to hounds, "with coyotes substituting for foxes."[190]

While well-heeled tourists were drawn to the charms of the "wild west," they had little interest in mingling with local Indians. The Utes, who long had used the mineral baths in the vicinity of the Colorado Springs resort, were removed. Likewise, fears that Indians who resided near Yellowstone Park would discourage the construction of hotels led to the removal of the native peoples of the park by 1879. As historian A. K. Sandoval-Strausz has noted, "the arrival of tourists meant exile for inhabitants."[191] Providing protection for European tourists in the Far West were U.S. army troops, half of whom were the Irish and German immigrants that these travelers found so contemptible.[192]

Also playing a role in the taming of the West was the transformation of the cattle industry into a legitimate business enterprise, claiming perhaps a higher proportion of European investment than any other American business.[193] The roots of the modern cattle industry were in Texas, and one of the pioneers was John Adair, a British investor who in the late 1870s partnered with American cattleman Charles Goodnight to create a prosperous cattle empire in that state. Inspired by this success, eleven other British cattle companies were established in Texas alone in the years ahead.[194] The cattle industry rapidly expanded elsewhere as well. Between 1870 and 1880 the number of cattle in Colorado increased by a factor of ten. Even more spectacular was the example of Wyoming, where the number of cattle went from 11,000 to 521,000 during this decade.[195] Especially enticing to the investor was that cattle could graze for free on the open range on public land. A good example of a British cattle baron is Moreton Frewen (future brother-in-law to Mrs. Randolph Churchill). An avid hunter, Frewen came to Rawlins, Wyoming, in 1878, attracted by the game. He stayed, and built an elaborate ranch house near the Big Horns in 1879 where he could entertain foreign visitors in style (especially prospective investors in his cattle scheme). By 1883 Frewen was presiding over Wyoming's Powder River Cattle Company, with some 50,000 head of cattle.[196] The amount of American beef imported into Britain increased by a factor of fifteen between 1876 and 1880. By 1884, there were over thirty English and Scottish cattle companies in America (making up some 15 percent of the total), and in the last quarter of the nineteenth century, British and Scottish investors put $34 million into the Western livestock industry.[197] The cattle industry peaked in the mid-1880s, then began to decline under the pressure of falling prices, overgrazing, droughts, and hard winters.

British cattlemen were also subject to the criticisms of an American public that was increasingly hostile toward foreign owners of large tracts of American land. In 1887, Congress passed the Alien Land Bill, requiring that an alien buying land declare that he would become an American citizen. The brutal winter of 1886–87 and the deaths of enormous numbers of cattle (some ranch owners calculated that they lost two-thirds of their animals) put an end to the open-range cattle industry in the United States.[198]

No other industry had a greater impact on the West than mining. Historian Patricia Nelson Limerick has emphasized that mining helped create territories and states, that it brought the West "into the forefront of industrialized life," and that it created an attitude in the West that persists down to the present day: "get in, get rich, get out."[199] The devastation of the Western landscape by mining was profound. In California, hydraulic mining operations employed powerful hoses to bring down entire hillsides, laying waste to the countryside. The rock and gravel that was carried downstream threatened towns with floods, and destroyed farms. Baron Hübner viewed "a chaos of rock, gravel, and mud" that had resulted from hydraulic mining, and William A. Bell saw "valleys obliterated, hills levelled to the ground, rivers turned from their course and fertile tracts of country covered with bare heaps of gravel miles in extent."[200] By the 1890s, the Army Corps of Engineers estimated that 39,000 acres of farmland had been buried under debris from hydraulic mining.[201]

Ordinary mining activities were no less invasive. "Of all the desolate, grim scenery to be found in America," said J. W. Boddam-Whetham, "that around Virginia City takes the lead. The great brown hills are scarred and seamed and bare."[202] English visitor James Thomson described the hills surrounding the mining town of Central City, Colorado, in a similar manner. They were "scarred and gashed and ulcerated all over from past mining operations; so ferociously does little man scratch at the breasts of his great calm mother."[203] J. Barham Zincke also noted of Colorado mining operations that the land had been stripped of its trees for building and fuel, to be replaced by "gigantic mole-hills" of earth the miners had excavated. "It will be a long time," said Zincke, "before the forest appears again."[204] By the end of the nineteenth century, the destruction from mining was even more stark. When Beatrice and Sidney Webb visited the once-thriving town of Leadville in 1898 they encountered an "acrid waste," a "vast grave ground of fir trees" with only charred stumps remaining.[205] In addition to denuding the natural environment, mining produced heavy pollution. At the Argo Works outside of Denver in 1881, William Howard Russell saw chimneys that "vomit out quite sufficient vaporous fumes and smoke to blight the vegetation."[206] An even more striking example was Butte, Montana, where by 1890 six smelters were spewing sulphur and arsenic smoke into the atmosphere, and in the process making Butte one of the most polluted cities on the planet.[207] The towns where gold was being mined were arguably even worse because in addition to the ordinary miseries of mining, there was the thunderous sound of heavy stamps crushing the quartz that contained the gold, and operating day and night.[208]

The social costs of mining were also considerable, with disturbing signs of an emerging Western mining proletariat. When she was in Butte in the mid-1880s, E. Catherine Bates described the miners as looking "pale and exhausted" after doing work that paid three dollars a day.[209] Just as in the industrial East, mining towns in the West developed tensions along class, ethnic, and racial lines.[210] When mine owners in Rock Springs, Wyoming, tried to replace white coal workers with lower-paid Chinese workers, angry whites burned Rock Springs' Chinatown to the ground and went on a killing spree against local Chinese.[211] In the years ahead, there would be violent confrontations between miners and forces hired by the mine owners at Coeur d'Alene, Cripple Creek, Ludlow and elsewhere.[212]

By the end of the nineteenth century, American historian Frederick Jackson Turner observed of the West that "the restless, rushing wave of settlement has broken with a shock against the arid plains."[213] In a plea for protection of the forests, the naturalist John Muir could clearly see that "the axe and saw are insanely busy, chips are flying thick as snowflakes, and every summer thousands of acres of priceless forests with their underbrush, soil, springs, climate, scenery and religion are vanishing away in clouds of smoke."[214] The wilderness of the Old West was quickly disappearing, and animating its destruction, according to Emily Faithfull, was worship of the dollar, with few Americans willing "to protest, like their countryman Thoreau, against railways, steamboats, and telegraphs."[215] A. Maurice Low agreed, insisting that between the end of the Civil War and the end of the nineteenth century, Americans had had time for nothing but "money-making and politics." Summing up what he called the "shocking improvidence" of Americans during this era, Low claimed that

> forests ruthlessly felled, the soil robbed so as to be made to yield with the least labor, animal life wantonly destroyed, water power sacrificed or allowed to go unused, is the story of those years. Extravagance, waste, a scorn of careful economies or details were seen everywhere.[216]

While the taming of the West was inevitable, James Bryce wistfully observed that "there will be something to regret when all is known and the waters of civilization have covered the tops of the highest mountains."[217]

Notes

1. Roderick Nash, *Wilderness and the American Mind* (New Haven: Yale University Press, 1982), 348. Even in 1912, the Santa Fe Railway estimated that one-third of the travelers who visited the Grand Canyon and Yosemite were foreigners. See Earl Pomeroy, *In Search of the Golden West: The Tourist in Western America* (New York: Alfred A. Knopf, 1957), 88.
2. James Fenimore Cooper, *The Prairie* [1827] (New York: Library of America, 1985), 892.

3. Charles Wentworth Dilke, *Greater Britain: A Record of Travel in English-Speaking Countries* (London: Macmillan and Co., 1890), 90; W. G. Marshall, *Through America: Nine Months in the United States* (London: Sampson, Low, Marston, Searle & Rivington, 1881), 123; Isabella L. Bird, *A Lady's Life in the Rocky Mountains* [1879] (Norman: University of Oklahoma Press, 1969), 29.

4. Marshall, 123.

5. Emily Faithfull, *Three Visits to America* (New York: Fowler & Wells, 1884), 214; Robert Louis Stevenson, "The Amateur Emigrant," in Robert Louis Stevenson, *From Scotland to Silverado* [1892] (Cambridge, MA: Belknap Press, 1966), 124.

6. Harold Brydges, *Uncle Sam at Home* (New York: Henry Holt and Co., 1888), 14; J. J. Aubertin referred to "the ingenious mode adopted to meet the difficulty of running to and fro with time and steam from east to west, and west to east, across an immense territory—a difficulty which we in England have never been called upon to meet." J. J. Aubertin, *A Fight with Distances: The States, the Hawaiian Islands, Canada, British Columbia, Cuba, the Bahamas* (London: Kegan Paul, Trench & Co., 1888), 49. Time zones were originally established by railroad companies. In 1918, the Standard Time Act made railroad time federal law. Thomas J. Schlereth, *Victorian America: Transformations in Everyday Life, 1876–1915* (New York: Harper Perennial, 1992), 30–31. William H. A. Williams also notes the frustrations of British travelers in Ireland when the locals could not express distances in miles. What was true of Irish peasants ("time was a more meaningful gauge of distance than some arbitrary, abstract measurement of space") was also true of Americans in the West. William H. A. Williams, *Tourism, Landscape, and the Irish Character: British Travel Writers in Pre-Famine Ireland* (Madison: University of Wisconsin Press, 2008), 67.

7. Edward A. Freeman, *Some Impressions of the United States* (London: Longmans, Green, and Co., 1883), 229. In a letter from America, Antoní Dvořák noted that Iowa, where he was to take up residence in the Czech village of Spillville, was some 1,300 miles from New York, "but here such a distance is nothing. Thirty-six hours by express and we are there." Dvořák to Dr. Emil Kozánek, Letter of 18 December 1893, in Antoní Dvořák, *Antoní Dvořák: Letters and Reminscences*, trans. Roberta Finlayson Samsour, ed. Otakar Šourek (Prague: Artia, 1954).

8. Baron Hübner, *A Ramble Round the World, 1871*, trans. Lady Elizabeth Herbert (London: MacMillan and Co., 1878), 65.

9. Iza Duffus Hardy, *Through Cities and Prairie Lands: Sketches of an American Tour* (London: Chapman and Hall, 1881), 222.

10. Windham Thomas Wyndham-Quin, *The Great Divide: Travels in the Upper Yellowstone in the Summer of 1874* (London: Chatto and Windus, 1876), 2.

11. Faithfull, 214; Dilke, 90; Marshall, 123.

12. Henry Sienkiewicz, *Portrait of America: Letters of Henry Sienkiewicz*, trans. and ed. Charles Morley (New York: Columbia University Press, 1959), 58–59.

13. Marshall, 135. The exclamation marks ranged freely in these travelers' descriptions of the Western landscape, such as in E. Catherine Bates' impressions of Santa Fe: "Such a sky! Such mountains all round us! Such billows of cloud of every conceivable shape and shade of pearl and opal!" E. Catherine Bates, *A Year in the Great Republic*, v. 2 (London: Ward & Downey, 1887), 25.

14. William Hepworth Dixon, *New America* (Philadelphia: J. B. Lippincott, 1869), 132.

15. W. F. Rae, *Westward by Rail: The New Route to the East* [1871] (New York: Promontory Press, 1974), 167.

16. William A. Bell, *New Tracks in North America: A Journal of Travel and Adventure Whilst Engaged in the Survey for a Southern Railroad to the Pacific Ocean During 1867–8* [1870] (Albuquerque: Horn and Wallace, 1965), 274.

17. William Howard Russell, *Hesperothen, Notes from the West: A Record of a Ramble in the United States and Canada in the Spring and Summer of 1881*, v. 2 (London: S. Low, Marston, Searle & Rivington, 1882), 16.

18. Parker Gillmore, *A Hunter's Adventures in the Great West* (London: Hurst and Blackett, 1871), 19; Faithfull, 157. Faithfull enthused that in Colorado "the very sense of *living* was an absolute delight which can not be realized by those who have never experienced the buoyancy of this electric air" [Faithfull's emphasis]. Ibid., 153. In contrast to a majority of European travelers who seemed to be in awe of the American landscape, James Bryce complained that "neither the Rocky Mountains, with their dependent ranges, nor the Sierra Nevada, can be compared for variety of grandeur and beauty with the Alps ... There are indeed in the whole United States very few quite first-rate pieces of mountain scenery rivalling the best of the Old World." James Bryce, *The American Commonwealth*, v. 2 (New York: The Commonwealth Publishing Co., 1908), 769, 770.

19. Lady Duffus Hardy, *Through Cities and Prairie Lands: Sketches of an American Tour* (London: Chapman and Hall, 1881), 128; Bird, 12–13. Hardy also mentioned "sparkling waters, so pure and bright they might be flowing direct from the throne of the Almighty God." Ibid., 129. Rose Pender referred to Yosemite's "soul-awing scenery," and when Baron Hübner viewed Yosemite, he found himself "filled with astonishment, admiration, and respect for the powerful Hand which, in modeling these rocks, has stamped upon them the impress of his own grandeur." Rose Pender, *A Lady's Experiences of the Wild West in 1883* (London: George Tucker, 1888), 17; Hübner, 173.

20. William A. Baille-Grohman, *Camps in the Rockies: Being a Narrative of Life on the Frontier, and Sport in the Rocky Mountains, with an Account of the Cattle Ranches of the West* (New York: Charles Scribner's Sons, 1884), 211.

21. Lepel Henry Griffin, *The Great Republic* [1884] (New York: Arno Press, 1974), 37, 36, 39.

22. Wyndham-Quin, 169.

23. Rudyard Kipling, *American Notes* [1891] (Norman: University of Oklahoma Press, 1981), 110. E. Catherine Bates was equally ravished by the sunset en route to Los Angeles: "Such colouring! Gold as deep as the Californian metal itself, faint greens and blues and greys and purples, rose and flame colour, all in the sky at the same time and ranging over such a continent of space!" Bates, v. 2, 68. In describing the colors of Mt. Shasta, J. W. Boddam-Whetham said that "the effects produced by the mingling colours of lava, snow, and ice, and the contrasting shadows of a deep violet hue are so varied, and the radiation of colour at sunrise and sunset so vivid, that it is difficult to keep the eyes turned from the mountain—for nothing seems worthy of consideration in comparison with Shasta." J. W. Boddam-Whetham, *Western Wanderings: A Record of Travel in the Evening Land* (London: Richard Bentley and Son, 1874), 210.

24. Boddam-Whetham, 140. Boddam-Whetham suggested that Yosemite could be "improved" if it was "cared for like a garden; trees and shrubs tended, swamps drained, bridges built, drives made, and grass sown where it is necessary." Ibid., 139. Historian Christopher Mulvey notes that the American wilderness filled foreign travelers "with a sense of threat and oppression" for which the Romantic sensibility had ill prepared them. Christopher Mulvey, *Anglo-American Landscapes: A Study of Nineteenth-Century Anglo-American Travel Literature* (Cambridge: Cambridge University Press, 1983), 11–12. William H. A. Williams emphasizes that early concepts of beauty in nature had been rooted in "harmony, balance, tranquility, and smoothness of texture," and that the wilder aspects of nature "could overwhelm the imagination, producing an aesthetic of terror." He credits the creation of the concept of the "sublime" as a way to "aestheticize" nature and to enjoy it in its wildest guise. Williams, 22–24.

25. Rose G. Kingsley, *South by West, or Winter in the Rocky Mountains and Spring in Mexico* (London: W. Isbinster and Co., 1874), 78.

26. Bird, 55.

27. F. Francis, "The Yellowstone Geysers," *The Nineteenth Century* 11, no. 61 (March 1882), 373.

28. Dixon, 52.

29. Dilke, 81.

30. Dilke, 83, 84. F. Barham Zincke also noted of Indians that "their complexion was not of so dark a copper colour as I had expected." F. Barham Zincke, *Last Winter in the United States: Being Table Talk Collected During a Tour Through the Late Southern Confederation, the Far West, the Rocky Mountains, &c.* [1868] (Freeport, NY: Books for Libraries Press, 1970), 173.

31. Faithfull, 212; Griffin, 166.

32. Freeman, 150, 151.

33. Pender, 8–9.

34. Robert G. Athearn, *Westward the Briton* (Lincoln: University of Nebraska Press, 1953), 126. At a station in Nevada, H. Hussey Vivian described "five of these ugly types of humanity" as "dirty and coarse looking to the last degree." H. Hussey Vivian, *Notes of a Tour in America from August 7th to November 17th, 1877* (London: Edward Stanford, 1878), 122.

35. Boddam-Whetham, 53.

36. Marshall, 117, 141. Marshall was hopeful, however, that the Indian could be Christianized and "won over to civilization from his wild and nomadic mode of life." Ibid., 244.

37. Kipling, 78. Not all Americans were convinced of the worthlessness of Indians. Kipling reported the following conversation with a cavalry officer in Yellowstone: "'Only,' as he said ruefully, 'there is no frontier these days, and all our Indian wars are nearly over. Those beautiful beasts will die out, and nobody will ever know what splendid cavalry they can make.'" Ibid., 98–99.

38. Griffin, 165. The worst extermination of native peoples occurred in California, where between 1848 and 1880 whites killed some 4,500 Indians. Civilians, rather than soldiers, did most of the killing. See Richard White, *"It's Your Misfortune and None of My Own": A History of the American West* (Norman: University of Oklahoma Press, 1991), 338–340.

39. Quoted in Philip Weeks, *Farewell, My Nation: The American Indian and the United States, 1820–1890* (Arlington Heights, IL: Harlan Davidson, 1990), 143. John Campbell Argyll spent an evening with Grant and other dignitaries in 1866 in which Grant told the company that problems with the Indians were directly related to the bad faith toward Indians by whites. John Campbell Argyll, *A Trip to the Tropics and Home Through America* (London: Hurst and Blackett, 1867), 250. General Philip H. Sheridan, who was charged by his commander William T. Sherman to subdue the Plains tribes, reportedly responded to the Comanche chief Tosawi's insistence that he was a good Indian by saying, "The only good Indians I ever saw were dead." Sheridan denied making such a statement, but a witness who was present recorded the remark. Weeks, 147, 148. The Savage Company advertised that its rifles made "Bad Indians Good." Lee Kennett and James LaVerne Anderson, *The Gun in America: The Origins of a National Dilemma* (Westport, CN: Greenwood Press, 1975), 136.

40. Dilke, 85.

41. Charles E. Rosenberg, *The Cholera Years: The United States in 1832, 1849, and 1866* (Chicago: University of Chicago Press, 1987), 115.

42. David Macrae, *The Americans at Home* [1870] (New York: E. P. Dutton, 1952), 429. One who made the extinction of Indians his life's work was "Comanche Bill," whom Isabella Bird met near South Pass. She was struck by "the number of weapons he carried. Besides a rifle laid across his saddle and a pair of pistols in the holsters, he carried two revolvers and a knife in his belt and a carbine slung behind him." She later found out that he was renowned as "the greatest Indian exterminator on the frontier—a man whose father and family fell in a massacre at Spirit Lake by the hands of Indians, who carried away his sister, then a child of eleven. His life has since been mainly devoted to a search for this child, and to killing Indians wherever he can find them." Bird, 173.

43. The United States had a population of about 40 million in 1872, while the Indian population from the Great Plains to the Pacific was under 239,000. See Weeks, 118.

44. Beatrice Webb, *Beatrice Webb's American Diary* (Madison: University of Wisconsin Press, 1963), 44.

45. Dan Flores, "Bison Ecology and Bison Diplomacy on the Southern Plains," in *Major Problems in the History of the American West*, ed. Clyde A. Milner, et al. (Boston: Houghton Mifflin, 1997), 110–111. Anne F. Hyde notes that "the region was probably being overhunted anyway, but when this was combined with an intense drought beginning in 1845, it spelled disaster for the Great Plains trade world. Hunger, and then disease, and then warfare stalked the people." Anne F. Hyde, *Empires, Nations, and Families: A History of the North American West, 1800–1860* (Lincoln: University of Nebraska Press, 2011), 344.

46. Yellow Wolf quoted in *Our Hearts Fell to the Ground: Plains Indian Views of How the West Was Lost*, ed. Colin G. Calloway (Boston: Bedford Books, 1996) 122.

47. Anne F. Hyde, "Round Pegs in Square Holes: The Rocky Mountains and Extractive Industry," in *Many Wests: Place, Culture, & Regional Identity*, ed. David M. Wrobel and Michael C. Steiner (Lawrence: University Press of Kansas, 1997), 99.

48. See Kennett and Anderson, 118–119. Gore's party moved on to the Big Horn mountains to shoot more game, but Indians attacked them and ran off with their horses and trophies. Gore and company were forced to walk 150 miles back to Laramie. See William F. Cody, "Famous Hunting Parties of the Plains," *The Cosmopolitan* 17, no. 2 (June 1894), 132.

49. See Peter Pagnamenta, *Prairie Fever: British Aristocrats in the American West, 1830–1890* (New York: W. W. Norton, 2012), 106.

50. Cody, "Famous Hunting Parties," 137–140.

51. Anne Farrar Hyde, *An American Vision: Far Western Landscape and National Culture, 1820–1920* (New York: New York University Press, 1990), 132.

52. Weeks, 162.

53. Ibid., 164.

54. *Reader's Encyclopedia of the American West*, s.v. "Buffalo," ed. Howard R. Lamar (New York: Thomas Y. Crowell, 1977), 136.

55. Quoted in David T. Courtwright, *Violent Land: Single Men and Social Disorder from the Frontier to the Inner City* (Cambridge, MA: Harvard University Press, 1996), 124.

56. *Our Hearts Fell to the Ground*, 123.

57. See Henry M. Stanley, *My Early Travels and Adventures in America* [1895] (Lincoln: University of Nebraska Press, 1982), 202.

58. Satanta quoted by Stanley, 249.

59. Ten Bears quoted by Stanley, 253.

60. Sherman quoted by Stanley, 210, 211. In October 1867, the Kiowas, Comanches, Apaches, Arapahos, and some Cheyennes signed the Treaty of Medicine Lodge. In 1868, the Sioux signed the Treaty of Fort Laramie. *Our Hearts Fell to the Ground*, 112, 121. In an 1868 letter to subordinate General W. B. Hazen, Sherman noted that Indians needed to be removed because "the co-existence of two races such as ours and the Indian in the same district of country is a simple impossibility, without a constant state of war." Sherman quoted in Colonel George Ward Nichols, "The Indian: What We Should Do with Him," *Harper's* 40 (April 1870), 735. Élisée Reclus summarized the grim options for Indians as "death or exile." Élisée Reclus, *The Earth and its Inhabitants. North America: v. 3, the United States* (New York: D. Appleton and Co., 1893), 452.

61. Stanley, 50, 51.

62. Ibid., 155–156. Thompson went back to England, and displayed his scalp in a carnival. Eventually, he contributed the scalp to the Omaha Public Library, where it now resides. See Tony Perrottet, "Lords of the Prairie," *New York Times*, June 24, 2012.

63. See also *Harper's* 17 (May 1873), 416.

64. Wyndham-Quin, 4.

65. Ibid., 114. Americans with knowledge of the situation, such as Colonel George Ward Nichols, agreed. Indeed, Nichols emphasized how "the Indian was wronged and

cheated in every way" by the white man. Still, Nichols placed much of the blame on the perverse nature of the Indian himself:

Neither by peaceful means nor by force of arms has he succumbed to the influences of civilization. Industry and frugal habits are foreign to his nature. He hates subjection to law; he despises thrift and order. Indians should be supplied with the necessities in return for peaceful relations, according to Nichols, but they should understand that "the hand that feeds can, and if need be will, strike." It was, he said, "'the iron fingers in a velvet glove.'" Nichols, 733, 732, 739.

66. Gillmore, 5, 329. Gillmore will make friends with an Indian woman and will travel with her for many days. Gillmore described her as one "who could live alone upon her own resources; who could handle a rifle or set beaver-traps, and unquestionably belonged to that strong-minded type for which I had always entertained the highest respect." Ibid., 68–69.

67. John Mortimer Murphy, *Rambles in North-Western America, from the Pacific Ocean to the Rocky Mountains* (London: Chapman and Hall, 1879), 286–287.

68. Bird, 184, 6.

69. Ibid., 184.

70. Lady Duffus Hardy, 26.

71. Rae, 217; Bell, lix.

72. Alexandra Gripenberg, *A Half Year in the New World: Miscellaneous Sketches of Travel in the United States* [1889], trans. and ed. Ernest J. Moyne (Newark: University of Delaware Press, 1954), 115, 116, 117.

73. Dilke, 88.

74. Anonymous, "The Antagonism of Race and Colour; or, White, Red, Black, and Yellow in America," *Blackwood's Edinburgh Magazine* 653, no. 107 (March 1870), 315.

75. Patrick Brantlinger, *Dark Vanishings: Discourse on the Extinction of Primitive Races, 1800–1930* (Ithaca: Cornell University Press, 2003), 6.

76. Quoted in Michael Fellman, *Citizen Sherman: A Life of William Tecumseh Sherman* (New York: Random House, 1995), 263.

77. Theodora Guest, *A Round Trip in North America* (London: Edward Stanford, 1895), 86.

78. Russell, v. 2, 78.

79. Bryce, v. 2, 782.

80. Stanley, 93.

81. Bryce, v. 2, 783. Paul de Rousiers took note of "the ease with which workmen of every industry in the West change their trade; so many ways are open to them, that they never definitely decide in favor of one or the other." Paul de Rousiers, *American Life*, trans. A. J. Herbertson (New York: Firmin-Didot, 1892), 149. R. W. Dale observed that "a judge who loses his seat on the bench will go out west and buy a farm, or he will start a manufactory in New England, or become manager of a bank." R. W. Dale, "Impressions of America," pt. 2, *Eclectic Magazine* 28, no. 2 (New Series, August 1878), 146. Baron Hübner observed of the American that he is "one day a butcher, or a waiter at an inn; to-morrow a banker; then go back to his first starting-point, to become in a year or two general of militia, a lawyer, or a minister of some religious congregation." Hübner, 63.

82. Quoted in Horace Annesley Vachell, *Life and Sport on the Pacific Slope* (New York: Dodd, Mead and Co., 1901), 133.

83. Bell, 240–241. One traveler commented that the American "is ready to be a lawyer, an official, a schoolmaster, a newspaper editor, a railway director, or to take up half a hundred other trades at a moment's notice; and it is hard if you cannot find some interests in common with so versatile an actor." Anonymous, "Some Remarks on Travelling in America," *The Cornhill Magazine* 19 (March 1869), 328.

84. Baille-Grohman, 53.

85. Vachell, 43.

86. Wyndham-Quin, *Great Divide*, 53–54.

87. Bird, 54.

88. Isabelle Randall, *A Lady's Ranche Life in Montana* (London: W. H. Allen & Co., 1887), 125–126.

89. Lady Duffus Hardy, 156.

90. Louis S. Warren, *Buffalo Bill's America: William Cody and the Wild West Show* (New York: Alfred A. Knopf, 2005), ix.

91. William F. Cody, *Story of the Wild West and Camp-Fire Chats by Buffalo Bill (Hon. W. F. Cody), A Full and Complete History of the Renowned Pioneer Quartette, Boon, Crockett, Carson and Buffalo Bill* [1888] (Freeport, NY: Books for Libraries Press, 1970), 501.

92. Ibid., 507–511.

93. Leroy Ashby, *With Amusement for All: A History of American Popular Culture Since 1830* (Lexington: University Press of Kentucky, 2006), 81.

94. Joy S. Kasson, *Buffalo Bill's Wild West: Celebrity, Memory, and Popular History* (New York: Hill and Wang, 2000), 17.

95. Cody, *Story of the Wild West*, 620.

96. Ibid., 625. See also Cody, "Famous Hunting Parties," 140–141.

97. Cody, *Story of the Wild West*, 640.

98. The origins of Cody's Wild West Show can be traced to North Platte, Nebraska. In 1882, the citizens of that town organized a Fourth of July celebration that featured an exhibition of cowboy skills, including roping, riding, and shooting. Cody had a ranch in the vicinity, and was appointed Grand Marshal. See, Henry Nash Smith, *Virgin Land: The American West as Symbol and Myth* (Cambridge, MA: Harvard University Press, 1950), 110.

99. Wilde said, "Better the Far West with its grizzly bears and its untamed cow-boys, its free open-air life and its free open-air manners, its boundless prairie and its boundless mendacity! This is what Buffalo Bill is going to bring to London; and we have no doubt that London will fully appreciate his show." Oscar Wilde, "Americans in London," in Oscar Wilde, *The Essays of Oscar Wilde* [1916], ed. Albert & Charles Boni (Bonibooks, 1935), 198. Irving quoted in Kasson, 78.

100. Queen Victoria quoted in Kasson, 81. The Sioux Black Elk also described meeting Victoria, whom he called "Grandmother England": "She was little but fat and we liked her, because she was good to us. After we had danced, she spoke to us. She said something like this: 'I am sixty-seven years old. All over the world I have seen all kinds of people; but to-day I have seen the best-looking people I know. If you belonged to me, I would not let them take you around in a show like this.' She said other good things too, and then she said we must come to see her, because she had come to see us. She shook hands with all of us. Her hand was very little and soft. We gave a big cheer for her, and then the shining wagons came in and she got into one of them and they all went away." *Black Elk Speaks: Being the Life Story of a Holy Man of the Oglala Sioux*, as told through John G. Neihardt [1932] (Lincoln: University of Nebraska Press, 1988), 221.

101. They were the King of Denmark, the King of Saxony, the King and Queen of the Belgians, and the King of Greece. Other royal personages attending the show included the Crown Prince of Austria, the Prince and Princess of Saxe-Meiningen, the Crown Prince and Princess of Germany, the Crown Prince of Sweden and Norway, Princess Victoria of Prussia, the Duke of Sparta, the Grand Duke Michael of Russia, Prince George of Greece, and Prince Louis of Baden. Cody, *Story of the Wild West*, 742.

102. Warren, 286.

103. Cody, *Story of the Wild West*, 735–737. Cody also quotes a London *Times* editorial that connected the establishment of a Court of Arbitration between Britain and America to the Wild West Show. "All London contributed to his triumph, and now the close of his show is selected as the occasion for promoting a great international movement

with Mr. Bright, Lord Granville, Lord Wolseley, and Lord Lorne for its sponsors. Colonel Cody can achieve no greater triumph than this." Quoted in Cody, *Story of the Wild West*, 748.

104. Warren, 286–287.
105. Kasson, 77.
106. Quoted in Cody, *Story of the Wild West*, 748. Louis S. Warren believes that show's royal patronage also helped to salve America's "cultural inferiority complex." Warren, 292.
107. James Fullarton Muirhead, *The Land of Contrasts: A Briton's View of his American Kin* (London: Lamson, Wolffe and Co., 1898), 97, 98.
108. Warren, 317, 306.
109. Kasson, 79.
110. Courtwright, 104.
111. Ashby, 83.
112. Black Elk's description of the battle with Custer's troops includes the following: "When we got farther up the hill, I could see the soldiers. They were off their horses, holding them by the bridles. They were ready for us and were shooting. Our people were all around the hill on every side by this time … Then we all went up, and it got dark with dust and smoke. I could see warriors flying all around me like shadows, and the noise of all those hoofs and guns and cries was so loud it seemed quiet in there and the voices seemed to be on top of the cloud. It was like a bad dream." *Black Elk Speaks*, 115–116.
113. Stanley, 86.
114. Ibid., 7.
115. George Ward Nichols published a story on Hickok in the February 1867 issue of *Harper's* in which he also included Hickok's claim that he had killed "hundreds of men." He was widely criticized by the press for including such inaccuracies.
116. Stanley, 97.
117. Ibid., 141. Custer said of Hickok that "on foot or on horseback he was one of the most perfect types of physical manhood I ever saw. His manner was entirely free from all bluster and bravado. He never spoke of himself unless requested to do so. His influence among the frontiersmen was unbounded; his word was law." Quoted in Daniel J. Boorstin, *The Americans: The Democratic Experience* (New York: Random House, 1973), 36.
118. William Saunders, *Through the Light Continent, or, The United States in 1877–78* [1879] (New York: Arno Press, 1974), 133.
119. Quoted in Athearn, 155.
120. Vachell, 177.
121. Pagnamenta, 195–229.
122. Gillmore, 309.
123. Bird, 79.
124. Stanley, 84; Dixon, 120.
125. Bell, 410.
126. Bell, 251, 252.
127. Gillmore, 311; William Francis Butler, *The Great Lone Land: A Narrative of Travel and Adventure in the North-West of America* [1872] (Rutland, VT: Charles E. Tuttle, 1968), 102.
128. See Patricia Nelson Limerick, *The Legacy of Conquest: The Unbroken Past of the American West* (New York: W. W. Norton, 1988), 126.
129. Quoted in Pagnamenta, 186.
130. C. F. Cumming, "Locusts and Farmers of America," *The Nineteenth Century* 17, no. 95 (January 1885), 133.
131. Faithfull, 256.
132. Quoted in Jeff Guinn, *The Last Gunfight: The Real Story of the Shootout at the O.K. Corral—and How It Changed the American West* (New York: Simon and Schuster, 2011), 17–18.

133. Quoted in Richard White, *Railroaded: The Transcontinentals and the Making of Modern America* (New York: W. W. Norton, 2011), 476.
134. Baille-Grohman, 321.
135. Vachell, 93.
136. Baille-Grohman, 363. Baille-Grohman added that "that marked feature of America, social equality, which, while it has often a way of expressing itself in a very extravagant and disagreeable fashion, is undoubtedly a main factor in the unusually rapid growth of the Great West, must never be forgotten by the English settler." Ibid., 364.
137. Randall, 71.
138. Quoted in Pagnamenta, 258.
139. Vachell, 94. Vachell emphasized that the person looking for trouble in the West could easily find it, but he who watched his mouth and minded his own business "is as safe in the wildest parts of the West as he would be in London—perhaps safer." Ibid., 101. What could happen if the foreign proprietor of a ranch failed to keep a tight control of his business is illustrated by the experiences of Lillie Langtry, who in 1888 bought a ranch in Lake County, California. Langtry noted that "the keyword of that ranch was 'Liberty,' and my cowboys, of every nationality, including a Chinese, walked in and out of my house in search of whatever they needed. Redskins from the reservation rode over my land at will from dawn to sunset, galloping about with rifles slung on their backs, shooting the game and poaching the trout. Some of the neighbouring ranchers, too, out of the kindness of their hearts, shot my deer (out of season), and presented me with them in token of welcome. Squatters annexed cows clearly marked with the brand of the ranch, in fact it was communism at its best." Lillie Langtry, *The Days I Knew* (New York: George H. Doran, 1925), 205–206.
140. Anonymous, "Ranche Life in the Far West," *MacMillan's Magazine* 48 (August 1883), 294.
141. Anonymous, "Ranche Life in the Far West," 295.
142. William H. Davies, *The Autobiography of a Super-Tramp* (New York: Alfred A. Knopf, 1917), 171.
143. Ibid., 189–190.
144. Charles C. Osborne, "Impressions of Klondike," pts. 3 and 4, *MacMillan's Magazine* 83 (November 1900), 49.
145. Ibid., 50.
146. Courtwright, 58.
147. Randall, 117.
148. Bryce, v. 2, 784; Faithfull, 341. William Hepworth Dixon claimed that in regards to horse stealing, "public opinion is far more strict than it is with respect to murder." Dixon, 103.
149. Quoted in Courtwright, 79, 133.
150. Iza Duffus Hardy, 242, 243. Henry Sienkiewicz also emphasized the perfect safety of the woman in America: "a hundred fists and revolvers will threaten the impertinent fellow who dares to offend her in any manner whatsoever." Sienkiewicz, 28. Nele Loring claimed that cowboys were soft-spoken because of the requirements of their job: "'Your genuine cowboy never shouts at his cattle. It is permissible to curse cattle, but this should be done in a conversational tone of voice, and you must depend for your effect, not upon noise, but upon a nice taste in profanity.'" Quoted in Athearn, 111.
151. Dixon, 100.
152. Courtwright, 150.
153. Bates, v. 2, 206.
154. Baille-Grohman noted that "many a time have I watched, with curiosity mingled with amusement, the behaviour of these uncouth men of the wilderness when in white woman's presence. The rough joke, the threatened oath, the careless fling of some saucy answer to a fellow craftsman, are hushed—stayed as abruptly as could the

hand, that in a child-like fashion is brought up to the mouth, thrust back the half-uttered jest, or the yet unpronounced name of the Deity." Baille-Grohman, 382. In the 1830s, Tocqueville noted that in the presence of women, the American man "minds his speech lest the women be obliged to listen to offensive language. In America, girls take long trips by themselves, without fear." Alexis de Tocqueville, *Democracy in America* [1835], trans. Arthur Goldhammer (New York: Library of America, 2004), 707.

155. Bird, 34. Bird claimed that, "Womanly dignity and manly respect for women are the salt of society in this wild West." Ibid., 18. Alexandra Gripenberg described American men as "paragons of neatness" in the presence of ladies, but when they were by themselves they "leaned back in their beloved rocking chairs, chewing tobacco and enjoying a moment of rest in their shirt sleeves." Gripenberg, 90–91.

156. Stanley, 106.

157. See Limerick, 49–52 and Courtwright 96, 133.

158. Dilke, 78. There were large parts of Western Europe in the mid-nineteenth century that also had not been touched by civilization. Speaking of Europe's most populous country, France, Graham Robb observed that, "As late as 1867, after more than a century of agricultural improvements, a national census estimated that 43 per cent of land that could be cultivated was 'dominated by the forces of nature': grasslands, forests and moors. Wolves were still a threat in several central regions, including the Dordogne, at the end of the nineteenth century." Graham Robb, *The Discovery of France: A Historical Geography from the Revolution to the First World War* (New York: W. W. Norton, 2007), 10.

159. Dixon, 42.

160. Dilke, 77. In 1868 F. Barham Zincke noted that the valley along the Platte "was strewed for hundreds of miles with the bones of the buffalo." Zincke, 208. The Europeans who came to the West as sportsmen and hunters generally condemned the wanton destruction of wildlife. Parker Gillmore, hunter and former British military officer, said that "the veteran soldier looks back with horror on the scenes which result from his own handywork. In same manner does the experienced hunter detest uselessly to sacrifice animal life." Gillmore, 333.

161. Faithfull, 212.

162. Baille-Grohman, 150–151. The hunter Parker Gillmore found that in isolated parts of the American wilderness "the mountain hares, instead of hurrying to place such a distance between me and them as would render them safe, would stop and gaze earnestly at me," allowing Gillmore to approach so close "that I might almost have captured them with the hand." "Man being a rare intruder on their solitudes," said Gillmore, "they exhibit the most remarkable confidence in his good intentions." Gillmore, 259.

163. Bird, 225.

164. Zincke, 84.

165. J. Valerie Fifer, *American Progress: The Growth of the Transport, Tourist, and Information Industries in the Nineteenth-Century West* (Chester, CN: Globe Pequot Press, 1988), 191.

166. Rae, 79.

167. Wyndham-Quin, *Great Divide*, 10.

168. Windham Wyndham-Quin, "A Colorado Sketch," *The Nineteenth Century*, 17, no. 43 (September 1880), 456.

169. See W. Henry Barneby, *Life and Labor in the Far, Far West: Being Notes of a Tour in the Western States, British Columbia, Manitoba, and the North-West Territory* (London: Cassell & Co., 1884), 42, and Phil Robinson, *Sinners and Saints: A Tour Across the States, and Round Them: with Three Months Among the Mormons* (Boston: Roberts Brothers, 1883), 297.

170. Boddam-Whetham, 212.

171. Robert Louis Stevenson, "The Silverado Squatters," in *From Scotland to Silverado* [1892] (Cambridge, MA: Belknap Press, 1966), 201.

172. Russell, v. 2, 27, 28.

173. Often these fires consumed the trees on other people's properties, but because these trees were regarded as "useless lumber," "no one thinks of complaining." Barneby, 72. In 1868, F. Barham Zincke took note of the devastation by fire of a great deal of the forests in the Rockies. "The fire," said Zincke, "generally occurs through the carelessness of persons who are camping out." Zincke, 206. J. J. Aubertin also noted that smoke from "frequent" and "extensive" forest fires obscured the air near Tacoma in 1886. Aubertin, 105.

174. Thomas Hughes, "A Week in the West," pt. 4, *MacMillan's Magazine* 25 (January 1872), 156.

175. Ibid., 158–159.

176. Saunders, 40.

177. Courtwright, 126.

178. Sienkiewicz, 78.

179. Robinson, 31. Lee Kennett and James LaVerne Anderson note that by the end of the nineteenth century, "this spirit of destruction brought the virtual extermination of the passenger pigeon, trumpeter swan, condor, whooping crane, ivory-billed woodpecker, some species of duck, as well as the buffalo." Kennett and Anderson, 120.

180. Kipling, 104. When she was in Yosemite in the 1880s, Lillie Langtry said that "on a medium-sized tree I nailed a silver tablet bearing my name." Langtry, 189.

181. Hübner, 169.

182. Gripenberg, 136.

183. Orvar Löfgren, *On Holiday: A History of Vacationing* (Berkeley: University of California Press, 1999), 277.

184. Fifer, 186.

185. Ibid., 301–306. One of Cook's popular innovations was the traveler's check. Ibid., 206.

186. See Cindy S. Aron, *Working at Play: A History of Vacations in the United States* (New York: Oxford University Press, 1999), 139; A. K. Sandoval-Strausz, *Hotel: An American History* (New Haven: Yale University Press, 2007), 112. See also Bates, v. 2, 77.

187. Colorado Springs resorts included Manitou House, The Cliff House, the Manitou Park Hotel, and The Mansions. Fifer, 257, 302.

188. See Hyde, *An American Vision*, 147–153; Kingsley quoted in Fifer, 260.

189. Athearn, 6. Adding a discordant note to the high-toned atmosphere were the tent encampments of the poor, who sought out the curative powers of the region's waters but who could not afford luxury accommodations. See Russell, v. 2, 87–88.

190. Earl S. Pomeroy, *In Search of the Golden West: The Tourist in Western America* (New York: Knopf, 1957), 21.

191. Sandoval-Strausz, 119. The Great Northern Railroad was given the concession to build the hotel at Yellowstone. See Schlereth, 217. E. Catherine Bates observed in the mid-1880s that "a few years ago the park was overrun by the Indians, but they have been successfully driven away now, only making occasional raids from the north-east corner, and then with a view to theft." Bates, v. 2, 189. Bates was also surprised to discover that that "*no hunting is allowed* in the park, and notices to that effect greet you at every turn" [original emphasis]. Ibid., v. 2, 188. Even as the West was becoming a premier tourist destination, Americans were remarkably slow to improve their roads. During her two-week stay in Yosemite in the mid-1880s, Bates noted that there were three stage coach accidents, two of which were severe. Ibid., v. 2, 91.

192. See Courtwright, 112. Louis S. Warren notes that Custer's Seventh Cavalry was one-third Irish, with the rest made up of Italians, Germans, and others. Warren, 97.

193. White, *"It's Your Misfortune,"* 261.

194. Pagnamenta, 232–234. The antecedents of the modern cattle industry were in the antebellum South, where there was extensive open-range herding of both cattle and hogs. Grady McWhiney cites an 1850 federal study that estimated that in one two-hundred-square-mile area of the backwoods South, a million cows per annum were

being raised for market. Grady McWhiney, *Cracker Culture: Celtic Ways in the Old South* (Tuscaloosa: University of Alabama Press, 1988), 55.

195. Richard W. Slatta, *Cowboys of the Americas* (New Haven: Yale University Press, 1990), 221.
196. See Pagnamenta, 246–261; Pomeroy, 77–79; Hyde, "Round Pegs," 97.
197. See White, *Railroaded*, 472–473; Pagnamenta, 259.
198. Pagnamenta, 279–280; David Lavender, *The Great West* (Boston: Houghton Mifflin, 1965), 424.
199. Limerick, 99–100.
200. Hübner, 144; Bell, 433.
201. White, *Railroaded*, 233.
202. Boddam-Whetham, 89.
203. Thomson quoted in Hyde, "Round Pegs," 104.
204. Zincke, 242. Isabella Bird also condemned mining in Colorado "with all its destruction and devastation, its digging, burrowing, gulching, and sluicing." Bird, 193.
205. Webb, 125.
206. Russell, v. 2, 95.
207. Hyde, "Round Pegs," 104.
208. See Stanley, 182–183.
209. Bates, v. 2, 205.
210. See Carl Abbott, *How Cities Won the West: Four Centuries of Urban Change in Western North America* (Albuquerque: University of New Mexico Press, 2008), 105.
211. White, *Railroaded*, 311. See also White, *"It's Your Misfortune,"* 342.
212. See White, *"It's Your Misfortune,"* 346–350.
213. Turner predicted that these "energies of expansion" would be pushed into the international realm. Frederick Jackson Turner, "The Problem of the West," *Atlantic Monthly* 78, no. 467 (September 1896), 296.
214. John Muir, "The American Forests," *Atlantic Monthly* 80, no. 478 (August 1897), 157.
215. "The trail of this restless, nervous, bustling, mammon-worship age is over all; the spirit which animates Wall Street asserts itself in the wild canyons of the Rocky Mountains." Faithfull, 154.
216. A. Maurice Low, *The American People: A Study in National Psychology*, v. 2 (Boston: Houghton Mifflin, 1909), 504.
217. Bryce, v. 2, 821. William T. Sherman observed in 1879 that, "People are fast filling up the Western Plains, and soon we shall have no Buffalo, no Elk or Bear, and it may be no Indians. I think in our new National Museum we will have to collect samples of them for preservation to show our children." Quoted in Fellman, 276.

AFTERWORD

Some 150 years have passed since the end of the Civil War, and life in America—and on the rest of the planet—has profoundly changed. Two brutal world wars have totally revolutionized both geopolitics and the technological world. Televisions, jet airplanes, nuclear weapons, satellites, and computers are among the commonplaces of twenty-first century society of which there was no inkling in 1865. Yet, it can be argued that technologies do not define us as a people today any more than steam power or the telegraph defined Americans of the nineteenth century. What is important is in the way we approach life, and Americans of the nineteenth century would find much that they would recognize in modern American life.

Gun ownership is still much more prominent in America than it is in Europe, with many Americans seeing gun ownership as a civil liberty which, as one writer observed, is "something that Europeans struggle to understand." The number of Americans with concealed weapons permits has increased from five million in 2008, to around seven million in 2011, and two-thirds of murders in the United States involve guns (compared to 10 percent in Britain). Justifiably garnering the most public attention are the spectacular mass murders that occasionally take place in the United States, such as the 2012 shootings in Aurora, Colorado, and the horrific killing of twenty-six (twenty school children and six teachers) in Newtown, Connecticut. But strict gun control laws in Europe did not prevent Anders Breivik from shooting sixty-nine people dead in Norway, nor did they prevent the killings in Dunblane in 1996 or Cumbria in 2010. The difference is that gun laws, such as the law the British Parliament passed in 1997 that outlawed the private ownership of nearly all handguns, have the overwhelming support of the public in Europe, while lobbying groups such as the National Rifle Association have played on deep-rooted American fears of an all-powerful central government oppressing an unarmed citizenry to defeat such measures in the United States. While the statistics are sobering—according to the Congressional Research Service, in 2007 there were 294 million guns in the country (roughly one gun for every man, woman and child in the United States)—the number of American households that have guns has steadily declined since the 1970s. Evidence further suggests that the Americans that already have guns are the ones who keep buying them, and that time is not on the side of the gun lobby.[1]

At this point, the leadership of the NRA and other advocates of permissive gun laws have a lot to answer for. A popular fallback position of gun rights organizations is that if a larger number of citizens carried guns, they would quickly be able to deal with an armed criminal and thus reduce death and injury to innocent bystanders. While this is an argument that only the simple or the shameless would make, there is no lack of either in this society, and one gun advocate had the astonishing nerve to crawl out of the gutter and make this claim in the immediate aftermath of the Newtown slayings.[2] In fact, a wider dissemination of firearms promises to increase the deadly toll simply because accuracy in armed confrontations is most often conspicuous by its absence. In contemporaneous New York City, for instance, police officers are extensively trained in the use of firearms, yet the accuracy rate for New York police using deadly force in the line of duty is 34 percent. With two-thirds of bullets shot from the guns of these highly trained individuals not finding their target, one can only speculate on what the dismal accuracy rate from America's weekend warriors might be.[3] Today, the two sides of the gun debate seem to be polarized between the extreme views of no gun restrictions versus no guns. But American views on guns have constantly shifted with the times, and as Adam Winkler emphasizes, "gun rights and gun control are not only compatible; they have lived together since the birth of America."[4]

Patriotism is still an important element in American society and especially in American politics where, as one person has observed, "voters can be vindictive toward anyone who dares criticize the country and, implicitly, the people."[5] In short, the nettlesome insistence on the superiority of all things American is as much a feature of the United States today as it was in the nineteenth century. The number of American flags on display in both public and private places is striking because there are no similar displays anywhere in Europe. Perhaps patriotism matters more to Americans because historically we have struggled to come to grips with what it means to be a citizen of the United States. While Europeans have found it easier to identify themselves as a people because of a shared race, national origin, or religion, Americans have none of these things in common. But what we do have is less concrete but perhaps more profound: a shared set of ideas from which we can take inspiration and of which we are rightfully proud. As G. K. Chesterton observed when he visited the United States in 1921, "America is the only nation in the world that is founded on a creed."[6] Making this vision a reality has been a struggle from the earliest colonial days, and too often Europeans have nurtured a smug superiority as they have watched the United States labor to assimilate a diverse population. But the current problems that European nations have had in assimilating their own immigrant populations should at least provide some perspective on an ordeal that has always been part of American life.

The rise of far-right anti-immigrant groups in Europe, and the cultural strains and even violence between immigrants and native populations are extremely troubling. Speaking of the situation in Holland, political scientist Henk Overbeek claims that, "The taboos are gone, and now you're suspect if you say anything positive about multiculturalism." Overbeek observes that while American citizenship is never questioned once it's granted, "in Europe it's never quite established, no matter how long you've been here. Here it's still, 'When did you get here, and when are you going back?'"[7] In a recent article, *The Economist* also noted the difficulty that European nations were having in bringing into the mainstream groups such as the Bangladeshis, Pakistanis, North Africans, and Turks, and concluded that "the United States, with its immigrant folklore and self-improvement ethos, seems to manage integration better than Europe does."[8] A recent survey by the Organization for Economic Co-operation and Development, a group made up of the thirty-four wealthiest nations, seems to indicate that hostility toward outsiders is indeed less prominent in the United States than elsewehere.[9]

The American energy and optimism that so many European travelers commented on in the nineteenth century also seems to have persisted into the twenty-first century. For example, during a recent visit to America, renowned Italian architect Renzo Piano was asked to comment on "the most surprising difference between building in Europe and in the U.S." He responded that it was, "The energy and optimism. I love Europe, I'm Italian, I live in Paris. But cities in Europe almost lack energy. This country is young. It's open."[10] These views are echoed by British Labour Leader Ed Miliband, who spent large amounts of time in America beginning as a child when his father was a visiting professor in the United States. At the age of eighteen, before entering Oxford, Miliband was an intern at *The Nation* and for *The MacNeil/Lehrer Newshour*, and in 2002 he took a sixteen-month sabbatical from his job as an adviser to Gordon Brown to teach a course at Harvard. In contrast to Britain, says Miliband, America is less of a "closed society," and "less of a class-bound country." And like Piano, Miliband admires "the sense of optimism and the sense of possibility" that he finds in the United States.[11] Finally, Scottish-born Craig Ferguson, who came to the United States and found great success with the *Late Late Show* (and then became an American citizen), recently returned to Scotland to do a series of shows. When Ferguson was interviewed by *New York Times* reporter Dave Itzkoff, Itzkoff observed that most Americans had formed their opinions of Scotland through either *Brigadoon* or *Trainspotting*. Ferguson replied that "my experience was 'Trainspotting.' And I went back and found a lot more 'Brigadoon.' I don't know if that's my age or I've developed a certain American optimism or what."[12]

Why should optimism be more characteristic of America than Europe? Searching for the roots of this attitude, Harold Bloom concluded that "the

American finds fault with nature, time, and history, but neither with God nor with herself or himself … it keeps us a republic of hope."[13] Half of Americans view religion as "*very* important in their lives," compared with 22 percent in Spain, 21 percent in Germany, 17 percent in Britain, and 13 percent in France.[14] Summing it up, British historian Niall Ferguson observes that "Europeans these days work a whole lot less than their American counterparts. And they don't only work less. They pray less."[15]

One thing that bewilders Americans about Europeans is their abbreviated work week. In 2005, the French were working 28 percent fewer hours than Americans and the Germans 25 percent fewer hours. A recent poll confirms that Parisian workers, followed by workers in Lyon and Copenhagen, enjoy the shortest work hours on the planet.[16] The European would argue that this frees up more time for the important things in life, but for Americans the overwhelming question is: How do they get anything done? This is another area of difference between Europeans and Americans in which economic and cultural elements become hopelessly entangled. On the cultural side, Max Weber and others have suggested links between Protestantism and capitalism, with both religion and a belief in a capitalistic system more prevalent in America today than they are in Europe.[17] This conjunction of capitalism and religion has led to considerable confusion, especially in France, as to the fundamental nature of the United States. As Denis Lecorne puts it, the French veer between the contradictory views that America is "either a godless nation dominated by the profit motive, or the very opposite: an intolerant Anglo-Protestant theocracy."[18]

Economically, the argument can be made that the differences between work hours in Europe and in America are of relatively recent origin. As James Surowiecki has noted, in 1970 the French worked 10 percent more hours than Americans. What has changed since then are higher tax rates in Europe (and therefore less incentive to work more hours), and the willingness of European labor unions to accept relatively stagnant wages in exchange for job security and increased vacation time. Lower-taxed Americans, however, spend more time on the job and less time at home, which means they must hire more people to do service jobs—jobs typically filled by young people, women, and immigrants. With fewer service sector jobs in Europe, unemployment among these groups is higher. As Surowiecki puts it, "voluntary leisure for some Europeans has helped lead to involuntary leisure for others."[19]

The divergence between Americans and Europeans can also be found in the confidence of Americans—and the skepticism of Europeans—that they can improve themselves economically. It is obvious that it is easier for a person *with* money to *get* money, but for centuries Americans have blithely ignored this economic fact of life. As one commentator put it, Americans seem to prefer "equality of opportunity rather than equality of outcome," even if that opportunity is less equal than they might like.[20] Historically, Europe presents a different case, and while it is difficult to know whether economic conditions there produced a fatalist mindset or vice versa, there is little doubt that European views of their own potential to accumulate wealth (and equally important, their views of the wealth of others) differ significantly from the American perspective. Contrasting Americans and Europeans in 1891, Hamilton Aïdé noted that American workers had "the well-founded hope of growing richer and rising in the social scale," and were therefore not "gnawed by envy and hatred of those born in another sphere, such as corrodes the peace of mechanics inoculated with socialistic doctrine in Europe."[21] How little things have changed. The French especially continue to nurture a considerable hostility toward the wealthy, and Socialist President Francoise Hollande has led the way, proclaiming, "I don't like the rich." He has proposed a 75 percent tax on upper incomes. As Parisian tax lawyer Vincent Grandil observes, "French people have an uncomfortable relationship with money. Here, someone who is a self-made man, creating jobs and ending up as a millionaire, is viewed with suspicion. This is a big cultural difference between France and the United States."[22]

Always, it seems, we return to class. Throughout American history, egalitarianism and the gospel of meritocracy has been the great lodestar that has guided the United States. Tocqueville himself proclaimed that the American insistence on equality was the convergence point of all his observations.[23] As historian Gordon S. Wood has noted, America has paid a steep price for creating a nation based on "common people with their common interests," including "its vulgarity, its materialism, its rootlessness, its anti-intellectualism." But Wood adds that "there is no denying the wonder of it and the real earthly benefits it brought to the hitherto neglected and despised masses of common laboring people."[24] For many Europeans, the possibility of ordinary humans rising in the hierarchy was a delusion that could only lead to disappointment. "How are men to be happy," asked Baron Hübner in 1878, "living in a narrow circle and constantly goaded on by the wish to be the equals of all the world? Their whole lives are a series of bitter deceptions, and aspirations which can never be realized."[25] There is little doubt that this class fatalism had a chilling effect on European ambition. George Augustus Sala was one of many European observers who took note of the expectation gap that existed in the nineteenth century between Britons and Americans. Sala found that the young English clerk "rarely cherishes the hope of being one day Her Majesty's Ambassador at Paris, Chief Secretary of State for the Home Department, or Governor of the Bank of England." The American clerk, however, could not look into the mirror without seeing "the features of a future President of the United States or of a Minister Plenipotentiary or Judge of the Supreme Court."[26] In *Britons View America*, historian Richard L. Rapson found that the single thing most commented on by nineteenth-century British travelers in America was egalitarianism. Rapson speculates that Britons might have exaggerated the opportunities that actually existed in America simply because "there was so little chance to rise, relatively speaking, for the British lower classes."[27]

Canadian writer Margaret Atwood claims that "America has always been different from Europe," and one of the most important areas of difference is in the maintenance of the European class hierarchy versus American social mobility.[28] Yassine Bellatar recently told *Le Monde* that "the Americans' 'strength' is that they put everyone on the same footing" and care more about results than pedigree. What concerns the French, however, is "'What is your degree?'" "'Where did you do your studies?'" "'Who is your father?'"[29] In Britain, the dominance of the established class system is reflected in widespread pessimism among those in the lower orders that they can better themselves. Today, the distribution of income in Britain and in the United States is about the same, with 5 percent of the population controlling over 30 percent of the wealth in both countries.[30] But confidence in the economic future diverges in roughly the same way as it did in the nineteenth century. Despite evidence cited by a number of observers that "inequality in the U.S., always high compared with that in other developed countries, is rising," 68 percent of Americans in 2011 said that "they have achieved or will achieve the American Dream" (this in the midst of the worst economic downturn since the Great Depression). In Britain, only about 40 percent believed that there were opportunities for economic or social advancement.[31]

Class, of course, is as much about social attitudes as it is about economics. One recent event in Britain that brought both aspects of class into sharp focus was the wedding of Prince William to the commoner Kate Middleton. Hoping for signs of gauche behavior from the middle-class parents of the bride, one British TV commentator staked out the hotel where they were staying and remarked that, "It's sometimes hard to tell who are Middletons and who are staff."[32] (Americans would say that that was to their credit.) *The Times* of London produced an even more hateful comment when it described Kate Middleton as the product of "shiny new money systematically raising a girl so perfectly to a prince's eye level that she is virtually indistinguishable from the real thing." The *Economist* added somewhat unnecessarily that, "Class shows up Britain at its worst."[33]

In France, the reaction to a much different incident brought up some of the same issues. When Dominque Strauss-Kahn, head of the International Monetary Fund and leading presidential candidate for the Socialists, was arrested in 2011 on charges that he sexually assaulted a chambermaid in New York, he was put in handcuffs by the police like any other suspect and, like other suspects, was subjected to the "perp walk" where he could be photographed by the press. Former French justice minister Elisabeth Guigou called Strauss-Kahn's ordeal "a brutality, a violence, of an incredible cruelty" and contrasted the American system of justice with the French, which is "more protective of individual rights." While it might seem to Americans that what is protected in France is the aristocracy's rights, at least this argument is in the realm of the reasonable. Other comments from the French have come perilously close to asserting that rank has its privileges and that Strauss-Kahn was merely claiming what was rightfully his. After all, the whole affair was merely a case of "*troussage de domestique,*" as Jean-Francoise Kahn put it, while Jack Lang commented that, "It's not like anybody died."[34]

Adding some perspective to this affair is Elaine Sciolino's recent book *La Seduction* (written before Strauss-Kahn's arrest) that proposes that seduction is simply the French style of negotiating life. Among the people that Sciolino interviewed was Alexandre Deschamps, a young physical therapist. Deschamps revealed that he would not hesitate to compliment a stranger on the Métro on her looks, nor would he hesitate to proffer the same comment to a colleague. As an example, Deschamps related an anecdote involving himself and a female physical therapist: "One day she asked me to give her a massage. So I said, 'Sure, but only if you're naked.' It was a normal joke." In a comment that perhaps Strauss-Kahn could appreciate, Deschamps observed, "I would be in prison if I had to work in the United States."[35]

The French seem genuinely baffled that the DSK affair has led to a renewal of "French bashing" in the United States, but American sensitivities to the faintest whiff of elitism and class privilege is an important element here. One of the few French commentators to have grasped the continuing importance of this to Americans is historian Max Gallo. While Gallo was disturbed that "a top-level figure is treated like a common criminal," he added that "it also manifests an egalitarianism in the American justice system that surprises us in France."[36]

The Strauss-Kahn story also pointed up more subtle cultural differences between Americans and Europeans. French reporters made their way to New York in droves, where they were easily indentifiable from their American counterparts by their better dress, their smoking, and their double kiss greetings. There were other differences as well. One French reporter cited the respect that American reporters gave the barricades put up by the police. "In France maybe the barrier would have been dropped on the ground," he said. "Here, you're more, how do you say it? *Civilisé.*" He was even more bemused by the sight of an American reporter helping a woman with a baby carriage down the steps. In an observation that might well have been made of Americans in the nineteenth century, the reporter from France declared, "That's American. That's not really French."[37]

Notes

1. "Arms and the Man," *Economist* 403, no. 8781 (April 21, 2012), 42; Matt Richtel, "New Fashion Wrinkle: Stylishly Hiding the Gun," *New York Times*, April 24, 2012; "Colorado's Dark Night," *Economist* 404, no. 8795, 12; Campbell Robertson, "Handgun Ban Tests a British Olympian," *New York Times*, August 1, 2012. There is also evidence that gun ownership breaks along party lines (about 25 percent of Democratic homes have guns compared to 60 percent of Republican households), and that persons in rural areas were more likely to own guns than persons in urban areas. Nate Silver, "Party Identity in a Gun Cabinet," *New York Times*, December 19, 2012.

2. Larry Pratt, executive director of Gun Owners of America, said, "Gun control supporters have the blood of little children on their hands. Federal and state laws combined to

ensure that no teacher, no administrator, no adult had a gun at the Newtown school where the children were murdered. This tragedy underscores the urgency of getting rid of gun bans in school zones." Pratt quoted in Charles M. Blow, "A Tragedy of Silence," *New York Times*, December 15, 2012.

3. See Michael Wilson, "After Bystanders Take Bullets, Questions on Police Protocol," *New York Times*, August 26, 2012.

4. Adam Winkler, *Gunfight: The Battle over the Right to Bear Arms in America* (New York: W.W. Norton, 2011), 12.

5. Scott Shane, "The Opiate of Exceptionalism," *New York Times*, October 21, 2012.

6. G. K. Chesterton, *What I Saw in America* [1922] in *The Collected Works of G. K. Chesterton*, v. 21 (San Francisco: Ignatius Press, 1990), 41. Chesterton added that "America, partly by original theory and partly by historical accident, does lie open to racial admixtures which most countries would think incongruous or comic." Ibid., 43.

7. Quoted in Steven Erlanger, "Amid Rise of Multiculturalism, Dutch Confront Their Questions of Identity," *New York Times*, August 14, 2011.

8. "Second Life," *Economist* 398, no. 8723 (March 5th–11th, 2011), 17.

9. The OECD found that to a significant degree Americans led all OECD member nations in "volunteering time, giving money, and helping strangers." Some 60 percent of Americans were involved in such activities, compared to the OECD average of 39 percent. "Society at a Glance—OECD Social Indicators," December 4, 2011, www.oecd.org/els/social/indicators/SAG.

10. Belinda Luscombe, "10 Questions," *Time*, July 4, 2011, 76.

11. John F. Burns, "A British Admirer of America Finds His Voice," *New York Times*, August 6, 2011.

12. Dave Itzkoff, "Never Too Late to Find His Brigadoon," *New York Times*, May 17, 2012.

13. Harold Bloom, *The American Religion: The Emergence of the Post-Christian Nation* (New York: Simon & Shuster, 1992), 260.

14. Pew Global Attitudes Project, "The American-Western Europe Values Gap," November 7, 2011, www.pewglobal.org, 8.

15. Ferguson quoted in Neil Genzlinger, "How the West Became the World's Alpha Culture," *New York Times*, May 22, 2012.

16. James Surowiecki, "No Work and No Play," *The New Yorker*, November 28, 2005, www.newyorker.com/archive. See also "Noway: Oslo Is Costliest City," *New York Times*, September 15, 2012. Drawing on 2010 data, Charles Siegel finds that Germany has shorter work hours than France, with Germans working 27 percent fewer hours than Americans. Charles Siegel, "Work Hours in Europe and America," January 15, 2012, preservenet.blogspot.com.

17. See Max Weber, *The Protestant Ethic and the Spirit of Capitalism*, trans. Talcott Parsons (London: G. Allen & Unwin, 1930) and Edmund S. Morgan, *The Puritan Dilemma, the Story of John Winthrop* (Boston: Little, Brown, 1958).

18. Denis Lecorne, *Religion in America: A Political History* (New York: Columbia University Press, 2011), xix. Among scholars who have tried to determine the basis of American national identity, Lecorne notes a split between those who identify "an Enlightenment narrative, based on a rational philosophy which excludes religion from the public sphere," and those who "are convinced that the nation is at its core religious and that government should support the free exercise of religion as far as possible." Lecorne holds out the possibility that a "faith-friendly secularism" will evolve. Ibid., 160. Canadian Margaret Atwood has also taken note of the contradictory assessments of American society: "Some have seen it as a dream world where you can be what you choose, others as a mirage that lures, exploits and disappoints. Some see it as a land of spiritual potential, others as a place of crass and vulgar materialism. Some see it as a mecca for creative entrepreneurs, others as a corporate oligarchy where the big eat the small and inventions helpful to the world are stifled. Others see it as the home of freedom of expression, others as a land of timorous conformity and mob-opinion

rule." Margaret Atwood, "Hello, Martians. Let Moby-Dick Explain," *New York Times*, April 29, 2012.

19. See Surowiecki.

20. "Lexington: Fat Cats and Corporate Jets," *The Economist* 400, no. 8741 (July 9, 2011), 32.

21. Hamilton Aïdé, "Social Aspects of American Life," *The Nineteenth Century* 29, no. 172 (June 1891), 890.

22. Liz Alderman, "A Plan for Higher Taxes Unsettles France's Wealthy," *New York Times*, August 8, 2012.

23. Alexis de Tocqueville, *Democracy in America* [1835], trans. Arthur Goldhammer (New York: Library of America, 2004), 3.

24. Gordon S. Wood, *The Radicalism of the American Revolution* (New York: Alfred A. Knopf, 1992), 369.

25. Baron Hübner, *A Ramble Round the World, 1871*, trans. Lady Elizabeth Herbert (London: MacMillan and Co., 1878), 179.

26. George Augustus Sala, *America Revisited: From the Bay of New York to the Gulf of Mexico and From Lake Michigan to the Pacific* (London: Vizetelly & Co., n.d.), 57–58.

27. Richard L. Rapson, *Britons View America: Travel Commentary, 1860–1935* (Seattle: University of Washington Press, 1971), 62.

28. Margaret Atwood, "Hello, Martians. Let Moby-Dick Explain," *New York Times*, April 29, 2012.

29. Quoted in Elaine Sciolino, *Le Seduction: How the French Play the Game of Life* (New York: Times Books, 2011), 288,

30. See Michael Kumhof and Romain Rancière, "Inequality, Leverage and Crises," IMF Working Paper, November 2010, 6, www.imf.org. See also Nathan Thornburgh, "London's Long Burn," *Time*, August 22, 2011, 30.

31. Rana Foroohar, "Whatever Happened to Upward Mobility?" *Time*, November 14, 2011, 28; "Economic Mobility and the American Dream—Where Do We Stand in the Wake of the Great Recession?" 2011 poll. Pew Charitable Trust, Economic Mobility Project, www.economicmobility.org; "Britons More Pessimistic About Social Mobility," September 2009 poll. The Sutton Trust, www.suttontrust.com.

32. Quoted in "A Traditional Royal Wedding, But for the 3 Billion Witnesses," *New York Times*, April 30, 2011.

33. "Bagehot: No More Royal Weddings," *The Economist* 399, no. 8730 (April 23—29, 2011), 61. The columnist concluded that the best wedding present for the royal couple would be the abolition of the monarchy and the creation of a republic. In *Snobs*, a contemporaneous novel of a middle-class girl who marries above her station, author Julian Fellowes brings some perspective to the English class system, observing that, "The English upper classes are, as a rule, not amused by upper-middle-class facsimiles of themselves. This brand of *arriviste* has all the dreariness of the familiar with none of the cosiness of the intimate." Julian Fellowes, *Snobs* (New York: St. Martin's Griffin, 2006), 197.

34. Maureen Dowd, "For Office Civility, Cherchez La Femme," *New York Times*, May 29, 2011.

35. Deschamps quoted in Sciolino, 115, 116.

36. Quoted in Steven Erlanger and Katrin Bennhold, "As Case Unfolds, France Speculates and Steams," *New York Times*, May 16, 2011. Former *French Vogue* editor Carine Roitfeld recently commented on clothing differences between Europeans and Americans: "I think the Americans, they love comfort more than Europeans. Americans created the T-shirt, the sweat pants, and they create the best sporting shoes. When I see a woman in the street, sometimes I think, Oh, it's a bit too comfortable the way she is dressing, you know? And not in a nice way." Andrew Goldman interview of Carine Roitfeld, "Fashion is Bondage," *New York Times Magazine*, September 4, 2011, 12.

37. Sarah Maslin Nir, "For French Reporters, Excitement and Shock Over a Big Story," *New York Times*, May 23, 2011.

BIBLIOGRAPHY WITH BIOGRAPHICAL NOTES

Henry Adams, The *Education of Henry Adams* [1907] (Boston: Houghton Mifflin, 1961). Journalist, historian, academic, and novelist, his *Education* is one of the most famous American autobiographies.

W. E. [William Edwin] Adams, *Our American Cousins: Being Personal Impressions of the People and Institutions of the United States* (London: Walter Scott, 1883). English journalist and Radical. From 1864 to 1900, Adams edited the *Newcastle Weekly Chronicle*, where he endorsed trade unionism and cooperatives.

Hamilton Aïdé, "Social Aspects of American Life," *The Nineteenth Century* 29, no. 172 (June 1891).

Anonymous, "American Humor," *The Cornhill Magazine* 13 (January 1866).

Anonymous, "The Antagonism of Race and Colour; or, White, Red, Black, and Yellow in America," *Blackwood's Edinburgh Magazine* 653, no. 107 (March 1870).

Anonymous, "The Education of the People in England and America," *Blackwood's Edinburgh Magazine* 627, no. 103 (January 1868).

Anonymous, "An Englishman in Vermont," *Eclectic Magazine* 18, no. 2 (New Series, August 1873.

Anonymous, "The Grand Anonymous, "A German Appraisal of the United States," *Atlantic Monthly* 75, no. 447 (January 1895).

Anonymous, "The Great American Language," *The Cornhill Magazine* 11 (New Series, October 1888).

Anonymous, "On Some Peculiarities of Society in America," *The Cornhill Magazine* 26 (December 1872).

Anonymous, "Ranche Life in the Far West," *MacMillan's Magazine* 48 (August 1883).

Anonymous, "Some American Notes," *MacMillan's Magazine* 53 (November 1885).

Anonymous, "Some Remarks on Travelling in America," *The Cornhill Magazine* 19 (March 1869).

William Archer, *America To-Day: Observations and Reflections* [1899] (New York, Arno Press, 1974).

[Sir] John [George Edward Henry Douglass Sutherland] Campbell Argyll (Marquis of Lorne), *A Trip to the Tropics and Home Through America* (London, Hurst and Blackett,

1867). Married the fourth daughter of Queen Victoria (Louise Caroline Alberta) and represented Argyllshire as a Liberal Member of Parliament before being appointed Governor General of Canada at age thirty-three. He and Louise travelled extensively in Canada, and made significant contributions to the arts before returning to England in 1883.

Army of the Republic," *MacMillan's Magazine* 65 (December 1891).

Matthew Arnold, "Civilization in the United States" in *Civilization in the United States: First and Last Impressions of America* [1888] (Freeport, NY: Books for Libraries Press, 1972). Poet, literary and social critic, and Professor of Poetry at Oxford. Best known today for his 1867 poem "Dover Beach."

Matthew Arnold, "General Grant" in *Civilization in the United States: First and Last Impressions of America* [1888] (Freeport, NY: Books for Libraries Press, 1972), 3–66.

Matthew Arnold, "A Word About America" in *Civilization in the United States: First and Last Impressions of America* [1888] (Freeport, NY: Books for Libraries Press, 1972), 69–108, 111–192.

J. J. [John James] Aubertin, *A Fight with Distances: The States, the Hawaiian Islands, Canada, British Columbia, Cuba, the Bahamas* (London: Kegan Paul, Trench & Co., 1888). A Spanish and Portuguese scholar who travelled extensively throughout North and South America.

William A. [Adolf] Baille-Grohman, *Camps in the Rockies: Being a Narrative of Life on the Frontier, and Sport in the Rocky Mountains, with an Account of the Cattle Ranches of the West* (New York: Charles Scribner's Sons, 1884). Wealthy hunter and adventurer best known as the promoter of the Baille-Grohman Canal built between the headwaters of the Columbia River and the upper Kootenay River in British Columbia. Completed in 1889, the canal was a failure, and was only used a handful of times.

W. [William] Henry Barneby, *Life and Labor in the Far, Far West: Being Notes of a Tour in the Western States, British Columbia, Manitoba, and the North-West Territory* (London: Cassell & Company, 1884).

E. [Emily] Catherine Bates, *A Year in the Great Republic*, vols. 1 and 2 (London: Ward & Downey, 1887). Maintained an intense interest in spiritualism throughout her life and produced a number of books on the subject, including *Seen and Unseen* and *Do the Dead Depart? And Other Questions*.

William A. Bell, New *Tracks in North America: A Journal of Travel and Adventure Whilst Engaged in the Survey for a Southern Railroad to the Pacific Ocean During* 1867–8 [1870] (Albuquerque: Horn and Wallace, 1965).

Sarah Bernhardt, *Memories of My Life* [1907] (Grosse Pointe, MI: Scholarly Press, 1968). The greatest French actress of the late nineteenth century. After appearing as Desdemona in Othello in 1878, she formed her own traveling company and toured extensively throughout the world, including eight visits to the United States.

Lucien Biart, *My Rambles in the New World* [1876], trans. Mary de Hauteville (London: Sampson, Low, Marston, Searle, & Rivington, 1877).

Isabella L. [Lucy] Bird, *A Lady's Life in the Rocky Mountains* (Norman: University of Oklahoma Press, 1969). A world traveler who also wrote *Among the Tibetans, Unbeaten Tracks in Japan*, and *The Golden Chersonese and the Way Thither*.

Black Elk Speaks: Being the Life Story of a Holy Man of the Oglala Sioux, as told through John G. Neihardt [1932] (Lincoln: University of Nebraska Press, 1988). Black Elk was a participant in the killing of Custer and his troops at the Little Big Horn and a performer in the Wild West Show that went to London in 1887.

Marie Therese de Solms Blanc, *The Condition of Woman in the United States: A Traveller's Notes*, trans. Abby Langdon Alger [1895] (New York: Arno Press, 1972). French novelist, literary critic, and promoter of women's rights.

J. W. Boddam-Whetham [John Wetham], Western *Wanderings: A Record of Travel in the Evening Land* (London: Richard Bentley and Son, 1874.) British writer and sportsman, whose books include *Pearls of the Pacific, and Roraima and British Guinea, with a Glance at Bermuda, the West Indies, and the Spanish Main.*

Paul Bourget, *Outre-Mer: Impressions of America* (London: T. Fisher Unwin, 1895). Novelist and poet. His best-known novel is *Le Disciple* (1889), which chronicles the impact of a mentor's advocacy of materialism on an impressionable student. Claude Debussy drew on Bourget's poems for some of his music.

Charles Loring Brace, *The Dangerous Classes of New York, and Twenty Years' Work Among Them* [1872] (Washington, D.C.: National Association of Social Workers, n.d.).

William Bradford, *Of Plymouth Plantation, 1620–1647* (New York: Modern Library, 1981). Arrived in America with other Separatists aboard the *Mayflower* in 1620. Would serve for many years as Governor of Plymouth Colony.

James Bryce, The *American Commonwealth*, vols. 1 and 2 (New York: The Commonwealth Publishing Company, 1908). Historian, constitutional lawyer, Liberal Member of Parliament, and British Ambassador to the United States.

James Bryce, "The Essential Unity of Britain and America," *Atlantic Monthly* 82, no. 489 (July 1898).

Harold Brydges (pseud. for James Howard Bridge), *Uncle Sam at Home* (New York: Henry Holt and Company, 1888).

Stephen Buckland, "Eating and Drinking In America:—A Stroll Among the Saloons of New York," *MacMillan's Magazine* 16 (October 1867).

Richard F. [Francis] Burton, *The City of the Saints and Across the Rocky Mountains to California* [1861] (New York: Alfred A. Knopf, 1963). Explorer, writer, translator, and ethnologist. Travelled in disguise to Mecca and was the first European to see Lake Tanganyika. Translated *One Thousand and One Nights and The Kama Sutra.*

William Francis Butler, *The Great Lone Land: A Narrative of Travel and Adventure in the North-West of America* [1872] (Rutland, VT: Charles E. Tuttle, 1968). Born of Irish parents, was a career military officer that included postings in Canada, Egypt, and South Africa.

Dudley Campbell, "Mixed Education of Boys and Girls," *The Contemporary Review* 22 (July 1873).

Mrs. E. H. Carbutt (Mary Rhodes Carbutt), *Five Months' Fine Weather in Canada, Western U.S., and Mexico* (London: Sampson, Low, Marston, Searle and Rivington, 1889).

François-René de Chateaubriand, *René, in Norton Anthology of World Masterpieces*, v. 2, sixth edition, ed. Maynard Mack et al. (New York: W.W. Norton, 1992). The father of French Romanticism, Chateaubriand was influential on the careers of both Lord Byron and Victor Hugo.

G. S. Clarke, "England and America," *The Nineteenth Century* 44, no. 258 (August 1898).

William F. (Buffalo Bill) Cody, "Famous Hunting Parties of the Plains," *The Cosmopolitan* 17, no. 2 (June 1894). Pony Express rider, army scout, Indian fighter, hunting guide, and creator of Buffalo Bill's Wild West Show.

William F. (Buffalo Bill) *Cody, Story of the Wild West and Camp-Fire Chats by Buffalo Bill, (Hon. W. F. Cody), A Full and Complete History of the Renowned Pioneer Quartette, Boon, Crockett, Carson and Buffalo Bill* [1888] (Freeport, NY: Books for Libraries Press, 1970).

James Fenimore Cooper, *The Pioneers* [1823] (New York: Library of America, 1985). One of the most popular of nineteenth-century American writers, Cooper is best known for his "Leatherstocking" series of novels, the most famous of which is *The Last of the Mohicans.*

James Fenimore Cooper, *The Prairie* [1827] (New York: Library of America, 1985).

Alexander Craib, *America and the Americans: A Tour in the United States and Canada, With Chapters on American Home Life* (London: Alexander Gardner, 1892).

Hector St. John de Crèvecoeur, "What Is An American," in Hector St. John de Crèvecoeur, *Letters From An American Farmer* [1782] (London: J. M. Dent and Sons, 1926). After serving France in the French and Indian War, settled in New York as a farmer. Became French Counsel at New York after the Revolution.

C. F. Gordon Cumming, "Locusts and Farmers of America," *The Nineteenth Century* 17, no. 95 (January 1885).

A Cynic, "National Antipathies," *The Cornhill Magazine* 21 (February 1870).

R. W. Dale, "Impressions of America," parts 1 and 2, *Eclectic Magazine* 27, no. 6 (New Series, June 1878), and 28, no. 2 (New Series, August 1878).

William H. Davies, *The Autobiography of a Super-Tramp* (New York: Alfred A. Knopf, 1917). Left England for America in his early twenties, drifting through the country between 1893 and 1899. After losing a foot in a railroad accident, returned to Britain and became a poet.

A. V. Dicey, "England and America," *Atlantic Monthly* 82, no. 492 (October 1898).

Charles Dickens, The *Letters of Charles Dickens*, v. 3, ed. Graham Storey (Oxford: Clarendon Press, 2002). Arguably the most popular novelist of the nineteenth century. His books include *Bleak House, David Copperfield,* and *A Christmas Carol.*

Charles Dickens, *Martin Chuzzlewit* [1843–1844] (New York: Penguin Books, 1995).

Charles Dickens, *The Speeches of Charles Dickens*, ed. K. J. Fielding (Hemel Hempstead: Harvester Wheatsheaf, 1988).

Antoní Dvořák, *Antoní Dvořák: Letters and Reminiscences*, ed. Otakar Šourek, trans. Roberta Finlayson Samsour (Prague: Artia, 1954). Composer of Romantic music, often employing folk elements of Bohemian and Moravian music. Works include New *World Symphony* and *Slavonic Dances.*

Charles Wentworth Dilke, *Greater Britain: A Record of Travel in English-Speaking Countries* (London: Macmillan and Co., 1890). Liberal critic and editor of the literary magazine *Athenaeum.*

William Hepworth Dixon, *New America* (Philadelphia: J. B. Lippincott, 1869). Historian, prison reformer, and writer of travel books. Among his most controversial works was *Spiritual Wives,* which dealt with Mormonism.

Edward Eggleston, "A Full-Length Portrait of the United States," *The Century Magazine* 37, no. 5 (March 1889).

"English and American Railways," *Harper's* 71, August 1885.

Emily Faithfull, *Three Visits to America* (New York: Fowler & Wells, 1884). Took up the cause of working women through *The Victorian Magazine.* Established a printing operation for women.

F. Francis, "The Yellowstone Geysers," *The Nineteenth Century* 11, no. 61 (March 1882).

Edward A. Freeman, *Some Impressions of the United States* (London: Longmans, Green, and Co., 1883). English historian chiefly known for his *History of the Norman Conquest.*

Parker Gillmore, *A Hunter's Adventures in the Great West* (London: Hurst and Blackett, 1871). Counted by many as among the great hunters of the nineteenth century, the Scotsman Gillmore explored extensively in South Africa and was employed by the British Army during the Zulu War of 1879.

Lepel Henry Griffin, *The Great Republic* [1884] (New York: Arno Press, 1974). Served in the Civil Service in India. Was Chief Secretary of the Punjab, and a diplomatic representative to Kabul at the completion of the Second Afghan War.

Alexandra Gripenberg, *A Half Year in the New World: Miscellaneous Sketches of Travel in the United States* [1889], trans. and edited Ernest J. Moyne (Newark: University of Delaware

Press, 1954). A leader of Finland's woman suffrage and temperance movements. Was a delegate to the first International Council of Women in Washington, D.C., in 1888.

[Lady] Theodora Guest, *A Round Trip in North America* (London: Edward Stanford, 1895). Worked to improve the lot of poor women, but was criticized by suffragists for not endorsing female suffrage.

Knut Hamsun, *The Cultural Life of Modern America* [1889] (Cambridge, MA: Harvard University Press, 1969). Winner of the Nobel Prize for Literature in 1920, Hamsun became notorious during World War II for his support of the Nazi regime and for eulogizing Adolf Hitler.

Iza Duffus Hardy, *Between Two Oceans: Or, Sketches of American Travel* (London: Hurst and Blackett, 1884). Daughter of Lady Duffus Hardy, she published in the 1870s and 1880s a large number of short stories and over thirty books, including *Oranges and Alligators—Sketches of South Florida Life.*

Lady Duffus Hardy [Mary (McDowell) Duffus], *Through Cities and Prairie Lands: Sketches of an American Tour* (London: Chapman and Hall, 1881). Like her daughter Iza Duffus Hardy, she published numerous novels and travel books, including *Down South.*

Joseph Hatton, *Henry Irving's Impressions of America, Narrated in a Series of Sketches, Chronicles, and Conversations* [1884], vols. 1 and 2 (New York: Benjamin Blom, 1971). Hatton was a novelist, journalist, and editor of *The Sunday Times* from 1874 to 1881. Renowned for his roles in Shakespearian plays, Henry Irving became the first actor to be knighted (in 1895).

Ernst von Hesse-Wartegg, "Across Nebraska by Train in 1877: The Travels of Ernst von Hesse-Warteg," trans. and ed. Frederic Trautmann, *Nebraska History* 65, no. 3 (Fall 1984). Austrian traveler and prolific writer who completed some forty books, including the four-volume set *Nord-Amerikca: Seine Stadte and Naturwunder, sein Land and seine Leute.* Hesse-Wartegg's memoir of his travels on the lower Mississippi was drawn upon by Mark Twain for his own *Life on the Mississippi.* Married the opera singer Minnie Hauk, who sang the first American *Carmen.*

Ernst von Hesse-Wartegg, *Travels on the Lower Mississippi, 1879–1880*, trans. and ed. Frederic Trautmann (Columbia: University of Missouri Press, 1990).

S. Reynolds Hole, *A Little Tour In America* [1895] (Freeport, NY: Books for Libraries Press, 1971).

George Jacob Holyoake, "American and Canadian Notes," *The Nineteenth Century* 14, no. 77 (July 1883).

George Jacob Holyoake, "A Stranger in America," *The Nineteenth Century* 8, no. 41 (July 1880).

Baron Hübner, *A Ramble Round the World, 1871*, trans. Lady Elizabeth Herbert (London: MacMillan and Co., 1878).

Thomas Hughes, "A Week in the West," parts 3, 4, and 5, *MacMillan's Magazine* 25 (November 1871–January 1872). Most famous for the novel *Tom Brown's School Days* (1857). An advocate of Christian Socialism, Hughes founded a cooperative, class-free colony in Rugby, Tennessee, in 1880.

J. W. C., "Social New York," *MacMillan's Magazine* 26 (June 1872).

Harry Kessler, *Journey to the Abyss: The Diaries of Count Harry Kessler, 1880–1918*, trans. and ed. Laird Easton (New York: Knopf, 2011). German patron of the arts and champion of aesthetic modernism. Kessler was director of the Museum of Arts and Crafts in Weimar and vice-president of the German Artists League. Served as a soldier during World War I, and was ultimately exiled from Nazi Germany.

Rose G. [Georgina] Kingsley, *South by West, or Winter in the Rocky Mountains and Spring in Mexico* (London: W. Isbinster and Co., 1874). Daughter of the canon of Westminister Abbey.

Rudyard Kipling, *American Notes* [1891] (Norman: University of Oklahoma Press, 1981). Among the most popular of writers in the late nineteenth and early twentieth centuries, Kipling was the author of novels, short stories, and poems. He won the Nobel Prize for Literature in 1907. His best-known works include the *The Jungle Book, Kim,* and the short story "The Man Who Would Be King."

Rudyard Kipling, "An Interview with Mark Twain," in *American Notes* (Norman: University of Oklahoma Press, 1981).

Lida von Krockow, "American Characters in German Novels," *Atlantic Monthly* 68, no. 410 (December 1891).

Lillie Langtry, *The Days I Knew* (New York: George H. Doran, 1925). Encouraged by her friend Oscar Wilde, Langtry began her acting career in London in 1881. Subsequent tours to the United States were great successes. She would become an American citizen in 1897, but would end her days in Monaco.

Henry Latham, *Black and White: A Journal of a Three Months' Tour in the United States* [1867] (New York: Negro Universities Press, 1969).

Hugues Le Roux, *Business and Love* (New York: Dodd, Mead and Company, 1903). French novelist, journalist and sénateur.

Émile Levasseur, *The American Workman*, trans. by Thomas S. Adams (Baltimore: Johns Hopkins University, 1900).

[Sir] A. [Alfred] Maurice Low, *The American People: A Study in National Psychology* (Boston: Houghton Mifflin, 1909). Chiefly a writer of non-fiction, Low's books include *Protection in the United States: A Study of the Origin and Growth of the American Tariff System, and Its Economic and Social Influences,* and *Woodrow Wilson, An Interpretation.*

J. R. [James Russell] Lowell, "On a Certain Condescension in Foreigners," *Atlantic Monthly* 23 (January 1869). American poet, literary critic and editor of *The Atlantic Monthly.* Served as both Minister to Spain and Minister to England.

David Macrae, *The Americans at Home* [1870] (New York: E. P. Dutton, 1952). Scottish patriot, temperance reformer, and Presbyterian minister.

W. G. [Walter Grove] Marshall, *Through America: Nine Months in the United States* (London: Sampson, Low, Marston, Searle & Rivington, 1881).

T. B. [Thomas Babington] Macaulay, "Letter of Lord T. B. Macaulay to Henry S. Randall, 9 October 1858," *Harper's* 54, no. 321 (February 1877), 460–461. Whig Member of Parliament, essayist, and historian. His most famous work is the five-volume *History of England.*

Jose Martí, *Martí on the U.S.A.,* trans. Luis A. Barlat (Carbondale: Southern Illinois University Press, 1966). Apprehensive about the possibility of an American annexation of Cuba, Martí died in combat fighting for Cuban independence in 1895.

John Muir, "The American Forests," *Atlantic Monthly* 80, no. 478 (August 1897). Among the most prominent of conservationists, Muir worked to establish national parks and protection of national forests in the United States.

James Fullarton Muirhead, *The Land of Contrasts: A Briton's View of his American Kin* (London: Lamson, Wolffe and Company, 1898). Author of *Baedeker's Handbook* for the United States and for Great Britain.

John Mortimer Murphy, *Rambles in North-Western America, from the Pacific Ocean to the Rocky Mountains* (London: Chapman and Hall, 1879).

Colonel George Ward Nichols, "The Indian: What We Should Do with Him," *Harper's* 40 (April 1870), 732–739. Served with the Union during the Civil War under both John C. Fremont and William Sherman, and published *The Story of the Great March* at the completion of the war. His 1867 *Harper's* article on Wild Bill Hickock was widely panned as inaccurate.

Oliver North (pseud. For W. Mullen), "Quail Shooting in California," in *Rambles After Sport, or, Travels and Adventures in the Americas and at Home* (London: The Field Office, 1874).

A. S. Northcote, "American Life Through English Spectacles," *The Nineteenth Century* 34, no. 199 (September 1893).

Jacques Offenbach, *Orpheus in America: Offenbach's Diary of His Journey to the New World* [1877], trans. Lander MacClintock (New York: Greenwood Press, 1969). A German-born French composer whose operettas include *Orpheus in the Underworld and Tales of Hoffman*.

Max O'rell [pseud. for Léon Paul Blouet] and Jack Allyn, *Jonathan and His Continent: Rambles Through American Society*, trans. Madame Paul Blouet (Bristol: J. W. Arrowsmith, 1889). French master at St. Paul's School, London, Blouet wrote the hugely popular *John Bull and His Island*. He married an Englishwoman, who translated his books.

Charles C. Osborne, "Impressions of Klondike," pts. 3 and 4, *MacMillan's Magazine* 83 (November 1900).

Our Hearts Fell to the Ground: Plains Indian Views of How the West Was Lost, ed. Colin G. Calloway (Boston: Bedford Books, 1996).

Rose [Mary Rose Gregge-Hopwood, Lady] Pender, *A Lady's Experiences of the Wild West in 1883* (London: George Tucker, 1888). Traveled with her husband James to the American West in 1883. Sir James Pender was a businessman and Conservative Member of Parliament for mid-Northamptonshire from 1895 to 1900.

W. F. [William Fraser] Rae, *Westward by Rail: The New Route to the East* [1871] (New York: Promontory Press, 1974). Scottish-born, worked in England as a barrister. Wrote several books on Canada as well as a biography of Sheridan.

Isabelle Randall, *A Lady's Ranche Life in Montana* (London: W. H. Allen & Co., 1887).

Arnot Reid, "The English and the American Press," *The Nineteenth Century* 22, no. 125 (July 1867).

R. L. S., "The Foreigner at Home," *The Cornhill Magazine* 45 (May 1882).

Phil Robinson, *Sinners and Saints: A Tour Across the States, and Round Them; with Three Months Among the Mormons* (Boston: Roberts Brothers, 1883).

Theodore Roosevelt, "Machine Politics in New York City," *The Century Magazine* 33, no. 1 (November 1886).

Paul de Rousiers, *American Life*, trans. A. J. Herbertson (New York: Firmin-Didot, 1892).

Mary Rowlandson, *The Sovereignty and Goodness of God* [1682] (Boston: Bedford Books, 1997). Survived eleven weeks of captivity by Indians before being ransomed. Her book was a best seller and is an important example of a captivity narrative.

Bertrand Russell, *The Autobiography of Bertrand Russell,* 1872–1914 (Boston: Atlantic Monthly Press, 1967). Philosopher, social critic, and mathematician. One of the founders of analytic philosophy, Russell won the Nobel Prize for Literature in 1950. Was a pacifist during World War I and a proponent of nuclear disarmament.

William Howard Russell, *Hesperothen, Notes from the West: A Record of a Ramble in the United States and Canada in the Spring and Summer of 1881, volumes 1 and 2* (London: S. Low, Marston, Searle & Rivington, 1882). British war correspondent who covered the Crimean War in 1854, the recapture of Lucknow, India, in 1858, and the American Civil War in 1861–1862. In his dispatches from the Crimea, he coined the term "thin red line." His descriptions of the atrocious medical conditions there revolutionized battlefield care. Knighted in 1895.

George Augustus Sala, *America Revisited: From the Bay of New York to the Gulf of Mexico and From Lake Michigan to the Pacific* (London: Vizetelly & Co., n.d.). Acquainted with both Charles Dickens and William Makepeace Thackery, who printed articles by him in their publications. Foreign correspondent and long-time contributor to the *Daily Telegraph*.

Madame de San Carlos, "Americans at Home," *Review of Reviews* 1, no. 5 (May 1890) and no. 6 (June 1890).

William Saunders, *Through the Light Continent, or, The United States in 1877–78* [1879] (New York: Arno Press, 1974).

M. E. W. (Mrs. John) Sherwood, "American Girls in Europe," *North American Review* 403, June 1890. Acquainted with many of the leading lights of the day, Sherwood wrote *Mrs. John Sherwood's Memoirs: Margaret Fuller, Lowell, Emerson, Dickens, Lord Houghton and Others*.

Henry Sienkiewicz, *Portrait of America: Letters of Henry Sienkiewicz*, ed. and trans. Charles Morley (New York: Columbia University Press, 1959). Polish Nobel Prize winner best known for his novel *Quo Vadis?* A group of Polish intellectuals charged Sienkiewicz with the task of going to California in 1876 to clear the way for the establishment of a utopian society near Anaheim. Because the colony did not include experienced farmers, it predictably expired. The Polish public learned of Sienkiewicz's experiences in the United States through a series of letters he wrote that were published in Polish newspapers.

S. C. de Soissons, *A Parisian in America* (Boston: Estes and Lauriat, 1896). Full name: Guy Raoul Eugene Charles Emmanuel de Savoie-Carignan de Soissons. Translator of Polish authors, including the works of Henryk Sienkiewicz and Joseph J. Kraszewski.

Robert Somers, *The Southern States Since the War, 1870–71* [1871] (Tuscaloosa: University of Alabama Press, 1965).

Herbert Spencer, "Mr. Spencer's Address" ("Proceedings of the Spencer Banquet") in Edward Youmans, *Herbert Spencer on the Americans and the Americans on Herbert Spencer: Being a Full Report of his Interview, and of the Proceedings of the Farewell Banquet of Nov. 11, 1882* (New York: D. Appleton, 1883). The most famous philosopher of his time, Spencer originated the phrase "survival of the fittest," rejected traditional religion, and described the human species in terms of evolutionary biology.

Herbert Spencer, "Report of Mr. Spencer's Interview" in Edward Youmans, *Herbert Spencer on the Americans and the Americans on Herbert Spencer: Being a Full Report of his Interview, and of the Proceedings of the Farewell Banquet of Nov. 11, 1882* (New York: D. Appleton, 1883).

Henry M. Stanley, "The Issue Between Great Britain and America," *The Nineteenth Century* 39, no. 227 (January 1896).

Henry M. Stanley, *My Early Travels and Adventures in America* [1895] (Lincoln: University of Nebraska Press, 1982). As a journalist, Stanley covered the U.S. army's negotiations with the tribes of the Great Plains in 1867, then was sent to Zanzibar by the *New York Herald* to find the missionary David Livingstone. In this and subsequent expeditions to Africa, Stanley's reputation was clouded by his alleged brutality to the natives.

William T. Stead, *If Christ Came to Chicago!: A Plea for the Union of All Who Love in the Service of All Who Suffer* [1894] (Chicago: Press of the Eight-Hour Herald, n.d.). English reform editor of the *Review of Reviews*. Came to Chicago for the World's Columbian Exposition in 1893, and developed an interest in the problems of the city. Stead went down with the *Titanic* in 1912.

Robert Louis Stevenson, "The Amateur Emigrant," in *From Scotland to Silverado* [1892] (Cambridge, MA: Belknap Press, 1966). Enormously popular Scottish essayist, novelist and travel writer. His works include *Kidnapped, Treasure Island,* and *The Strange Case of Dr. Jekyll and Mr. Hyde.*

Robert Louis Stevenson, "The Old and New Pacific Capitals," in *From Scotland to Silverado* [1892] (Cambridge, MA: Belknap Press, 1966).

Robert Louis Stevenson, "The Silverado Squatters," in *From Scotland to Silverado* [1892] (Cambridge, MA: Belknap Press, 1966).

Frank R. Stockton, "On the Training of Parents," *The Century Magazine* 28, no. 1 (May 1884).

Bram Stoker, "A Glimpse of America" [1886] in *Bram Stoker's A Glimpse of America and Other Lectures, Interviews and Essays,* ed. Richard Dalby (Westcliff-on-Sea, UK: Desert Island Books, 2002). Personal assistant to actor Henry Irving and business manager of Irving's Lyceum Theatre. Stoker may have modeled the title character in his novel *Dracula* (1897) after Irving.

R. H. Inglis Synnot, "The Pacific Express," *The Contemporary Review* 17 (June 1871).

Peter Tchaikovsky, *The Diaries of Tchaikovsky,* trans. Wladimir Lakond (New York: W. W. Norton, 1945). Composer of operas, ballets, and symphonies, his works include *Eugene Onegin, Sleeping Beauty,* and *The Nutcracker.*

Alexis De Tocqueville, *Democracy in America,* [1835] trans. Arthur Goldhammer (New York: Library of America, 2004). In 1831, Tocqueville and his friend Gustave de Beaumont traveled to America to examine prison conditions in the United States. Overshadowing Tocqueville's prison report was his treatise on American society, the hugely influential *De la Démocratie en Amerique.*

W. P. Trent, "Dominant Forces in Southern Life," *Atlantic Monthly* 78, no. 471 (January 1897).

Anthony Trollope, *The American Senator* [1876–77] (Oxford: Oxford University Press, 1991). One of the most popular British novelists of the nineteenth century. Trollope visited the United States during the Civil War, and recorded his impressions in *North America.* Many American characters found their way into his novels, and in contrast to his mother, Frances, Trollope was more generous in his overall assessment of America.

Anthony Trollope, *The Last Chronicle of Barset* [1867] (New York: Penguin Books, 2002).

Anthony Trollope, *North America* [1862] (New York: Alfred A. Knopf, 1951).

Frances Trollope, *Domestic Manners of the Americans* [1832] (New York: Alfred A. Knopf, 1949). Traveled with her family to America in 1827 to the Nashoba Commune, a utopian society, then to Cincinnati. After returning to England, she published a number of social protest novels and miscellaneous works.

Frances Trollope, "Selections from Mrs. Trollope's Notebooks and Rough Draft," in Frances Trollope, *Domestic Manners of the Americans* [1832] (New York: Alfred A. Knopf, 1949).

Frederick Jackson Turner, "The Problem of the West," *Atlantic Monthly* 78, no. 467 (September 1896). Turner's "frontier thesis," which was described in an 1893 paper titled "The Significance of the Frontier in American History," made Turner among the most influential of American historians.

Mark Twain, "Concerning the American Language," [1882] in *Collected Tales, Sketches, Speeches and Essays, v. 1* (New York: Library of America, 1992). American humorist and novelist. Best known for *The Adventures of Tom Sawyer* and *The Adventures of Huckleberry Finn.*

Horace Annesley Vachell, *Life and Sport on the Pacific Slope* (New York: Dodd, Mead and Co., 1901). After spending seventeen years operating a ranch in California, Vachell returned to England and wrote fifty volumes of fiction. His *The Case of Lady Camber* (1915) was turned into the Alfred Hitchcock film *Lord Camber's Ladies* (1932).

Charles W. Vincent, "The Dangers of Electric Lighting," *The Nineteenth Century* 27, no. 155 (January 1890).

H. Hussey Vivian, *Notes of a Tour in America from August 7th to November 17th,* 1877 (London: Edward Stanford, 1878).

Beatrice Webb, *Beatrice Webb's American Diary* (Madison: University of Wisconsin Press, 1963). The daughter of a wealthy capitalist, Beatrice Potter became a Fabian socialist. She married Sidney Webb in 1892 and together the two produced *The History of Trade Unionism* and the fifteen-volume *Industrial Democracy*. In 1898 they toured the United States, New Zealand and Australia.

W. C. M., "American Traits," *Eclectic Magazine* 16, no. 1 (New Series, July 1872).

Horace White, "An American's Impression of England," *Eclectic Magazine* 22, no. 5 (New Series, November 1875).

Oscar Wilde, "The American Man," in *The Collected Oscar Wilde* (New York: Barnes and Noble Classics, 2007). An Irish aesthete known for his witty epigrams and plays. His best remembered works include his only novel, *The Picture of Dorian Gray*, and the play, *The Importance of Being Earnest*.

Oscar Wilde, "American Women" in *The Works of Oscar Wilde* (New York: AMS Press, 1972).

Oscar Wilde, "Americans in London, " in *The Essays of Oscar Wilde* [1916], ed. Albert & Charles Boni (Bonibooks, 1935).

Oscar Wilde, *Decorative Art in America: A Lecture by Oscar Wilde Together with Letters, Reviews and Interviews,* ed. Richard Butler Glaenzer (New York: Brentano's: 1906).

Oscar Wilde, "The English Renaissance of Art," in *The Essays of Oscar Wilde* [1916], ed. Albert & Charles Boni (Bonibooks, 1935).

Oscar Wilde, "Impressions of America" in Oscar Wilde, *The Works of Oscar Wilde* (New York: AMS Press, 1972).

Oscar Wilde, "Soul of Man Under Socialism," in *The Essays of Oscar Wilde* [1916], ed. Albert & Charles Boni (Bonibooks, 1935).

Henry Trueman Wood, "Chicago and Its Exhibition," *The Nineteenth Century* 31, no. 180 (February 1892).

Windham Thomas Wyndham-Quin (Fourth Earl of Dunraven), *The Great Divide: Travels in the Upper Yellowstone in the Summer of 1874* (London: Chatto and Windus, 1876). An avid hunter, Wyndham-Quin arrived in the United States in 1872, and by 1874 had decided to turn Estes Park, Colorado, into a game preserve for well-to-do sportsmen by appropriating it through the Homestead Act. While this scheme was unsuccessful, he was able to build the first tourist hotel in the area in 1877. The gaudy career of Wyndham-Quin included covering the Abyssinian War, the Franco-Prussian War, and witnessing the signing of the Treaty of Versailles as a correspondent. Owner of a yacht that participated in the America's Cup competition in 1893 and 1895. He was a member of the first senate of the Irish Free State.

Windham Thomas Wyndham-Quin, "A Colorado Sketch," *The Nineteenth Century* 17, no. 43 (September 1880).

Therese Yelverton [Maria Theresa Longworth, Viscountess Avonmore], *Teresina in America, v. 1* (London: Richard Bentley and Son, 1875). Chiefly remembered for her role in the Yelverton case, in which she claimed to have secretly married William Charles Yelverton, Viscount Avonmore. The viscount later used his influence to annul the marriage. Afterward, Yelverton supported herself by writing. She met John Muir in 1870, and made him into a fictional character in one of her novels.

Edward Livingston Youmans, "Preface" to Edward Youmans, *Herbert Spencer on the Americans and the Americans on Herbert Spencer: Being a Full Report of his Interview, and of the Proceedings of the Farewell Banquet of Nov. 11, 1882* (New York: D. Appleton, 1883). Youmans was the founder of *Popular Science* magazine.

F. Barham Zincke, *Last Winter in the United States: Being Table talk Collected During a Tour Through the Late Southern Confederation, the Far West, the Rocky Mountains, &c. [1868]* (Freeport, NY: Books for Libraries Press, 1970). Author of numerous non-fiction works, including *On the Duty and the Discipline of Extemporary Preaching,* and *Egypt of the Pharaohs and of the Khedive.*

INDEX